KU-426-562

SAINTE-BEUVE

BY

LEWIS FREEMAN MOTT

PROFESSOR OF ENGLISH IN THE COLLEGE OF THE
CITY OF NEW YORK

D. APPLETON AND COMPANY
NEW YORK 1925 LONDON

COPYRIGHT, 1925, BY
D. APPLETON AND COMPANY

1580

PRINTED IN THE UNITED STATES OF AMERICA

PREFACE

SAINTE-BEUVE is universally recognized as the greatest literary critic of France, and this reputation, established during his lifetime, has not faded in the half century since his death. No writer of any sort is so frequently cited in current French literature, nor are our own critical reviews far behind in reference to his life and works. Taine called him "one of the five or six most useful servants of the human mind" produced by France in the nineteenth century: Matthew Arnold was his professed disciple; a whole generation of critics have looked up to him as their master.

From his youth, when he first came to Paris as a schoolboy, to his last days, Sainte-Beuve was in the midst of every intellectual movement of his time. He belonged to the staff of the *Globe*, considered by Goethe the most interesting group in Europe; he was Victor Hugo's closest friend and a mainstay of the Romantics; he was a Saint-Simonian, a revolutionist, an intimate of Lamennais, of Chateaubriand and Madame Récamier, and of countless other famous people. Then he shut himself in to write his *Lundis* and, when he emerged, he was the center of a new circle, Princess Mathilde, Renan, Taine, Gautier, Flaubert and the Goncourts. There was, indeed, not a single distinguished author of his time, from Mérimée, Lamartine, Balzac and George Sand to Baudelaire, Verlaine and Zola with whom Sainte-Beuve did not have more or less close associations. The present biography places the author in his surroundings, pictures all these groups, and shows their relations with the critic. The history of literature is here treated, not as

1077

an abstract subject, but as the product of living human
beings and reflecting their reactions on one another.

Sainte-Beuve has naturally been the subject of an enormous quantity of writing, and he has furnished matter for
bitter controversy. He had a habit of becoming very intimate with people, and then dropping them or quarreling
with them. It is of interest to find out how far such dissi-
dences affected his taste, particularly since there are widespread misconceptions on this subject. A great amount of
biographical material is accessible, and there are numerous
studies of special phases of Sainte-Beuve's career, but no
one has yet attempted anything like a complete biography.
This is a gap which this book aims to fill.

The first biography of Sainte-Beuve was published in
1875 by Count Othenin d'Haussonville, of the de Broglie
family, in the form of three articles in the *Revue des deux
Mondes* (Jan. 1, 15, Feb. 1), later reprinted as a volume.
The work, besides being marred by family, social, religious
and political antagonism, preceded the appearance of most
of the important documents. As soon as upset conditions
allowed, Jules Troubat, Sainte-Beuve's last secretary and
his literary executor, began his contributions to his master's
history, *Souvenirs et Indiscrétions* (1872), *Lettres à la
Princesse* (1873), *Premiers Lundis* (1874-75), *Cahiers*
(1876), *Correspondance* (1877-78), and *Nouvelle Correspondance* (1880). Meanwhile, Morand had given out the
letters to Barbe (1872) and in the same year Jules Levallois
had produced his valuable book of appreciation and reminiscence. In 1876 appeared the *Chronique Parisienne,* and
in 1879, the recollections of Olivier and *Sainte-Beuve et ses
Inconnues* by Pons. During the quarter of a century that
followed, a variety of other less important documents were
given out and there was much discussion.

The centenary of Sainte-Beuve's birth furnished occasion for the publication of a voluminous mass of new

material: the letters to Collombet (1903), to the Oliviers (1904); and works by Michaut and Séché. Many details have been added by Spoelberch de Louvenjoul and by articles in the *Revue d'histoire littéraire*, in the *Annales romantiques*, and in other periodicals.

I have made use of all these works, gleaned the biographical information so copiously scattered in Sainte-Beuve's own writings, and consulted contemporary magazines and newspapers, as well as volumes in which the authors republished their critical essays; but I have not considered it advisable to burden my pages with the immense apparatus of footnotes which constant reference to authorities would entail. From the recent biographies by Harper (1910) and Michaut (1921) I have taken nothing, since these works contain no documents. Choisy, in his charming book, gives some extracts from a correspondence, which I have made use of.

Of the three secretaries, Levallois, Pons and Troubat, the first is an excellent writer, and can be depended upon for opinions as well as for facts. The chief sins of Pons are two pieces of flagrant dishonesty: his book claims a "preface by Sainte-Beuve," which is nothing but a collection of quotations from the critic's published writings, and a poem is quoted as taken from the *Livre d'Amour* which does not belong there and which is not in the tone of the volume. In addition to the revelations of Sainte-Beuve's amatory life, the book contains some valuable first-hand biographical information and it voices a sincere admiration for the personality and the intellect of the master. Troubat, in his numerous publications, is repetitious and utterly unmethodical, but indispensable for the facts of the last eight years.

Coming to more recent writers, the two volumes of Séché must be used with great caution, for, while containing a great amount of documentary information, they abound in assertions which are incredible blunders on the part of a

man who knew so much about the subject. Confusing
chronology, the author jumps to conclusions which he sometimes proceeds to utilize as facts from which to draw
further inferences. Michaut is a thorough scholar as to
investigation, but his exaggerated language gives a false
color to many of his statements. "Malignant joy,"
"malevolent judgment," are of frequent occurrence; when
Sainte-Beuve visits Hugo to ask for his vote, he "implores
his protection."

To put, as many antagonists do, the worst interpretation
on everything Sainte-Beuve did or said, to attach insinuations to guess-work when no pretext is furnished by fact,
and thus to construct a monster of unrighteousness, meanness and trickery—such a procedure is assuredly not the
one most favorable for a plausible portrait of a human
being. The idea that a writer can be a great critic, and at
the same time be governed by rancor, envy, malignity,
jealousy, self-seeking servility and whims, is self-contra-
dictory. Such a view is not borne out by the essays and
the correspondence and it is contrary to the express and
unanimous testimony of the three secretaries who knew
Sainte-Beuve best. Hillebrand, an impartial contemporary
observer with no ax to grind, is a further witness.

About Sainte-Beuve's sexual irregularities, it is sufficient to state the facts, remembering, however, that he was
not altogether exceptional. Few of his eminent literary
contemporaries were in a position to cast many stones at
him. That he should excite much political, social and clerical animosity was natural enough, and some of it was not
unearned. For forty-five years, as Schérer said, there was
no other writer who mingled so extensively among literary
men, and no one personally traversed so many diverse
societies and centers of opinion. The contacts, and particularly the separations, excited hard feeling, which critical
outspokenness did not alleviate. Sainte-Beuve was irritable,

but irritability is not the same thing as rancor. A personal dislike flashes out, but a moment later the critic is entirely occupied with the merits of his subject, merits which no momentary exasperation can obscure. His fundamental quality is large mindedness and a justice of judgment that always in the long run outbalances occasional overflowings of vivacity or bile. I am no apologist or advocate, and I have tried not to color my statements; let the record speak.

L. F. M.

CONTENTS

xi

PAGE

CHAPTER XIII

1861–1864

CHAPTER XIV

1865–1869

SAINTE-BEUVE

CHAPTER I

1804—1827

CHARLES-AUGUSTIN SAINTE-BEUVE was born December 23, 1804, at Boulogne-sur-Mer. His parents had married—a first marriage for both—on March 21, the father being fifty-two and the mother forty. On October 4 the father died. Charles-François by name, he was of Picard origin and had been head of the tax office of Boulogne. The mother, Augustine Coilliot, was the daughter of an Englishwoman and of a Boulognese seaman, who came of an old and locally well-known middle-class family. The boy, brought up by the mother and an elderly aunt, attended a lay school kept by a M. Bleriot, where he studied under a good humanist, M. Clouet. Finishing the course here before he was fourteen, he was sent to Paris in September, 1818, where he lived in the boys' boarding house of M. Landry, attending the Collège Charlemagne. Here one of his teachers was Paul-François Dubois, who soon lost his position because of his liberalism. In 1821 Sainte-Beuve transferred to the Collège Bourbon, studying under Pierrot and Planche, with Damiron in philosophy. At the same time he attended lectures on physiology, chemistry, natural history and literature every evening from seven to ten at the Athénée. At Landry's table he met the academician Picard, and in 1819 he became well acquainted with his own fellow-townsman, Daunou, professor at the Collège de France. In college Sainte-Beuve was an excellent scholar, winning many prizes. In 1823 his mother came to Paris, and the young man entered the medical school, in which he continued as "externe" for four years. While still a student, he began to contribute to the *Globe,* founded in 1824 by Dubois. A review of *Odes et Ballades* in 1827 initiated his intimacy with Victor Hugo.

Sainte-Beuve attributed a certain restlessness and melancholy in his nature to his having been born in the immediate

1

sorrow over his father's death. Poverty was also an early affliction. Yet there were compensations. His childhood was passed apart from the world in an isolated provincial town, studying much, dreaming much, serious, pious, pure, with even a touch of religious fervor. By such a life the mind is kept fresh; before entering the turmoil of the age, it attains a certain maturity; ideas have not become commonplace before they can be understood. For physical vigor, too, "it is not a matter of indifference to have been born and brought up near some beach, in daily clash with the ocean."

Good health also was inherited. In physique Sainte-Beuve resembled his mother to an unusual degree, and she exercised a strong influence on his early years, not indeed an intellectual influence, her culture being quite ordinary, but in the formation of character, for from her the son acquired his habits of method and order, which, after all, became also mental traits. To this maternal influence must be added that of his aunt, Marie-Thérèse, his father's older sister, a widow who lived in the same house and afterwards accompanied the mother to Paris. His childhood, thus passed in association with people well advanced in years, was favorable, if not for joyous exuberance, at least for precocious development. Listening to the talk of those who had passed through the Revolution—among these his relatives, the d'Alton-Shées, and Michaud, a journalist who had been obliged to flee from Paris and who had been imprisoned—he came to know the personages and the episodes of that troubled epoch as realities rather than as history. Carried back into the preceding age by family and local traditions, he almost felt that he had actually lived amid the events of which he had so often been told.

Intellectually, the chief inheritance of Sainte-Beuve came from his father, who, though dead, exercised a most important influence upon the boy, not only through the rem-

iniscences of both mother and aunt, who sedulously kept a
cherished memory alive, but more particularly through his
favorite books, some of which he had annotated, often with
quotations from Voltaire, Horace and Virgil, in a hand
scarcely to be distinguished from that of his illustrious son.
Among these books were pamphlets and journals of the
Revolutionary days, from which the boy got an additional
first-hand knowledge of that period. Sometimes in the
margins were written reflections in which the Revolutionary
movement is analyzed, calmly, philosophically, without passion, but with a tone showing a horror of the crimes and
the criminals of the Terror, a state of mind equally averse
to despotism and to anarchy. One volume of particular
interest is a Virgil, the very copy afterwards used by
Sainte-Beuve for his lectures, to which the father had appended a multitude of comments. "In these margins,"
said the son, "he left me all his soul, his mind and his
taste."

In regard to Sainte-Beuve's childhood we have much information from his own writings. *Volupté* must indeed
be used with some caution, for while it is based on introspective study, the analysis is overdone. The recollections
of Dubois, on the other hand, are sufficient evidence, if any
evidence were really needed—for Sainte-Beuve himself acknowledges the identity—that the introduction to *Joseph
Delorme* is very close to a statement of actual fact. Here
we are told that the boy was guided by moral precepts and
formed to laborious habits, and that he was early noted
for application to study resulting in continued success at
school. "Brought up amid the miracles of the Empire,"
we read, "and attracted by military splendor, how many
hours did he pass far from the games natural to his age,
apart on some secluded path, in imaginary monologues, cre-
ating at will a thousand perilous adventures, seditions, bat-
tles, sieges, of which he was the hero. . . . In the midst of

3

his triumphs, he would see on a screened balcony, behind
a half-open Venetian blind, the ravishing form of a young
girl, partly veiled, a slender, graceful figure in white, leaning from above to salute the conqueror and smile on him as
he passed.''

That any boy should have indulged in such dreams is
by no means extraordinary. The surprising feature is that
a man of twenty-five should think it worth while to recall
and publish them. It is a procedure that shows Sainte-
Beuve's native interest in introspective psychology, the
basis of the absorbing interest in character displayed in his
portraits; and it also manifests his sentimentality, which,
when subdued and chastened by experience, becoming sentiment, sympathy, poetic atmosphere, sheds so delightful
a charm over his later essays.

The school at Boulogne, though thorough in the elements of Latin, did not carry its pupils very far. Sainte-
Beuve, therefore, persuaded his mother to send him to
Paris, where his uncle, a wine merchant, entered him in a
school boarding house, then attached to the Collège Charlemagne and afterwards to the Collège Bourbon, institutions
which the boy attended for three and two years respectively,
spending his vacations each year at Boulogne. Among his
teachers in the first, during the year 1820, was Dubois,
already something of a journalist, who lost his position
before the end of the term on account of his liberal political
ideas. In the second, his most distinguished professor was
Damiron, submissive disciple of Cousin, whose eclectic and
spiritualist philosophy, however, the boy was not entirely
willing to accept.

At school, Sainte-Beuve was always one of the best students, and several of his teachers became his close friends.
At the age of nine he had carried off all the prizes in his
class. Nor was he less successful in Paris. In his library
were found various volumes given him at term-ends for

4

superiority over his fellows. In 1819 he won the general competition in history, naturally receiving a copy of Rollin, and in 1822 he headed the list of all the Paris lycées in Latin verse, for which he received a fine Virgil in four volumes. A good many of his college exercises were preserved and published by Pierrot, one of his teachers at the Collège Bourbon, in a collection of such things by various hands. They are of a type then current, imaginary speeches of historical characters, *Defense of Phidias by Pericles, Dying Speech of Alexander, Cato to the Senate, The Duke of Anjou to Duguesclin,* excellent task work for an able boy. That he also wrote French verses on his own account is shown by a piece found among the papers of Dubois, *A Young Italian Poet at the Tomb of Tasso,* inspired by his early enthusiasm for Delavigne, with a touch, perhaps, of André Chénier.

Many of his school companions remained close friends throughout life. At Boulogne, on long remembered Thursdays, he used to take extensive strolls on the sands and about the town and country with his schoolmate, Eustache Barbe, afterwards a priest and professor of philosophy in his native town, with whom he maintained a somewhat intimate, but not very frequent, correspondence, extending from his first year in Paris to 1865. These strolls were occasions for infinite discussions, Sainte-Beuve already allured by vagrant thoughts, Barbe solid on the rock of Faith. At Paris there were new "relations." While his associates at the Collège Bourbon were in later life acquaintances rather than friends, some of his classmates at the Collège Charlemagne remained among his intimates, and even in his last years addressed him with the familiar *tu*. Among these were Nestor Roqueplan, a journalist, Charles Potier, actor and dramatist, who in his blind old age still visited his friend, and above all, Loudierre, who became an admirable professor at the Lycée Saint-Louis and to whose revision and verification the critic in his days of greatest celebrity and authority submitted his not infrequent translations from the classics. The two always corresponded when separated and when in Paris saw one another frequently. In boyhood, Loudierre had become the Parisian successor of Barbe for long walks and interminable discussions.

The topics of such discussions, we may be sure, were not only philosophy, politics and classical literature, but also the poetry of the day. "One is always inspired at first by his immediate contemporaries, by the poet of the eve or of the morning," says Sainte-Beuve. As a boy of nine he had been enraptured by Delille's verses on Rousseau; in 1822 he had professed himself "crazy" for Delavigne, whose rhetorical and patriotic *Messéniennes* had appeared some three years before. This ardor was soon moderated. The poet "of the eve" was André Chénier, first made known in 1819, who became at once, as he remained permanently, a type of the new spirit, a master of the new school of singers. But above all others was the poet "of the morning," Lamartine, whose *Méditations* (1820) from the very beginning carried Sainte-Beuve away, and throughout his whole life did not at any time cease to make him vibrate as no other verse ever did. It was one of these poems that he read aloud one evening shortly before his death in a voice that seemed inspired. To the schoolboy the book had been a revelation, "large, abundant, truly inward, elevated, altogether divine."

The young Sainte-Beuve lived in one of those establishments where boys attending a neighboring lycée boarded and were drilled in lessons to be learned out of school. This house was kept by a former professor of the Lycée Louis-le-Grand, named Landry, a mathematician and free-thinker of the eighteenth-century type. At his table the youth, who because of his intelligence was treated as a grown-up, listened to discussions on all sorts of topics. One of the

frequent guests was Louis-François Picard, actor, theatrical
manager, author of a multitude of successful comedies and
novels, and now past fifty and a distinguished member of
the Academy. In constructing one of his own *dramatis
personæ* and also in studying a character in the works of
other authors, Picard had the habit of writing out the
whole life of the personage from birth to the opening of
the piece in question, a procedure which must have attracted
the attention of the eager boy and stimulated his interest
in personalities.

Late in life Sainte-Beuve recalls certain features of this
period; Sunday afternoon talks (1821) on the Emperor
Joseph II by a former professor of rhetoric, Jules Pierrot,
giving information freshly obtained from an old Austrian
gentleman who had been a personal friend of the monarch;
a visit to an exhibition in the studio of Horace Vernet
(1822), which indicates an early interest in art; a book that
had influenced him, Chabanon's *Tableau de quelques cir-
constances de ma vie,* to which a tribute of gratitude is
paid. "My dreamy youth," says the critic of sixty-three,
"formerly loved to seek therein a foretaste of those intimate biographies, of those true romances, such as I have
sought to accredit."

At the age of fifteen Sainte-Beuve became acquainted
with Daunou, most distinguished of the sons of Boulogne.
He thenceforth visited him frequently and became as
nearly one of his familiars as difference of age and situation would permit. The influence of this relationship upon
the boy would be difficult to overestimate. Daunou, "the
wise old Daunou," was at that time one of the most distinguished scholars of France, member of two Academies
(Moral and Political Sciences, and Inscriptions and Belles-
Lettres), professor in the Collège de France, and a writer
of eminence. Behind him, moreover, lay a political career,
which made him a noted historical figure. Born in 1761,

and entering life as an Oratorian and a priest, he had become one of the leaders of the Convention, and a "philosopher" in the eighteenth-century sense, a disciple of Condorcet and Condillac. He had spoken against the execution of Louis XVI, had suffered imprisonment under Robespierre, then had become secretary of the Convention, one of its chief orators and the author of the Constitution. To the Council of Five Hundred he had been elected from twenty-seven departments, and he was its first president, as well as the deviser and first president of the Institut and the organizer of the Republic of Rome. Finally under Napoleon he had retired from politics and become keeper of the archives. Listening with deference to this retired statesman and to his friends and contemporaries in reunions at his house, the young Sainte-Beuve learned at first hand a thousand details and stored his mind with anecdotes of the Revolutionary period, not the dull spoil of books, but living fragments of actuality, which he later used to such good effect to enliven and furnish point to many an essay.

Daunou is drawn full-length in one of Sainte-Beuve's best portraits. Timid and retiring in his old age, but firm in his ideas, he told the youth that the period in which he would have preferred to live was that extending from the last years of Louis XIV to the verge of the Revolution, a peaceful age, enlightened and without catastrophe. In later life, Sainte-Beuve himself expressed a preference for the ultimate fifteen years of this same epoch. Daunou's philosophy was that of experience and analysis, skeptical, materialistic, regarding anything beyond the senses as non-existent. A man of method and precision, ruled by the spirit of order and classification, he placed perfection of diction above enthusiasm and inspiration and preferred a style in which the expression never goes beyond the idea. As a critic, he demanded exactness in literary appreciations and, with his moderate, lucid, smiling sagacity, he would not overpraise. "Veritable permanent secretary of the eighteenth century at its close," Sainte-Beuve calls him; surely a guiding influence of the utmost importance.

In scholarship, Daunou was rather a humanist than a man of erudition. "Classic Italian, that of Ariosto and Tasso, he knew well; he read English prose, chiefly of the age of Anne; knew no German; did not read Herodotus or Thucydides fluently, but well enough to verify a quotation. What he knew marvelously well and with incomparable distinction was French and Latin." In French, his preference was for the prose of the seventeenth and eighteenth centuries. Bossuet he appreciated and praised from the heart, and he would recite long passages of Rousseau as models of harmony. In Latin, "he liked Seneca, but without prejudice to Cicero; he adored Tacitus, but without losing his appreciation of Livy. To Horace and Virgil he attached all his sensibility, his moral delicacy, the youthfulness of his impressions, just as in the days when he talked about them under the trees at Montmorency. His intellectual make-up was wholly Latin, exquisite and completely rounded." A discussion of these favorites always aroused and interested him. In modern literature, he had stopped at a certain point and he judged everything new from his fixed ideas. From him the Romantic School naturally got little appreciation. On Lamartine's lines: " 'Tis thus all changes and passes, and we too must pass," he made the characteristic comment that the verb was well conjugated. Daunou did not like the *Globe* and the younger man's Romantic escapade also put a slight barrier between them, but Sainte-Beuve later returned to him and was with him on the eve of his death. The funeral of the critic in the early morning and without ceremonies was modeled upon that of Daunou.

"He was a rare being," says Sainte-Beuve in concluding his essay, "not only distinguished, but unique in his kind, one of those men who must be personally known in order that you may receive from them the tradition of an epoch, and yet a man who had his own distinct stamp among all the individuals reputed to represent the eighteenth century; a character and nature original in its combination of qualities, relic of a former age preserved to ours entire and without a line effaced." [1]

While attending the Lycée, Sainte-Beuve had his evenings free and, since he never abused his liberty, he was allowed to attend lectures on natural science and literature from 7 to 10 at the Athénée in the Palais Royal. Among the teachers was Magendie, the physiologist, who had a horror of premature generalization, who demanded facts instead of theories, and who used to say that he had eyes, not ears. The boy was even introduced to Destutt de Tracy, member of the Academy and of the Chamber of Peers, and a typical materialistic philosopher of the school of Auteuil. Such associations fitted a tendency already developed in Sainte-Beuve and aided his progress toward rationalism. He had got comfort from saying his prayers and, up to the age of sixteen, he had been sufficiently religious, though not particularly devout except on special occasions. As in most cases of the sort, it is impossible to say just when he ceased to believe. At any rate his first year at the Medical School, which he entered in the autumn of 1823, made him a thoroughgoing positivist. Being sensual as well as sentimental, he at the same time yielded to the attraction of lewd women, though his taste and intelligence induced revulsion and disgust, and his ideal dreams of

---

[1] This sketch, together with the quotations, is taken from the essay on Daunou in *Portraits Contemporains*, vol. iv. Other sketches given in this and the succeeding chapters are, as a rule, taken from this collection.

pure love and of the charms of family life rose in flagrant contradiction with his practice. The oscillation between sensual indulgence and tenuous Platonic worship of the eternal feminine gave him many regretful hours, yet furnished him with an irresistibly attractive subject for analysis, an anguish not without its element of delight. His temperament was such that his very pleasures were grievous and melancholy, enveloped in a dreamy mystery, which he was at great pains to observe and to record, perhaps to exaggerate, for his mind dwelt upon sexual matters frequently and with great intensity. He indeed ascribed to the exercise of these functions most of the vividness of emotional life and of the creative faculty.

A youth, during the four or five years that center about his twentieth, is not infrequently restless, unsatisfied, heartsick and melancholy, an unhappy disposition which is accentuated when he is also afflicted by lack of vocation, uncertain prospects and present poverty. More grievous still is his condition if the religious belief in which he had been nurtured should crumble before the attacks of doubt. Let him then feed his soul on some despairing book, such as *Werther, René, Obermann,* the whole brood of Byronic morbidness, and his thoughts will naturally linger upon the picture of an early death, perhaps suicide, with friends, especially one female friend, weeping at his tomb. All these conditions combined in the case of Sainte-Beuve. He lacked unity. His poetical tendencies were crossed by a love of science, and science, in its turn, could not long hold out against literature.[2] It is characteristic that, as a student of medicine, he read the series of obituary notices of physicians which had been pronounced before the Acad-

---

[2] On June 28, 1824, Sainte-Beuve writes his fellow-student Emler that he is buried like a rat in chemistry, physics and other such things and will in a week take his examination for *bachelier-ès-sciences.*

emy of Medicine in the reign of Louis XIV by the permanent secretary, Vicq d'Azyr, and as he read, he felt his own aspirations change in accord with the subject treated, being attracted in turn by the dominant feature of each life portrayed, even of the most modest.

If his true vocation had been that of the physician, he could have gone straight ahead, as others have done, toward the accomplishment of a fixed destiny; but the impelling inward force was not there. He had a choice among alternatives. Excluded from politics by his humble situation, and simply looking for a career by which he could make a living in troublous times, he selected medicine in preference to law, because he saw in that profession the opportunity of doing good to his fellowmen. As for religion, he had abjured his simple Christian beliefs for the incredulity of the eighteenth century, or rather for "that somber and mystic adoration of nature which, in Diderot and Holbach, seemed almost a religion." Though he would not set foot in a church, he would yet give of his meager substance to the poor. His mother, who adored him, used to scold. "He never has even shoes," she said; "he gives everything, like Béranger." "An infinite love for the suffering part of humanity and an implacable hatred of the powerful, divided his heart: injustice suffocated him and made his blood boil" (*Joseph Delorme*). Not by nature of a joyous disposition, he exaggerated an unhappy enough situation. Writing to a friend of their boyish discussions at school, he says (1826): "I remember that I had then, as now, terrible attacks of melancholy and disgust over everything"; and in the same letter, he adds the essential point: "It is useless to say that the material of our happiness is within us; that is correct only if you add that what sets the material to work comes from outside. As for me, the only one I know whose clothes can fit my shape is the tailor of the good King Midas." This was

12

a tailor whose services Sainte-Beuve could command only in the very last years of his life.

Though he had no specfic misfortunes to complain of, the young man was in straitened circumstances and without prospects, though rich in sentimental and ambitious dreams; he was studying human bodies while longing to express his own soul in poetry; he was eager for leisure, yet with every moment occupied; solitary, yet with a hunger for human intercourse. Is it at all strange that, in his youthful and romantic reveries, he should have pictured himself as one consumed by a lingering malady, beaten by frightful tempests, branded on the brow, haunted by a phantom that seated itself between him and his happiness, reduced to despair; and that the vision of himself as a suicide on a solitary rock by the sea should have replaced the child's vision of a conqueror received with acclamation by the multitude?

While usually reserved and reticent about his soul struggles, Sainte-Beuve had periods when his spirit burst the bounds and he felt an imperious need of confession. The first of these confessions of which we have record was made to his former teacher, Dubois. On being dismissed from his professorship, Dubois had taken up literary work, contributing to periodicals and preparing historical material for Guizot. In 1824 Pierre Leroux, who was employed in the printing office which published the *Mémorial Catholique,* broached to Dubois the idea of a new periodical, the *Globe,* a rival publication, to consist largely of translations from foreign magazines. As Leroux, in spite of his thorough education, was at this time no writer, Dubois was to be the editor of the new paper. Enlarging the scope of the enterprise, he associated with himself a group of brilliant young graduates of the École Normale, most of them under thirty, and thus established an organ of liberal opinion and of psychological and his-

torical criticism. Made up of serious literary and philosophical articles, this sheet at once became the most
distinguished critical periodical of its time.

Here Sainte-Beuve saw an opening. Cherishing literary
aspirations and thoroughly dissatisfied with his situation
as a student of medicine, he rushed to his former teacher,
the new editor, and poured out to him a confession which,
as Dubois remembered it many years afterwards, revealed
a somber melancholy, a sensual voluptuousness, an imagination excited by the lyric passion of the poets, and a young
soul devoured by the doctrines of Hobbes and Helvetius.
Dubois was deeply moved. He advised the youth not to
give up his medical studies, since literature offered him
slight prospects of a livelihood, but to try writing for the
Globe in his spare moments as a relief and an outlet for
his overcharged mind; and he assigned as an initial task
a series of historical and descriptive articles on localities
in Greece, these places being of public interest at the
moment because they had been scenes of important events
in the Greek war of independence then in progress.

Goethe told Eckermann (1826) that he found the *Globe*
one of the most interesting journals and that he could not
get along without it. There is, indeed, no periodical so
frequently noticed by him. The editors, he says, are men
of the world, bright, clear and bold; they know how to
blame without exciting enmity. "What men they are!"
he exclaims; "Daily they become larger and more important, and all are penetrated with the same spirit." It was
on this journal that Sainte-Beuve got his first practical
schooling, and no schooling could have been better. "My
masters of the *Globe*," he remarks in reminiscence, "truly
masters so far as philosophy and history were concerned."

Dubois himself never produced the distinguished literary work of which his friends considered him capable,
for he became absorbed in politics after 1830—"Dubois of

14

the Loire-inférieur"—and also in education as Director of
the École Normale and member of the Educational Council;
and though he retired in 1852 and lived till 1874, he never
could complete his scattered compositions and bring them
together into a whole. He was a pupil of Cousin, but hardly
one of his disciples. The real disciples among the editors
were his comrades and friends, Jouffroy and Damiron, who
were, to use his own words, "the two master friendships
of my life." Through them eclecticism became the philosophy of the *Globe,* "spiritualism" as opposed to the
"sensualism" of the eighteenth century. Jouffroy, also
an ex-professor dismissed for liberalism, was particularly
the generalizing and dogmatic philosopher, while Damiron
was the analytical and penetrating psychologist. History
and literature were especially represented by Charles de
Rémusat, the first man of universal tastes; by Vitet, the
man of the fine arts, passionate student of the Middle
Ages and pilgrim to Gothic cathedrals; by Magnin, organ
of new, just and opportune ideas, wisely progressive, armed
with an excellent, incisive pen; by Duvergier de Hauranne,
penetrating, exact, pungent; and by Jean Jacques Ampère,
the best-informed man in France on foreign literature.
Guizot, Cousin and Villemain, the great university triumvi-
rate, were indeed friends of the editors, but from none of
them was a single article received. Thiers contributed only
on the exhibition of paintings in the Salon of 1824, a subject generally regarded as lying outside his field, though he
afterwards became a well-known collector of works of art.
Pierre Leroux exercised the self-effacing functions of secretary and business manager, though he, too, gathered
material and occasionally produced an essay.

Because of the censorship and the enormous deposit required of political journals, the subject matter was at first
confined to general literature, though the articles showed
clearly enough that they were written by opponents of

the reactionary Restoration government, which had destroyed their École Normale and deprived so many liberal professors of their chairs. The point of view was equally antagonistic to revolutionary anarchy, being the golden mean often identified with the doctrinaire school. In literature, too, moderation and liberty were the guiding principles. The editors were partisans neither of the old nor of the new, accepting neither the most advanced Romanticism, nor yet the routine and formal correctness of the fossilized Classicism of the preceding century. "I do not know whether this is Classic or Romantic," says one writer, "but it is admirable." The great writers of the age of Louis XIV they held in due honor, yet, while respecting the national taste, they sought the best form and thought offered by foreign literatures, going even to such unexplored regions as Portugal and Brazil. Germany and England were, indeed, largely revealed to France by the *Globe,* and doubtless some of Sainte-Beuve's largeness of view, perhaps even his first acquaintance with the critical writings of Goethe, may be ascribed to this source. At first the paper appeared Tuesdays, Thursdays and Saturdays; then, in 1825, Wednesdays and Saturdays, as a political journal, the censorship having been relaxed; after 1830, it became a daily and passed into the hands of the Saint-Simonians, but it did not long survive the change.

In the "Profession of Faith" that Sainte-Beuve wrote for this new Saint-Simonian organ (Jan. 18, 1831), he says:

The first idea, the conception of the *Globe,* when it was founded about seven years ago, was to gather and present to the French public all the scientific, literary and philosophical works of any importance in the great peaceful movement which had begun to sweep along together the civilized nations of the world. . . . By extracts from books of travel, by translations and analyses of foreign works, by all sorts of studies on the past, the *Globe* sought to put into the hands of its readers the principal elements of various questions; to offer them a view of preceding works and of the position of contemporary science on each point in controversy; to bring to them and set forth in order the most complete materials for the broadest and most conciliatory solutions. . . . The principle of liberty, professed frankly, and rigorously pushed to its last consequences in political economy, in philosophy, in art—such was the general doctrine of the *Globe*. . . . If you recall the hostile intolerance of the liberals against all that was Catholic in religion, and German or English in poetry, it will be understood that the path followed by the *Globe* was at once a very original novelty and a very real progress. It powerfully aided in the destruction of the prejudices and the barriers that still remained in the fields of liberalism. And in this work of demolition it was moved, not by hatred and rage, as were the other liberal sheets, but by a generous sympathy for a future epoch which it confusedly perceived and whose coming it wished to hasten. . . . Freeing itself from the bonds of national egotism, it admired and it glorified in the sight of France the great poets of England and Germany; it generalized ideas of art, dragged them out of the rut of past centuries, provoked new works, without flattery applauded national efforts, and deserved the declaration of Goethe that he saw in this combination of accomplishments and efforts the symptoms of a *new European literature*.

These words are, it is true, the introduction to a program; but with all allowance for this fact, they show to what an extent Sainte-Beuve had grown in harmony with the *Globe,* and what a school had been his association with this able group of writers. We have from him no portrait of Dubois, though abundant record has been left of his high regard for the talent of the chief editor; nor have we any of Damiron, the philosopher being nevertheless treated fully enough in connection with other subjects. Thorough studies were made, however, of several of his associates who attained literary distinction in later years, most having won admission to the Institut, and half a dozen even to the Academy.

Jouffroy (*Revue des deux Mondes,* 1833) is pictured as

a tall mountaineer, with simple and open manners, who came to Paris and, with Damiron and a few others, formed the first group of Cousin's pupils at the École Normale, a group dominated by an exalted sentiment of justice and duty. Lecturer at the École itself and at the Collège Bourbon, he became associated with Cousin, Thierry and their band of Carbonari in "civic demonstrations," and was consequently dismissed from all teaching positions at the time the École Normale was closed in 1822. Then he wrote in solitude his most brilliant essay, *How Dogmas Come to an End,* a description, entirely abstract and impersonal, of the slow decline of ancient religious and political beliefs, with an indication of the rise of the new, his thoughts being obviously concerned with the Catholicism and absolutism of his own day and with his ardent hopes for a glorious future. An outburst of persecuted virtue and faith, Sainte-Beuve calls it, and it certainly is a piece that should not be conceded to oblivion.[3] In 1824 Jouffroy joined the staff of the *Globe,* bringing as his distinctive quality comprehension, intelligence and a large manner. His function was to observe, to understand and to explain. "He sought to deduce from the historical antecedents of nations, from their geographical conditions and their religious spirit, the law of their progress and destiny." Everything was viewed in masses and general forms, as from a mountain top. He had, without doubt, his aristocratic, disdainful and ironical side, but more usually he was good-humored, plebeian, affectionate, interested in those who came to him, benevolent and humane. Though able to write so well, he preferred the liberty and ease of speech and, in spite of his numerous publications, became rather a philosophical demonstrator than an author. As professor, after the Revolution of 1830, and even in the Chamber of Deputies, he gave up his polemical ardor and grew con-

---

[3] It is the first essay in *Mélanges philosophiques,* par Th. Jouffroy.

templative rather than active. Like the river Loire, his discourse was slow, broad and of varying depth, often overflowing its banks beyond measure. Sainte-Beuve addressed two poems to Jouffroy and, though not feeling bound to conceal weaknesses, he invariably speaks of him with affectionate regard.

In the portrait of Charles de Rémusat (*Revue des deux Mondes*, 1847) the words that constantly recur are *rare, delicate, fine, varied, rich, distinguished, graceful, elevated.* Here is an extraordinary enthusiasm, yet an accent that echoes the contemporary impression. The count seems to have been the first aristocratic gentleman of the finest type of manners and culture that Sainte-Beuve had met. It is a type, indeed, never very common in any land, and always delightful. In the life of this youth, the salon had preceded the college, and he united the tone and taste of the old society with the democratic principles of the new, principles of which he accepted all the political consequences. The indifference to thought and the stagnation of the old order excited his antipathy; thereafter his liberalism never flagged and at the age of fifty his youthful ardor was still unabated. A free and brilliant talker, abounding in ideas, prodigiously precocious, he began his literary career, under the auspices of Guizot and the Doctrinaires, with some thoughtful and eloquent political articles. His early songs and elegies he did not publish, nor did he produce his dramas, though he read them to gatherings of friends.[4] He plunged deeply into the philosophy of Condillac; then into that of Cousin; then into that of Kant and the whole German school. His youthful enthusiasm for Cicero led to a translation of *De Legibus,* with a scholarly introduction. He made a version of Goethe's plays, *Faust* excepted; at the same time, he wrote

---

[4] *Abélard,* however, he published. It is quoted in *Port-Royal,* book v, chap. ix.

notable literary essays for Thiers, with whom he became closely associated; no two brains in France more continuously fertile, says Sainte-Beuve, adding: "and let us join to them also Cousin." To the *Globe* de Rémusat brought "his richness of ideas, with his experience and a tact which corrected the roughness of certain other valiant pens." He was a penetrating critic, open, sympathetic, impartial, and always polite. Breadth and delicacy marked his views, and he exhibited the taste and courtesy of a man of the world, qualities which forbid those direct hostile judgments that give pain. And withal he was enormously productive. When the *Globe* first became a political daily, he wrote two-thirds of it, and one issue, on the day of the Revolutionary outbreak, was wholly from his pen. Later, as deputy and minister, both in office and out, he invariably displayed the grace and ease and dignity of a high-minded gentleman. When he stood for the Academy, no candidate ventured to enter the lists in competition, the feeling of his superior merit being universal and subduing even the promptings of vanity and ambition. Then he gave himself almost exclusively to philosophy, often abstruse and technical philosophy, though always expressed in literary style. He was gifted, says Sainte-Beuve, with the most penetrating analysis and also with the finest raillery; and between the two was fixed the most solid conviction. Among all changes, he was never indifferent in matters of truth. "Being one who understands everything and who is tempted to excuse much, whose taste can be gratified and who might thus become too indulgent, he yet has his fixed points, his natural heights, on which he renews his force. He continues under all conditions to respect the thoughts and aspirations of his youth." [5] At the time

---

[5] The phrase is borrowed from the last sentence of de Rémusat's essay on Jouffroy: "Schiller somewhere says that the grown man ought to respect the dreams of his youth; the first mark of such

Sainte-Beuve wrote this article, he must have been on terms of rather close friendship with de Rémusat, for he had been supplied with family information and private documents for the portraits both of the mother (1842) and of the son (1847).

Two other writers for the *Globe* were painted full-length by Sainte-Beuve, and for each of these he made a new portrait after a considerable interval of years. The two thus favored were Charles Magnin (*Revue des deux Mondes,* 1843 and 1863) and Jean Jacques Ampère (*idem.,* 1840 and 1868), both men of learning and both allied to the Romantic School, though not absolutely of it. Magnin may be said to have been born in a library, and he was himself a librarian from the age of twenty, though in youth he was essentially a critic and his organ was the pen; Ampère, son of the famous scientist, after travels that took him from Scandinavia to Italy, became a professor in the University and in the Collège de France, and produced vast studies in the history of early French literature. Both were Sainte-Beuve's personal friends, and they communicated to him much that did not appear in print. In later years, he was an assiduous attendant at Magnin's little dinners, where the host served and eulogized the wine grown in his own humble vineyard. For a brief space, too, he was Ampère's most intimate confidant, and he also heard and made notes of his lectures. "For years, I was a faithful auditor of these courses," he says, "and, though of the same generation, I am a pupil of Ampère."

Magnin's special subject was the drama. In the *Globe,* he wrote not only of Scribe, but of the English theater, particularly of Shakespeare, in connection with the performances given in Paris at the Odéon and Favart from

---

respect is not to acknowledge that they were dreams." Like other great writers, Sainte-Beuve took from others whatever suited him but modified his borrowings, as here, to fit his purpose.

September, 1827, to July, 1828, by Charles Kemble, Kean, Macready and the adorable Miss Smithson, afterwards Mme. Berlioz, performances which furnished much Romantic ammunition.[6] He "put the qualities of a classic writer in the service of Romanticism." Nevertheless, he kept his grasp upon the old, while adopting the new, and was the bitter adversary only of false Classicism. Open and flexible in mind, he was learned and sane, and, as critic, impersonal and unprejudiced.[7] In the Romantic system he saw no miraculous virtue which could dispense with talent. *Hernani* he received with fervor. "Come, Magnin, let fly your *admirable*," exclaimed a fellow-editor in the hearing of Sainte-Beuve and a crowd of other enthusiasts, fresh from the first performance. At the breaking up of the *Globe*, Magnin passed to the *National* and the *Revue des deux Mondes*, and then, as keeper in the Library, grown the very type of the retired scholar—the day spent among the shelves, the stroll for a breath of fresh air, the frugal meal, the long evening's indefatigable agglomeration of notes—he devoted himself to amassing materials on the early history of the drama for a book of which the first volume only was completed, his accumulations becoming too much for him and merely furnishing separate articles for the *Journal des Savants*.[8]

On the other hand, Ampère, while sober and judicious, revealed the poet under the critical writer and beyond this,

---

[6] A large group of these essays appears in his *Causéries et Méditations*, vol. ii.

[7] The following furnishes an example: "It is evident that today the form of Shakespearean drama has fallen in England into the hands of mediocrity, just as the form of Racine's tragedy has among us. The romantic form has its *classics* at London, and their force is about the same as that of ours. Nowhere has the nineteenth century shown dramatic originality, and in this line England is no further advanced than the continent" [1828]. He always deplores the mutilation of Shakespeare's text.

[8] We find Sainte-Beuve using these articles for his lectures in the École Normale.

true son of the great physicist, he introduced the scientific spirit into the literary field. His ingenious combinations, it is said, were always verifiable. From Fauriel, under whom he studied Sanscrit, he acquired a taste for origins, and for a long time he lived among the Latin writers of the fourth century, lavishing upon them his talent, imagination, sagacity and learning. Versatile, and yielding to many intellectual attractions, he was led by a wonderful linguistic facility to learn even Egyptian hieroglyphics and chinese; after living many intimate years with the orientalist, Mohl, he became for another series of years the closest friend of de Tocqueville; and at the end, attaching himself to a family in Rome, he made himself in spirit a Roman citizen and produced a learned, if somewhat arbitrary, history of his adopted city. But all this came later. Rome he had first visited in early life in the train of Mme. Récamier, for at the age of twenty, the brilliant young scholar had become the devoted slave of this enchantress. In the atmosphere of the Abbaye-au-Bois, he had absorbed tact and taste and urbanity. To the *Globe* he was welcomed in 1825. The next year he published an article on Stapfer's translation of Goethe's plays, which elicited the old poet's admiration for its divination of his moods at the various epochs of composition; and in May, 1827, Ampère actually visited Goethe at Weimar, where every one was surprised to find that a man whose writings had given the impression of such maturity was still under thirty. On his return, after an excursion to Scandinavia, he naturally produced further articles on Goethe, and he could not have failed in his animated and brilliant talk to recount his experiences. Through Ampère, therefore, Sainte-Beuve was brought almost directly under the influence of this great modern liberator of the human spirit.

Between Sainte-Beuve and most of this group, the generation that came to young manhood in the year of the

Restoration, lay that distance which separates an undergraduate from a young college teacher, not large in years
indeed, for in later life the two merge into absolute contemporaries, but a considerable gap at the moment. The
teacher seems to belong to a preceding age, and he exacts
what he considers due respect. Sainte-Beuve, who had sat
in the classes of both Dubois and Damiron, his seniors by
ten years, was thus in a subordinate position, which he
soon found irksome. His work, however, is always conscientious and, for a student of medicine, astonishing in
quantity.[9] Before his first assignment, the five articles
on Greece, had been completed, he began writing book
notices, some mere hack work, but others concerned with
memoirs of the French Revolution, a topic that he had
made particularly his own, having devoted the summer of
1823 to extensive and careful reading of this sort. At
what moment (probably early in 1826) Dubois said to him:
"Now you have command of your instrument, you know
how to write," we do not know; for none of his articles,
even the slightest, shows any immaturity. Usually they
are very good book notices, opening with some general
remark, then giving a competent analysis of the work,
noting points of special interest, and finally pronouncing
a judgment. "To appreciate the literary merit of a book
of whatever sort," he says, "is usually to give the exact
measure of its real merit." He tries to understand; he
seeks truth, "What is false is never useful." Of one character he says, "What makes him a profoundly original man
is his good sense"; he is very severe on falsifications of
either history or human nature; he praises good taste,
revolts against the unnatural, hates abstract language, is

---

9 His first article appeared Oct. 10, 1824. Up to Dec. 30, there
were nine articles. In 1825 there were twenty, in 1826 twelve, in
1827 twenty-five. He wrote little for the *Globe* in 1828, and hardly
at all in 1829, when he began to contribute longer essays to the
Revue de Paris.

delighted by even a fugitive appearance of real poetry; Scott and Cooper he admires; Marie Antoinette fascinates him by her beauty and grace, but he salutes the Revolution and decries the meanness and frivolity of the old régime. The strictly Romantic seems to him "the vaporous and melancholy poetry of our age." He speaks of "lack of study buttressed by intrepid presumption," of "routine combined with disdain of facts," of "taking a generous intention for a poetic inspiration and every heartbeat for a stroke of genius," adding that "in poetry as in philosophy, there may be genius in the mere possession of good sense." The author of the *Lundis* hardly thought otherwise.

The first articles that the mature Sainte-Beuve (1845) recalled as of any importance, articles to which he would not even then be ashamed to put his name, were a series of five, published 1826-1827, reviewing the last six volumes of Thiers' *History of the French Revolution*. A rapid analysis of the work under review exhibits all the salient points of the history in their relation to the current of events. Enthusiastic appreciation for the skill of the author in presenting the complicated narrative is slightly mitigated by censure of something scattered and incomplete in the construction and by a friendly reproach for an incorrect and negligent style. Here is no portrait of a writer, but definite criticism of an actual book, solid, clear-sighted, and vigorously written. A goodly number of such articles might well have carried Sainte-Beuve in the course of time safely into the Academy, but they could never have made him permanently famous.

That books of this character—Thiers, Mignet, Scott's *Life of Napoleon*—were intrusted to a mere youth shows the high regard in which Sainte-Beuve was held by Dubois, and this regard was justified, for in thoroughness of knowledge, maturity of judgment, and grace and force of style, these articles are worthy of a distinguished critical writer. When one compares them with the accessible *Globe* essays of de Rémusat, Jouffroy, Magnin and Ampère, one notes in the younger journalist even elements of superiority. All four were writers of unusual excellence, both for ideas and for expression, but when read today, they often fail to hold our interest. De Rémusat and Jouffroy are almost always abstract and impersonal, proceeding step by step, discussing, generalizing; they are always good logicians, with the gift of clear exposition; in Jouffroy, indeed, there is even a limpidity of style that may be called beauty; but to both the fact is less than the reasoning, and the image, the detail that gives life, hardly exists at all.[10] Magnin, while more lively, is apt to insist too much, repeating and driving in his point, where Sainte-Beuve merely gives a vivid touch and passes on. Magnin also exhibits an occasional negligence, as when he says: "Some of our poets have strangely abused this remark." Such a fault would be impossible to Sainte-Beuve, for above all things, he thought straight. Of the four critics named, the one whose style resembled that of Sainte-Beuve most closely, though still some distance off, was Ampère. He often writes with color, and he has a keen interest in personality. Not seldom do we find in him strokes that give life to the picture. Of the unexpectedness of Goethe, for example, he says: "The ordinary road is the only one on which you can be sure never to meet Goethe; do not be surprised, however, to find him on any other." Yet that last clause one feels Sainte-Beuve would have omitted. The manner of all four

[10] De Rémusat's point of departure, even in his critical essays, is almost invariably political. His strictly political writings, indeed, he himself considered his best. Both he and Sainte-Beuve later wrote articles on Jouffroy, de Rémusat treating the development of Jouffroy's opinions, Sainte-Beuve the development of his personality. Here we have the fundamental distinction between the two, and, to my mind, the essence of Sainte-Beuve's superiority.

is, in fact, somewhat pedagogical and, in the long run, dry. While they are all sound and learned critics, their style lacks one or another of the qualities of which Sainte-Beuve already displays such an easy mastery—liveliness, precision, symmetry, a perfect gradation in which each element has the right setting and the exact emphasis it needs, and furthermore a continuity and variety of movement, without jerks, yet never monotonous. Such mastery for the first time invests the articles contributed to the *Globe* in 1826. These are, indeed, real precursors of the *Lundis*. Already, for the most part, Sainte-Beuve plunges into his subject at once, instead of prefacing it with a passage of futile introductory generalities in accordance with the respectable and rather tedious tradition of the *Globe*. He even produces his first portrait, that of Mme. de Maintenon (September, 1826). What insight he manifests! What an intuitive grasp of characters and situations in their entirety! He is, besides, almost always sparkling and colorful. While he would doubtless scorn so dusty a jest as Magnin's on Colley Cibber—"a man of brains although poet-laureate"[11]—his wit yet embellishes every page. He especially delights in little pictures of life, sketched with one vivid stroke. Volumes of anecdote about Voltaire, he suggests, are received by the public with the same avidity as scandalous stories told in an undertone to a select circle by Mme. De Genlis or Mme. Suard, just back from Ferney. "Rabaut consecrated to his friend's memory a touching *Hommage* in which La Harpe deigned to recognize true eloquence"—a whole literary epoch and a professional type in the one word *deigned*; "His pieces were thrown off in the intervals of passion, between remembrance and desire"—criticism illuminated by a flash of experience. Moreover, he had ac-

---

[11] He blames Victor Hugo for writing: "For me thou canst people a desert, even a city."

quired the skill to insinuate far more than he directly said. We cannot, therefore, be surprised to find that Dubois, who heartily admired his young collaborator's work, should, when he had a troublesome book on his hands, turn it over to Sainte-Beuve.

Such a book was Scott's *Life of Napoleon*, which must be castigated, while the author must retain the admiration due to his genius (July, 1827); such a book, also, was the *Odes et Ballades* of Victor Hugo. "One morning," says Sainte-Beuve, "when I went to see M. Dubois, he pointed to two volumes on his table, *Odes et Ballades*, which he had just received and which he asked me to review. 'They are,' he said, 'by that young barbarian, Victor Hugo, who has some talent and besides is interesting on account of his life and character; I am acquainted with him and meet him occasionally.' A few days later," continues Sainte-Beuve, "I read Dubois my article, at the same time telling him that I had not found the author so barbarous." Two essays appeared in the *Globe*, Jan. 2 and 9, 1827. The opening pages display, as was suitable in that staid liberal periodical, a somewhat hostile attitude toward the Romantic group. Hugo's dictum that "the history of mankind presents nothing poetical unless viewed from the altitude of monarchical ideas and religious beliefs" is quoted, and the quotation is followed by sneers at the solemn, sermonizing tone of the holy, militant tribe. Yet, to the critic, Victor Hugo's hatred of the Revolution and adoration of the monarchy are redeemed by his fire, his sparkling images, his ravishing harmony. The Lamennais of poetry, his bad taste is the product of force, never of deliberation. If he is grotesque, it is an orgy of imagination. Sainte-Beuve notes the progress of the poet's talent. Much of the blame is softened by being reported as what people are saying, and the praise, when it comes, is unreserved. Of certain love poems, he says: "If you should dream of delight rapt to heaven on the wings of prayer, you could imagine nothing that Victor Hugo has not realized and indeed surpassed in these delicious pieces.''

In the second article, the critic assumes the rôle of a monitor. He dwells on faults because they spring from traits inhering in the very nature of Hugo's talent, faults which must be sought out and combated. Here follows a keen, profound and sympathetic analysis of the processes of the poetic imagination, the work of a novice, but not unworthy of a Coleridge. We quote the application:

Most of M. Hugo's ideas, before being put into French and into verse, have existed in his mind as original and often sublime reveries. But in passing into the form of style and of poetry properly so called, they have often undergone strange shocks of violence. Far from being weakened and effaced, as happens in the case of certain talents incapable of reproducing anything, they have been forced and overcharged beyond measure. . . . In poetry, as elsewhere, nothing is so dangerous as force; let it go its own way, and it commits every abuse; by it, what was simply original and new is near to becoming bizarre; a brilliant contrast degenerates into an affected antithesis; the author aims at grace and simplicity, and he attains mannerism and silliness; he seeks the heroic, and finds the gigantic; if he ever tries the gigantic, he cannot avoid the puerile.

On the other hand, personal impressions are rendered by Hugo with perfect naturalness and melody. In the fantastic, too, he is found superior, but here again the poet is warned against excess and lack of gradation and proportion. To those who accuse Hugo of offenses against the language, Sainte-Beuve replies that in grammar and vocabulary he is always perfectly correct, his only offenses being those against good taste. The final counsel to the poet, enforced, perhaps maliciously, perhaps as a sop to Dubois, by the example of Racine, is that, on the whole, to fall a little short of the ideal is better than to leap beyond it.

Victor Hugo, not yet grown vain and domineering, and indeed really pleased to find an old opponent at last in a half-yielding mood, called to thank Dubois for the notices, and having learned that Sainte-Beuve was the author of them, he also visited him, leaving his card when he did not find him at home. The next day at lunch time, Sainte-Beuve hurried to Hugo's house, two doors from his own in the rue Vaugirard, where he was most cordially received. A new epoch was opened in his intellectual and moral life.

CHAPTER II

1827—1830

SAINTE-BEUVE became at once an intimate friend of Hugo's, soon visiting his house daily, and becoming acquainted with a new group, called by him the Cénacle, who read one another their poems and who were recognized as leaders of the Romantic School. To these gatherings at Hugo's house Sainte-Beuve was encouraged to present his poetical compositions. He soon became known also as the principal critical expounder of the new views. In August, 1826, the Académie Française had announced as subject for a prize a discourse on French literature in the sixteenth century. At the suggestion of Daunou, Sainte-Beuve had entered the competition, but becoming absorbed in the verse of the period, he renounced all effort to gain the prize, confined himself to poetry and drama, and published in the *Globe* a series of articles which, with extensive additions and corrections, appeared as a volume, *A View of French Poetry in the Sixteenth Century*, in 1828. A companion volume of selections from Ronsard was also published. Immediately after this, he made a brief trip to England. On his return, he prepared himself for a professorship in a lycée. In 1829, he published his own poems as the production of a recently deceased medical student, Joseph Delorme, together with a biography of the supposed author and an appendix of critical remarks upholding the Romantic principles of versification and language. Offended at his treatment in the *Globe,* he began in the *Revue de Paris,* a new periodical, a series of seventeenth-century portraits, in order indirectly to support the Romantic movement and particularly Victor Hugo. At the close of the year 1829, he made a trip to the Rhine with the artist Boulanger and another friend. All this time, he was very intimate with the Hugos, whose influence had brought him into the realm of mystical religious sentiment. This sentiment, together with Hugoölatry, adoration of Mme. Hugo, and friendship with Lamartine, de Vigny and several others, is expressed in *Les Consolations,* a volume of poetry published in March, 1830.

31

The first interview with Victor Hugo being at luncheon, Mme. Hugo was naturally present. Looking the young man straight in the eye, she asked who had written the disparaging review in the *Globe* of de Vigny's *Cinq-Mars*, and Sainte-Beuve was obliged to acknowledge the offense. To wound one of the group was to arouse the ire of all. Alfred, moreover, was Victor's particular and intimate friend, the first among the witnesses who had signed the record of his marriage to Adèle. As an outsider, Sainte-Beuve had been irritated by de Vigny's distortion of historical fact and his injustice to historical characters and, though praising certain features of *Cinq-Mars*, he had spoken very severely of its faults. Now, from the first moment, he was made captive; within a month he was invited to a reading of *Cromwell*, Alfred being also present; he became one of the inner circle, and for some years ventured upon no further severities toward the initiated. He soon came to visit the Hugos daily, often twice a day, and when the two families moved to neighboring houses in rue Notre-Dame-des-Champs, he continued these visits.

Victor Hugo was already celebrated, and within a year his *Cromwell* was to become the Bible or Koran of the Romantic groups. Théophile Gautier's description of his appearance in 1830 will hold good for this period.

The first thing that struck one in Victor Hugo was his truly monumental forehead, which crowned his placid and serious countenance like a marble façade. It did not actually attain the proportions that David d'Angers and other artists afterwards gave it in order to accentuate the genius of the poet; but it was nevertheless of a superhuman beauty and amplitude; there the vastest thoughts could write themselves; there might be placed crowns of gold and laurel, as on the forehead of a god or of a Cæsar. It was a symbol of power. The head was framed with light chestnut hair, allowed to grow rather long. No beard, mustache, side-whiskers, or goatee; a face carefully shaven, and with a particular pallor, hollowed-out and illuminated by a pair of reddish-brown eyes, like the pupils of an eagle; a mouth with sinuous lips, the corners turned down, showing firmness of will, and when he smiled, displaying teeth of shining whiteness. He wore a black frock coat, gray trousers, a small turned-down collar—a costume most scrupulous and correct. You could not have suspected this perfect gentleman to be the chief of those long-haired, bearded bands, terror of the smooth-faced bourgeois. The image has remained ineffaceable in memory, a precious portrait, handsome, young, smiling, radiating genius and spreading around an aura of glory.

In contrast, we have the following portrait of Sainte-Beuve by his friend Juste Olivier: "Middle stature, rather irregular features, pale, a round head, almost too big for his body, very abundant red hair; not handsome or even passable, but not disagreeable, and, in the long run, even pleasing." Lamartine brings out the poetic side: "In 1829 I was very fond of a pale, blond young man, frail, morbidly sensitive, poetic to the verge of tears: he was named Sainte-Beuve. With his mother, who was old, tranquil and absorbed in him, he lived in Paris in a little house with a quiet garden in the Luxembourg quarter. He came often to see me, and I was also happy to visit him. The retirement, the mother, the retreat, the garden, the doves delighted me, too much carried along at that time by the currents of literature, society and politics. It made me think of the country parsonage and the friends I had so much loved in my childhood."

"Morbidly sensitive, poetic to the verge of tears," here is the key to one of the richly stored chambers of Sainte-Beuve's soul. He was timid, retiring, impressionable, and he readily took the tint of his environment; yet, like many timid people, he was proud and had a sense of his own value, though without the ability to push himself forward, as Victor Hugo did, and as all typically successful men can and do. Lacking this hard wedge of aggression, he

33

had yet a hard surface of resistance, which surprised people when they bumped against it, and their surprise often led them to suspect duplicity. At certain points Sainte-Beuve was susceptible to a degree that can best be expressed by the vulgar word "touchy." Here, too, he surprised people. Though normally quick-tempered, he would yet go along, often for a considerable period, perfectly unruffled and reasonable, and then suddenly, without warning, he would flare up, and take offense and give offense—one of his mother's traits, it is said. His reserve underwent a similar mutation. Every now and then a bottled-up accumulation would burst forth in frank confession, perfectly heedless of reputation, whether presented in intimacy to a friend or published freely to the world in books or journals. Custom wore down the primitive barrier, so that reserve soon came to be the least of Sainte-Beuve's defects. As often with young people who suppress themselves, his imagination seems to have been excessively preoccupied with sexual images; sometimes purely sensual —sometimes domestic, presenting wife and children in a cottage listening to father reading aloud—sometimes of the most tenuous Platonic idealism, all air and fire. Beneath this emotional turmoil lay an insatiable curiosity and an extraordinary capacity for intellectual toil, unremittent and without apparent fatigue, yet shadowed ever with a haunting dejection that sought relief in some uplifting enthusiasm, all the while dimly aware that such an enthusiasm was fated to shrivel the instant it might be captured.

The promise of something exciting and admirable was at first the chief attraction of Victor Hugo and his circle. Sainte-Beuve had already written poems, but he had not dared to exhibit them in the matter-of-fact office of the *Globe*. At last he found a sympathetic audience. Hugo had divined his new friend to be a poet even before the

fact was confessed; a batch of manuscript verses confided
to him was commented upon; soon a reading was called
for, while Sainte-Beuve begged the children to make a
noise at their play in order to cover his confusion. In this
springtime of Romanticism, each youth seemed as eager
to hear and applaud another's poem as he was to read his
own. At Hugo's house Sainte-Beuve met a new group of
writers, through whom, added to his friends of the *Globe,*
he shortly came to be personally acquainted with everyone
of literary importance in Paris. Some of the group had
published novels, some volumes of poems, some had produced or were about to produce plays—all seemed on the
road to glory. There were also painters and sculptors
looking forward to artistic triumphs, and meanwhile furnishing vignettes for the volumes often published by their
literary friends at their own expense. They were vivacious
young figures then, all of whom might cherish legitimate
hopes of the most brilliant triumphs. A few years sufficed
to tarnish much of this sparkle, but a handful attained
permanent fame, among these being Alexandre Dumas,
Charles Nodier, Gérard de Nerval, Alfred de Vigny, in the
flower of his genius and not yet retired to his "ivory
tower," and Alfred de Musset, a mere boy, but already a
dandy, producing disdainful and passionate verse. Ulric
Guttinguier and Victor Pavie, among the poets, and Louis
Boulanger and David d'Angers, among the artists, may be
mentioned as the particular friends of Sainte-Beuve.
Others, not strictly of the Cénacle, whom he met at Hugo's,
were Mérimée, Lamartine and, later, Lamennais. In 1830
Hernani brought into the circle the art-student, Théophile
Gautier. To know him was to love him. Others might
become estranged, but three decades later, in the dried-up
Sixties, Théo still used *tu* in addressing *Oncle Beuve.*

Without delay Sainte-Beuve began what he calls his
campaign in the *Globe.* The effect of his recent Romantic

associations appears already in a review of Delavigne's new *Messéniennes* (March 20, 1827), particularly in his discussion of the versification, a subject of which the critic had begun to learn the secrets in his talks with Victor Hugo. Yet he was not free to put the *Globe* at the service of his new friends. He was an underling, and very soon an embittered underling. *Cromwell* (December, 1827), the sacred book of volcanic youth, he was not permitted to review. The task was assumed by de Rémusat, who solemnly refuted the thesis of the sophomoric preface, which divided the poetic history of the world into three successive epochs, lyric, epic and dramatic. With characteristic strategy, Sainte-Beuve conducted an indirect attack. In August, 1826, the French Academy had proposed as subject for the next year's competition for the prize in "eloquence" a *Discourse on the French Language and Literature from the Beginning of the Sixteenth Century to 1610*. It was at the instigation of Daunou, who had himself won his first literary success by a prize essay for the Academy of Nîmes, that Sainte-Beuve determined to compete, and it occurred to him quite naturally, it seems to us, though in connection with such contests the idea was at that time wholly novel, that he had better read up on his subject before writing. Daunou lent him many books and he himself bought others, then despised and cheap. He became so interested in the poetry that he gave up all thought of the prize—ultimately divided between Philarète Chasles and Saint-Marc-Girardin—and, confining himself to a single aspect of his subject, he produced his first volume, *A Historical and Critical View of French Poetry and Drama in the Sixteenth Century*.

About three-fifths of the material was published in a series of twelve articles in the *Globe* (April 14, 1827—April 30, 1828), opening with Malherbe, and then going back to Charles d'Orléans and continuing in chronological sequence till Malherbe was reached again. From the very first, though Sainte-Beuve is never recreant to his classics, either Latin or French, there is evidence of his sympathy with the Romantic group, particularly in his treatment of versification. The chief of his other articles during this period, though not the only ones, are those on Thiers and Scott, already mentioned. One little essay on a transla-tion of Anacreon (March 1, 1827) bears clear marks of his sixteenth-century studies.

The volume,[1] which Sainte-Beuve calls his literary début, was published in July, 1828, "a work of rare merit," de Rémusat calls it in his *Globe* review, adding praise for the "erudition and sagacity of the young critic." The work would, indeed, making allowance for the learning available at the time, take a high rank among the most excellent of the theses for the French doctorate. Much space is giving to quotation and analysis. For facts Sainte-Beuve consulted not only books, but the authors of books, and he knew the difference between the best and the medi-ocre in scholarship. One is surprised at the extent and the minute care of his reading. As a critic, he seizes the trait and attaches it to the current, pursuing this current far beyond his time limit. In contrast to many literary critics who venture into the older literature, he is willing to find beauties even in dull surroundings. His good taste always distinguishes the simple and natural wherever dis-covered. "It would be hard to put more imagination into criticism," says de Rémusat. "His style has color, force, brilliance. But," and here the pedagogue shakes his finger, "severe taste and natural grace and ease we sometimes

---

[1] The *Globe* essays were extensively altered when they appeared in book form, these alterations being in favor of the Romantic ideas. See Michaut, *Études sur Sainte-Beuve.* Possibly Sainte-Beuve's views had changed as he advanced; on the other hand, he may not have been free, in the *Globe*, to say all he wished. The footnotes date mostly from the edition of 1843.

seek in vain.'' The many striking portraits, condensed into a page or less, could hardly constitute an offense against this ''severe taste,'' but the vivid anecdote perhaps, such as that of the flea on the bosom of Mlle. Des Roches, celebrated in verse by a swarm of distinguished scholars, jurists and statesmen; or that of the dying Malherbe scolding his nurse for faults of language while his father-confessor remonstrated in vain; or that of Buffon sweating all day over a majestic period and then exploding in a flood of vulgarities that shocked men of taste and put ladies to flight. It is in the flash of such vivacities that we recognize the essential Sainte-Beuve.

De Rémusat objects to a return to the procedure of Ronsard and his school in verse. Imitation, says he, is artificial; let the style be molded by the thought. But this is precisely the sense of Sainte-Beuve's advice. That the versification of the new school was in certain features a return to the old was all that he claimed. Nothing was proposed for imitation; the whole aim was exactly the opposite. After all, we can see that the chief admiration of Sainte-Beuve is for the acknowledged masters; for Racine, in whom ''the perfection of Virgil was equalled''; for La Fontaine, ''the most naïve, the most delicate''; for Molière, ''the most Gallic of our poets''; in short for the first modern literature that applied ''the most exquisite taste to its noblest masterpieces, that employed reason to caution and assist genius, and like a vigilant mother, to teach it elevation and chastity of sentiment, grace and melody of language.'' The special point of support for the Romantics, in addition to the claim for freedom of versification, is his treatment of the theater, yet even here there is always a defense or excuse of the great century. In the epilogue we find his hopes for the new school. As André Chénier had remade the poetic line, so Victor Hugo has remade the strophe, and many—Lamartine, Béranger,

Hugo, Mme. Tastu, de Vigny—are pressing forward toward the creation of masterpieces. But here, too, he checks his enthusiasm. The example of Du Bellay casts its shadow upon his hopes. Perhaps this new school will also prove abortive. May he be pardoned for saluting what has seemed to him the dawn.

The *Historical and Critical View* was accompanied by a volume of selections from Ronsard with extensive annotations. For fourteen years Sainte-Beuve continued to gather material for his footnotes, and he also wrote new articles for the *Revue des deux Mondes,* dealing more fully with certain poets and certain aspects of literary history, until in 1842, with an essay on Anacreon, he came to what he calls the bottom of his basket of flowers. The notes added then, notes embodying wider knowledge and indicating changes of taste, show the disillusionment at last accomplished. Not only does he here revise a too enthusiastic judgment of the older poets and, often with a charming irony, substitute sober reality for a poetized view, but he has, alas, discovered that, where he had believed liberty alone lacking for a great poetic outburst from his Romantic friends, experience had proved that the lack was in truth elsewhere. In this edition he returns frankly to the *Globe* spirit. The book is dedicated by "his devoted and grateful pupil" to Dubois.

At the time of first publication, however, Sainte-Beuve was getting out of sorts with the *Globe* editors. For over a year (July 5, 1828—August 12, 1829) not an article from him appeared, and it was only in April, 1830, that he began again to contribute regularly. The reason for this abstention can hardly have been that the *Globe* had turned to politics, nor can Sainte-Beuve's trip to England in August and September serve as an explanation. Probably he had been offended. His last article, one on Durand, was an open, almost violent proclamation of Romantic principles, with a prophecy of the imminent conquest of the theater by the new writers. Had he not recently heard Hugo read his *Cromwell*? A continuation of the article was promised, but this never appeared, a circumstance sufficient to arouse the suspicion that Sainte-Beuve had been called to order by his superiors. At any rate, Joseph Delorme's complaint of being exploited by those pretending to be his patrons has generally been regarded as referring to Dubois, and Sainte-Beuve states flatly in a letter to his friend, Loudierre, that he has broken with Dubois, though the show of courtesy continues, and that at the *Globe* office he is considered a trifle crazy. The following February, the editor wrote deploring the separation and urging his former pupil's return.

The real basis of Sainte-Beuve's withdrawal was, we may be sure, his ambition to become a poet. A second visit to Hugo had completed his conversion. Returning home, he selected some of his poems and sent them to his host, receiving a prompt reply, the praise in which, he realized, indicated itself the weak spots in his pieces. From that day, Sainte-Beuve was won over to the branch of the Romantic school of which Hugo was the head. He became one of the innermost circle, from which the profane were banished. A period of three enthusiastic years was opened. He "drifted without resistance from the forbidding coast of the *Globe* toward the enchanted isle of poetry." Here, amid illusions and caresses, he was consoled and sustained against outside indifference. Yet there were drawbacks.

In this school, he writes, of which I was a member from the end of 1827 till July, 1830, no one had any *judgment,* not Hugo, nor Vigny, nor Nodier, nor the Deschamps brothers; and during this time I was much like the rest; I put my judgment in my pocket and gave myself up to fantasy. Coming from a wholly rationalistic and critical school, like that of the *Globe,* and from close association with M. Daunou, this was an altogether new world to me, and in it I forgot myself, relishing the sweetness of the praise, which they certainly did not stint, and giving rein for the first time to certain poetic and romantic qualities and faculties that I had hitherto painfully suppressed. At times I felt, indeed, the false atmosphere; no absurdity or exaggeration escaped my notice; but the accompanying talent that I perceived reanimated my courage and I persuaded myself that these defects would probably remain a family secret.

"Nodier had the gift of inexactitude," Sainte-Beuve once noted in a memorandum book; in an article published at the time of his death (*Revue des deux Mondes,* 1844) he writes: "His true gift was to be inevitably loved." Between the two remarks there is no contradiction, even in spirit. Charles Nodier was the typical man of letters, not exclusively scholar or poet, but a little of everything, producing romances, poems, criticisms, and works on natural science and philology, brilliant, delightful, scrappy, unmethodical. Coming of age either too soon or too late, just between the eighteenth century and the Restoration, he was now nearing fifty, the elder brother of the coming poets, without pretension, without conceit, "a comrade, good-humored, charming, enthusiastic, encouraging, disinterested, becoming anew often the youngest of all in heart." A Wertherian in his own youth, he regarded the extravagance of these youngsters with a benevolent, ironical smile and greeted the budding Romantics with admiration and affection. Yet, conciliating as was his nature, he frankly contradicted his friends when he thought them in error, and he opposed all literary abuses with perfect independence. Sainte-Beuve compared him to a generous wine, growing mellower with each succeeding year. The so-called first Cénacle—we must keep in mind that there was in reality no such thing, only rapidly varying associations and gatherings—had been largely superseded by Victor Hugo's circle and other groups, but Nodier still received Sunday evenings at his apartment in the Arsenal Library. Sainte-Beuve pictures him standing by the fireplace in a reminiscent mood that banished whist for that evening. "One who has not heard him talk," he says, "only half knows and appreciates him as a story-teller. His youth attempted all sorts of things, risked every adventure, political and sentimental in turn, passing from conspiracy to idyll, from innocent and austere studies to romantic delirium, but stopping short, cutting off every risk just in time to gather nothing but the emotion and the substance of a dream."

Some ten years younger than Nodier came Émile Deschamps, who had met most of the earlier poets at his father's house and who now brought to these same home receptions the youthful band just entering the field. To his friend, Soumet, the dramatist, also of the older group, he once presented an eagle feather, reputed to have served as the pen with which Soumet's *Divine Epic* was written, but which did not after all enable that work to soar. Émile and his younger brother Antony, translator of Dante, had collaborated with Hugo in publishing the *Muse Française,* organ of the new literary ideas, a periodical hardly to the taste of the stiff-necked *Globe.* Having produced a successful comedy, Émile published, in 1828, a volume of poems, with a preface which, as a manifesto, rivaled for a time Hugo's famous preface to *Cromwell.* Later he collaborated in drama and in an opera libretto (*Huguenots*), and produced romances, criticisms and translations, yet, though universally considered fit, he was never elected to the Academy. In an epigram on the subject, he genially expresses a preference that the world should demand in surprise why he was not a member, rather than wonder how he ever managed to get in.

Alfred de Vigny, a frequent early visitor at the Deschamps home, and coming thence to Hugo, was a character of another stamp, though the self-importance and susceptibility displayed in his later career had not yet become conspicuous. At this time, he manifested, to quote Sainte-Beuve, "the pride of a lofty independence under the perfect forms of elegance and urbanity." As a poet, he was highly prized by a few; to the general public, he was known as the author of a widely popular historical novel; after some moderate successes in the theater, he was shortly to win a complete triumph with his *Chatterton*. To the private reading of his plays Sainte-Beuve was invariably invited during this period of ardor and mutual sympathy. His former harsh judgment on *Cinq-Mars* had been forgiven in the admiration felt and expressed for his friend's poetry. If we may estimate the repicrocal adulation from de Vigny's letters to Sainte-Beuve regarding the *View of Sixteenth Century Poetry* and *Joseph Delorme,* it must have been almost ludicrously beyond measure. Though ten years cooled friendships and developed antagonisms, Sainte-Beuve retained to the end his admiration for de Vigny's genius. "He is of that chosen band of poets who have said things worthy of Minerva," is a final judgment; and as a summary, "He has inscribed his name in tongues of fire among those placed highest on the ideal dome of art." This eulogy Sainte-Beuve can pronounce at the very moment he recalls his impatience with de Vigny at the Academy, futile, long-winded, perpetual, supporting impossible propositions or discussing motions already passed, while Patin, seated between the two, indulgently murmurs: "Sainte-Beuve is impatient, but it must be confessed that de Vigny is a bit trying."

The babe of the group was Alfred de Musset; and what a babe! No solemnity, no sentimentality for him! The adorable moon he likened to the dot on an *i*—irreverent, shocking image! Hugo's friends were exacting in matters of technique, scrupulous above all concerning perfect rhymes. De Musset was incorrect and negligent on purpose. One ballad he willfully un-rhymed, just to give the Cénacle a jolt. "He jumped into the poetic sanctuary through the window and with his spurs on," says Sainte-Beuve. "He was Cherubino at the masked ball disguised as Don Juan," insolent, audacious, "with the grace and effrontery of a page." Rosy-cheeked, fair-haired, with a bold, proud forehead, he had at eighteen the aspect of adolescent genius. Having heard Sainte-Beuve read some of his poems one evening at Hugo's, he visited him the next day and recited some of his own, a discovery of lyric talent reported at once to headquarters. It was a genius that Sainte-Beuve loved, one that caught in its flight something that no effort or study could give, possessing a virtue of style that in a flash lifts up to heights not to be reached by climbing; "the god, say if you choose the demon, had passed there." On his death, Sainte-Beuve recalls his note, "so dear from the first day, going so deep into the heart with its freshness and its vernal novelty"; and, coming from his funeral, the man past fifty lingers under the weight of this thought: "Our youth died long ago, but we have just buried it with him."

While youth lasted, it was a time of intoxication. Sainte-Beuve had never been so happy. If his poems are often weighted with dissatisfaction and grievous melancholy, we may take his word for the fact that, when a poetry altogether intimate and wet with tears comes to be expressed in harmonious verse, the wounds are already cicatrized. Even had this not been so, sympathy would have added to bitterness a rather agreeable taste. He was at last a poet among poets. Emulation, not yet hardened into rivalry, stimulated production. On the other hand, there were a few accompanying drawbacks. In some ways, indeed, inspiration was diminished, narrowed, stunted. Every technical device was noted, every brilliant expression or image remarked and saluted. The laudation was indiscriminate.

Then, too, visitors would slip in, mere imitative rhymers, tolerated for their applause and avid in their turn for a like recompense. Sometimes two or three poets would happen to meet in some salon; the mistress of the house would beg for a recitation, to be listened to by a circle of elegantly gowned ladies, an altogether insipid and counterfeit performance. At the moment, however, a flood of enthusiasm submerged matter-of-fact motives, and all the duller and more sober monitors were silenced. Sainte-Beuve and his friends did not perhaps do utterly absurd things, but the fine old folio of Ronsard from which he had culled his selections he gave to Victor Hugo, with a dedication "To the greatest inventor of lyric rhythms that French poetry has seen since Ronsard," and on the margins of the stately volume each poet of the group inscribed some verses.

Among Sainte-Beuve's poems, there are several that we can imagine him reading to the faithful: *The Cénacle,* a poem which seems to have attached this name to all the innovating associations, magnifying the chosen group in the midst of a mocking world, with Hugo, de Vigny and Delacroix as types; *The Yellow Rays,* coloring a host of recollections with a maleficent tint; *To My Friend Victor Hugo,* the soaring eagle contrasted with the caged bird (himself), a piece in which he has caught a few echoes of Hugo's strain; *To David d'Angers* dreaming in his studio, while his statues come to life, glory being promised to the sculptor. Other pieces are almost equally fitted for such recitation; the poet does not demand Chateaubriand's American wilderness, Lemartine's Alps, Hugo's medieval ruins on the Rhine, but only a common field, a little murmuring water, a tree; a spring-like autumn day in the Luxembourg gardens suggests a happy momentary return of youthful feeling in old age; sometimes, leaving a serious task, he launches his bark on the sea of poetry—a dead calm—night falls—the keel is still motionless, the mast fades from the pilot's sight in the gloom; poetic inspiration flown for a moment, he turns to books, not great achievements of genius, but ten, twenty, a hundred volumes of anecdotes and chat of bygone celebrities—then he takes delight in buying from a dealer on the quays a precious parchment-bound edition printed on vellum—one evening Nodier beckons him from the dance to pore for the rest of the evening over some recently acquired treasure—after a while, he begins again to read the poets, from Pope to Goldsmith and Gray, coming at last to Mme. Tastu's "adored lute," till he is anew possessed by the impulse to sing,

> "Eyes raised to heaven and wings outspread to soar,
> Lo! I become a rhymer as before."

Perhaps we could even imagine him reading a poem warning the dreamer against gazing too fixedly into the lake of his own soul, for deception awaits the victim; plunging in, he will find shapeless monsters, serpents, dragons, crocodiles and a frightful, voracious shark—after which there is for him no possibility of happiness.

During 1827 Sainte-Beuve had attended lectures on philosophy given by Jouffroy in his two small rooms, rue Four-Saint-Honoré.

These courses were much sought after, he says, persons with minds already mature—comrades of the teacher, physicians since celebrated, some choice intellectual spirits of the salons, a few young peers and heirs to the peerage—composed the usual audience, limited in number, indeed, for the apartment was small, and besides any marked gathering might easily have become suspicious in the years preceding 1828. Once a week they resorted to these philosophical preachings; they entered with fervor and discretion, for they seemed to imbibe a new and forbidden science, to absorb by anticipation the purified faith of the future. When, one by one, the company of fifteen or twenty had assembled, when the key had been withdrawn from the outer door and the last ring of the bell had ceased, the professor, standing

propped against the mantelpiece, after some moments of silence,
began in a low voice. The countenance, the whole appearance of
M. Jouffroy is of a kind that is most striking at first sight, on
account of some indefinable quality of melancholy and reserve
that brings up an involuntary idea of a mysterious and noble
enigma. He began to speak; he talked of the Beautiful, or of
Moral Goodness, or of the Immortality of the Soul; in those
days, his faint color, his slightly furrowed cheek, the deep blue
of his glance were united in our minds with ideal memories of
the *Phaedo*. For a time, he spoke in a monotone, then he raised
his voice and became animated: the intervals between his words
diminished, or seemed to be filled with sparkles. His eloquence
spread out, prolonged itself beyond the assigned hour, and could
not bring itself to end. The declining day intensified the im-
pressiveness of the scene; all came away in a mood of belief,
deeply penetrated, and happy for the seeds of inspiration they
had received. Since lecturing in public, M. Jouffroy has justified our expectations, but to those who heard his private teaching, nothing he has since done has revealed, or can ever reveal,
the old charm, the old preëminent power.[2]

Sainte-Beuve addressed two poems to Jouffroy: in one,
he admires the philosopher's vigilant reason, victorious over
his dreams, yet he utters a warning lest romance insinuate
itself and invite passion to upset that tranquil equilibrium;
in the other, he blesses Jouffroy for his consoling utterance,
which inculcates truth, divine justice and eternal beauty.
At the opposite pole are two poems to de Musset, written
in a mood of disillusionment, ennui and cynicism; one
expressing the crude sensuality of a young fellow at a
dance; the other describing a moment of gratified passion,
invaded in the very act by disgust, an odious thought, like
a night bird, obscuring his heaven, a shadow seating itself
between him and his companion and corrupting the present

---

[2] The public lectures Sainte-Beuve knew about, for he had attended
them at the reëstablished École Normale, as he so often attended
public courses at the University and the Collège de France, and he
gave an account of them in three issues of the *Globe*, December, 1830–
January, 1831.

delight. On the birth of Hugo's son, a poem is addressed to the father, composed while Sainte-Beuve watches throughout the night by the corpse of an old man who had died of the stone, the monotony being broken at last by the noise and flare of a city conflagration. Forty-one years later, less eight days, Sainte-Beuve succumbed to the same malady from which that old man had died.

His poems of this period were published as the works of a fictitious medical student, Joseph Delorme, premature victim of tuberculosis, whose biography, which served as an introduction, was nothing but a slightly poetized and strongly sentimentalized version of his own career, while the poems themselves are almost without exception expressions of his personal moods and experiences. We all, he says in a later essay, like to pose before ourselves a type, to exaggerate it, to put into it our qualities, our faults; we caress it, we ill-treat it, and generally we kill it off in our impatience. The general idea of struggle, early death and posthumous publication with a memoir by a friend, seems to have been suggested by Southey's edition of *Henry Kirke White*, a book which enjoyed an astonishing transient popularity and which was often cited by Sainte-Beuve. There is little in the poems themselves which recalls the unfortunate English youth, and that little may be ascribed rather to the general temperament of the times than to direct influence. Even Sainte-Beuve's professed imitations of White, Wordsworth and other British poets have little resemblance to the originals. What he took from them was principally a taste for the humble and homely, close observation of nature and of the soul, frank, sometimes crude naming of common objects, a preference of the cottage to the drawing-room, and an effort to relieve the prosaic character of domestic details by the human sentiments attached to them—qualities which were indeed innate rather than acquired, though they may have been fortified by sympathetic reading. There is an occasional queer obliquity; we find masts made of oak and an æolian harp hung on the branch of a tree.

Assuredly not a third of the poems fit the character of the imaginary Joseph Delorme, a more or less Byronic sentimentalist, a defeated, disillusioned youth, whose life is withered in its springtime, who dreams in the moonlight and in solitary places, who pictures the details of his suicide and the finding of the body, who suffers from doubt, emptiness, disquiet, melancholy, a nameless, secret malady, and who sheds vast quantities of tears. To a general hopelessness are added the more substantial miseries of poverty and lack of prospects. The youth longs in vain for leisure, for a cottage out of sight of Paris, for opportunities to indulge in revery, for a friend, for a bride, for kisses, for various kinds of mistresses, including a rich widow and an ignorant Italian peasant girl. His destined love he has perhaps passed unaware in the crowd. Yet he would not poison an innocent life with his bitterness. He is eager for some great crisis, for some noble activity or, failing that, for some more modest occasion for self-sacrifice. All this fits Joseph Delorme and, without doubt, it also fits Sainte-Beuve. Where Joseph Delorme has no part is in such pieces as we imagined Sainte-Beuve reading to Hugo's circle, or in those addressed to Alfred de Musset, and also in a multitude of others, such as a poem depicting an evening with a prostitute,[3] or one describing a commonplace, ugly, squalid landscape, both bits of crass realism. It is especially the pieces that could hardly be ascribed to Joseph which are, as Sainte-Beuve calls them, serious and frank studies, severe in art, though in a limited frame.

To the poems were added as an appendix some thirty pages of "Thoughts of Joseph Delorme," but it is evident

---

[3] Kirke White has a poem on a prostitute, but it is separated from Sainte-Beuve's by a greater space than the breadth of the Channel.

to the least observant that these are the reflections, not of
our imaginary consumptive, but of the vigorous and pug-
nacious convert to the new school. Here Sainte-Beuve
takes up the cudgels for his friends, Hugo, de Vigny,
Deschamps, designating André Chénier as their master; he
discusses and defends their technical procedures in great
detail and with frequent examples; he sarcastically assails
the critical attitude of the *Globe*. At last we see the new
champion unencumbered and in the open. And there is
ample evidence that this champion is a great critic. He
can draw fine distinctions. In his condemnation of the
conventional Delille, he purposely employs a disgusting
image. That is *bad* taste, he adds, I admit it, but it is not
false taste. Though for the moment a partisan, he proclaims universality to be the essential quality of true criticism. In the following passage we find Sainte-Beuve—the
young, the medial, the mature Sainte-Beuve:

The critical spirit is in its nature facile, insinuating, mobile
and comprehensive. In serpentine course it encircles poetic
works and monuments, as a great, limpid river twines about the
rocks, the fortresses, the slopes embroidered with vineyards and
the wooded valleys that border it. While each of these objects
in the landscape remains in fixed position, without regard to
the rest, while the feudal tower disdains the valley and the valley
ignores the hillside, the river passes from the one to the other,
laves them without injury, embraces them all with its fresh flowing water, *takes them in,* reflects them; and when the traveler is
anxious to know and visit these varied sites, it takes him in a
boat, which carries him without a jar and unfolds to him suc-
cessively the whole changing spectacle of the river's course.

On December 6, 1828, Sainte-Beuve wrote Loudierre:
"I have sold the first edition of my poems at four hundred
francs for a thousand copies to Delangle, and the printing
will begin toward the end of January." It was in the last
days of March that the volume appeared. A month later,

he again wrote: "This wretched book has had all the success I could have hoped; it has excited and irritated the proper more than might seem credible; Mme. de Broglie deigns to find it *immoral;* M. Guizot discovers in its author a *Wertherian and Jacobin Medic.*" The *Globe,* Sainte-Beuve says, was divided, the high and mighty, including de Rémusat, opposed; Leroux, Jouffroy, Damiron, Magnin in favor. It was Magnin who wrote the advance notice (March 26) and the review (April 11). In the first article, he speaks of this good Joseph Delorme, who died last autumn, as his friend, thus keeping up the very thin disguise. The modest book, he thinks, will make a stir; it is "true, profoundly felt, frank," severe in form and showing the influence of Victor Hugo, but no imitation. Joseph Delorme is a dreamy spirit, of the family of René, Werther and Obermann; not an imitator, but a rival of Kirke White. He further notices that, in the "Thoughts," several opinions of the *Globe* are treated with disdain, revealing even irritation and bitterness, and he advises that a few of these passages be suppressed. In the review, Magnin says that the book has made a noise, almost a scandal. Praise and blame have both been excessive, especially the blame, for the "Thoughts," which are those of an exalted disciple of André Chénier, have offended the classic school, the salons and even the author's friends. Joseph has neither the consuming passion of Werther, nor the distinguished manners of René. A poor medical student, proud, timid and knowing nothing of the world, he has a heart under his worn coat. No mere copy of the "Lakists," he produces a sort of elegy of intimate analysis hitherto unknown in the language. Some of the moral situations, however, are so special, so far from the common experience, that they must be taken on faith. The idea and the style are one, language without decoration, thought without illusion, things seen in their repulsive nudity. The forms, common to the

Romantic School, some being revivals from the old poetry, are objectionable; also the pleasure in difficulty vanquished. *The Yellow Rays* is delirious, outside the realm of art. As for *My Muse*, "we could pardon the poet for showing us his Muse poor, sad, ill-clad, but with pulmonary disease, excuse us!" [4] On the whole, "it will never do to toy with the false." In spite of these strictures, when Magnin, in another article of this same year, has occasion to enumerate the great poets of the century, he includes Sainte-Beuve.

Lamartine was born with the gift, not to be acquired, of melody; Victor Hugo saw the idea as an image that vibrated into rhythm; de Vigny lived in the image he had sought and found, till it molded a poem; in de Musset, sentiment and disdain sang themselves without forcing; Sainte-Beuve, on the other hand, had a disposition to poetry rather than an inspiration, the poetic heart rather than poetic genius. He was moved by a vague poetic emotion that he strives to express instead of by an imperative poetic concept that creates its own expression. He was aware of various ways of saying things, on one level or another, and he selects according to his judgment. The poetic apprehension of a subject was not the first that came to him, dominating his idea; it was something added by reflection to his thought or feeling, a modification wrought in an originally different mental picture. Nevertheless, all his poems are readable, most are interesting, and half a dozen deserve to live.

In his trip to England (August-September, 1828) Sainte-Beuve had visited, of course, London for a fortnight, though all the monuments were closed, and had spent two months with friends in the country near Oxford; he had also made a special point of admiring those "sublime

---

4 This poem depicts the Muse as a hard-working peasant girl, who cares for an aged, blind father in a sordid hut and who interrupts her song to expectorate some lung cells.

cathedrals before which our miserable insignificance stands confounded and overwhelmed''—the phrase sounds like one of Victor Hugo's, but it is quoted from the *View of Sixteenth Century Poetry*. The savage, as the traveler calls himself, had been initiated into art by his new friend.

On his return to Paris, Sainte-Beuve's chief preoccupation was the problem of earning a livelihood. Medicine he had renounced, the date of his last matriculation being November 13, 1827. With his literary training and aptitudes, he naturally turned to teaching, and at the close of 1828 he was preparing for the examination for the license, Jouffroy trying to procure him a professorship in the Lycée at Besançon, where Amédée Thierry was eager to have him for a colleague. Even Villemain was ready to aid, and Cousin gave advice. Before the appointment was made, however, Dr. Véron, an enterprising and successful journalist, secured Sainte-Beuve's services for the *Revue de Paris*, which the doctor had just founded. There was a group of notable contributors, the articles were signed, and the remuneration seemed to the young critic ample, two hundred francs a sheet, that is, sixteen pages. With untiring work, such pay meant a competence.

In this periodical, Sainte-Beuve tried for the first time in extended essays his special method of criticism, the literary portrait, in which he passed from the man to his work, seeking in the inner life of the author the germ of his production. His series of articles [5] constituted what he called a campaign, heartily and openly Romantic, yet always, in characteristic fashion, respectful of established reputations. In the first issue of the new magazine (April,

---

[5] These articles are republished substantially as they appeared in the *Revue*. Sainte-Beuve has made a few typographical corrections and sometimes, though not more than two or three times in an essay, inserted a short sentence, usually adding some relative fact. The only real modification is the provision of footnotes, there being none in the *Revue*.

1829) the subject is Boileau, no new theme, it must be confessed, but it is good in each new literary epoch to review the great names. The intention is, not to conduct a regular suit and pronounce a definitive judgment, but to talk freely with the reader, to study Boileau intimately, and look on details from the point of view of the present, passing from man to author, from bourgeois to court poet. In spite of the disclaimer, there are resolute judgments, though these are often half concealed among appreciations. If imagination is the test, Boileau is not a poet; he reformed verse as Colbert reformed the finances, not on a general plan, but by details; he was the editor of a poetic code, since repealed. In treating Mme. de Sévigny in the second essay, the polemic is interrupted, and the fascinated critic yields himself up to the charm of his subject, presenting a delightful portrait with consummate grace. His single reservation regards the cold-hearted references of the great lady to the sufferings of the unfortunate Breton rebels. One sentence may be emphasized for the light it throws on Sainte-Beuve's life at the time: "Our days are passed in study, our evenings in serious discussions."

With Jean-Baptiste Rousseau we come back to the campaign. In a later note, indeed, he calls this essay "an example of the literary paroxysm of 1829," just as he calls the Boileau piece an "impertinence." A lyric poet is a soul that bares itself to the world in song. Because Jean-Baptiste had been set up as a rival to the Romantics, he is utterly and, according to a later view, unjustly disparaged. Lebrun, on the other hand, is tolerated as a precursor, whose literary relations, at the same time, enable Sainte-Beuve to exalt André Chénier, a poet who "leaves far behind him Boileau and the ordinary prose of his axioms." The styles of Maturin Régnier and André Chénier are "a perfect model of what our language permits to genius expressing itself in verse." They exhibit the graces and ornaments that grammarians have foolishly purified away. The one closes an old epoch, the other opens and reveals that which is now coming to fulfillment. Yet all these judgments are pronounced, says the critic, "without erecting our opinion into a precept." "It is not our purpose to wreck reputations in order to establish new principles," is another remark, made this time in discussing La Fontaine, "the only personal poet, the only dreamer, before Chénier."

The propaganda reaches its climax in some essays on Corneille and Racine. In August and September, Sainte-Beuve interrupts his series in the *Revue de Paris* and publishes in the *Globe* two articles reviewing a life of Corneille, these being his first contributions to this journal for over a year. The opening is perfectly innocuous, the biography being praised as disclosing the man beneath the poet. Then comes the deployment of strategy, certainly unnoticed by the *Globe* editors, a strategy which consists in praise of the old dramatist's Spanish inspiration at the very moment that Victor Hugo was meditating *Hernani*. Sainte-Beuve must have chuckled over his successful ingenuity in palming off these two pieces on the unsuspecting and unsympathetic *Globe* under the guise of a book review. After this triumphant trick, he returns to the *Revue de Paris* to treat Racine, praising him, of course, but making reserves on just those points in which Victor Hugo was considered strongest. "Racine was dramatic, without any doubt, but in a type of play that was essentially undramatic. In another epoch, in times like ours, when the proportions of the drama must be different from what they were then, what would he have done?" Not a soaring untrammeled genius like Shakespeare and some others, but lyric and elegiac, confined to general terms, indirect expressions and circumlocutions, instead of having the liberty of directly naming things, he is the perfect expression of a vanished society. When Sainte-Beuve published the last of these articles, January 17, 1830, *Hernani* had already been a month in rehearsal.

This method of indirect attack, of producing by insinuation more durable effects than could be wrought by frontal blows, is typical; but not only did Sainte-Beuve thus pave the way for *Hernani*, he also lent his pen to Victor Hugo for undisguised propaganda on occasions when the poet could not speak for himself. In order that the critic should not be compromised by the advertiser, he sent these pieces out under other names or initials. An account of Hugo's defense of liberty of art in an audience with Charles X, after *Marion Delorme* had been suppressed by the censor (August, 1829), is signed by the editor, L. Véron; a prospectus of Hugo's works, a bookseller's puff, published with *Les Orientales* (December, 1829), is signed E. T. Both pieces betray Sainte-Beuve's style, and even his critical judgment, though he was, of course, not free to mingle reserves with his encomium.

During the period preceding the appearance of *Hernani*, he was much occupied with that piece, apparently securing recruits. These effervescent youths, strangely garbed, wearing a "Merovingian prolixity of hair," and ferociously prepared to eat any stray Academician, youths who drank healths out of a skull and who tore the green coat from the back of Dumas after a theatrical success and distributed the fragments as relics, these enthusiastic and volcanic combatants were of a different type from the Hugo Cénacle, and their irruption into Hugo's house was looked upon by the elect as a calamity. They were necessary to the triumph of *Hernani*, however, and all shared in that glory. Sainte-Beuve himself was one of the crowd that flooded the *Globe* office after the performance (February, 1830) and rejoiced in the conquest of that staid organ.

It was just at this point (March, 1830), when differences

were about to arise, and each of the group of friends was to go his own way, that David d'Angers, their sculptor, sent Goethe a box of bas-relief portraits in plaster of Hugo, de Vigny, Émile Deschamps, Mérimée, Mlle. Gay, Mme. Tastu and others. The portrait of Sainte-Beuve is not mentioned by Eckermann, but we are told that his autographed works were among those that came in the same chest, a gift from the young writers of France which made Goethe profoundly happy and gave him, he said, new life.

During 1829 Sainte-Beuve had considerably widened his circle of distinguished friends. He is on very close terms with Mérimée, who had just published his *Charles IX*. Lamartine, to whom, through Hugo, he had the year before addressed an elegy reflecting the style of *Les Méditations*, made a visit to Paris in June and became his intimate in long conversations on human ills and on the needs of their souls. Sainte-Beuve even met the veteran statesman, Royer-Collard, who lauded his treatment of Jean-Baptiste Rousseau. Villemain, the idolized lecturer on literature at the Collège de France, he often heard, as he also heard Cousin, Guizot, Jouffroy and others. With Villemain he would sometimes walk after the lecture and the professor would talk copiously, reminiscence, quotation—a distich of Martial, if they passed some roses—"perpetual thought without effort, animation without smoke or flame, prose and poetry intermingled as in the Dialogues of Cicero." One evening in July, Villemain called, and led Sainte-Beuve to the home of Chateaubriand in the rue de l'Enfer, thinking that the great man, who was about to leave on an embassy to Rome, would soon head the ministry, and might then be useful to a literary aspirant. The visitors found him in his garden. He began, in contrast with Royer-Collard, by reproving Sainte-Beuve for his treatment of Jean-Baptiste. In the house, later, he talked of La Harpe, whom he had known. After Chateaubriand's return from Rome, Sainte-Beuve made several morning calls on him and tried with little success to win him for Hugo and the new school. Chateaubriand, indeed, urged his caller to shake off this dominating influence and be himself. In November, Sainte-Beuve, in company with the painters Boulanger and Robelin, made a trip to the Rhine, traces of which may be found in his first essay on Racine. His letters to "My dear and great Victor" show the taste for the Gothic and the medieval that he had acquired.

Some poems written to Boulanger during this trip are among the verses of *Les Consolations,* a collection which appeared anonymously in March, 1830. In Sainte-Beuve's eyes, this volume remained to the end "the ardent and pure sanctuary of the most beautiful hours of my youth." Composed during "six celestial and fugitive months" (July-December, 1829), the poems express his exalted affection for the Hugos and the religious fervor generated by that affection. In both these intermingled streams of sentiment is embodied the excessive emotionalism of the Romantic spirit, an extreme that seems to sober judgment infected with affectation, but which, however exaggerated in joys and sufferings, was undoubtedly sincere while it lasted. Unbalanced in its emotional manifestations, this season of excitement, for Sainte-Beuve as well as for the rest of the group, can be comprehended only on its own principles, which obviously do not accord with the precepts of reason.

While in poetry Sainte-Beuve seems to us mostly a villatic fowl, Hugo calls him an eagle. In return, Hugo is idolized as something divine, crowned with a pure aureole, a radiance in which Sainte-Beuve humbly glories, a purity of which he feels himself unworthy. He is as a reed that bends before the potent breath that might uproot it; he will be saved, as a foundling babe might be taken up by the valiant warrior and carried in his helmet. In fact, the vigor, the energy, the authoritative character and dominating personality of Hugo constituted part of the attraction to Sainte-Beuve, whose inconstancy during these years sought a master for the moment. In the letters exchanged they talk much of their mutual affection, and Hugo often signs himself "Your brother." One prosaic touch, however, seems worthy of notice: to one another the members of the group are always Victor, Ulric, Alfred, Delphine, Émile, but we never hear of Charles; when Sainte-Beuve is to be addressed affectionately, the formula is "My dear friend"; even his mother called him "Sainte-Beuve."

Les Consolations is dedicated to Victor Hugo in a long epistle. "My friend," it begins, "this book is yours; your name occurs on almost every page; your presence and your remembrance are mingled with all my thoughts. I give it to you, or rather I return it to you; without you it would not have been done." The author finds repose in God, in the soul, in the soul of a friend. After a moral malady, he has achieved a victory, possessing a sentiment of inward well-being, like that which succeeds an agony. He will find nourishment in study, but above all in lyric and elegiac poetry. Friendship, the union of souls, attaches him to life and to society. The only friendship which is not vain is that based on religion and tending toward a future life. "Such," he continues, "I have found in your spirit. You have borne me to the source of all consolation, to God and all the consequences of his being, immortality, reward and punishment, prayer. This is the only way out of emptiness."

The poems, which the author calls a faithful image of his soul, are overflowing with religious sentiment, worship and repentance, though there is nothing in the expression that is distinctly Catholic, or even Christian. He begs forgiveness for his sins of sensuality, laments relapses, begs for love; he would be content with a quiet home in the country, even with the solitude and severity of the cloister.

Why doubt Sainte-Beuve's sincerity? His spirit here may indeed be characterized as "a pronounced vein of religious sensibility," rather than a true conversion, but it was real, as far as it went. Even in his prose essays, this turning to religion appears. He regrets in Chénier the absence of the magnificent and fertile idea of God, as well as the fact that nature does not lead the poet to prayer. He expatiates with predilection on Racine's late religious epoch and on La Fontaine's conversion. Yet, while Sainte-Beuve was led into the regions of belief by pious fervor, it was not possible for him to be truly a believer. Speaking of seventeenth-century converts, he says: "They were not, as in our days, pursued right into the arms of a vaguely reviving faith by terrifying doubts and eternal obscurities, an abyss yawning perpetually at their feet."

Sainte-Beuve's absorption in Victor Hugo and his wife is subject to no greater doubt than his religious sentiment. "Brilliant and happy pair, in you alone I *live*." It was a period of poetry and enthusiasm, and whatever undertone of calculation and suspicion he afterwards remarked was at the moment certainly no more than a half-conscious uneasiness. Analyzed after the heat is gone, these skeptical undercurrents moving against the stream seem to have been more conspicuous than was actually possible during the flood. For a brief space, in truth, Sainte-Beuve was carried away by an idealism which seemed to point to a *Vita Nuova* and which elevated human relations into the divine. Even the opportunity of visiting Goethe in company with David d'Angers (August 28, 1829) was rejected on account of this fervor.

Most of the poems in *Les Consolations* are addressed to friends, the Hugos, de Vigny, Émile and Antony Deschamps, Lamartine, Guttinguer, Boulanger and others, but among these friends, the reckless de Musset is conspicuously absent. Mysticism and young Alfred would ill fit the same cradle, as we realize from the picture handed down of him and his inseparable friend, Tattet, roaring with irreverent laughter when Guttinguer once treated them to some unctuously devout preachment.[6] In Sainte-Beuve's book there may be contradictions, but no dissonances. Whatever the variations, the pieces all strike the same chord of humility, repentance and desire toward God. To the pious old beau, Guttinguer, after confessing his vain loves for Lucile, Natalie, Emma and others whose names he has forgotten, he acknowledges that these attachments were mere debasing pleasures and that only God gives the true love for which he begs. In the same breath, he writes to the priestly Barbe admitting that, after a few hours of good resolutions, he again falls a prey to his passions. Such vacillation is among the moral conditions soon to be analyzed in *Volupté*, and while it seems almost abnormal, it should not be called theatrical. The mutual confessions of Sainte-Beuve and Lamartine, the confidences and tears exchanged with Mme. Hugo, the angry word to her for which he begs forgiveness, the picture of Boulanger sketching an old façade at Strassburg, such things are fresh impressions caught at the moment. And the same is true of the poet's self-abasement and of his aspirations. Mysticism cannot be judged by stereotyped standards.

The book made a considerable impression. Though *Joseph Delorme* attained a second edition in less than two years, Sainte-Beuve himself expressed the opinion that the only collection of his poems to which the public paid much attention was *Les Consolations*.

---

[6] In connection with this picture, Sainte-Beuve adds: "Poetry in shirt-sleeves. There ought to be in each biography of a poet a little secret chapter reserved wholly for the right-minded and for those capable of bearing the truth, the whole truth, without twisting it awry and turning it to abuse. In the times of Horace this could be done, but one does not dare nowadays."

CHAPTER III

1830—1834

FINDING himself in love with Mme. Hugo, wife of his best friend, Sainte-Beuve, in 1830, kept much away from Paris, visiting Guttinguer at Honfleur and Rouen and beginning in collaboration with him a novel, *Arthur*. When he learned of the Revolution of July, he hurried back to the capital, but arriving too late to take part in the struggle, he soon returned to Rouen. With Hugo he kept up a painful correspondence. Most of the editors of the *Globe* obtained office under the new government; there were quarrels over the management of the paper, in which Sainte-Beuve took part with such vivacity that Dubois struck him, and a bloodless duel ensued. When Leroux continued publication, Sainte-Beuve joined him, and even after the journal was sold to the Saint-Simonians, he remained on the staff, becoming imbued with the ideas of this new religion and writing heartily in its spirit. He soon broke with the Saint-Simonians, however, and in 1831 came largely under the influence of Lamennais, though not connected with his organ. He was a republican in politics and, in religion, he seemed for several years to be approaching Catholicism. At the close of 1831, he joined the *National* under Armand Carrel, and wrote revolutionary political articles. Perhaps he even took part in a conspiracy. Meanwhile, he published a few last essays in the *Revue de Paris*. In 1831 appeared his first article in the *Revue des deux Mondes,* and the next year he began to write for that periodical pretty regularly. During these years, he continued to proclaim and support Victor Hugo and the Romantics. He was, however, almost entirely banished from Hugo's house. In 1832, Mme. Hugo began secretly meeting him away from home, and Sainte-Beuve wrote her love poems, some despairing and others representing his happiness over some undivulged pledge of her affection. The same subject is treated under a thin disguise in his novel, *Volupté,* which he was composing at this time. A fitful correspondence with Hugo shows the grievous strain in

62

their relations. In 1834, after some unknown offensive words in a lost letter, Hugo definitely renounced Sainte-Beuve's friendship.

In the seventh volume of the *Revue de Paris* (October, 1829), Latouche had exercised his wit, justly enough, on the Cénacle, as a mutual admiration society (*La Camaraderie littéraire*). Victor Hugo himself was ridiculed, and there was special mockery of Joseph Delorme's *Rayons Jaunes* and *Creux de la Vallée*. In the first heat of passion, Sainte-Beuve wrote Hugo from Worms that he would never again write a word for the *Revue*, any more than he would set foot in a salon or a café where an insulter was installed; and indeed he abstained for several months. After an interval he replied to Latouche indirectly (1831) and with perfect calm, acknowledging the drawbacks of such associations, but maintaining their advantages to "the poet who is not a prey to too much glory, nor addicted to the tumult of the drama." Before *Hernani,* he could not have taken this tone, but in the months following theatrical success, the Cénacle, choice gathering of apostles, sanctuary sacred from the multitude, had been invaded by the mob and profaned by vulgar contact. In February, 1830, in the midst of the maneuvers preceding the first performance, Sainte-Beuve wrote to Victor Hugo:

And she, whose name should never echo from your lyre except when listeners are on their knees, even she is exposed to profane eyes all day long, distributing tickets to a hundred young fellows scarcely known the day before; this chaste and charming intimacy, this prize of closest friendship, forever deflowered by the rabble; the word devotion prostituted, the *useful* appreciated above all, material combinations carrying everything before them!!!

Sainte-Beuve's adoration of Mme. Hugo was on the verge of becoming a passion.

The last poem of *Les Consolations,* the one addressed to Mérimée, forebodes political disaster. Sainte-Beuve recounts his redemption and expresses his fear of a relapse. He is living under the law of a holy friendship and his mind is occupied with art. Without ambition, his sole desire is a bride, a humble cottage, peace in his heart and love for humanity. Suddenly he is saddened by the tears of his country; he hears clamors of rage and grievous lamentations. Civil war theatens; hate regains him—ill indeed for one who longs to be healed—but he cannot remain indifferent. Yet he prays that suspicion may die out and that God will save France from armed duels between the people and their king under the hot August suns. From childhood he had palpitated for France; he had shed bitter tears over Waterloo; a devotee of Liberty, brother to André Chénier and Charlotte Corday, he had come too late for the sacrifice; he could only sing, thus to conquer his senses and attain peace. Must he tear himself from his repentance at the sinister cries of a shaken country, the dynasty a victim to its ministers and to priests who entangle the old king in their meshes? The age, they say, is impious. No, it is sick; it sighs, it hopes.

> Faithful to guard the past, it treasures her behest,
> And bears it through the waste—show it a holy place,
> A temple newly built, wherein the ark may rest,
> This age will fall in prayer prostrate upon its face.

The explosion did not wait for the hot days of August, but came in July (27-29), at a time when Sainte-Beuve was absent from Paris. Meanwhile literary labors, all in favor of Romanticism, had occupied his attention. He had taken part in the triumph of *Hernani,* but had refused to write on the subject, partly because he would not be duped by Véron into returning to the *Revue de Paris,* but chiefly because the clamor over the play excited his disgust, and the irruption of a mob into a region he had felt sacred to himself irritated and afflicted him. In the *Globe* (April 3), to which he now returned, he rejoiced in a great literary event, the reception of Lamartine into the Academy, which seemed to open to the new poetry the ancient path to the highest public honors. In comment on Lamartine's speech, approbation is expressed for his severe judgment of the eighteenth century, for his appreciation of the present religious, political and poetical regeneration, and for his prediction of a still happier future, while there is disappointment that the great Cuvier, who received the candidate, should have been so dry and meager in his praise of the poet. With obvious reference to Hugo, the Academy is warned against the narrow policy of electing mediocrity instead of genius. With the same aim, Sainte-Beuve, a week later, holds up Pongerville's translation of Lucretius to ridicule and contempt, not simply because it is false, but most obviously because the author was a candidate for the Academy in place of those more worthy. In June there are three articles announcing and reviewing Lamartine's *Harmonies,* poems which satisfy our "need for love, for religion, for infinite tenderness." With the exception of a short list of faults at the close, thrown in as if to save the critic's face, these articles, with their analyses and quotations, are an ecstatic dithyramb to the singer who has "opened for poetry the path to heaven." Even here, though Lamartine is the hero, admiration for Hugo is not forgotten.

As has been remarked, the sight, often the thought of a skirt made Sainte-Beuve palpitate. Voluptuous and at the same time romantic, his one dream of happiness, even from early childhood, had been love. Besides yielding to his senses, he had, as Joseph Delorme, laid siege to a Mme. Gaume, a frequenter of Nodier's receptions, who seems to have enjoyed dangling him. Now his long confidences with

Mme. Hugo had stirred in him the romantic surge and made it predominant. With this surge came a mystical religious sentiment. In many natures sensuality lies close to worship, the beautiful and pure being idealized by contrast with the low; and a feminine type, particularly a dreamy, abstracted, somewhat mysterious type, becomes angelic. A continuation of such worship, however, demands a certain distance. If there be intimate companionship, reciprocal melancholy and feminine sympathy with moral or sentimental woes, a rather insidious heat begins to accumulate; add a husband intent on glory, absorbed in the task of overwhelming a hostile world, and the situation becomes dangerous.

We cannot know all that happened between Sainte-Beuve and the Hugos, and less than all merely gives rise to infinite guessing. What is obvious is that all three were guided by emotional exaltation rather than by reason. "To be wroth with one we love doth work like madness in the brain." The suggestion advanced by some to the effect that Sainte-Beuve, on his part, was merely acting a rôle, a false, perfidious, infamous rôle, and that Hugo, on his, was merely trying to keep his hold on the critic as a valuable advertising agent, is too contemptible for belief. In the complex of feelings that go to make up a motive, there may well be half-buried unworthy elements, but in elevated natures these never direct, or even much accelerate the current. The letters of Hugo and Sainte-Beuve show, on the one side, passion and adoration for the wife, irritation and jealousy toward the husband, mingled with affection and admiration; and, on the other side, longing for the friend when he was absent, uneasiness amounting to misery when he was present.

Early in the year 1830, Sainte-Beuve wishes to quit Paris; he seeks a teaching position abroad; he will be glad to become secretary to Lamartine, who expects to be envoy at Athens; and meanwhile he frequently visits Guttinguer at Rouen and Honfleur, where we find him in April, in May, in July, and again in August. In May, the Hugos had moved from the street in which Sainte-Beuve lived to a house in the district of the Champs Élysées, then really fields. Sainte-Beuve, writing from Honfleur, doubts that he is of any use; "blame me," he adds, "but do not believe in any lessening of my affection." "We miss you," answers Hugo, "more than you can think; we miss your advice, your good offices, your conversation." Back in Paris, Sainte-Beuve cannot visit them, it pains him too much; he has evil thoughts, hatred and jealousy: "Adieu, for ever." At the same time, he writes to his friend, Pavie, that he suffers horribly from love without issue; he has no aim; from childhood his one dream had been love, and this had never been obtained; he was not loved as he wished; this was the secret of his foolish life. He stays away but is induced to act as godfather to Hugo's daughter, Adèle. After the melancholy reflections in the review of *Joseph Delorme* (November), Hugo expresses sympathy and invites Sainte-Beuve to visit him. Then, in December, comes a despairing letter. Sainte-Beuve even wants at times to kill Hugo; he begs for pardon; his friendship is slain by excess of love. "What can I do henceforth by your fireside; I have deserved your suspicion; it slips in between us; you are so disquieted and vigilant that Mme. Hugo cannot even glance at me without looking to you for permission." His friendship, which was a sort of worship, is killed, buried in his heart; "you, too, bury it in your hearts." Perhaps, after many years have passed, they can come together again. "Adieu." "Come often," answers Hugo, "let us keep our friendship chaste and holy." But after another letter, in which Sainte-Beuve speaks of a thought that prays eternally at the tomb of their friendship, Hugo's chief comfort is that they should write one another frequently. On the first day of the new year, thanking Sainte-Beuve for presents sent the children, Hugo invites him to dine. "1830 is past."[1]

These agitations, though they wrung the hearts of the two friends, did not monopolize their minds. Both were enormously busy. At no time, indeed, did any distraction keep Sainte-Beuve from at least five or six daily hours of serious study and reading, an occupation that brought him both calm and very great delight. He had, besides, new literary projects. Almost all the poets of the Cénacle had also written novels. In April, 1830, Sainte-Beuve began an attempt of this sort, *Arthur,* in collaboration with Guttinguer, a queer mixture of piety and licentiousness, "the lovable, the weak, the fickle, the tender Ulric," who lent a bit of his own career for the subject. They sought to represent the passionate youth of the time, the Werther, the René, the Obermann, saved in the end by Christianity. Arthur—none other than Guttinguer himself—after the death of a young wife, had spent his time in pursuing all sorts of women, from duchess to chambermaid; finally he retires from the world, marries a former mistress who had borne him a child or two, and concentrates upon books of devotion. After a few chapters, Sainte-Beuve's work was interrupted by the Revolution, and he never returned to it, substituting a story of his own case, *Volupté,* in its place. Guttinguer, however, completed and published the tale, which made somewhat of a stir, being indeed so well known that the audience at Lausanne could, two years after its appearance, be referred to its pages for extracts from d'Andilly's translation of the *Pères du Désert.* Sainte-Beuve in the *Revue des deux Mondes* (1836) consecrated

---

[1] We find a record of Sainte-Beuve dining at Hugo's on Jan. 15, 1831, other guests being Leroux, Boulanger and Guttinguer. Sainte-Beuve and Leroux were at this time warm partisans of the Saint-Simonian doctrines.

an article to his friend and to this romance. "Religious ideas," he says, "which are indeed love, only rightly directed and eternized, came to this voluptuous and sensitive soul. This negligent and tender elegiac poet, flung into a country retreat, read the Gospels, the Fathers of the Desert, the theosophist Saint-Martin, etc., and from this seed of readings cast abroad sprang a final and bitter harvest, *Arthur.*" The bitterness must not be taken too seriously. In his fragment, Sainte-Beuve makes his hero confess what we should in any case guess to be the fact: "I took pleasure in my sufferings, in my tears, in the feeble murmur of my repentance."

The instant Sainte-Beuve learned of the Decrees by which Charles X abrogated the liberty of the press and destroyed constitutional government, he took the coach to Paris. Among his fellow-travelers from Rouen was the royalist, Ballanche. Unfortunately the speed of the vehicle could not keep pace with the eagerness of the passengers. Before they reached their destination, the victory had been won. That he had thus been deprived of a chance to offer his life in an insurrection caused Sainte-Beuve the deepest chagrin. He envied, rather than regretted, his friend Farcy, a more or less kindred spirit, brilliant disciple of Cousin and writer for the *Globe,* who had been killed on the barricades; and in the course of a review in the *Globe* of a new edition of his own *Poems of Joseph Delorme,* he said:

If Joseph Delorme had lived till the end of July, 1830; if, instead of being in Paris during those days, he had been dreaming somewhere in the country, at Amiens or Rouen; if he had not been able to hasten back in time to receive, like his friend Farcy, a ball, one among all those that whistled through the streets in those sublime days; I can well imagine the vexation of the estimable young man and his excess of ill humor.

Among the varying motives of this period, one of those most frequently expressed is this strong desire to sacrifice his life for some cause. Several years later he wrote of the Revolution of '89 what was an obvious reminiscence of his own feelings: "At the outbreak of the Revolution, every young head was seized with a fever of enthusiasm, every young heart beat high; they were at length to find their deliverance, and they consequently imagined that, even then on the eve of it, they must still be suffering from grievous oppression."

In the *Globe* office there were quarrels. Dubois and most of the principal writers obtained office, either administrative or educational, under the new government. They were therefore ready to cease publication, while Leroux and a few others desired to continue, and Sainte-Beuve sided with Leroux. One day early in August he was impudent to his former teacher, who slapped him. A duel in the woods at Romainville ensued, made famous by the fact that, as it was raining, Sainte-Beuve carried an open umbrella. Each discharged two shots without accident, using pistols that had been taken by the poet Fontaney during the July fighting from the corpse of a gendarme. A reconciliation is said to have occurred on the field. At any rate, we find Dubois a year or two later supplying Sainte-Beuve with confidential documents for an essay on Jouffroy, and throughout life the two respected and admired one another.

When Dubois left the *Globe* (August 14), Leroux attempted to continue publication, but owing to lack of funds he sold the paper in November to Enfantin, leader of the Saint-Simonians. Early in 1831 it appeared under the direction of Michel Chevalier as the avowed organ of the new religion, *Journal of the Doctrine of Saint-Simon*, its aim being "the betterment of social institutions for the benefit of the poorest and most numerous class." This venture ended in April, 1832, but Sainte-Beuve had ceased to contribute a year earlier (March 22, 1831).

At first he flung himself heart and soul into journalistic

controversy, giving all his ardor to politics, as he wrote Pavie. An anonymous combatant in the daily struggle, he did not sign a single article, though a few of the more important have been distinguished, and these give some notion of his eager proletarian aggressiveness. He maintains that, unlike the English Revolution of 1688, the Revolution of 1830 is a continuation and complement of '89 (August 24). As the Revolution was made by the people, the government must act according to the wishes of the people (August 31). Why should the authorities fear the celebration in honor of the conspirator Bories, the heroic sacrifice of 1822? And Sainte-Beuve himself proceeded to take part in the public demonstration in memory of Bories and the Sergents of La Rochelle (September 22). The government should march with the social movement and develop and apply the principles of '89, instead of being prejudiced, petrified, reactionary, an object of scorn (September 20).

Moreover, a revolution in art must accompany that in politics. He introduces Victor Hugo in his new rôle as a liberal by means of a note (August 19) accompanying the poet's ode to *La jeune France*. Here, by a reference to Chateaubriand as an old man who had relinquished his hopes of a public career and sacrificed a possible future to the unity of a fine life, he aroused the great author's resentment and elicited a message to the effect that M. Chateaubriand was not old and furthermore was not so sure to abdicate in politics. But what Chateaubriand might feel mattered little to the enthusiastic Sainte-Beuve. He saw danger in isolation, in breaking up into little groups; literature must become broader, more profound, accessible to all. The time of the Cénacle is past; the Romantic reversion to the Middle Ages, the solitary inward revery, the detachment from reality, these features are swept away by the crisis of 1830; literature has now entered the arena, side by side with the struggling populace, reflecting the sentiment of progressive humanity (October 11).

This is the revolutionary and proletarian Sainte-Beuve. On the other hand, his individual interests are not suppressed. His essay on his own *Joseph Delorme* has already been mentioned. It is almost entirely a confession. In reviewing the letters of Diderot (September 20), he shows a literary touch as delicate as ever; he presents charming pictures of the eighteenth century and, with his own personal feelings in mind, takes the deepest interest in Diderot's love for Sophie, particularly in its ideal and ecstatic manifestations. Treating Hoffmann's tales (December 7), he takes pleasure in the delirium, disorder and tumult, in the unbounded desire for something undefined, in art as a feverish malady, in the portrayal of ''mystics without faith, geniuses without works, souls without organs.'' Even here, however, he is pleased also by the occasional victorious return of good sense and reality; he in fact praises Hoffmann for exciting ''all our superstitious inclinations without too violently shocking our obstinate good sense.'' Autobiography, this, slightly veiled—for Sainte-Beuve's own vague and passing half-beliefs in the supernatural, in spirits, in mystic influences, never completely obscured in him that obstinate basis of solid material fact.

The conflict in his soul opened the way, some thought, for the acceptance of religious belief. One of his friends, Buchez, former fellow-student at the Medical School, also revolutionary fighter and propagandist, in a letter (March 31) praising *Les Consolations,* urged Sainte-Beuve to join the religion of the future. This religion—for Saint-Simonianism was not only a form of socialism, but also a religion, the religion of humanity—made a strong, though temporary, appeal to men of brains—scholars, engineers, physicians, lawyers—as is vouched for by such names as

Thierry, Comte, Littré, Carnot. On the socialistic side, Sainte-Beuve would be attracted to the new doctrine by its disquietude over the sufferings born of industrial excess; by the transfer of the golden age to the future, a result of the perfection of the social order; by the demand for the abolition of privilege, the state bcoming the universal legatee and common parent; by the ideal conception of a world governed by its best intellect, each laboring according to his ability and receiving corresponding compensation. On the religious side, the notion of the order of nature as the will of God, with positive knowledge replacing theology, could not have failed to appeal to him, as well as the placing of the reign of God, not in heaven, but here on earth, the result of the progress of a regenerated humanity. At any rate, Sainte-Beuve became for a few months a sincere and enthusiastic adherent of the school, although he did not adopt the fantastic costume or take part in the esoteric ceremonies of the disciples of Enfantin.

In some of the *Globe* essays already mentioned, the influence of the Doctrine may be distinctly observed; it flames forth without disguise in three articles (December 13, 27, 1830; January 6, 1831) devoted to Jouffroy's course on philosophy, a course that dealt with human destiny. The substance of the lectures is to some extent summarized, but over three-quarters of the space and practically all the emphasis are given to an ardent and closely reasoned refutation of Jouffroy's individualistic psychology. Here is a transfiguration; nowhere else in the collected works do we find this Sainte-Beuve. The criticism is that of an expert dialectician; the proclamation of belief, that of a fervid orator. "Humanity is more than a collection and succession of individuals; it exists and lives by itself in nature; it is a continuously perfectible manifestation of God. Man is a feeling, intelligent and active being only through his relations with humanity and nature, that is to say, with

God. The revealer, the inspired leader, does not study psychology; he founds a religion. All progress is revelation of God to man, a lifting up of man to God. The new conception is utilized *socially*. No one man makes a religion; one man conceives it, others transform and realize it. Religion makes men, and men make religion. There is no division of the human being into the *me* and the *not me;* it is a unity and tends to join itself with the universal life, with God, of which it feels itself a part. It conceives God only as itself raised to the infinite, and itself only as God finite and localized in man. Harmony is attained by the new conception that conjoins matter and spirit in the substance of the human being, soul and body in the unity of life, man and nature in the bosom of God, science and industry in religion. Material activity becomes as holy as thought, participating in the same God under a different aspect." Such are a few of the ideas, but a brief abstract can give little impression of the eloquence, the heat and passion with which Sainte-Beuve exalts inspiration at the expense of reason, and condemns the solitary thinker and poet in favor of the association of all.

Although in the "Profession of Faith" that introduces the new *Globe* (January 18, 1831), Sainte-Beuve lent his pen to Leroux, at that time a clumsy writer, the beliefs are nevertheless his own. In a formal and official style, with only here and there a trace of his usual manner, he seeks to present this transformation of the paper as a natural development of its original ideas of liberty and the intellectual association of all peoples. While the unity of the old *Globe* lay in one dominant and remarkable personality, Dubois—and how generously is Dubois appreciated!—the unity of the new *Globe* will rest on a precise doctrine, new, full of ardor, tending to realize the age to come, Saint-Simonianism, which has openly proclaimed its possession of the key to the future. This doctrine intermingles religious inspiration with industry and science in order to unite and fertilize them. The emancipation of the poor and the classification of men according to capacity and work had always been the writer's instinctive beliefs; the new dogma, indeed, answered both the predilections of his intellect and the desires of his heart. The present venture is not really a change in direction, but a consummation of the thought that presided over the foundation of the *Globe* six years before.

In a few weeks, however, Sainte-Beuve's enthusiasm for the new faith had begun to evaporate. On February 13, it is true, he published a fervid propagandist review, which closes with a lyric passage contrasting Lessing and Saint-Simon, the marble statue of the philosopher being saluted with respect as one passes, while into the arms of the builder of the altar one flings oneself with tears; but on the same day he wrote to Paul Foucher, Victor Hugo's brother-in-law: "I am no more Saint-Simonian than you have known me, that is, with moderation, sangfroid, and a belief in the future, mingled with scepticism for the present." About a month later he retired from the *Globe,* still apparently looking forward with ardor to "the new birth that is to become the hope, faith and love of the world." During his brief immersion in the Doctrine, in which he believed he had found a final progress, a basis, a crowning of his agitated life (to Hugo in March), he does not appear to have come at any time completely under the spell of Enfantin, though, in spite of this leader's many absurdities, revelations, trances, inspired prophecies, Sainte-Beuve always speaks of him with respect. There was soon a general desertion. Carnot, Leroux, Reynaud, Charton could not follow the new Messiah. Several of these associates in the movement remained Sainte-Beuve's good friends in later years, some to the very end. Of Leroux he had been really fond, but with him there came a breach.

When the reformer invented a new socialism and set up as a god to be worshiped by women and laborers, Sainte-Beuve thought him a charlatan, though still recognizing that he had ideas and a certain confused power. As for Saint-Simonianism, which he had observed at close range, and indeed behind the scenes, it served to make all religious movements intelligible, including Port-Royal and Christianity itself. An overhasty solution of social problems, its brief destiny had yet left many seeds. "No one," writes Sainte-Beuve in 1863, "who has passed through Saint-Simonianism, or even come into somewhat close touch with it, has done so with impunity. Beyond its economic and industrial bearing, it gave to more than one who lacked the idea, not only some sense of a religion, but also a respect for religion as a social form, a form which is in truth the loftiest of all."

Among the believers, apostles, "Pope-spirits," those who always urge upon you some faith, the name of Lamennais is coupled in Sainte-Beuve's note-book with that of Buchez. The priest, indeed, as well as the layman, had perceived in the poet of *Les Consolations* a promising proselyte. Interviews begun at Hugo's house were continued in the clerical establishment where Lamennais lived in the rue Vaugirard and also in the Oratorian college at Juilly, under whose trees, it was thought, Malebranche had once meditated. This new venture followed hard upon the venture into Saint-Simonianism. On May 16, 1831, Sainte-Beuve wrote to a friend: "I have just passed some days at Juilly with M. Lamennais, where I have gained calm and greater and greater detachment from Paris and the life led there." To intimacy with the master was added intimacy with his disciples—Lacordaire, not yet celebrated, but a brilliant talent, a militant orator, whose sparkling word was like the sword of the Levite; Montalembert, just turned twenty-one and still unknown; Gerbet, modest, simple, learned, moderate, lovable, yet a man of rare distinction, persuasive with unction, possessed of logic and of a calm and reflective lucidity. All three are portrayed in the *Lundis*.

With Gerbet Sainte-Beuve kept up relations for many years, greeting him with effusion and visiting him as late as 1852 at Amiens, where he lived near his friend Salinis, the bishop. Beginning as an author in the *Mémorial Catholique*, the rival of the *Globe*, Gerbet became in the critic's opinion one of the best writers of France, though his delicate health and feeble voice withheld him from effectiveness in the pulpit or in the professorial chair. With Lamennais his relations were those of affectionate devotion, without limit until the final revolt. The asperities of his master he softened as far as he could and clothed his doctrine with the character of persuasion and conciliation. Association with Lamennais was, indeed, the one considerable episode in a simple and unified life. Afterwards, for ten years, Gerbet lived in Rome, where, in 1839, Sainte-Beuve visited him in his cloister. In 1853 he became a bishop, the meek, in this case, inheriting ecclesiastical authority. One of the *Lundis* celebrates his benign countenance, his delicate, affectionate smile, his amenity and social charm, his conversation, flavored with happy expressions and agreeable anecdotes, rich in reminiscence, without an evil thought, and sparkling with the joyousness of a pure soul. He was, it seems, the single flawless gem of the group. Montalembert and Lacordaire might occasionally make disparaging remarks about one another, but nobody had anything but good to say of Gerbet.

It was in this year 1831 that the two orators, who became distinguished, the one in the senate, the other in the pulpit, sprang into immediate fame. Together they had started a free school in disobedience of government regulations, and they defended themselves so eloquently before the bar of the Chambers that their reputation was made at a stroke.

Montalembert in his maturity was, according to Sainte-Beuve's view, the intrepid and brilliant champion of a cause. He defended Poland, assailed the University, and demanded unlimited freedom for church schools and for the religious orders. Elegance and perfect breeding enabled him to say bitter things without giving offense, while his happy inspirations and complete ease always fascinated even his opponents. Lacordaire, on his part, was characterized by a hardy flight of ideas and by happiness of expression. Beginning as a lawyer, he had turned at twenty-five to the priesthood, and later he joined the Dominican order and was the first monk to enter the Academy. With his brilliance and ardor of speech, his imaginative and poetic phrases, he was a fit preacher for the generation brought up on Chateaubriand. Speaking the language of the young, he might be called the Romantic pulpit orator. Like Gerbet, both Montalembert and Lacordaire separated from Lamennais when he broke with Rome, but the old Breton used to say justly enough that they were a brood he himself had hatched.

When Sainte-Beuve joined this group, all were engaged on *L'Avenir,* preaching, under the motto "God and Liberty," doctrines that seemed at the time revolutionary—democracy, universal suffrage, separation of Church and State, freedom of the press, of association, of teaching, and, with a special coloring, the principles of the "party of movement." This general tendency harmonized with Sainte-Beuve's mood, though he did not himself contribute to the paper. How close he was to the leader is shown by the fact that Lamennais urged him to join Montalembert, Lacordaire and himself when, having suspended publication (November 15, 1831), they went to Rome to plead their cause before the Pope. Retained in Paris by "a charm," he refused the invitation, but his sympathies were deeply engaged.

Lamennais, or "M. Feli," as he was familiarly named, was "sympathetically plebeian and fraternal." With his alternations of ardor and sweetness, violence and tenderness, he had the gift of attaching people, and one was never half bound to this soul of wrath, this soldier, excessive in love or hate, to whom all that was moderate appeared insipid. He had found society indifferent, cold, corrupt, material; it must be aroused and spiritualized. The *Essay on Indifference* had forced the attention of all and helped revive Catholicism in France. *L'Avenir,* his new journalistic creation, was marked by talent and generosity, mingled with venturesome imprudence. Here he preached the public union of democracy and Catholicism in the tone of a prophet. Unable to carry Rome with him, he finally renounced Catholicism and plunged wholly into democracy. "He is the soldier of the future," wrote Sainte-Beuve in 1861, "the democratic soldier, fervent and full of faith, without peace or truce, knowing but the one word *Forward!,* extravagant often, out of all measure indeed, but with a profound feeling for social infirmities and popular sufferings, to whom much will be forgiven."

Such, however, was not Sainte-Beuve's attitude in 1831. He had come to Lamennais, *Papa* he sometimes called him, as a sick soul, an intelligence without faith or will, seeking moral energy through adherence to truth recognized as perpetual, universal and holy. He longed for a sacred union of will and intelligence under the seal of faith. The master, too, as he learned, had cherished solitude, revery, retirement from the world, melancholy converse with memories, the vagueness of indefinite passions; but duty had won him to violent effort, to indefatigable exercise in the rude path of sacrifice; and grace and prayer had helped him over hard places. Sainte-Beuve, as Lamennais read passages of his Christian philosophy at Juilly, had studied the man soul to soul, obtaining revelations of the intimate depths

79

of his being. Overpowered by a dominating personality, he had become "Christian and Catholic, if not in faith, at least by affinity and desire."

When the doctrines of *L'Avenir* were condemned by Rome, Lamennais seemed at first to submit with the others. Then, one day, on the verge of leaving Paris, he handed Sainte-Beuve a manuscript with instructions to have it published, adding, "Change what you choose." This was the *Paroles d'un Croyant*. Only two lines about the Pope were crossed out as an impropriety from the pen of a priest. The published work Sainte-Beuve hailed as a prophetic book (1834). It was, however, condemned by the Church. Two years later, *Affairs of Rome* made the breach irreparable. By becoming purely democratic, Lamennais seemed to Sainte-Beuve to have compromised the unity and authority of his life. "Nothing is worse," he writes, "than to provoke souls to faith, and then go off suddenly and leave them there. Nothing so flings them into scepticism. . . . How many hopeful souls have I known, whom you possessed and carried in your pilgrim's sack, and who, now that the sack is cast on the ground, are left lying alongside of the ditches."

One of the hopeful souls was surely his own, though there can be little doubt that, even without this change in Lamennais, Sainte-Beuve would, after his first enthusiasm, have reverted to what he was at bottom, a critic. He had formed an ideal and traced a program for the great priest, but when the program was not followed, what right, he asks, had he to complain? Yet he considered that he really had the right to demand, in place of faith, at least a wise moderation. He could not follow the leader when he thought him a demagogue. He even wished Lamennais had died in 1833. At times, up to '48, they met and Lamennais was gay, natural and affectionate, as he had always been, but the Revolution of February wrought a complete separation. The great character and the great writer, however, continued to be appreciated. In his moral nature Lamennais was one "who never sacrificed an idea or a sentiment to an interest." Long after his death he seemed to Sainte-Beuve a soul of sorrow, anguish and torment.

How many varied experiences fertilized the soil out of which the *Lundis* grew! Coincident with Sainte-Beuve's approach to religion, through Lamennais and his circle, was his plunge into revolutionary radicalism. Being free from his connection with the *Globe,* he was, through his friend Magnin, attached to the *National,* a paper edited by Armand Carrel, to whom it had been abandoned by Thiers and Mignet when they took office. After a brief period of half-hearted adhesion, Carrel turned against the new government, first against the Chambers, then against the ministry, and finally against the monarchy itself. Independent and revolutionary from his school-days, resigning from the army to combat monarchy in Spain, and almost brought to the scaffold when captured by the French royalist troops, Carrel, a man of action, a man of the sword, was driven to letters by force of circumstances, rather than by genius or inclination. After assisting Thierry and writing two or three historical works, he entered journalism and became the most remarkable leader in the press of the opposition to the dynasty of Louis-Philippe. A strong, tenacious, vehement and courageous individuality, ardent and extreme in his polemic, always ready for a personal encounter, he was in constant turmoil and met his death in a duel at the age of thirty-six. At first favoring constitutional monarchy, he became republican in January, 1832, conducting a guerilla warfare, and, though blaming insurrection and an utter stranger to all conspiracies, he felt it a point of honor to defend the too impetuous partisans of his cause, even when they initiated such movements. Some of his assistants on the *National* were, indeed, far more violent

than the editor-in-chief. Sainte-Beuve himself, who joined
the staff late in 1831, wrote, if we may trust Barbier,
political articles of a frightful sans-culottism.

A report contained in a document of doubtful authenticity places him in a group of twelve conspirators, one of
whom was to be chosen by lot to shoot at the King. He is
even said to have been among the last three from whom a
final choice was made. The shot was actually fired by
Bergeron, student of law and a writer for the *National,*
and he was arrested, tried and acquitted. Doubtful as it
is, there is no inherent improbability in this story. Indeed,
several circumstances confirm the suspicion that in some
secret political society, some lodge of the *Droits de l'homme*
perhaps, Sainte-Beuve had taken a pledge against the Government of July. "To youth," he wrote in 1865, "violence and error may be excused, but not exhumed."

He was at this time in a condition of exaggerated sensibility. He regretted that his generation had been at school
during the first ardor of the Carbonari and could do no
more than absent themselves from their classes the day that
Manuel was expelled from the Chamber. In a letter he
speaks of "the rotten race of Orleans." Not a literary
article in the *National* for 1832, not even that on the death
of Scott, but contains some stroke at the government with
its cynical negation of all human progress; and he steadfastly refused any favors whatsoever from the monarchy,
while not at all averse to accepting them later from the
Empire. When he found that his post as secretary of a
historical commission was a sinecure, he promptly resigned,
although he needed the salary; the decoration of the Legion
of Honor he absolutely and repeatedly refused, even going
so far as to send the minister his resignation as librarian
of the Mazarine to force the withdrawal of the offer. When,
after 1848, his name was found on a list of those who had
received payment from a secret fund, his agitation was in-

comprehensible and beyond bounds. He wrote letters and paid visits in every direction, and he consented to remain at the library only so long as his friends, Charton and Reynaud, continued in the Ministry of Public Instruction. It is significant that these friends "of eighteen years" had been his fellows in both Saint-Simonianism and the succeeding radicalism, and it was to them naturally that his defense, a most fervent exposition of his life-history, was sent.

Was Sainte-Beuve's change of residence connected with this episode? He left his mother's house and lived under the name Joseph Delorme in two student rooms in the Cour de Commerce at twenty-seven francs a month, breakfast included.[2] There is no thoroughly satisfactory explanation of this move. Pavie said it was in order to escape service in the National Guard which Sainte-Beuve and all the young intellectuals hated; others have thought he sought freedom for amorous adventure, a reason Sainte-Beuve would not have been ashamed to avow. He does speak of needing quiet for his work. In 1826, when attending the School of Medicine, he had, according to Schérer, so that he might study in peace, a room, rue de Lancry, where he made his own bed and lived absolutely in solitude; but he was living at home again the next year. We know that his mother, fearing for her son's future, could not bear the compromising Carrel and Bergeron, and refused to see them. In later years, Sainte-Beuve wrote that he went to these rooms in 1830, which seems to be a blind. His memory was accurate, wonderfully accurate in the smallest matters, and he has apparently given a false date. On December 18, 1831, he wrote to Barbe that he was still living with his mother, rue Notre-Dame-des-Champs. A

---

[2] The sum is small even for the prices of those days. In 1838 Reuchlin wrote Sainte-Beuve that he could live in Germany on 120 to 140 francs a month.

letter of June, 1832, shows him at the Cour de Commerce. This is precisely the period of his extreme radicalism. Bergeron's shot was fired in November of that year.

Writing to Zola thirty years later, Sainte-Beuve says: "As to what happened to me after July, 1830, of crossings in every direction and of internal conflicts, I defy anybody except myself, to find the key." But he himself indicated where this key was to be looked for, though characteristically putting the indication in such a form as to lead the seeker astray. In a footnote to the essay on Sénancour (*Portraits contemporains,* I, 170), he writes:

My young imagination, in those years 1830-1834, embraced indifferently several systems. I was sick at heart, I was suffering, a prey to passion, and, in order to distract or benumb myself, I played with every conceivable sport of thought. I went into these things ardently, very sincerely at the time, and without reserve or calculation; but for the reason I have given. There will be found in a passage of *Volupté* (Chapters XI and XII) a picture of the same moral condition, with a transposition of names to fit the date, when Amaury, for relief from the passion that possesses him, gives himself to every intellectual curiosity and takes up in turn and almost simultaneously the system of La Marck, of Saint-Martin, etc.

That word "intellectual" is designed to throw the reader off the scent. On turning to the chapters indicated, we find Amaury not only finding distraction in systems, but plunging heart and soul into a conspiracy, though he never actually commits an overt act. The conclusion of Chapter XII reads:

I hurried to the valley in search of the sage [Saint-Martin]. I reëntered the city on the trace of the warlike conspirator. I invoked the bloody encounter, I launched my soul into the fluidity of air, up to the skies. Then some gross form of beauty dragged me down. And behind it all, a faithful thought, a veiled sentiment, powerful in its languor, permeating everything and present everywhere, desire without hope, a lamp without brightness—my love!

The gushing and splashing of this agitated emotional experience, however it might muddy the stream, did not at any time long interrupt the steady current of intellectual labor. In an essay on Diderot (*Revue de Paris,* June 26, 1831), Sainte-Beuve says:

I have always been fond of the correspondence of great men, of their conversations, their thoughts, all the details of their character and manners, of their biography in short; and especially when this biography has not already been compiled by another, but may be constructed and composed by oneself. Shutting yourself up for a fortnight with the writings of some dead celebrity, some poet or philosopher, you study him, turn him over and over, and question him at leisure; you make him pose for you; it is almost as though you passed a fortnight in the country making a portrait or a bust of Byron, Scott or Goethe; only you are more at *ase with your model, and the tête-à-tête, at the same time that it requires strict attention, permits much closer familiarity.

Soon, he continues, an individuality takes the place of the vague, abstract type. The moment the familiar motion, the revealing smile, the vainly hidden crack or wrinkle is seized, "at that moment, analysis disappears in creation, the portrait speaks and lives, you have found the man."

Of such portraits of the dead, only two, those of Diderot and Prévost (September, 1831), belong to this epoch, both appearing in the *Revue de Paris* and both, though ripe in manner, being obviously studies of a sentimental life related to his own, preparatory to the composition of *Volupté*. To the still living Sénancour (January, 1832) he is also attracted by affinity of sentiment, and he even breaks the continuity of his essay by quoting over two pages on love, an echo of some of his own reflections. This was his last contribution to the *Revue de Paris*.

SAINTE-BEUVE

In 1831 Hugo introduced Sainte-Beuve to Buloz, who had just secured the management of the *Revue des deux Mondes* and who, changing it from a magazine of travel and description, was eager to enlist in his enterprise every writer then prominent before the public, for he had conceived the ideal, which his persistence and ability realized, of a literary periodical without a rival in the world. Sainte-Beuve's first article (June 15, 1831, written as an introduction to a volume of Farcy's prose and verse) celebrated his friend, George Farcy, slain in the street fighting of July, and his second article celebrated Victor Hugo (July 2). He did not contribute again until December, about which time he also became a regular writer for the *National*, an anonymous journalist, producing political articles, reports of receptions at the Academy, very disparaging to all concerned, and book reviews, better on the whole than the generality of such things, yet really nothing more than good, honest daily work. Sainte-Beuve later regretted the sharp personalities and the lack of impartiality of these articles. There are few of them, indeed, that are not distorted by political favor or animosity. Even the contributions to the *Revue des deux Mondes* are more or less propaganda rather than disinterested criticism. "We perform," he says, "the functions of the lookout, and our cry of discovery will always be mingled with emotion and joy."

This cry was for his personal friends, for Lamennais, Lamartine and Béranger in 1832, and for de Musset and Jouffroy in 1833; but Victor Hugo is still foremost, both in asides inserted in these articles about others and in essays entirely devoted to himself and his work. Referring to this period in letters written in 1837, Heine mocks Sainte-Beuve's ardor, comparing him to the announcer running before the chariot of an oriental potentate and crying: "Behold the Buffalo, son of the Buffalo,

Bull of Bulls; all others are mere oxen; he alone is the true
and perfect Buffalo!''

This rôle, vociferous, excited, enthusiastic, prejudiced,
partisan, is not that which we usually associate with the
name of Sainte-Beuve, but it was the rôle that, with occasional misgivings and reactions, he actually performed for
five or six years. An article written for a biographical
dictionary, but first published in the *Revue des deux
Mondes* (July 2, 1831), after opening with the quotation
of Hugo's poetic account of his childhood—"Two years of
age the century"—recalls the evening when the poet read
these verses to a private circle of friends "in a voice full of
feeling and still palpitating with the spell of creation."
The life of Hugo is "pure, grave, honorable, independent,
introspective, magnificently and disinterestedly ambitious,
more and more turned toward the grandiose work he feels
himself called upon to accomplish." It cannot perhaps be
said that so great a book as the *Feuilles d'Automne* is over-
praised in the next essay (December 15, 1831), but note
the vehement tone: "For criticism there are true triumphs; these come to it when the poets it has early appreciated and celebrated and for whom, flinging itself into
the throng, it has not feared to risk mockery and insult—
when these poets surpass themselves and go even beyond
the magnificent promises that such criticism, as a harbinger,
dared to set before the public in their name." Such criticism "names its heroes, its poets, is attached to them by
preference, surrounds them with love and counsel, casts
upon them the words *glory* and *genius* . . . cries out before them, like a herald, 'Make room!' " The whole article
consists of ecstatic laudation, without a shadow of reproach,
though Hugo's loss of religious faith is noted. Sainte-
Beuve even went so far as to write for Hugo a sort of
mitigated advertisement of the novels, which was inserted,
unsigned, in the *Débats,* a journal with which, on account

of its politics, the critic refused to be connected in any way, though Hugo could do what he liked in it, because of his close friendship with the owner, Bertin.[3] Even the plays, which Sainte-Beuve never wholly liked, he supports both by his presence and by his pen, giving up a visit to Juilly for the first performance of *Marion Delorme* (August, 1831), and celebrating the triumph of *Lucrezia Borgia* (February, 1833) in the *Chronique* of the *Revue des deux Mondes*.

Sooner or later, no doubt, under any circumstances, a breach between Hugo and Sainte-Beuve must have occurred. Both, as they developed, became alienated from their most important early associates. After 1840, in fact, the Cénacle 'met only at funerals. Of Hugo, Heine wrote (1836): "Almost all his old friends have given him up and, to tell the truth, it is his own fault, for they have been hurt by his egotism." On the part of Sainte-Beuve, the fault was not so much egotism as a truant disposition, to which was added a sudden irritability, unexpectedly taking offense, as a result apparently of some accumulation of bile, for the bursting forth of which the external incident was an occasion rather than a cause. "I am a victim of spleen," he once wrote to Marie d'Agoult; "when I have an attack, I hide myself, as I ought. I abominate the world and hate the light; and the light and the world reciprocate." During these years, according to his own statement, he was full of sensibility and enthusiasm, feeling the need of admiring, of exalting each object of his fervor into an ideal. Indeed, he classes himself among the secondary souls that espouse the illustrious and become servants of their glory. Yet, on the other hand, his was not the soul of a disciple. He hated pretentiousness, self-sufficiency, self-

---

[3] In 1829 Sainte-Beuve had been among the candidates for a place on the *Débats* who met one Sunday at Bertin's country place, Les Roches. See *Nouveaux Lundis*, iii, 223.

glorification, **arrogance**, the spirit of the sacred priest, the
solemn pontiff; witness his sarcasms later vented on Hugo,
de Vigny and Leroux. In this regard, he was thoroughly
honest; he never at any time set himself up as an oracle,
or allowed others to do so. He had, it is true, a sense of
his own value, which was a little more than self-respect,
since there was in it often an element of irritation; yet it
was decidedly less than egotism, for there was never mingled with it the slightest trace of conceit. When, in later
life, he could easily have had his little band of adorers,
he was to these younger men nothing more exalted than
"Uncle Beuve." Not enshrined himself, he could not long
worship at any shrine. Reality inevitably brought diminution of the idol's radiance, disillusion, an impulse to push
the sacred thing off its throne and roll it over, so as to observe and exhibit even the unsightly parts, though without
derogation to what was really admirable. There followed
misunderstandings and perhaps even quarrels before the
final emancipation. When Béranger in a letter calls Fontanes "one of our most distinguished poets," Sainte-
Beuve slyly comments: "I wonder what one of our celebrated poets to-day would say if he heard himself called
simply a *distinguished poet*." Anger on the part of the
poet. "In every emancipation," he remarks elsewhere,
"there is a sprig of revolt." Provocation on the part of
the critic.

In the relationship with Hugo, what should have been
a natural emancipation was complicated by Sainte-Beuve's
passion for the wife. The agitation on both sides was
excessive, breaches being followed by desperation, and then
by reconciliation, only to be succeeded by fresh jealousies
and mutual expressions of anguish. When one of the parties gets irritated, the other grows humble, and the irritated
one, in turn, begs pardon. At one time, Sainte-Beuve reproaches Hugo for not having been *unique* in his attitude;

at another, he accepts all the blame: "It is a necessity for me that those whom I have injured should love me and forgive me." On the other side, Hugo, who frequently signs himself "Your brother," finds Sainte-Beuve dearer than his own life: "I must hear you tell me that you love me in order to believe it"; "Do not forsake me." Yet he cannot bear this friend's presence; his wife has asked him always to be in the room when Sainte-Beuve calls; and the caller is requested to come no more (July, 1831). An appointment of the trouble-maker to a professorship at Liège [4] (1831) delights Hugo, who is happy all summer, and he expresses deep disappointment when the position is resigned in September. "When you are not here, I feel at the bottom of my heart that I love you as of old; when you are present I am in torture." Sainte-Beuve is one of the two beings whom Hugo loves most in the world. "I had to choose between her and you," he writes. In one letter, he announces his certainty that his wife has ceased to respond to his affection. "It is your fatal imagination," rejoins Sainte-Beuve, "that magnifies your suspicions and is reflected from her, because her heart is frightened and compressed by a force so beyond all our vulgar dimensions." Hugo was again touched and grateful. Even as late as the end of August, 1833, he wrote: "O Sainte-Beuve, two friends like ourselves ought never to part. It would be impious."

[4] At the instance of his friend Charles Rogier, whom he had met as a Saint-Simonian and who had been a leader of the Belgian revolution in 1830, Sainte-Beuve was appointed Professor of Comparative or General Literature, May 31, 1831, on condition that he should become naturalized. At first willing to accept, he then kept silence for two months, and on Sept. 4 resigned the position on the ground that certain private and personal matters had taken a favorable turn. He appears to refer to some clandestine meeting ·with Mme. Hugo, which is thought to have taken place Sept. 1. For this love affair Sainte-Beuve, poor as he was, relinquished a salary of 2,200 florins, or 4,510 francs.

Such are a few of the high lights in this correspondence. In the midst of all this frenzy, there is place for practical matters, literature, propaganda, theater tickets, politics, articles in the press. The friends dine together in restaurants or meet at Nodier's. In October, 1833, Hugo invites Sainte-Beuve to a reading of *Marie Tudor* at his home, and Sainte-Beuve predicts a triumph for the piece. Meanwhile, perhaps in September, 1831, Sainte-Beuve and Mme. Hugo begin a clandestine correspondence. They do not, however, often see one another, for the next April he laments that he has not set eyes on her for nine months, and in July, a two months' interval is deplored. At about the same time, he begins to open his heart to her in a series of intimate poems, which represent various phases of their love, but particularly his own feelings. Soon they arrange to meet, without Hugo's knowledge, in churches and parks; once she even visits his rooms, and leaves a permanent fragrance there. His godchild, the little Adèle, also blesses his bachelor quarters with her presence. In any ordinary case, we should be sure that the affair had gone to its utmost limit, but, considering Sainte-Beuve's exaggerated state of mind, remembering also the relations portrayed in *Volupté,* and with due regard finally to Mme. Hugo's physical condition after the birth of Adèle, we are led to conclude that the romance must have been enacted exclusively, or almost exclusively, in the region of imagination and sentiment and words.

Hugo, "Buffalo of Buffaloes," acted quite otherwise in his love affairs. He plunged ahead with a robustious frankness that disdained, as much as it excited, publicity. All Paris knew that, after the performance of *Lucrezia Borgia* (February, 1833), he had carried off the beautiful Princess Negroni, Juliette Drouet, who became his lifelong, if not exclusive, mistress. No hesitation, no repentance could stem the torrent of this poet's passion. To

Sainte-Beuve he wrote in the midst of the scandal: "I have never been more *worthy* of your love."

Early in 1834, however, trouble was brewing. Sainte-Beuve published in the *Revue des deux Mondes* (February 1) an article dealing with Hugo's *Study on Mirabeau,* and this Hugo complained of as "not benevolent." Sainte-Beuve, in reply, cannot understand how, writing merely as a critic, he has wounded his friend, and the disagreement is patched up. In this case, at least, the poet cannot be regarded as thin-skinned; he had assuredly not been accustomed to such point-blank contradiction from his neophite. Especially important, in view of Sainte-Beuve's characterization of himself as a secondary man, is a passage on Hugo's conception of the historical relation of great men to men of this smaller type: .

When the idea of the predestination of great men is pushed too far, one is led, if care be not taken, to be severe and unjust toward a multitude of secondary, though estimable persons, who, in their time, and because of their good sense or virtue, and also because of their passions, have dared to contradict the triumphant ones on certain points and retard them for a time. . . . As he goes along, the poet [Hugo], without any ill intention, insults these accidentally from his lofty chariot of fire. . . . All the genius of the author, all the brilliance of his colors, cannot convince me here; arches of triumph and breaches in the wall for some; then, for all those below a certain stature, for the largest number, the Caudine Forks, unless they belong to the retinue. Once the great man is conceived in this spirit, note what becomes necessary in respect to him; in all points he must be upheld on this enforced elevation, and, as in the panegyrics of the Roman Emperors, so here, there is nothing in regard to him that does not become strange and supernatural. . . . If he merely recalls parenthetically that Admiral Coligny was *his cousin,* this is transfigured into *sublime,* instead of seeming simply a piece of vanity.

What happened at the end of March (1834) no one knows; Sainte-Beuve wrote a letter, which has not been recovered. Perhaps the passage just quoted will enable us to hazard a fairly probable guess as to its tenor. At any rate, Hugo, on the evening of April 1, sent the following reply: "There are so many hatreds and cowardly persecutions to share with me to-day that I understand well enough how friendships, even the most thoroughly tested, are renounced and sundered. Farewell then, my friend. Let us bury in silence, each on his own part, that which was already dead in you and which your letter kills in me. Farewell. V."

The friendship was ended, and for Sainte-Beuve this severance was truly an emancipation; for, if Marc Antony's genius was rebuked by Cæsar's, Sainte-Beuve's was almost cowed by Victor Hugo's. It was good, no doubt, that he had come for a time under the dominance of that energetic and violent personality, but it was good also that he should be at length liberated. His liberty was, however, not yet complete. For some three years more he continued, though with progressively decreasing ardor on both sides, under what he calls the charm of Armida, a charm in conflict with reason and compelling constraint in critical expression. This broken, he became, unwillingly enough, it is true, entirely himself.

CHAPTER IV

1834

IN 1834, besides breaking with Hugo, Sainte-Beuve also severed his relations with Carrel and the *National,* on account of a quarrel over an article on Ballanche contributed to the *Revue des deux Mondes.* For about two years, he had been losing his revolutionary fervor under the influence of several aristocratic salons that he frequented, notably those of Count Molé and the Countess de Boigne. Ampère, after much resistance, introduced him into the circle of Mme. Récamier, where Chateaubriand presided, and Sainte-Beuve was completely conquered by the grace and charm of beauty and the force of genius. He heard the *Memoirs* read, and reported the occasion in the *Revue des deux Mondes.* Many of his essays embodied themes more or less connected with his novel, *Volupté,* which finally appeared in July, 1834. Though not a great success, it attracted considerable attention. Meanwhile, he had offended Balzac by a critical essay and he had become a familiar friend and adviser of George Sand. A professorship in the École Normale was sought for him, but refused by Guizot. At the close of 1834, he gave himself earnestly to the study of Port-Royal, a subject on which he had been reading extensively during the four preceding years.

A second emancipation, that from the political yoke, occurred also in 1834. After Carrel's duel with the royalist Laborie in the preceding year, Sainte-Beuve had felt that the editor should have made some accommodation with his antagonists, who had shown themselves so sympathetic to the wounded antimonarchical champion. Although in two delightful essays on Jefferson (*National,* February, 1833), the critic's republicanism seems undiminished, he does not any longer look for immediate fulfilment, and he soon abandons entirely a political propaganda which had, indeed, for some time been growing less and less pronounced. Liberty is now thought of as something to look for in the future; the insurrectionists who died at Saint-Merry, fighting to the last, were deceived, though self-sacrificing (July 8); doctrinaire cant is no longer popular, nor is there any call for young Jacobins, since, even in the salons, one may say what one chooses, provided it is said with effectiveness and courtesy (August 8). The critic, furthermore, shows a revived interest in excellence of language, in Atticism; he delights in skirting the indecencies of Casanova with delicacy and charm, giving the full flavor of naughtiness but avoiding the offensive; he repents injustice formerly done to Racine, and he takes up Chénier again with renewed pleasure (January, 1834). He has, indeed, traveled far from his painful disappointment over the results of the July Revolution, the disappointment "of every soul devoted to ideas and to honor" (1831); he is convalescent from what he later termed the current smallpox of the time, a savage, ulcerated discontent that avoided and refused what was possible in practical political achievement. In short, he was returning to reason and common sense. Even the two Jefferson articles, as Carrel wrote to Thierry, "were in the old manner, or rather mania, of the pupils of Dubois."

Toward the close of 1833 there was, indeed, a decided coolness between Sainte-Beuve and Carrel, usual precursor of definite estrangement; but the actual breach came the next September. On the fifteenth of that month, Sainte-Beuve published in the *Revue des deux Mondes* an article on Ballanche, adorer of Mme. de Récamier and author of prose poems on human destiny and of works on political philosophy. According to his habitual method of criticism, Sainte-Beuve took the point of view of his author, effaced and forgot himself and identified his thought with that of Ballanche. Now to Ballanche, an antirevolutionist, "true institutions are daughters of time." They have their roots in the traditions and memories of a nation, as a tree has its roots in the soil. Even the best theoretical constitution is only provisional and without essential life. Legitimacy means, not divine, but historical right. "Glorious dynasty," exclaims the writer, "hasten to identify yourself with our destinies that are crying out for you, for these our destinies are immortal." To quote things of this sort, without reprobation and, at the same time, to speak respectfully of such authors as de Bonald and de Maistre, clerical enemies of the Revolution, made Sainte-Beuve look to his associates on the *National* like a renegade. Bastide and Raspail, chiefs of the republican party, expressed astonishment and indignation. The word "sectary," applied by the critic to Coëssin, an unbalanced religious and political fanatic, led one of this writer's equally unbalanced followers to attempt to provoke Sainte-Beuve to a duel. Carrel, at the time in prison, refused to utter a word to calm the turmoil; a tempest in a teapot, it seems from this distance, but one which then made stir enough for a few weeks. "I acquired from this affair," says Sainte-Beuve, "very useful enlightenment on the spirit of party and on the small profit that men of letters and critical thinkers draw from mingling with political groups, which are always more or less intolerant; for one is obliged, on one side or the other, to close one's eyes and to consent absolutely to shut out light from the intelligence." These are second thoughts, however; at the moment, passion dominated reflection. Angered at Carrel's obstinate silence in the matter, Sainte-Beuve left the *National* abruptly. Hypersensitive, perhaps, though in this case the cause of offense was certainly adequate, he did not go back to the office even to collect pay due him for articles already published. To the biographer, this incident is precious. Sainte-Beuve's unbridled resentment over the treatment accorded him casts a revealing flash upon his natural disposition.

Having suffered severely for bringing all his "sincerity and tenderness of soul" into his political and literary relations, he now gave himself more than ever, he says, to study and to intimate personal poetry, the charm and consolation of his youth. He found time, however, both before and after this episode, to mingle in cultivated and aristocratic society, and this fact possibly irritated his republican associates quite as much as anything he had written.

For fifteen years, he tells us in the preface of *Chateaubriand*, that is from 1833 to 1848, he lived much in the world, "in a society where a man of letters without fortune or ambition, of modest manners and knowing his place, might, by brains perhaps, and character and tact, hold an honorable and most agreeable position, and stand on a footing of equality with personages of every rank, even the most distinguished, a feature which constituted the charm and honor of French social life." At this time (1833), he became a familiar at the home of Count Molé, a more or less liberalized representative of an ancient family, who had served both the Empire and the Restoration, and was now foreign minister to the July Monarchy. Sainte-Beuve was also on friendly terms with Salvandy, member of the Council of State and later ambassador. In the salon of the Countess de Boigne, one of the rarest and most distinguished survivors of the old society, a perfect embodiment of propriety, uniting feminine grace and elegance with wit and originality, he came in close contact with Pasquier, later Chancellor and President of the Chamber of Peers, an able administrator, the very type of moderation and wise liberalism, an ornament of society and an accomplished man of the world. In such company Sainte-Beuve acquired first-hand information about leading political, literary and social personages of the preceding age and, at the same time, his plebeian savagery of disposition was considerably mitigated.

The civilizing influence of such an experience was of inestimable value to the critic.

I have remained thoroughly classic, he avows (1861), in regard to the salon. For me a salon is a circle presided over by a woman, whether old or young matters little, though perhaps it is best she should be neither too old nor too young, so as not to overshadow her surroundings. You come there with pleasure and you frequently return; you talk of everything under the sun; there is general conversation on certain subjects that everybody is interested in, and slight discords and dissonances arise, but here a skillful mistress of the house, like an orchestral leader, though without baton or gesture, either maintains or else quickly restores harmony. No important subject is forbidden; on all topics, there is entire liberty; for once a certain conclusion is prescribed, once any political or religious orthodoxy is fixed in advance, a *credo* or a *veto*, a *nec plus ultra*, farewell to that free and charming variety of talk which goes along as it may, and finds in the heat of contradiction its liveliest sallies and its unpremeditated stimulation. From time to time, some of the great athletes come to take one another's measure in duels of ingenuity; they enter the lists and exhibit their brilliancy; all pause to listen and to applaud, but soon each regular guest takes up again the thread of his own reflections in consecutive separate conversations, which, after the imposing display, make up in combination a softer hum. While thought and wit are never neglected, there is room also for the play of sentiment. A salon in which you may not follow or join the woman you prefer, take her out of a group that surrounds her, chat with her in an undertone for a few moments where the lights are low, repeat to her a bit of the general talk in which you have surprised yourself by making some clever remark, and as a recompense receive an appreciative glance—a salon in which you cannot do this is to me no salon at all. Our French salon, may it never lose its animated and unremitting alertness and its lively desire to please —the attractive graces these of France.

Unequaled, or rather unapproached, in any other social gathering, was the fascination exercised by Mme. Récamier.

MME. RÉCAMIER

This exquisite lady held court in her modest apartment on the first floor of the Abbaye-au-Bois, surrounded by a group of eminent admirers, whom she, by some magic of which her heart alone possessed the secret, had tamed from ardor to devotion, transmuting adoring lovers into no less adoring friends. Unique among women who reigned by their beauty and grace, she held a salon that united under a charming influence the most illustrious and diverse personages; yet even the most obscure might have the good fortune to enter. It was a literary center.

Here, writes Sainte-Beuve (1849), Chateaubriand dominated, and when he was present, everything revolved around him; but he was not always present, and even when he was, each of the others had his own place, his rank and his individual rights. Every subject was talked over, but as if in confidence, and a trifle less emphatically than elsewhere. Everybody, or nearly everybody, visited this salon, yet there was nothing ordinary about it. On entering, one inhaled an atmosphere of discretion and mystery. Kindliness, but a real and diversified kindliness, something special addressed to each individual, put you immediately at your ease and tempered the first effect of an initiation into what seemed, however slightly, a sanctuary. Here you found distinction, and with it familiarity, or at least naturalness, great liberty in the choice of subjects, a feature of prime importance for the play of intercourse, and promptitude in entering into ideas, which was not mere complaisance and graceful courtesy, but bespoke a real interest in what you were saying. Your glance never failed to meet a smile which plainly said *I understand*, and which brightened everything with its sweetness. Even on leaving the place for the first time, your mind and heart were touched in a peculiar way, so that you felt flattered and, at the same time, grateful. There had been many distinguished salons in the eighteenth century, such as those of Mme. Geoffrin, Mme. d'Houdetot and Mme. Suard. Mme. Récamier knew them all and talked of them excellently; anyone who might have wished to write of them with taste should have talked them over first with her; but none of these could have resembled her own, the reason being that she herself resembled no one. M. de Chateaubriand was the pride of this salon, but she was its soul. . . . She disarmed anger and softened asperities, banished rudeness and infused mutual indulgence. She could not rest until she had brought together at her home her friends of opposite sides and had reconciled them under the sway of her compassionate mediation. It is from such influences as this that society becomes, as far as possible, society and acquires all its affability and grace. . . . In her little salon at the Abbaye, she thought of everything. She spread abroad the net of her sympathies. Not a talent, not a virtue, not a distinction of any kind that she did not wish to know, to attract, to oblige, to set prominently in the light, and above all, to put in relation and in harmony with herself and to imprint on its heart some little mark that was all her own.

Sainte-Beuve was exceedingly shy of allowing himself to be brought under this benign influence. His relations with Chateaubriand had been interrupted in 1830, and he had even gone so far as to express doubts concerning the permanence of the great man's works. "One begins to think," he writes (1831), "that, without the solitary tower of René, which detaches itself and lifts itself up to the sky, the entire edifice of Chateaubriand would be perceived rather vaguely in the distance." But his friend Ampère was insistent, talked of Mme. Récamier to Sainte-Beuve and of Sainte-Beuve to Mme. Récamier, coaxed and pleaded, and finally, in 1834, victoriously led the strayed sheep into the fold. Sainte-Beuve capitulated utterly. He gave himself up without reserve to this charming society of the élite, where polish and taste presided, and where a glorious old man, happy to be understood and liked by the younger set, was often provoked by their vivacity to flights of lofty eloquence. The critic, indeed, soon became one of the most assiduous visitors, going to the Abbaye two or three times a week, sometimes a solitary caller, sometimes a dinner guest, sometimes a participant in the larger gatherings; and he also attended the Fridays of Mme. Lenormant, Mme. Récamier's niece. Yet, while he yielded to the charm and acted as all the others did whom Mme. Récamier had conquered, he nevertheless felt that this sweet influence paralyzed his judgment and abridged his freedom. In the vicinity of the siren, verdicts were softened at the expense of truth. Soon, therefore, this intimacy, too, was thrown off as a burden, though there was no open breach. Of Sainte-Beuve Mme. Lenormant wrote: "You are very much taken with the almost caressing grace of his manners, with the subtlety, delicacy and unaffected style of his conversation; you see him often, and flatter yourself that the pleasure is reciprocal; but all of a sudden you lose him; he escapes you."

Before he escaped, however, he had as usual picked up all sorts of personal information about distinguished people of the preceding generation, and stored away inestimable treasures for his future professional career. He eagerly absorbed Mme. Récamier's gossip about Mme. de Staël, Benjamin Constant and other remarkable friends; he became acquainted with Mme. Tastu and Mme. de Sousa, both of whom he also visited and to both of whom he consecrated essays; he met in familiar intercourse, not only men of note whom he already knew, but a great number of others, whose recollections of the Revolution, the Consulate and the Empire, when added to those of Daunou and his group, made the young inquirer almost a contemporary of that period. Above all, he came into intimate relations with Chateaubriand, and was enabled to study at close range all the greatness, as well as all the pettinesses and inconsistencies of that extraordinary character.

It was at the Abbaye-au-Bois in March, 1834, that Chateaubriand's *Memoirs* were read, and this occasion became the subject of one of Sainte-Beuve's important *Revue* essays. The eminent author, it may be said, was not averse to this kind of advertisement. Some years before, in Volume III of the *Revue de Paris*, Latouche had given an account of the reading at the Abbaye of Chateaubriand's *Moïse* by Lafond of the Comédie Française, an account in which the reporter, in journalistic fashion, depicts several of the celebrities among the sixty auditors and quotes from the drama extended passages, which he must have been allowed to copy for this purpose from the manuscript. In the same way, Sainte-Beuve was allowed, not only to take copious notes during the reading, but also to transcribe here and there bits of the text, so that his note-books preserve readings which the author afterwards altered or omitted.[1]

The essay on Chateaubriand and his *Memoirs* (*Revue des deux Mondes,* April 15, 1834, under the heading *Poètes Modernes de la France, XI*), as was obligatory under the circumstances, is written in a tone of almost ecstatic admiration and enthusiasm. Chateaubriand is the "founder in France of the poetry of imagination, the only one whose words do not pale before the glory of Austerlitz"; his style

---

[1] There has been a fierce debate on this subject. The evidence for the above statement, however, seems decisive. At the end of his article in the *Revue,* Sainte-Beuve inserts six pages of Chateaubriand headed *Avenir du Monde.* The *Memoirs,* indeed, were widely known, and many must have had access to the manuscript. In March Janin, who had not been present at the reading but had obtained his information from others, published in the *Revue de Paris* an article on the subject with long quotations, and in April, in the same periodical, Quinet, an auditor, added his impressions, which were followed by a passage communicated by Chateaubriand on his crossing to America and his halt on the Isle Saint-Pierre. The next year further extracts were published in connection with a notice of the translation of *Paradise Lost.*

While speaking of the *Revue de Paris,* attention may be called to an article (February, 1836) on the salon of Mme. Récamier by Édouard Gauss of Berlin, translated from *Der litterarische Zodaicus.* Besides giving special attention to the hostess and to the chief figure, the author describes at some length Ballanche, Cousin and Lerminier; somewhat less fully de Tocqueville, de Beaumont, Valéry, Edgar Quinet and Mlle. Clarke; then in one paragraph he mentions Sainte-Beuve, Pasquier, Fauriel, Guizard, de Kergolay, the two Ampères and Tourgueneff. At five Chateaubriand disappeared without ceremony and at six all the rest took their leave.

resembles "Greek columns, with wreathing vines of the wilderness for capitals"; yet he displays "a solid good sense mingled even with the splendor; measure and proportion in grandeur"; he is at times Homeric and Sophoclean, for the *Memoirs* are not so much a history as a poem, full of beauty and epic sublimity. And the setting and the scene of the reading were worthy of such a work of genius. The hostess, a renowned and sovereign beauty, uniting sweet kindliness and infinite grace; the salon, its door open to the world and its clamors; its windows looking upon a quiet conventual garden, symbol of retirement and peace; one wall covered with a vast painting of Corinne at Cape Miseno, linking a lofty friendship to a world-established fame; vases of flowers and oak leaves on the marble mantelpiece, and on the table nobly bound autographed volumes of the greatest contemporary authors; a select audience, to be one of whom was in itself a proud distinction, who listened with a respect almost akin to awe; amid such surroundings were read the *Memoirs* of the most illustrious of living men, a work of the most intense personal, literary and historical interest, but destined to be published only after its composer and its theme had ceased to live. And although another read, he himself was present, with his grave leonine head, a triumphant amplitude of brow, and eyes, now humid with tears, now flashing like the eyes of a young eagle. Under the spell of the moment, even Chateaubriand's political career is found noble and chivalrous. "This is not a judgment," wrote Sainte-Beuve two years later; "it is an impression, a faithful reflection."

The article, then, is not to be classed among the critical essays. On the other hand, it is of considerable biographical importance, not only as showing how Sainte-Beuve at the age of thirty could still be carried away by enthusiasm, but also for the points upon which his personal interest chiefly focused. These points all center in René; they are his *ennui,* his Sylphide and his religious faith, the very topics that haunted Sainte-Beuve's imagination during this period and that he embodied in his poems and in his novel *Volupté.*

In the first place, this *ennui* is real. To those who ask, "What ails him? His step is sprightly and he goes along smiling?" Sainte-Beuve replies: "Good people, can you not understand that one may have a pleasant smile, and at the same time feel the utter nothingness and the endless tedium of everything?" Every ardently desired delight ends in disenchantment; achievement means inevitable disillusion. Then comes age, full of suffering and regret. Even the objects that should make you happy strike death into the heart. And René is not alone in his intense feeling of the emptiness of life. Less glorious as we are, inestimably smaller, never honored by the heaviest blows of fate, we are yet all of us in this regard his brothers.

The Sylphide, inspirer of Chateaubriand's poetry, was "a composite of all the women he had known or dreamed of," heroines of history and romance, the ideal allegory of visions, and also a cloudy figure rising at the feet of some real object of adoration. At this point Sainte-Beuve stops, leaving the Sylphide as the sole possession of René; but if it was the still surviving Joseph Delorme who analyzed the *ennui,* it is surely the poet lyrically inspired by Mme. Hugo who speaks here, and who fathoms the nature of this mysterious apparition.

As a final personal interest, and this is developed at greater length than the other two, the religion of the champion of Christianity is found to be an alternation of faith and doubt, the history of many another soul. "As for these contradictions, struggles, oscillations between the Christian spirit just grasped anew, and the world with its passions, its doubts and its combats, who of us has not endured such in his heart? Who of us, instead of making accusations and of doubting the sincerity of him who created René, should not rather admire and respect in him this intermingling of desires and efforts towards that which we feel the need of believing, and this reiterated attraction toward that which it is so hard to abandon?'' In this query, we have what truly amounts to a confession.

Sainte-Beuve's preoccupation with religion dated, as we have seen, from his intimacy with the Hugos. His affection for both, and particularly his passion for Mme. Hugo, stimulated a desire to enter the same region of Christian faith in which they dwelt. This influence was reënforced by his relations with Guttinguer, who seems to have initiated him into the writings of Port-Royal and led him also to sympathetic appreciation of Saint-Martin, the eighteenth-century theosophist and mystic. "Love of all is a celestial love"; "Ye learned, forget your sciences; they have put a bandage on your eyes"; such maxims certainly appealed to Sainte-Beuve. In some essays, indeed, we perceive even traces of a leaning toward the occult and of a half-way belief in intermediate spirits. When Amaury in *Volupté* found in Saint-Martin the sentence "Man is born and lives in ideas," it opened to him a new vista; material objects acquired the moral significance of thoughts. In this writer Sainte-Beuve noted a perpetual incense of love, mysterious relationships, communications of spirit with spirit, a view into the beyond across the hindrances of the visible world. Yet the basis for such mysticism was, after all, purely emotional, with Mme. Hugo as the ultimate source. The lover readily enters into strange, cloudy heavens, if these are the habitual dwelling place of the beloved, hardly realizing that his intellect has not accompanied him and that he could not, in any case, transport its weight into this rarefied atmosphere. When, in later life, this realization comes to him, the adventure is apt to be recalled with a sort of sarcastic contempt, the revenge of mind on heart. Thus Sainte-Beuve, who is usually loyal to the vagaries and even the aberrations of his youth, wrote mockingly of this episode (1863): "I indulged in a bit of Christian mythology in my day; but it has evaporated. It served me as a swan of Leda, a means of approaching beauties and weaving a tenderer love. Youth has plenty of time and makes use of everything. Now I am old, and I have driven away all clouds. I mortify myself less, and my sight is more accurate."

"Christian mythology" is by no means a correct characterization of Sainte-Beuve's religious interests and efforts from 1830 to the publication of *Volupté*. His letters, his poems, his articles, his intimate converse with Lamennais and his circle, all show the seriousness of his studies and meditations upon worship and dogma. His mind dwells upon sin and grace. To Barbe he writes that peace is to be found only in religion, in orthodox Catholicism; and his letters to others often echo like thoughts. At Précy-sur-Oise, where he sometimes passes his two weeks' vacation with Mme. Pélegrin, mother-in-law of Théodore Gaillard, one of his old teachers at the Collège Charlemagne, he contemplates an evening landscape, "bare-headed, in adoration, reciting the *Ave*" (sonnet to Mme. P., 1834). He laments Hugo's departure from faith in *Feuilles d'Automne* (1831); he exalts Lamartine's *Harmonies,* not as dogma, wherein they are weak, but for moral elevation and Christian feeling (1832); in article after article he reviews the religious aspect of his topic, and his phraseology in these passages is often the phraseology of the priest. Yet we cannot say that Sainte-Beuve was actually a believer. A person who firmly holds to Christian dogma is in a certain spiritual condition in relation to the moral forces of the universe. Sainte-Beuve was, not continuously, but intermittently, and for a considerable part of the time, in this spiritual condition, yet without really embracing the dogmatic beliefs.

VOLUPTÉ

In his reflections on life—a not unusual proceeding with him—he identifies his epoch with himself:

Its intelligence has broadened, its knowledge increased; it has studied, learned and grasped many things and in many ways; but it no longer possesses the power and it has no longer *willed* to exercise its will. . . . We wish to understand without believing, to receive ideas after the manner of a clear mirror, without being thereby impelled, let us not say to acts, but even to conclusions. . . . There is, experience shows, in many young and open minds a perilous facility for prematurely adopting and professing certain doctrines that are taken hold of and loved, but in which there still remain elements that trouble us. This is an intellectual aberration which leads naturally and by rapid decline to indifference, clothed in a new and more specious form and adding another insult to the thrice sacred character of Truth. (Essay on Lamennais, 1832.)

Practically the whole of Sainte-Beuve's moral life during this period is expounded in his novel *Volupté,* which thus becomes an autobiographical document of the highest import in the light of what we know from other sources. No sane man, and least of all the studious Sainte-Beuve, ever lived a life of such uninterrupted agitation as is represented in this book. "I know the race of René," wrote the mature critic; "it has moments of suffering, when it cries from the housetops and complains to the world; it has day after day of happiness, which it buries in silence."

In an essay on the "Roman intime" (July, 1832) Sainte-Beuve lays down the principles which he followed in writing both *Volupté* and the poems afterwards collected to form the *Livre d'Amour.* With regard to the lover who composes confidential confessions, he says:

He presents to readers eager for such emotions either a history which is somewhat altered, but which, under the disguise of apparent fiction, is animated by profound truth; or, on the other hand, he keeps for himself, and prepares for a time when he will no longer be living, a confidence, a confession, which he perhaps calls, as Petrarch called one of his books, *his secret*. [The form, if one has not the genius of a Raphael or a Lamartine, must not depart from] the pure and naïve detail of things experienced. The best, in our opinion, is to keep closely to the truth and to pay the least possible regard to romance, omitting sometimes with taste, but being scrupulous to add nothing. Thus letters written in the moment of passion and reflecting, without any effort of memory, its successive movements, are of inappreciable value and offer a particular charm in their very disorder.

The fiction in *Volupté*, then, is simply a slight disguise for "profound truth"; we are to look for "pure and naïve detail of things experienced," omissions when advisable, but nothing added. For the fictional framework Sainte-Beuve adopted the same epoch as that of his abandoned *Arthur*. At the dawn of the Empire, a young man, Amaury, who has all the morbid nervous characteristics of the youthful Sainte-Beuve, becomes intimate in the family of M. de Couaën, a gentleman of dominating personality, and falls in love with his wife, a dreamy and pensive lady, with two children. In Paris, Amaury complicates his idealistic love for Mme. de Couaën with indulgence in sensual pleasures. He also has an intrigue with another lady, who dangles him without giving him any satisfaction. In the end he turns to religion, enters a seminary and becomes a priest. In form, the book consists of the autobiography of this priest, written as he sails for America, his purpose being the deliverance of a young man of similar character from the same sort of temptations.

This young man to whom the book is addressed is plainly enough Sainte-Beuve himself, but, lest any reader should have doubts on this point, we are almost directly told the fact. In a passage referring to the Feuillantines, where Victor Hugo spent many early years, Amaury calls it a place "made dear to you by the childhood of one of your illustrious friends."

VOLUPTÉ

The character of this young person, Sainte-Beuve's self-portrait, is presented at the outset:

It is not by false science, nor by proud love of domination, nor by the factitious need of dazzling or making a show that you are beset. Your tastes are humble; your modest heart, after the first intoxication of various doctrines, has warned you that truth was not there, although scattered fragments were to be found everywhere. . . . Neither have you any of those foolish artificial passions that encrust the surface of old societies, like monstrous or grotesque superfetations; you are of a true nature and you have remained sincere. Having reached, while still young, an honorable rank in public esteem by your intelligence and talents, you appreciate this success at its true value; you do not make it the point of support for helping yourself to climb further up, and it is by no means by this fragile handle that you seek to grasp your future. . . . Yet you are always lamenting; you do not believe in your own force, in your self-direction. . . . A single attraction, but that the most treacherous, the most insidious of all, has long seduced you, and to it you have imprudently yielded. Voluptuous pleasure has hold of you. . . . For you such pleasure was early a shining desire, a dewy flower, a savory fruit toward which your longings tended. . . . This strange fruit your youth has gathered, and yet has not been satisfied; drowned in this perfume, life has not appeared more fresh or more beautiful. You have, nevertheless, continued to pursue that which fled from you, to press from these petals new odors, ever quickly dissipated. Sensual pleasure, which was at first an inexpressible seduction, has become by degrees a habit, but its monotonous wearisomeness dispels none of its empire. You know beforehand what it is worth, what bitter deceptions and regrets it has in store for you; but what shall you do? . . . You are aware of the precipice, and you slide insensibly down. Hasten to lift yourself up, my friend; you must, and you can, if you only will. . . . I have lived a life much like yours; . . . the particular accidents that have marked it and changed its course resemble your case more than you might think.

We are here explicitly informed, and the information is repeated often enough in other places, that Amaury's life and its "particular accidents" resembled the case of Sainte-

Beuve. In these accidents, indeed, it is easy to recognize
the author's dreams, his *ennui,* his impotent desire for
action, his love of study, the variety of his interests, his
association with a conspiracy, his attachment to a young
girl and to a married flirt, but above all, his ideal passion
for a dreamy, abstracted lady and his simultaneous yielding
to venal beauties. Amaury's salvation through entering
the priesthood corresponds, of course, to nothing actual,
but merely to Sainte-Beuve's aspirations, to his frequently
expressed feeling that in religion alone could lasting peace
be found.

Of the other characters, we know, on the authority of
the author himself, that the gentleman of Normandy, who
excited Amaury by showing him his love letters, and who,
after serving as a model for his fall, became one of the
instruments of his return to grace, represents the volatile
Guttinguer. Mme. R., the flirt, is probably Mme. Gaume.
M. Couaën is not Hugo, except for his decided, com-
manding character, his absorption in a cause, and his dominating personality, in which, along with fascination, there
is something excessive and false; but his wife, the woman
Amaury loves, is, in all important respects, Mme. Hugo
herself. She is, like Adèle, tender, religious and mystical,
devoted to her children, abstracted and given to revery,
sometimes apathetic and scarcely noticing what goes on
around her, romantic, yet with underlying good sense. "To
write a romance," said Sainte-Beuve in later years, "was
for me an indirect way of loving and of saying so."

Let us note, in addition, a few coincidences, together with
some episodes that bear strong marks of actuality. After
meeting Mme. Couaën, it is six months before Amaury pays
much attention to her; one day he sees the husband caress
his wife, and it goes through his heart like a sword; in the
following days, his vacillating ideas begin to move in one
direction, he emerges from chaos, he loves; he finds mo-

ments when, with swimming eyes, languorous movements, negligently arranged hair, the purest woman is seductive; on one occasion, Mme. de Couaën begs Amaury never to leave her husband and herself, and, indeed, whenever she expresses the desire to hold him, she stresses his value to the marquis; Amaury wishes to exist wholly in these two beings; at one time, he is entirely contented with their long talks together, talks which connected everything with two or three ideas of the invariable, of the invisible, of the inward triumph of the soul, not thinking his happiness can ever change, desiring nothing more; at another time, it is intolerable to him that he is not first in her heart, not even second, but perhaps fifth.[2] Occasionally, he thinks of emancipating himself; one evening he wounds the lady by his harshness, and the next day there is a reconciliation with tears (subject of a poem in *Les Consolations*); she lets him read her husband's love letters, but refuses to show him her own; she allows him to take and keep the trimming of her wedding gown; she once visits him in his apartment and seats herself in his chair, and the place is thenceforth consecrated (poem in *Livre d'Amour*); she grants him as much love as she bestows upon her eldest child; he writes to M. de Couaën, asking if he thinks the relationship improper; he is irritated when he finds the lady occupied with other matters in preference to himself; he contradicts and wounds the marquis, and jealousy springs up between them, so that thereafter the presence of the husband becomes a hindrance. to Amaury's intercourse with the wife, and one day, finding the two together, the marquis even exclaims, "Are you still here?" Such are a few of the situations, which are either known to represent, or may be fairly

---

[2] Sainte-Beuve seems here to have completely identified Amaury with himself. Mme. de Couaën had her husband and two children to prefer; Mme. Hugo, her husband and three children. This is not the only discrepancy of this sort in the book.

presumed to represent the relations of Sainte-Beuve and Mme. Hugo while they were playing with fire.

One further episode has been thought significant in relation to Sainte-Beuve's rapturous poems on the satisfaction of his love, written in the summer of 1832. When Amaury protests that it is hard for him to keep his passion within bounds, Mme. de Couaën announces that she has found a means of overcoming the trouble, and, after much insistence on his part and much embarrassment on hers, she stammers out amid blushes: "If desires diminish when they have been satisfied, why not imagine your own to have been so satisfied long ago, and enjoy the tender sentiment that endures thereafter?" Extraordinary as such a proposal may seem, it is perfectly possible in the incoherent and excessive emotionalism of the epoch of Romanticism.

Amaury-Sainte-Beuve was born near the ocean, passed a studious, reflective, religious and pure childhood apart from the movement of the century, was afflicted with morbid sensitiveness, displayed excessive modesty in public, yet secretly dwelt in imagination on sexual matters and was perpetually haunted with the idea of woman. He passes through an episode of "moral hysteria" regarding certain physical characteristics. For him there is no pure normal love leading to peace and uninterrupted unity in marriage, but, with a fantastic and perverted imagination, he seeks an intoxicating tumult. On the one hand, he is stirred by immediate and brutal desire without choice and, on the other, by refined and subtle romantic passion, Platonic, breaking all connection with the senses and lifted up to an inaccessible summit, the senses being abandoned grossly to themselves down below. He makes good resolutions, but fails, and after every such failure, he feels shame in the presence of the loved one. He is incapable of true love, because he had given himself up to sensual pleasures, and such pleasures, instead of calming his early obsession with

sexual matters, have exasperated it. He perceives the abyss
that separates true love from sensual, and as the latter
grows, the former dries up. Full of desires that cannot
be satisfied, he recognizes himself in René, though he is
less exalted and more definite in his discontent. He feels
the necessity of entering into all sorts of ideas, running
the gamut from Lamarck to Saint-Martin. He wishes to
be at once scholar and poet and man of action, and longs
for a chance to offer his life for a cause, for his heroes are
Barnave, Hoche, Mme. Roland and Vergniaud. When nothing can satisfy him, he seeks out the conspirator Georges,
offers himself to him, and takes an oath, not out of hatred,
but for the sake of some kind of chivalrous employment.
Since all the rest of this character is self-confession, why
not this episode too? The conspiracy that Sainte-Beuve
was possibly connected with belongs to the year 1832.
Apparently he sought for a parallel to fit the case of
Amaury, and this he found in a book on the Napoleonic
police which he reviewed for the *National* (April 20, 1833).
In this review we come upon a passage, entirely dispropor-
tioned to the rest of the article (four pages out of eleven),
devoted with much detail to the affair of Georges and his
associates.

Sainte-Beuve's feelings as a conspirator and, incidentally,
as a duelist, may fairly be inferred from Amaury's confession:

I had neither hatred nor fanaticism as an excuse; the need
of change and of extraordinary emotion that incited me was,
crudely speaking, nothing but a delirium of the most exigent
egotism. It was this fact that I could not hide from myself.
On the eve of a conspiracy, as on the eve of a duel, it is vain to
try to distract yourself; you feel at the bottom of your heart that
your conduct is neither true nor right, and yet you feel bound
by honor, and you go on. While saying such things to myself
under my breath, I nevertheless did not repent.

The serious religious atmosphere amid which *Volupté* closes emanates from association with Lamennais and his group. To Sainte-Beuve it now seemed that, in his medical school period, he had merely wandered away from the spiritual point of view, instead of deserting it. His religion, however, is far from the simplicity of childhood. In his relations with Mme. Hugo, he is dominated by an idea akin to that which inspired Guido, Dante and Petrarch, declaring love the unique good, and attaining the love of God through the idealization of an actual woman. Yet in his case, this was not, as it might at first seem, a mere factitious literary revival of Beatrice and Laura; it was truly a repetition in his own personal experience of the feelings that underlay and gave birth to this medieval love philosophy, the pure heart of his lady becoming to him a refuge from inferior pleasures and worldly pursuits. Lofty as it appeared, this spiritual, intellectual and Platonic adultery, as Dupanloup once termed it, proved in the end to be no true ideal, but merely an ideal of the imagination. A passionate love of such a type cannot remain pure, and ends in libertinage of heart. Love thus failing to cure the voluptuary, there remains religion, the human will guided by divine grace, and with this religion earnest prayer, salutary in effect even when not attaining its direct aim. Such is the result to which Sainte-Beuve is led by his own experience and through his own sentiments, under the influence of intercourse with his ecclesiastical friends. In the book itself, Lamennais is named as the guide and helper of the young man to whom the narrative is addressed; even the tranquil, distant Barbe is indirectly celebrated. As might be supposed, there was no active collaboration, with the exception of a single bit of incidental assistance on the part of Lacordaire. To him Sainte-Beuve appealed, with characteristic thoroughness, for a correct representation of Amaury's theological studies, and the young priest conducted the author through the seminary at Issy, also sending him afterwards for his use a written account of the daily routine of the school exercises, an account which, with some necessary adaptations, Sainte-Beuve inserted in the body of his narrative. To the theological portion of the work, a further important contribution is furnished by Sainte-Beuve's studies on Port-Royal, begun superficially with Guttinguer in 1830 and taken up seriously in 1834. The Jansenist library described in the novel was a real library visited by the author. Yet in spite of thorough preparation, this portion of the book is unconvincing; it has not been lived. The unconverted Amaury is the only one Sainte-Beuve really knew, the Amaury who states his own situation in the words: "Durable and vital faith is made up of both atmosphere and the rock; I had only the atmosphere." Amaury the priest, indeed, is no more possible than a truly virtuous Guttinguer.

As to passion, we get the impression that Sainte-Beuve was by no means a man who goes frankly and heartily into a love affair. He examines his condition, makes a commentary on every emotion, and comes to disdain, even to despise himself, as a result of dissecting his motives, separating the theatrical from the real, and distinguishing in every idealism of the soul a sediment of sensuality. There results a subtle self-comprehension, without self-mastery, superfine intelligence at the expense of will. He does not plunge into either sin or repentance vigorously and with his whole nature, but slinks into both partially and with reserves. In life, as in literature, he is not the poet, but the critic. Victor Hugo smashes his way into his various love affairs with the regardless violence of a tempest; Sainte-Beuve, a sort of moist November breeze, blowing now from one direction, now from another, sighs and moans intermittently about the object, and occasionally turns over a dead leaf to show that the under side has begun to decay.

115

Volupté is a story, not of events, but of inward situations, a personal and confidential novel, based on reminiscence, such as, according to Sainte-Beuve, every observant person of sensibility could write once, and once only, in his lifetime. There are few acts, but sentiments, strained and attenuated sentiments, without end. The reader, indeed, becomes a trifle impatient over the hero's ceaseless vacillation and introspection. Sainte-Beuve is always dissecting a motive with a view to finding out what part of it may be base or corrupt or unhealthy, instead of accepting its dominant tone. Professedly the novel represents a malady. It is doubtless advantageous to get such a malady out of the system, and some have maintained that the only remedy is to put it into a book, but the result is not favorable to the author's moral reputation. The confessional is not normally a publication office. Yet when, in later years, people complained that Sainte-Beuve had been too frank in communicating to the world the weaknesses and follies of his former friends and acquaintances, they might have remembered in palliation his formidable sincerity in divulging his own.[3]

Published anonymously by Renduel[4] (July, 1834), though the authorship was no secret, *Volupté* was rather widely read and, in general, seriously reviewed. Grateful words of commendation came from Chateaubriand; Michelet thought the work expressed the moral psychology of the time with finesse of observation; Nisard found in it the sharpest and most delicate instrument of analysis and moral revelation; Lamennais, on the other hand, judged it too subtle; Lamartine saw in it a double purpose; for Magnin, it represented, not a normal state, but a rare

---

[3] What most people hide from themselves and from others, notes Ampère in his review of *Volupté* (*Revue de Paris*, July, 1834), Sainte-Beuve makes the subject of his study.

[4] It was the fashion among many of the Romantic writers not to sign their names to their publications.

exception; while George Sand, steeped in romance, maintained that every excessive situation is poetic. Sainte-Beuve himself declared that the book answered to a morbid disposition that brooded within the youth of the time; again, it seems, identifying the youth of the time with himself. It was six years before a new edition was called for, but four more succeeded this within Sainte-Beuve's lifetime.

The *ennui* which depresses Amaury, "a grief without a pang," a dreary longing for something entirely indefinite, permeated the typical literature of the early years of the century and found its chief expression in *Werther, René* and *Obermann*. It haunted Chateaubriand to the end of his days; Goethe found his remedy in work; and for Sénancour, alleviation, not cure, lay in resignation. Sainte-Beuve's theoretical remedy was religion; his real remedy was ultimately the same as Goethe's.

Before writing his novel and while composing it, Sainte-Beuve made preliminary studies, often reflected in his published essays. In addition to those previously mentioned, we find for *ennui* two on Sénancour (1830, 1831) and one on Chateaubriand (1834). There are portraits of Diderot and the Abbé Prévost (1831). Even earlier (1830), it is found that Diderot's letters to Sophie reveal "a subtle analysis, the infinite and detached pursuit of certain shades of passion and of certain hidden places of the heart"; and a similar quality is noted in Stendhal's *Amour* and in Prévost's *Jeune Grècque*. In other ways, many passages in the essays manifest Sainte-Beuve's preoccupation with the work he had in hand. He even exhorts Jouffroy to write a psychological romance. Novels, moreover, are treated by him to an extent not paralleled in other periods, there being articles on Mme. de Sousa and Mme. de Duras, both of whom had written fiction of the Revolutionary epoch, and others on Balzac and George Sand. It is, indeed, in a review of *Valentine* (1832) that he says: "Every one who, in youth, has lived a life of stormy emotion, and who dares to write with simplicity all that he has felt, is capable of a novel, of a good novel, the more excellent the less his recollections are altered by outside fancies. It would be sufficient for the author to tell, almost directly and with but little rearrangement, the story of two or three years taken from his personal experience."

The essay on Balzac (1834) led to a feud, possibly a continuation of Hugo's quarrel, for Balzac had found everything to blame and nothing to praise in *Hernani*. Though Sainte-Beuve praised the novelist as "a magnetizer, an alchemist, a master of occult science," and though he wrote that "*Eugénie Grandet* lacks but little of being a masterpiece to be classed with the best and most delicate single-volume novels," he also found much to blame, particularly in the matter of language. "A talent often bewitching and seductive," he says, "no less frequently contestible and illusory"; and further, "Most of his openings are delightful, but his endings degenerate or become excessive." The critic, in addition, made a careful list of Balzac's pseudonymous failures, published before he had attracted public attention, works that the author hoped had been forgotten. "He shall pay for that," exclaimed the victim; "I will thrust him through the body with my pen."

In an entirely different spirit, George Sand welcomed both praise and faultfinding. After the review of *Valentine* (*National*, December 31, 1832), Gustave Planche, chief literary critic of the *Revue des deux Mondes*, conducted Sainte-Beuve to her apartment to receive her thanks. There ensued a close intellectual companionship, undisturbed by passion. Sainte-Beuve became a sort of confidential counselor and almost a confessor. She found in him something angelic and even childlike, a discovery that rather surprises us, though we cannot doubt the sharp-eyed lady's word. They read to one another passages of *Volupté* and *Lélia,* and she was ever eager for his criticism, though not always ready to follow his advice. Often she intrusted to him the publication of stories and the correction of faults of spelling and of diction. As she was retiring and taciturn, he sought out for her suitable friends, de Musset, Dumas, Jouffroy, Lamennais, Leroux, and throughout the later phases of the affair with de Musset, he was often her confidant. Whenever a coolness arises between them, he refers to her in his letters as Mme. Dudevant. Her adventures into communistic philosophy, with Leroux for high priest, alienated his sympathies for a time, yet in spite of some eclipses, there was never any real break in their relations. To the end, he admired her generous and superior personality. In 1850 he reviewed some of her rural stories, but though he contemplated a complete study of the writer, he shrank from the task, and it was never accomplished.

In spite of the variety of his social affiliations, Sainte-Beuve cherished the impression that his life was "wholly devoted to thought, revery and study," and it is true that the hours stolen by the world from such occupations were comparatively few. "At thirty, as a rule," he writes, "the first impetus of youth grows feebler. Taking the point of view of strict reality, you know the unfavorable aspect of everything, the emptiness of friendships, the underside of enthusiasms, the insufficiency of exalted stoic doctrines." Philosophy has lost its glamour.

We confess that, as a branch of knowledge, philosophy appeals to us less and less, and that we see in it little more than a noble and necessary exercise, a gymnastic of thought which every vigorous youth should practice for a time. For each generation without exception during the past three thousand years, philosophy has had to be begun over again, and in this respect it is beneficial; it is an exploration in the direction of lofty places,

far from those near-by objects that shut out the view; it brings
to mind in their true importance the vast eternal questions, but
it never solves them, it never even attains them. Accompanying
philosophy, however, there are a number of truths of detail,
wholesome roots that our feet strike against on the road; but in
its chief pretension, the pretension of which it in reality consists,
and which aims at the infinite depths of heaven, philosophy does
not reach its goal. I may thus say of it, much as Paul-Louis
Courier said of history: "Provided that it be remarkably expressed, and that there be plenty of truths, plenty of wholesome
and precious observations of detail, it makes no difference to me
on board of what system all this is embarked or what method
it pursues." (*Jouffroy*, 1831.)

As to politics, Sainte-Beuve is no longer troubled over
the afflicting spectacle of a society and government from
which all noble and lofty ideas had disappeared. He has
no further immediate hopes for the achievements promised
by the generation of 1815. The permanent obstacles to
progress loom up discouragingly, but he also perceives a
general and continuous movement of society which ultimately surmounts them, a movement always obscure, doubtful as to the means it employs, and which at times seems
almost entirely to cease, leaving mankind as in the hollow
of the waves, without sight of the distant horizon. Judging
from such ideas one might suppose all youthful ardor
quenched. Yet, in a private letter (1833), Sainte-Beuve
confesses that there is within him a savage and revolutionary region, not perhaps very large in itself, but which
might make trouble if he went into active life.

Personal confessions, usually more or less veiled, are
frequent enough in the essays. On the other hand, Sainte-
Beuve had with regard to himself a curious habit of harmless mystification. Not infrequently he introduces feigned
quotations, and sometimes translations of nonexistent works.
In his review of his own *Joseph Delorme*, he speaks of "the
famous 'Yellow Rays,' which has been so widely and so

justly ridiculed," and then proceeds to defend his poem; in another place, he says: "I have read somewhere," and the passage that he has read is quoted from the "Thoughts" appended to his first volume of poems; he cites his own words as those of another, forgets who has written a phrase of which he knows that he is the sole inventor, and often says *on dit* when he himself is the authority. Such deceptions, even when not seriously misleading, ought not to be practiced by a critic, whose function, without question, is to inform, and not to hoodwink his readers. Indeed, Sainte-Beuve himself came to feel a bit uneasy on this score, for in his later footnotes, he very often either states directly, or with a roguish reticence insinuates the truth of the matter. Nevertheless, he continued the practice to the end of his days and *Port-Royal* is crowded with such passages, though we are openly warned that *on* means *I*.

In form, both in the newspaper criticisms and in the review essays, he almost invariably opens with a general introduction, not infrequently of disproportionate length. The approach is sometimes philosophical, more often historical, and in a few cases personal. For Béranger there are several pages on the development and character of the *chanson;* for Lamartine, a review of the eighteenth century; for l'Abbé Prévost, a series of melancholy reflections on the mortality of popular books. A favorite topic is the headlong haste of the age, which seizes every new object that appears in literature, bringing all of them indiscriminately to the surface, so that there is no weighing of merits, the young not having time to grow, nor the mature the leisure for development, every talent fatigued and driven to create out of season, thus multiplying the swarm of ephemeral mediocrities—words that might have been written yesterday. Over and over again, Sainte-Beuve speaks of the dispersal of the Romantic group, a dispersal which was on the verge of taking place from natural causes when the Revolution of July exploded, and broke the connection with sudden violence.

Almost all Sainte-Beuve's essays of this period touch upon his own life, either indirectly through subject-matter, or undisguisedly in the first person. In dealing with Sénancour, for example, he states that he had first read *Obermann* in 1828 or 1829 (Ampère had in fact introduced him to the book), and that he had been attracted by affinity of sentiment; he quotes long passages on the ills of poverty; Obermann is "the type of a majority of the somber and suffering souls of our time, the type of all warped geniuses and limited existences"; as a contrast, Christianity furnishes "the rectitude of universal beliefs, the central axis that fixes the meaning of all deviations"—a sort of phraseology that he had learned from Lamennais and Gerbet, just as he had previously acquired for a season the jargon of Saint-Simonianism.

A majority of his portraits, it should be observed, were those of personal friends and acquaintances, in which case his relations with the subject demanded a certain attention to propriety and a reticence, later abandoned. The personal equation slightly disturbs the critical balance. While, considering the circumstances, his appreciations and criticisms are remarkably just and clear-sighted, they lack perfect surety of touch. He is indeed rather too kindly to almost any minor poet who expresses real feelings, though he always distinguishes sackpoets from the truly great. Even the absurd Petrus Borel gets a good word in the midst of many reproaches. The style, too, is apt to be a little diffuse, lacking simplicity and directness. Metaphor is frequently overworked and there are too many long digressions. And yet the Sainte-Beuve charm is here, grace, delicacy, insight, equilibrium, solid learning, and, only slightly veiled, openness of mind and a judgment both wise and just.

CHARACTERISTICS

In 1832 Sainte-Beuve published his first volume of collected essays, *Criticisms and Literary Portraits,* a series increased by volume after volume in later years, and finally distributed into *Contemporary Portraits* (five volumes), *Literary Portraits* (three volumes), and *Portraits of Women* (one volume). He was growing in reputation, but his means of support were precarious. In 1834 his friends, particularly Mme. Lenormant, tried to secure from Guizot, then Minister of Education, an appointment at the École Normale, but Guizot refused pointblank, and demanded that the candidate should first produce a learned book as proof of his fitness for such a post. It was probably with this purpose in view that Sainte-Beuve set to work with the utmost diligence on his new task. "I have altogether taken up the study of the holy hermits of Port-Royal," he writes Ampère (December 18, 1834). "This is a Rome within my grasp, and I already love it as much as you love your Vatican."

To us the demand of Guizot is somewhat surprising; yet it is at the same time illuminating, for it was after all natural enough. Sainte-Beuve, author of a novel, of two volumes of poems, of a book on the sixteenth century, and of a variety of critical articles in newspapers and magazines, a few of which had been collected, did not in 1834 appear to the world of erudition in his just proportions. Nothing he had done seemed a sufficient guarantee of professional scholarship. Indeed, even in literature, if he had died at thirty, he would fairly have been dismissed with a few pages in histories of the Romantic movement and with two or three poems in anthologies representing that period. He would have left the impression of an enthusiast and a partisan, and also of a soul struggling through doubt toward religious faith. He had, indeed, already made some mark as a critic, but it was not yet *his* mark.

CHAPTER V

1835—1838

THE *Revue des deux Mondes* was now (1835-1837) Sainte-Beuve's only resource, slender enough indeed, for, though an assiduous contributor, he barely earned a subsistence. He was, nevertheless, completely identified with the struggling magazine, being one of its mainstays. Besides twenty-six articles, he wrote during these three years minor literary notices and showed his devotion to the undertaking by all sorts of services in the office, as well as by enlisting eminent writers and seeking out new talents. His essays exhibit his preoccupations. It is easy to distinguish in them traces of his love affair, of his poetical ambitions and of his studies upon Port-Royal. A history of these Jansenists had already been promised to his publisher, Renduel, by whom it had been publicly announced, but Sainte-Beuve could not find the time for consecutive composition, though he constantly amassed materials and meditated his plan. Entering sympathetically into his subject and always seeking moral support, he was yet without actual religious faith. In poetry he was composing, on the one hand, ardent verses of love setting forth his relations with Mme. Hugo, and on the other hand, a group of rather dry occasional pieces, descriptive, narrative and reflective. The first he assembled as the *Livre d'Amour,* kept as a precious manuscript for some indefinite future; the second he published in 1837 with the title *Pensées d'Août,* his most unsuccessful venture in any field. In 1835 he was, for a few months, secretary to a government historical commission, which accomplished so little that he resigned. To this epoch belong fresh volumes of his *Critiques et Portraits.* Among new social relations, not, however, interfering with those previously established, was a temporary association with the pious Mme. Swetchine, as well as permanent friendships with the aristocratic Mme. de Castries, with the poetess Mme. Desbordes-Valmore and with Collombet, a writer of Lyons. A breach with Mme. Hugo came in 1837. Personal allusions in a review of Victor Hugo's *Chants du*

124

Crépuscule almost brought about a duel, and later the two estranged friends faced one another at a funeral without mutual recognition. What moved Mme. Hugo is not absolutely known. At any rate, Sainte-Beuve attempted in vain to win her back by means of a story, *Mme. de Pontivy,* published in the *Revue des deux Mondes.* Much hurt by her indifference, he traveled in Switzerland in July and August, 1837, and, visiting the Oliviers at Aigle, he talked of his desire to complete *Port-Royal.* From these talks arose the proposal of a professorship in the Academy of Lausanne. The authorities, on Olivier's insistence, offered the appointment to Sainte-Beuve, who really wanted the position, but yet hesitated to accept it. Though he continually attended lectures at the University in Paris, he had never taught, nor had he ever even spoken in public, and, however excellent the substance, his delivery was in fact wretched. Nevertheless the course, which lasted from November 6 to May 31, was a success, and Sainte-Beuve won in Switzerland a host of friends. Full of affectionate remembrances, he was back in his old student rooms in Paris in the first days of June, 1838.

Among the literary campaigns enumerated by Sainte-Beuve, the longest is that undertaken in the *Revue des deux Mondes* (1831-1848), a campaign that "mingled an occasional bit of polemic with many analytic and descriptive portraits—a war of scholarly maneuvers, somewhat neutral in form and on the whole defensive and conservative, rather than aggressive, a long sequence of operations, which was interrupted by the trip to Lausanne (1837-1838) when *Port-Royal* was constructed."

Buloz, who had been a proofreader in a printing house, entertained rigid and insistent notions of style and diction, and he did not hesitate to correct the work even of his most eminent contributors. Sainte-Beuve's notions were equally fixed and, though willing to yield on some minor points of punctuation, he would not otherwise endure having his work tampered with. Not a word should be changed. There were certainly quarrels, and lively quarrels. Speaking of a later time, Hillebrand tells us that the vociferous

disputes between Buloz and some contributor might often
be heard by a passer-by in the street below. The acrid
manager was, without question, a rigorous taskmaster and,
in spite of much mutual respect, of complete devotion on
the part of both to the *Revue,* and of real community of
ideas and feelings, Sainte-Beuve felt "the collar" that
poverty obliged him to wear. In these years, a two weeks'
autumn vacation not far from Paris was all his resources
would allow him. Indeed, he wrote to Barbe (February
1, 1835) that he was not even earning a living.

For the *Revue,* besides regular articles, he produced many
notes in the *Chronique,* anonymous for the most part, but
signed S-B when important, and he even at times saw the
magazine through the press. Always on the lookout for
contributors—Cousin and Lamennais were among his recruits—he was at the moment indispensable, and Buloz,
though asserting editorial authority, looked to him constantly for help and counsel. Indeed, so far as public
consideration was concerned, the critic could have had no
complaint. "M. Sainte-Beuve," says the prospectus appended to the last issue of 1831, when the new policy was
completely inaugurated and the geographical matter eliminated, "M. Sainte-Beuve, whose fine historical and critical
work on the poetry and drama of the sixteenth century
has preluded so high a reputation, and who, by his *Joseph
Delorme* and his *Consolations,* is placed naturally by the
side of Lamartine, has promised us a sequence of pieces in
the manner of William Hazlitt on the leading modern poets
of France."

In spite of the foregoing promise, the series on modern
poets was extremely irregular, and it was not by any means
entirely from the pen of Sainte-Beuve. Indeed, he himself
is the subject of the thirteenth (July 15, 1834), which was
occasioned by *Volupté* and written by Gustave Planche,
the author also of several of the others. From Sainte-

126

Beuve, before 1834, we have Brizeux and Barbier, Hugo, Lamartine, Béranger, and others of less note, including also prose writers of various types. After that date there seems little further thought of this series as the study of selected representative authors, Sainte-Beuve's contributions being largely governed by circumstance. His essays on contemporaries, indeed, become almost exclusively simple book reviews, though not without interesting outlooks, as in the case of Quinet's *Napoléon* (February, 1836), an article which has value chiefly from a discussion of the possibilities of Bonaparte as an epic subject. Among his friends who are reviewed we find Lamartine, de Musset, Guttinguer and Montalembert, besides Lamennais, who was alienated by the critic's strictures, and Hugo, who was infuriated. Though he made no disturbance at the time, de Vigny, too, was displeased when Sainte-Beuve and Buloz took advantage of his absence from Paris to concoct a portrait without consulting him and with the design that he should have no chance to modify it. While the result might not have squared with his own aristocratic conception, he could make no reasonable complaint, for his faults are not overemphasized and his great merits are adequately appreciated.

Circumstances, rather than choice, also led Sainte-Beuve to publish as magazine articles several studies written to serve as introductions to editions of authors, such being his Molière, Mme. de Staël and Mme. Roland in 1835; to this group, though not a magazine article, belongs also Bernardin de Saint-Pierre (1836): and no work he ever did is superior to these pieces. There is not a student of Shakespeare who would not gain by being familiar with the notable analysis of essential dramatic genius in the Molière essay. As for Mme. de Staël, she had been one of the "religions" of Sainte-Beuve's youth, a worship never relinquished; Mme. Roland, too, had been an object of adoration, whose personality and social environment he knew as though he had been her contemporary, or perhaps even better; for *Paul et Virginie* he again professes extreme admiration, proclaiming Bernardin de Saint-Pierre one of his favorite authors. Yet his enthusiasm is always controlled by taste, and his sentiment by reason. In this group of essays, indeed, we find the most consummate skill both in portraiture and in the interpretation of an epoch, and this skill is combined with subtle moralizing and with the highest type of literary analysis and criticism.

In the allusions scattered through all the work of this period, Sainte-Beuve's studies on Port-Royal may be divined. Some pieces, indeed, are directly based on his researches. In 1835, while copying some manuscript correspondence of Mme. de Sablé, he came upon a letter to Mme. de Lafayette, and around this he wove his essay on this distinguished lady (September 1, 1836), an essay of such high quality that Géruzez apologizes for treating a phase of the same subject at a later date (*Revue de Paris,* July, 1838). To the same general studies belong the portraits of La Bruyère (1836) and Bayle (1835), and these critical writers then suggested his own contemporaries, Villemain and Nisard (both 1836). For the portrait of Mme. Guizot (May, 1836), which opens with a passage on the seventeenth century, full of suggestions used in *Port-Royal*, Sainte-Beuve was supplied with material by Guizot himself, and possibly the article was partly intended to gratify this statesman, who had been consistently ill-treated in the *Revue's* political *Chronique*. In the same way, for Mme. Krudener, in her prophetic religious rôle, certain documents from Benjamin Constant had been supplied by Mme. Récamier, from whom Sainte-Beuve had also derived indispensable personal information regarding Mme. de Staël and others. Entirely occasional is the essay on the elder Ampère (February, 1837), published shortly after the philosopher's death, and followed in the next number by Littré's estimate of his strictly scientific achievements. There is considerable science, however, in Sainte-Beuve's article, though the charm lies in the personal touch, for the subject was the father of one of the author's best friends. From this piece we learn the interesting fact that Sainte-Beuve, insatiable learner, had attended in 1832 the lectures of both Ampère and Cuvier at the Collège de France. But science was a mere side issue. As the date for the publication of a new volume of verses approached, two poets of the preceding age are noticed, Millevoye (January, 1837) and Delille (August, 1837), and meanwhile, a new star of Provence, Jasmin (May, 1837), had been flatteringly introduced to French literature and to the salons.

The group of pieces on the critics offers material of most obvious significance, the fundamental essay being that on Bayle. Here two sorts of criticism are distinguished; one which explains and reanimates the past or treats of subjects already fixed and established; the other journalistic, alert, working day by day, audacious, always on the watch, often mistaken, but correcting its faults, and with no system beyond instinct and experience. To this second sort belongs Bayle, not a philosopher, but a critical genius, never fanatical or too firmly convinced, but tolerant, infinitely curious, indifferent to substance, taking keen pleasure in all phenomena, and seeking rather for the spirit and genius of an author than for the subject of the book. The excellence of such a critic is that he should have no style or art of his own, a point at which Sainte-Beuve parts company with his predecessor. Bayle never wrote youthful verse, or dreamed in the meadows, or gave himself to passionate love, or even, though sincerely religious, experienced any real religious fervor. As a consequence of this absence of passion, he shows a lack of delicacy and finesse, and a certain dryness which draws a smile from those of us who, "by introducing art into criticism, as they say, have cut off so many other qualities no less essential." This art, combined with an incomparable talent, Sainte-Beuve finds in his personal friend, the critic-orator Villemain, whose lectures he attended so frequently and with such fruitful results for both learning and inspiration. It is in this essay on Villemain that the distinction is drawn between two kinds of literature, one of which is "official, written, conventional, taught, Ciceronian, set up to be admired," and the other "oral, in fireside chats, anecdotal, mocking, irreverent, correcting and often effacing the first, but sometimes dying almost completely with the men of its time." This second type, though fatal to the "statue" of the great writer, is favorable to truth, and not really harmful to admiration, that "vivifying soul of criticism."

We get here Sainte-Beuve's critical principles, not his method, for he never had a critical method. It is not the principles that are new, only the formulation of them, and the characteristic in which his growth is most evident is his tolerance. When he deals with Nisard, he does not present a portrait, but a criticism of a critical attitude, the attitude based on a system and exhibiting the prejudice resulting from a system. Nisard is censured for studying the later Latin poets through the distorting lens of his hatred of contemporary Romanticism.[1] Sainte-Beuve himself is no longer Romantic; he admits that solid prose is best for instruction, but claims that genius is the exception, and he defends the exception, while at the same time allowing due weight to tradition. "If nowadays Boileau's *Art Poétique* has been abrogated," he had remarked in another essay, "let us at least read for our profit La Bruyère's chapter on *Les Ouvrages de l'Esprit.*"

---

[1] Many years later, after quoting Chateaubriand's remark that there is no genius without religion, and Daunou's that there is no genius without the republican soul, Sainte-Beuve says: "Let us see natural things in all their breadth and with a generous indifference."

In an ephemeral but delightful article of 1835 upon *Foreign Judgments on our Contemporary Literature,* which is nothing but an answer to a review translated from the *London Quarterly,* Sainte-Beuve's habit of tolerance appears in a charming turn given to his condemnation of the English point of view. Its insufficiency, he says, is such as ought to make us very humble and a bit skeptical concerning our own judgments on the foreign literature of today. Even while defending French authors, he admits that beauty, harmony and moderation are not perhaps sufficiently sought; these we have a right to demand, not any direct moral purpose, taste itself being a sort of morality; there is, indeed, "a certain good sense indispensable to genius." [2]

Genius, an exception to all rules but not escaping the control of good sense—within such limits there is room for much tolerance, as well as for much severity of judgment. Hugo's discords and lack of Attic taste do not prevent hearty appreciation of his exuberant powers: Lamartine's incorrections and negligences are mere defects in "one of the most divine poetic organizations accorded to the world"; de Musset's crudities, his style at times confused like a translation over which we exclaim, "That must be fine in the original"—such faults cannot interfere with the warmest enthusiasm for his extraordinary gifts; and in the moral sphere, Lamennais, become "Coriolanus at the head of the Volscians," is still the ardent, the honorable, the great-hearted. In one essay Sainte-Beuve presents two methods, without pretending to judge them or express a preference, but usually his opinion is very decided, and in

---

[2] In his private note-book Sainte-Beuve writes: "Not to have the literary sense is to lack the sense of virtue, of glory, of grace, of beauty, in a word, of all that is truly divine on earth." And again: "It is the glory and eternal honor of the things of the mind, of art, that charlatanism does not enter there; this constitutes the inviolability of this noble part of man."

this period, it is turning more and more toward Atticism, a quality which he finds even in Jasmin, though of a dialect variety. In the essay on Quinet, he professes himself "French of the rejuvenated but uninterrupted Greek and Latin tradition, a friend particularly of a polished, studied, elaborated and perfected culture, of the poetry of Augustan epochs, and in default of these, of epochs of Renaissance." In La Bruyère he admires the careful artist, who never mingles trash with gold. It was not against such perfection, but against colorless imitation that Romanticism had won its victory, and Sainte-Beuve rejoices in this victory. When his cause has triumphed, however, he finds it pleasant to be just to the vanquished, and he can accord some merit even to Delille, a writer "without poetic art or style."

The justice cultivated in the essays was not always preserved in conversation. Sainte-Beuve has frequently been blamed for his disparagement of contemporaries, and he really seems to have carried this practice to excess. A young Swiss, Charles Didier, who saw him many times in 1831, is at first much attracted. "Sainte-Beuve," he says (October 31), "talks a great deal, and in a lively way that interests me. He has no settled ideas. A true man of imagination, very inconstant, passing from one influence to another, from one opinion to another; but frank, sincere, engaging; he is sympathetic to me." A few weeks later (December 15), however, the same young man reports that, though the critic has wit, he lacks force, elevation and greatness, and that his conversation consists entirely of personalities and emanates from a spirit of detraction. Such testimony is amply corroborated by others, yet we find Sainte-Beuve in a different mood honoring genius, appreciating sensibility and defending character. In his writings the two attitudes, often separated in personal talk, coexist and contribute to the truth of the picture. In an article in the *National* (July 18, 1833), Sainte-Beuve wrote: "One day the poet Béranger said to me that, once great living men became types and statues (and he named some), we must take care not to break these or to diminish them for the sake of making them more true to life in detail; for even if not exactly resembling the real persons, these consecrated and improved statues become an additional noble image offered to the admiration of men." But while recognizing the fitness of such "statues" for certain occasions, Sainte-Beuve grew more and more to feel that not only truth, but appreciation could be better served by the portrayal of the whole human being, weakness and pettiness as well as lofty power and nobility, in a combination not devoid of harmony and opening our hearts to sympathies that the "statue" could never evoke. However bitter the tone of a passing conversation, the mature writings of Sainte-Beuve are more genial than severe, and he almost invariably makes an effort to be just.

An example of the difference between private and public expression is furnished by two judgments on Montalembert's lack of originality. In a note dated 1836 we read: "*Phanor* has always been the disciple of some one; of Lamennais for his political Catholicism, of Hugo for his cathedrals. Whose disciple is he at present? He comes from Germany? Whom has he seen? I do not know. But why ask the name of his master? Be assured he has one. *Phanor* is a born disciple." The tone is unmistakably derogatory. In the essay (January, 1837), the effect is entirely changed, though the thought is essentially the same. "There escapes from him on almost every page a candor that his piety has not lost, a faculty for enthusiasm, a delight in admiration and adoration, a docility, an impulsiveness, a simplicity of heart, all those fine qualities of the disciple and the youth, so rare in our days and so ill-treated and exploited where they seek to show themselves." In the interval between the two pages, Sainte-Beuve had thought of his own case, and it is characteristic that, in the last phrase, an attentive ear catches an echo of his latent grudge against the *Globe,* Hugo, Carrel and all others who had made use of his talents and, as he thought, cast him off.

It is in the notes added in later years, rather than in the body of the essays, that the disparaging remarks appear in print, but these comments are generally corrective of some undue embellishment of the "statue," though often enough based on unpleasant personal experiences, in which we may judge Sainte-Beuve quite as much at fault as his adversary. In the end, however, reason dominates. After being unexpectedly irritated, Sainte-Beuve becomes, through a certain largeness of mind, unexpectedly indulgent, and, in spite of all that has been adduced against him, it may be affirmed that he does not in the long run allow his personal feelings to influence his artistic judgment. He is said to have hated Hugo for a time, and he certainly hated Balzac, yet, even when most antagonistic, he praises both highly for qualities that he deemed praiseworthy. What he blamed in their writings, was what offended his taste; and the arrogance of character that irritated him, perhaps unduly, both in these two men and in others, was surely more offensive to a contemporary than it can be to us. Sainte-Beuve's own irritability, though unquestionable, has been overemphasized by many biographers; it really stands out, prominent but occasional, on a large background of tolerance, which was habitual. Approaching men through admiration and praise, as he wrote to Barbe (1836), he soon got to the bottom and perceived their secret vanity; but such vanity does not, he adds, destroy talent and worth, for we are all of us a mixed product, false and true, petty and great.

During the period under consideration, Sainte-Beuve's situation, while socially agreeable, left much to be desired financially. Instead of taking his life energetically into

his own hands and making a career, he allowed his course
to be governed by the cravings of his nature and by circumstances, becoming thus a better critic, but a less fortunate, some might say a less happy, man. "After the
earliest youth and the first triumphs," he says in his essay
on Villemain, "there comes a decisive and fatal day; then
hopes must be realized, the conquest pushed, a definite
destiny settled. . . . How many talents have succumbed at
the test! This day distinguishes the leader in a skirmish
from him who, even if not a conquering genius, is at least
a brain with breadth, skill and resources." This decisive
moment Sainte-Beuve seemed unable to grasp or, let us
rather say, to create by deliberate and voluntary effort.
Results were achieved by internal forces of which he was
aware, and which he could analyze, but which he did not
direct. Appearing to drift, he was nevertheless actually
steered by an inward necessity which, in spite of all vicissitudes, and thanks to the happy intervention of others, either
friends or "exploiters," prevented shipwreck, limited dispersion and built up a final unity as complete as though
there had been from the first a definite aim.

This unity was now gradually emerging from arduous
work on the *Revue des deux Mondes*. Sainte-Beuve would
often have been glad to show Buloz that he could get along
without his review, but he really had no other resource.
In 1835, it is true, he became for a short time secretary
to the Historical Commission for Language, Literature and
Art, founded by Guizot as Minister of Education, a commission which included among its members Lenormant,
Montalembert, Hugo and Ampère, "a matter of luxury and
superfluity in which pleasant company played a large
part." They made archæological trips in Paris and to
neighboring towns, offering opportunities for instruction
from which Sainte-Beuve, who worked "poetically, vaguely
and in a dreamy spirit," profited little. He did, however,

draw up a circular of instructions on medieval researches for provincial correspondents, published in the *Moniteur* and signed by Guizot, and he undertook the preparation of a memoir on the trouvères, but finding his place a sinecure, he soon resigned. It is curious to conjecture what Sainte-Beuve might have become as director of erudite search for manuscripts on medieval science, philosophy and literature. His resignation of the post, in spite of pecuniary need, exemplifies not only his refusal to accept favors from the July Monarchy, but also his rejection of what was repugnant to his nature. Traces of his investigations are found in several of his essays, and the published circular, while naturally based on the notes of his colleagues, bears unmistakable marks of his composition. Furthermore, in the *Revue de Paris* (January, 1838), Didron says that Sainte-Beuve had, as secretary, already gathered all the materials for a history of works on French literature for the past three centuries.

New volumes of his *Critiques et Portraits* occupied more time than he had expected, for, harassed by the "demon of exactitude," he spared no effort in providing a humble note or an additional sentence. There were also distractions to which, after resistance, he capitulated. The social relations already indicated were continued and to them were added, among others, the salon of the religious propagandist, Mme. Swetchine, too sanctimonious in his judgment for a real salon, and the homelike afternoons of the Duchess de Castries, with whom he established an affectionate friendship; he also saw much of the actress-poetess, Mme. Desbordes-Valmore, unhappy magnet for calamities; and he began a long-continued correspondence with Collombet, a writer of Lyons, whose translations of early Latin theologians he noticed in a friendly spirit in the *Chronique* of the *Revue*. Every one he met contributed to his fund of information; he quizzed Mme. Swetchine, for example, and pursued Collombet for hidden facts about Joseph de Maistre, displaying a curiosity worthy of a larger subject. He also haunted the University and the Collège de France, sometimes attending individual lectures, sometimes following an entire course, taking notes, and not confining himself to any special field. To lectures already mentioned may here be added a series on Latin poets by Patin, subject of some verses in *Pensées d'Août*. In those days it was not unusual for an eloquent professor at the Collège de France to attract a distinguished audience. Even Chateaubriand in 1827 slipped in to hear an interpretation of *Paradise Lost,* a scene perfectly preserved for us in the essay on Villemain. What makes Sainte-Beuve's attendance remarkable is his assiduity extending over so many years, a manifest indication of his insatiable eagerness to learn.

Port-Royal was now the center of his studies. To Barbe he wrote (February 1, 1835):

I am engaged at present on a literary history of Port-Royal and of the recluses attached to it; that is a fine part of the literary history of the seventeenth century, the finest perhaps, when one includes Racine, even Despréaux, and a little of Mme. de Sévigné, and when one speaks occasionally of Bossuet and Fénelon, who had relations, of contradiction it is true, with Jansenism. I hope by the end of the year to be well advanced in this work, from which, however, I am too often drawn away by secondary labors, *Revue* articles and others. As for the journals, I have given them up entirely, and shall not resume.

In 1836 he had spent six weeks in the country at work, though Port-Royal was still far from completion. In the early stages, Lammenais had given encouragement and had helped with his knowledge of theological literature. The opening sentence of the essay on *Paroles d'un Croyant* (1834) shows that Sainte-Beuve was already deep in his study of Nicole and Arnauld. In 1835 we find him copying

manuscript letters of Mlle. de Vertus. His essay on
Molière (January, 1835) is permeated with ideas which
were later developed in relation with Pascal and more
restrictedly applied in harmony with the religious subject.
Hardly an essay from this time on, no matter what the
subject, that does not show some trace of Port-Royal and
its personages, Arnauld, Nicole, Du Guet and others. Even
where we should least expect it, we come upon symptomatic
phrases, such as the remark that talent is a gratuitous
gift, like Grace.

What is to be thought of Sainte-Beuve's religious sentiment at this time? Sentiment, for it can hardly be called
belief. That he was a hypocrite parading in the garments
of piety is a view that can be held only by those who
distinguish no shades between black and white, no nuance
between complete belief and complete negation. "Religion
and science," he writes in the essay on Ampère (1837),
"undying double need. In a strong mind, scarcely is one
of these requisites satisfied, considered sure of its object
and settled in peace, when lo! the other rises up and in
its turn demands nourishment. And if care be not taken,
it is the one which was considered assured that will be
shaken or consumed." Sympathy warms him in the atmosphere of Faith; then a thought comes like a frost and
he stands hardened in unbelief. He turns the page of a
book of piety, and on the other side finds Voltaire. In
1832 and 1833 he had attended the spiritual talks of Gerbet
and the Sunday receptions of Montalembert, gatherings at
which there were eager discussions of plans for a new
Port-Royal at Juilly or in Paris; by morning all had
evaporated. Yet even in the midst of error, combat and
doubt, he exclaims (*Pensées d'Août*, verses attached to
Volupté), "let something ideal remain, a spirit of forgiveness, of indulgence and tears, a willingness to pray under
arms . . . something truly good, trusting Heaven, tolerant

toward all . . . universal Christianity.'' On the other hand, he finds difficulties: ''If Christ softens my heart, Rome troubles me.'' In a poem to Barbe, he contrasts his friend's faith, solid on the rock, with his own everlasting search, ''an ill for me and a pain, but a charm as well.'' When he enters the delightful and elevated home life of the Oliviers, he renews his lost belief. Alternate attraction and repulsion, with no voluntary decision in either direction, such was his situation for several years. ''Since you are such as you are,'' wrote one of his Catholic friends, ''would that you were one of us!''

During the period here treated, the poet in Sainte-Beuve was perpetually more or less in conflict with the critic, no permanent concord having been established between senti-ment and reason. Sentiment, indeed, not infrequently de-generated into sentimentality, an exaggerated emotion over the insignificant. His heart is haunted and agitated by romantic situations of which he has been deprived. He sympathizes with suffering natures, with the melancholy and the exalted; he feels himself akin to those who admire with tears an ideal they can never hope to attain. He, in truth, overestimated the grievousness of pains that were chiefly endured on paper. Much of this sort of thing be-longs doubtless to the literary tone of the age, but Sainte-Beuve had, in addition, a real tendency toward depression. He also had special reasons for personal sadness, reasons that are more potent than is commonly allowed. He longed to be a poet, and the daily grind quenched his spark; he was poor, and he had absolutely no future. Here, as may be seen from his verses to Mme. Tastu, the study of Port-Royal was salutary. After regrets for vanished literary companionships and complaints against the labors that slay the Muse, he comes at the end of the piece to find the abhorred daily task even fairer than the Muse herself, for the Master, he sees, is God.

Beyond teaching patience, Port-Royal deflated sentimentality and showed the vapidity of gush. Was it then
an actual, though unsuspected, cause of the final break
in Sainte-Beuve's relations with Mme. Hugo?

Victor Hugo he had seen from time to time on public
occasions up to the publication in the *Revue des deux
Mondes* (November, 1835) of a review of *Chants du
Crépuscule*. In this essay, while happy that a great genius
has returned to pure poetry after his novels and dramas,
and while according high praise to elegies and meditations
that *came* instead of being *willed,* Sainte-Beuve finds a lack
of delicacy, a lack of Attic tact, and he speaks of Hugo
as an "energetic and subtle Frank," "a Goth back from
Spain and become Roman, refined even in grammar,
learned in the style of the Later Empire and in all sorts
of Byzantine ornamentation." "This lofty and imposing
belfry," he adds with a reference to *La Cloche,* "where he
has placed the bell to which he compares himself, represents
wonderfully well the principal and central view of his
work; everywhere the vast horizon, a rich landscape, smiling cottages, and also, as one comes nearer, formless ruins
and roofs bizarrely heaped together." Here was sufficient
occasion for disturbance, but this was not all.

Hugo, disregarding conventions, included in his volume
passionate love poems to his actress-mistress, Juliette, together with respectfully affectionate verses to his wife.
Writing to Béranger before the appearance of the volume,
Sainte-Beuve had said of it: "There will be verses of
love. . . . Another unity in his poetic life broken, the
domestic after the political and the religious"; and to
Pavie he had predicted uproar and malignant curiosity
when the book should appear. To both of these evils his
own article contributed. It is true that he had made the
same sort of objection to Lamartine's *Méditations* in 1832,
not indeed to love songs inspired by others after Elvire, but

to the mingling of the two. "And yet," he says, "Elvire herself reappears, the *Crucifix* attests the fact in immortal accents. Why then this *Chant d'Amour* immediately after the *Crucifix*? Poetically that is impossible." We hear of no objection from Lamartine, but Lamartine was not Victor Hugo, and the criticism itself seems less personal, certainly less meddlesome, than the page about Hugo's *Date Lilia*. This poem Sainte-Beuve considers an attempt to blind the public by throwing lilies in their eyes, and the respected object, he says, would have been better honored and praised by entire omission. The rage of Hugo was unbounded; there was prospect of a duel, so imminent that Sainte-Beuve made his will and put a package of precious papers into the hands of Renduel; but this publisher of the works of both accommodated the affair, at least to the extent of averting bloodshed.[3]

This was Sainte-Beuve's last article on Victor Hugo, and there were excellent reasons for silence, even had Mme. Hugo exacted no promise. References to the poet, which are still fairly frequent in essays on other subjects, always recognize his genius, and this even at the moment of most violent rupture (1836). Nor was such artistic detachment the only form of Sainte-Beuve's tolerance. Hugo's greatest fault, he wrote in a letter of December, 1835, was "immense pride and infinite egotism"; his other weaknesses call for indulgence; if our idols disappoint our expectations, we should not get angry that they act without consulting us.

Such tolerance, however, broke down on personal contact. When Hugo was reconciled with Dumas (1836) Sainte-

---

[3] Sainte-Beuve was not the only critic to refer to Hugo's liaison. Reviewing the same volume in the *Revue de Paris* (November, 1835), A. R. Bouzenot writes: "We cannot understand the blindness that has induced M. Hugo to perpetuate the memory of a moment of error." He could not of course foresee that the moment was to be a lifetime.

Beuve wrote Pavie that in his case no resumption of relations was possible. In 1837 the two met at the funeral of Gabrielle Dorval, daughter of the famous actress and wife of the poet Fontaney. Having avoided one another in the church, they were accidentally seated face to face in the carriage going to the cemetery. It is reported that Sainte-Beuve showed his embarrassment by gazing fixedly out of the window; doubtless he was composing some verses on the episode for his *Pensées d'Août,* the point of these being that the former friendship is quite as dead as the young woman in the coffin.[4]

It was shortly before this incident that Mme. Hugo herself broke with Sainte-Beuve. In spite of the estrangement between him and her husband, she had continued to meet her lover away from home, in streets and squares, churches and cemeteries, and on charitable missions to the poor. Many essays of these years, even when they seem to be wholly concerned with the emotions of their subject, betray Sainte-Beuve's preoccupation with his own love. He dwells, for instance, on Molière's tenderness and, in illustration, quotes verses about the little signs of passion that come without design, the betrayal of the heart by a sigh, a glance, a blush; or again, a passage declaring it false that one loves at first sight; or, still more clearly referring to his personal situation, a bit containing the words, "The least conversation with the beloved becomes, when forbidden, a supreme favor." In the midst of a discourse on Mme. de Lafayette, he has a vision of love, not voluntary, but mastering us in spite of ourselves, and he gives assurance that, when love has fled, there remains nothing but death, or God; all of which is quite in harmony with what

---

4 In 1840 Sainte-Beuve wrote that he and Hugo were no longer deadly enemies. A handshake followed a New Year's gift to the goddaughter. The children's illnesses always touched a sympathetic chord, as is shown in letters to Pavie.

he wrote in a copy of the *Livre d'Amour* about antique and fatal love mingling with that which is Christian, mystical and ideal.

The intimacy between his emotions and his poetry, moreover, is disclosed in a passage in the essay on Bernardin de Saint-Pierre, where Sainte-Beuve thinks it the ideal of romantic love "to be a great poet, and to be loved before attaining glory; to exhale the first fruits of a soul of genius, deeming oneself nothing but a lover; to reveal one's being entirely for the first time in a sort of mystery." Who can fail to understand, after that, why the *Livre d'Amour* was precious to Sainte-Beuve? Such passages, to which others might be added, demonstrate the absorbing intensity of his romantic feeling for Mme. Hugo. At Angers and Nantes, on the occasion of Pavie's wedding (1835), the two were together for several days, she being accompanied by her father and her daughter, while Hugo was off on an excursion elsewhere with Juliette. Sainte-Beuve was so happy that he overflowed in song. But Mme. Hugo was romantic, apparently too romantic for a taste now sobered by constant association with the recluses of Port-Royal. He urged upon her a little more reason, and thus offended her, at the same time causing her to reflect on the proprieties and on her duty to her daughter. Such, at least, is the story to be disentangled from Sainte-Beuve's own version, a sonnet that has been barbarously misinterpreted, and a story, *Mme. de Pontivy.*

The sonnet, which begins "Madman, what have I done!" and ends "I sought the nuance and spoiled the ardor," is entirely unintelligible without the story, in which we read that the lover, desiring a nuance of reason in his lady's ardor, she grew cold, thought of the proprieties and of her daughter, and neglected the object of her former flame.

Victor Hugo, in his youth, had written *Han d'Islande* as a message of love to be understood only by Adèle; now

Sainte-Beuve in imitation published in the *Revue des deux Mondes* (March 15, 1837) *Mme. de Pontivy* with the object of winning back the affection recently lost to him. Though the scene opens at the close of the reign of Louis XIV (epoch of Port-Royal), and the circumstances are far from identical with his own case, the sort of relation between the lovers exhibits a sufficiently close correspondence with the reality, even Mme. Hugo's physical condition being indicated, for Mme. de Pontivy by a fall sustains internal injuries that prevent childbearing. M. de Murçay, the hero of the story, urges and regains the lost fervor, and harmony is reëstablished. "Her ardor renounced nuances; his glow developed into ardor"; and the two, as they grow old, look forward to "sentiments every day deeper and more sacred."

The story, however, failed of its purpose; Mme. Hugo remained indifferent, and Sainte-Beuve was so wounded by her indifference that he vowed never to see her or write to her again. In this frame of mind he sought and found distraction in travel. He had commonly spent his two weeks' holiday with Mme. Pélegrin at Précy—not in 1835, however, since the trip to Angers and Nantes for a fortnight in May consumed his spare time as well as his funds—but in 1836 he spent six weeks in the country near Chantilly and in July and August, 1837, he traveled for about a month in Switzerland, visiting every place on his route which had literary associations and recalling not only Voltaire, Rousseau and Mme. de Staël, but Byron, Shelley and Gibbon. Sometimes a bit of crass realism interposes itself in the poetic reminiscence. Finding a trace of Chénier, he remembers that André wished a mountain maid for a wife. "Ideal André," he adds, "he forgot one thing, the *goitre*." Sainte-Beuve went as far as Lake Lucerne and returned by way of Lyons, where he had delightful intercourse with Collombet and his circle.

At Aigles he had visited the Oliviers, entering "a sweet and simple life" such as had been little known to him. To these good friends he expressed his regret that he could not have a year of respite to complete his work on Port-Royal, long meditated and already outlined. After sounding the authorities at Lausanne, Olivier proposed a course of lectures in the Academy there, and Sainte-Beuve, after some hesitation, accepted, the hardest part being, as he expressed it, the fixing of his *will*. His friends in Paris, Ampère, Lerminier, even Buloz, approved, as also Renduel, "my indispensable adviser." Among the difficulties was Cousin, who had just gone to Switzerland and who might be depended upon to make trouble, thus from the outset casting his shadow across *Port-Royal*. "He will praise me," wrote Sainte-Beuve, "in such terms as to depreciate me, but without ill-will; it is his way and one must not get angry at him." "A great mind, but the soul of a lackey and of mud," was the characterization sent in a letter to Buloz.

An appreciative article on Vinet (*Revue des deux Mondes*—September 15, 1837), who had recently been appointed professor of practical theology at Lausanne, seems, though honest in its praise and not without indication of faults, to have been designed to smooth the way for a friendly reception. Meanwhile the sedentary Sainte-Beuve was much upset, "sick in soul, heart and mind," living in Paris like a traveler, and longing for a studious, settled life. He reached Lausanne about October 20, very short of money, for it had cost 105 francs to transport his books; and he at once plunged headlong into work.

About a fortnight before leaving Paris he had published a volume of poems, this time under his own name, the *Pensées d'Août*. During the years since *Les Consolations*, he had written a large quantity of verse as a sort of double sequel to that collection. One group of compositions were passionate and dealt with his relations with Mme. Hugo, the *Livre d'Amour*. Frequently referred to rather indefinitely in letters to personal friends as confidential poems of his inner experience, and somewhat mysteriously announced to the public in the preface of the *Pensées d'Août* as his favorites and indeed the real revelation of his soul, these were not, he said, to be published for many years, being in fact something that he cherished for himself and for posterity. He nevertheless read these pieces to trusted friends.

To many the predilection of Sainte-Beuve for these poems has seemed fatuous and, indeed, it is an example of the victory of his sentiment over his critical taste and judgment. To the end of his life he hoped, against the warnings of the still, small voice, that his poems, these and the others too, were better than they actually were. To write verses, he told Béranger, was better than to construct books of erudition, and once, when George Sand called one of his essays *admirable*, he reproved her on the ground that the word *admirable* should be reserved for poetry and art. He envied those who had undoubted poetic genius, not with the malignant envy of which some accuse him, but with regret that he had not himself the gift, a feeling prettily expressed in the final pages of his 1833 essay on de Musset. There is a sort of wistfulness in his praise of Delavigne for being only a poet and never, though far from rich, seeking office. This wistfulness clings especially to the story Sainte-Beuve tells of the poet's answer, when asked if a piece of land he was obliged to sell had brought in much, the answer: "It brought in verses."

If Sainte-Beuve put his trust in others, indeed, he could well feel that he occupied an important place among contemporary poets. In 1832 the *Revue des deux Mondes* had spoken of the present great poetical epoch which had produced "Béranger, Sainte-Beuve, de Vigny, Victor Hugo

and Lamartine,'' and in 1834 Gustave Planche, whose
authority as a critic was at that time quite equal to his
own, in an article on *Les Royautés Littéraires,* again ranks
Sainte-Beuve with de Vigny and Lamartine. ''If he has
not Lamartine's overflowing spontaneity or de Vigny's
patient coquetry,'' says Planche, ''he yet lifts himself to
their level by treading other paths.'' Granted that Sainte-
Beuve committed a critical sin in tasting the sweet fruit of
an overestimated poetic fame, his fall was yet not without
conspicuous and perfectly intelligible temptation.

Pensées d'Août was received, not only with disapproval,
but with parody and ridicule, a treatment against which
the *Revue* protested, apparently at the instigation of Sainte-
Beuve himself. The *Revue's* own notice (October 1, 1837),
written by Planche, is a valiant effort not to condemn too
harshly, and though portions of the book are thoroughly
analyzed, fully half the article consists of digressions.
There is some rather faint praise of the simplicity of the
means used to produce a profound impression, and there is
a sort of half praise, if it be praise at all, for pieces the
accuracy of which must be trusted because the form of
expression is like that of a legal document; but the style
of the new volume, we are told, has unhappily not the
clarity and transparence of *Joseph Delorme* and *Les Consolations;* between the poet and the reader there comes a
cloud that fatigues attention, and in the end the obscurity
and confusion cause impatience. By multiplying nuances
the poet abolishes color. There are also improprieties of
diction, violations of syntax and poor analogies in the
images. After the labor of thought is completed, it is
necessary for a writer to begin work on expression, and
not leave his productions unfinished. In conclusion, the
reviewer urges an effort toward clearness. The poet ''has
elevated thoughts and true sentiments, but to obtain due
esteem, he must cease to veil what he feels and thinks; at

this price, he will have, as soon as he desires, the glory and the popularity that he deserves.''

The linguistic distortions, about which there seems to be pretty general agreement, are not for a foreigner to judge. Sainte-Beuve himself considered them liberties that Boileau would have taken, had he written in the nineteenth century. The other strictures of Planche appear also to be merited. Readers attuned to the low-pitched poetry of Cowper, Crabbe and Wordsworth, so often lauded by Sainte-Beuve, do not find the same sort of thing here. Along with the humble subjects and the plain style, there is usually something strained or sentimental, such as the old man at Patin's lectures transfigured into Voltaire, or, though this piece was written later, the little Portuguese girl's hair saved by a kind patron from the barber to whom her impecunious mother had sold the tresses. In the essay on de Vigny, Sainte-Beuve had proclaimed that poetry was ''no longer a happy natural faculty, but a penetrating and subtle malady, an affliction rather than a gift, a bitter dew on a suffering forehead.'' It might have flowers of brilliant hue, but their beauty was really a disguised degeneration. From another angle, it is a consolation in distress, a response to inward suffering, an instinctive plaint which, when all else is silent, gives vent to our tears. This sort of sentimentality does not harmonize with the grimness of homely subjects in homely verse, and the discord produces an impression of morbidity.

Pensées d'Août contains sonnets and epistles addressed to various friends, including graceful compliments to ladies, praise of the retired life, defense of homely poetry that attains the ideal through truth, and appreciations of religion and self-sacrifice and devotion. There are also reflections, regrets, a series of scenes viewed from the top of a stage-coach, anecdotes of a little girl, a priest, a schoolmaster, and histories of other humble lives, some translations and, at the end, a group of pieces written in Switzerland, which show that the author, in order to be moved, needs the charm of ideas and of human beings mingled with the aspects of nature. The volume is of a kind that might interest personal friends, and for us, too, it is interesting, not in itself, but because it was Sainte-Beuve who wrote it.

Though the unfavorable reception of his book vexed and disheartened him, he did not entirely relinquish poetical composition, but his later efforts are sporadic and cannot modify an estimate based on the published collections and on the one he still treasured in manuscript. He had not the gift of spontaneous verse. In a little piece included in *Pensées d'Août*, the fluidity of which is in striking contrast to his own response, de Musset urges him to return to poetry, calling his attention to a harmonious line that had escaped him unawares in his article on Millevoye; but while the idea is poetical—"the man surviving the poet, who died young"—and becomes indeed a harmonious line in the hands of Musset, to Sainte-Beuve it came distinctly in prose. Verse, he had once said, should be born and come into being with the thought itself, and his own verse did not come that way. Great talents of all kinds, he realized, require special endowments. "The true scientist," he wrote in the essay on Ampère, "the discoverer of the laws of the universe and of natural phenomena, when he comes into the world, is endowed with a special organization, just as much as the poet or the musician. . . . He is led to seek the cause, the reason of things, to find their laws, and where others pass by with indifference or permit themselves to be lulled by sentiment into revery, he is urged to look beyond and to penetrate the hidden depths." With such a special organization Sainte-Beuve was assuredly gifted, but instead of being purely or mainly poetical, it was mixed with a preponderant and infallible alloy of science and of prose. He was never captured and enslaved by his inspiration. He had emotion enough, but this was forced into a roundabout course, having no direct and immediate link with poetic expression. He was, besides, so saturated with literature that even when the flame of passion began to blaze, some analogy would intrude itself and make the lights burn blue. Even the *Livre d'Amour* is annotated with indications of all sorts of parallels, and Beatrice and Laura haunt the poems themselves.

What was thus injurious to the poet was, however, highly advantageous to the critic. In each of his essays Sainte-Beuve's immense range of knowledge is felt to be present, forming a background on which the particular subject is developed and from which objects are from time to time brought forward in relation to some part or phase of the matter under consideration. In other respects, too, the hostility of the critical and the poetical faculties may be noted. The critic is disinterested; the poet must be a partisan, not necessarily of a sect, but of his own conception, of his own nature, forcing everything into the mold of a dominant idea or emotion, subjecting fact to the vision. Such subjection was antagonistic to Sainte-Beuve's innate mental structure. Yet, while in creative imagination, as well as in rhythmical impulse, he came short of the abundance essential to poetry, he had ample provision of both to lend exceptional color and movement to his prose.

Up to the season at Lausanne, there might have seemed some doubt of Sainte-Beuve's vocation, his three volumes of verse and his novel having made much more noise in the world than his three volumes of collected essays. Now, however, the die was cast, cast *for* him rather than *by* him, and all uncertainties were resolved. When the year's labor was completed, a path had been trodden which admitted no return.

As visiting professor, he received 3,000 French francs,

which amounted to a little more than the 2,000 Swiss francs paid the regular professors. In all he gave eighty-one lectures, three a week, on Mondays, Wednesdays and Fridays, from three to four P. M. Imitating the Collège de France and contrary to local custom which limited the audience to students enrolled in the Academy, he threw open his course to all comers, men and women alike, so that, poor speaker as he was, he was obliged to make use of the large hall of the library. All his lectures were carefully written out, an immense labor, since every page of the writing had to be done as the course proceeded. In order to accomplish his task, he took a room at the Hôtel d'Angleterre, in spite of the Oliviers' invitation to their home, and there he shut himself in till afternoon, three o'clock on lecture days and four on others, always dining at the Oliviers' and spending his evenings there, with occasional visits to Vinet, whom he greatly admired, and to other friends. For his working hours he thus reproduced his life in his student rooms in Paris, a régime which he followed with slight interruptions until his death. His enormous capacity for intellectual work was seconded by a perfect regularity of hours and an abstemious habit of life.

As one might naturally suppose, there was considerable diversity of opinion regarding his effort. Some praised without measure, others thought him dull, and the press, as usual, was discontented. One group had expected a typical Parisian, lively, sparkling, elegant, who would make them laugh, tell naughty anecdotes with pleasing delicacy, and ridicule superstition in the spirit of Voltaire. They found, instead, a little, awkward, homely, baldheaded man, wrinkled and oldish, though still young, who chanted in monotonous recitative a series of solid and learned theological and literary essays. One lawyer is reported to have endured the martyrdom of attendance for a month for the purpose of raising a laugh each evening among the frequenters of the Café Morand by taking the lecturer off. On the other hand, there were many, particularly among the women, who followed the course with enthusiasm, and Sainte-Beuve could count on the approval and support of all that was most intelligent and serious in the town. "I confess that his delivery is a bit heavy," writes one auditor, "that he half sings his course, and that his reading is deplorable, but he has real merit, which causes his faults to be overlooked." After two months, there was still an attendance of between two and three hundred.

At Lausanne, allowing for the difference between Catholic and Protestant, Sainte-Beuve found in Vinet and a few others living examples of the charity and faith, the inward Christianity, he was portraying in the personages of Port-Royal. Surrounded by a religious atmosphere, studying a religious subject, and daily discussing religious topics with earnest friends, he came indeed so close to Christianity in sentiment that he gave the impression of being himself a believer. "He is Christian," says our letter-writer, "or at least friendly to Christianity, . . . and he has in his faith, still too literary perhaps, a candor and sincerity that make him loved." In Vinet's opinion, he had not reached the port, but did not deceive himself or seek to deceive others. And Sainte-Beuve's own analysis harmonizes with the impressions of others: "A sober life, the heavens overcast, some mortification of desire, a secluded and solitary mode of existence, such influences penetrate, touch the heart, and incline insensibly toward belief." It is not only an injustice to Sainte-Beuve, a matter of little consequence to a man long dead, but it is duping ourselves to consider the tone of these lectures to have been hypocritically assumed for effect.

The venomous and bitter Sainte-Beuve, always eaten up with disappointment, always filled with envy of the more

fortunate, always harping on some personal grudge, is
also largely a fable. Quarrels he had, and he said caustic
things, but his generosity was stronger than his virulence
and, after every explosion of temper, after every mood of
sneering, he reverted to an habitual equilibrium and equity.
Though he had a tendency to melancholy, he was by no
means morose, and his extant letters frequently exaggerate
his depression. With no trace of a sunny disposition, he
yet found life always endurable—consoled by the "animated solitude" of study—and often exceedingly enjoy-
able. "Sadness apart, I am contented enough," he writes
Marmier from Lausanne, and he looks forward to enjoying
their peals of laughter when they next meet to dine in the
little private room at Pinson's restaurant. Even in the
midst of a period of seeming agitation and high tension
(1836), he wrote to Mme. Pélegrin that he did not laugh
so heartily in Paris as at Précy, implying surely much
merriment during the short vacation, and no very somber
existence in town. This gayety is a note, unobtrusive
though it be, that should not be omitted if we are to appreciate the full harmony of Sainte-Beuve's character. In
spite of *Volupté* and certain poems, he was a normal human
being, with plenty of faults and weaknesses, it is true, but
sincere with himself and others, remarkably endowed, universally interested and indefatigably laborious.

The winter at Lausanne was one of few diversions, excepting such as were furnished by the happy home life of
the Oliviers. His course, Sainte-Beuve wrote, was his only
thought; he had put his hand to the plow and he looked
eagerly for the end of the furrow. Though the actual
lectures were written day by day as delivered, the plan
had been made and the materials—not every detail, of
course—completely assembled during the years of preliminary study in Paris, a fact made evident by the inaugural
lecture published in the *Revue des deux Mondes* (Decem-

ber 15, 1837) and reprinted without change as the introduction to the history. When Sainte-Beuve finished his course in May, he had a manuscript that a less exigent scholar would have thought ready for publication, but verifications and corrections were demanded, new facts came to light, and the added labor put into the work became unending. During the thirty years that ensued, much was added and many changes were made, for, in spite of multitudinous occupations and distractions, Sainte-Beuve allowed nothing that appeared on his subject to escape his attention. He corresponded with scholars, he visited libraries and collections of manuscripts, he sought pertinaciously, and neglected no source of information. In his own library he accumulated some seven hundred volumes on Jansenism, many of the utmost rarity, as though the topic were a hobby. Indeed, "due proportion being observed," *Port-Royal* is for him as much a central life work as *Faust* was for Goethe.

CHAPTER VI

EARLY in the seventeenth century, Angélique Arnauld, daughter of a celebrated lawyer of Paris, was, when a mere child, made Abbess of Port-Royal. At the age of seventeen, in an access of religious fervor, she instituted reforms in the convent. She soon came under the direction of Saint-Cyran, who had formed himself by the study of Saint Augustine. The closest intellectual associate of Saint-Cyran was Jansenius, afterwards Bishop of Ypres and author of *Augustinus,* a work condemned by Rome, but accepted by many priests and laymen called Jansenists, who denied the *fact* that the condemned doctrines were to be found in the book of their leader. Under Saint-Cyran's influence, Angélique's nephew, M. Le Maître, the greatest orator at the Paris bar, became a recluse, living in an apartment close by the convent. Other members of the Arnauld family and several of their friends retired to lead a life of penance either as nuns within the walls of the convent or as hermits nearby, all strongly penetrated with the doctrines of Predestination and Free Grace, and differing from the Calvinists chiefly in their attitude toward the Sacraments. Their independence aroused the opposition of the authorities, Richelieu first and then Louis XIV, and particularly irritated the Jesuits, with whom they conducted a controversial warfare, famous for the *Provinciales* of Pascal, who had joined the group when he abandoned science and the world. Racine was also of Port-Royal, both through his early education and through his later years of repentance. Several high-born ladies,

the most illustrious of whom was the Duchess de Longueville, sister of the Great Condé, lived in close association
with the nuns and their theological advisers. At length,
after intermittent persecutions extending over many years,
Louis XIV, irritated at resistance to his orders and resolved to extirpate Jansenism in France, banished the
counselors, dispersed the last handful of nuns, razed
the buildings and dug up the dead bodies of those
buried in the sanctuary—the final triumph of a glorious
reign.

Outside of Pascal, Racine and two or three high-born
ladies, what was there in such a subject to interest Sainte-
Beuve?

In the first place, he was attracted to Port-Royal by his
own experience of sin and repentance. Not only *Volupté*,
but many scattered remarks in letters and essays manifest
his feeling of the need of some higher power to give such
authority to the will as would prevent relapse. There can
be little doubt that it would at times have been a real satisfaction to him, had he been able to become a recluse after
the pattern of those he portrayed. If in practice he could
not long confine himself either morally or intellectually
within narrow limits, he yet admired those who honestly
and tenaciously subjugated flesh and spirit to a severe
ideal of Christian life. Furthermore, Port-Royal was
bourgeois; it despised trappings, show and brilliance; its
common sense and straightforwardness exploded all empty
and windy rhetoric, as its humility, surmounting pride,
overpeered aristocratic disdain. Such qualities, on the
whole, harmonized with Sainte-Beuve's nature, and,
though consistent humility cannot perhaps be reckoned
one of his outstanding characteristics, he was not himself
vainglorious and he found it hard to endure a display of
arrogance in others. Fundamentally his sympathies were
with the meek, and he had, even after he came to feel re-

ligion futile or hopeless for himself, a sincere admiration for the holy.

In the second place—and here he departed widely from the spirit of his theme—he found satisfaction in securing a subject which was so largely his own. He is pleased that Royer-Collard should say, "You and I are the only two in France who take any interest in such things," and he withholds his third volume until the general excitement aroused by the publication of Cousin's studies should subside. His indignation at Cousin, indeed, is the result, not so much of any fear for the sale of his book, as of resentment over the invasion of his territory, his own personal domain.

This domain might appear restricted, yet here again Sainte-Beuve's genius rebelled against confinement. In one way or another, Port-Royal touched every distinguished personality of the reign of Louis XIV, political, social and literary, as well as ecclesiastical. What a region for excursions! This feature, indeed, is one of the chief merits of the book, the epoch seen through the gratings of a convent or, at the widest, through the half-open door of a recluse. Sainte-Beuve, it is true, sometimes wanders a trifle beyond this field of vision, but we are mainly within rather strict limits and, if we escape for a truant hour or so, a rigid hand inevitably leads us back to the fold.

As we should naturally expect in a task spread over so many years, the aim of the volumes on Port-Royal is not absolutely uniform throughout, yet the leading purpose is sufficiently maintained. Though Sainte-Beuve often speaks of himself as an historian, a "pacific and curious historian," he is equally positive that what he attempts is, not to write the history of Port-Royal, but to paint its portrait, to present its heart and soul as revealed in the most notable circumstances and by the most marked personages. For a continuous narrative the reader is referred to other works. It is not the external fact that is

157

followed or stressed, but its significance. Truth is almost always covered by a veil; if we can find some little breaks in the drapery, let us peep through. And let our report be faithful. With no cause to plead, with no view of propaganda, dealing with disputes long dead, the author can be just, where partisans had been heated, and, instead of reviving buried quarrels, he can explain the conduct of antagonists by differences in their points of departure and by their varying environment. He thus seeks to define the principles of these Jansenists, not so much in doctrines, as in the inclinations and in the physiognomy of men, to restore a flavor that has evaporated, to portray the true, humble and great Christian spirit of Port-Royal in living models and in original works.

The plan is indicated under the image of the exploration of a monumental church. Passing up the nave, we view chapels to right and left, with tombs, shrines and confessionals that invite attention; several times these are seen and named before being actually visited; only after reaching the central point from which all radiate, do we enter these separate sanctuaries. The further we proceed in the main edifice, now grown thoroughly familiar to us, the more frequent our excursions into side aisles and outer rooms. There will at length come a time when, fully possessed of the dominant features of church and cloister, and even of the whole domain of the abbey, we need not reject any expedition into the outside world, if offered by related objects, not hesitating to go so far as to lose sight apparently of our sacred buildings; but to these we shall always return. Every road we take, whatever the direction in which it may seem to diverge, will lead inevitably, and often by a most unexpected turn, back to the holy precincts.

Our summary given in the appendix to this chapter will offer some idea of the way in which Sainte-Beuve branches out in every direction from the main trunk of his history. Indeed, as in some richly foliaged trees, the branches bulk larger than the trunk itself, which in places is only dimly perceived, though always felt to stand as a support to the whole. Port-Royal is treated, not as a collection of doctrines or a series of incidents, but as something alive, and, as its life is the life of a group of men and women, each of these is introduced to us personally and made to speak his characteristic language. Indeed, a large part of the text, perhaps over a quarter, consists of skillfully selected and always significant quotations. There is also much anecdote, almost gossip, which brings the reader close to these bygone personalities.

And Port-Royal is placed in its environment. The careful study of this group becomes a means of traversing an epoch, for the distinguished men of those days were few enough to allow even a handful of notables to come into contact with almost every important figure at the court or in the city, that is, in France. A liberal interpretation of such contact widens the circle to any extent desired. François de Sales is included because he was acquainted with Mother Angélique and Saint-Cyran, Corneille because he awarded a prize to little Jacqueline Pascal and because his *Polyeucte* was made possible by an age that could produce the scene at the Wicket, even Molière because *Tartufe* aroused against him the same enemies as those who assailed Port-Royal. Sainte-Beuve knew his seventeenth century from many angles; here it is looked at almost exclusively from a single point of view. It is surprising, to take but one instance, how different Harlai (or Harlay) appears, though unmistakably the same man, first, in the two *Lundis* devoted to his career, where, in spite of faults, he shines in the atmosphere of the world, and then in these pages, where the strict and somber atmosphere of the cloister somewhat darkens his lineaments and magnifies his evil features. And this is only one example out of many that might be cited.

Of historical events the same one-sided view is taken. The death of Richelieu is important in this narrative because it permitted the release of the imprisoned Saint-Cyran; the Age of Louis XIV, which might be divided according to treaties of peace or according to the succession of royal mistresses, is here divided according to the king's confessors; we forget the political aspect of the wars of the Fronde and simply observe that they brought roving bands of pillaging soldiers into the valley and filled the precincts of the convent with the cattle, fowls and crops of refugee peasants, even the church being encumbered with their belongings, while the retired military hermits fortified the place and mounted guard.

This limited view has the advantage of being more intimate. We come across things never met on the high road of history. A thousand little affairs, soon forgotten, but making noise enough at the time, help to form a realistic picture of the epoch. When d'Andilly's adroit practice of sending choice peaches to the queen procures a revocation of the order for his expulsion, or when Louis XIV reverses himself and sends back the nuns he has removed because he gets tired of paying their expenses in other convents, or when the new and hostile abbess hurries from Port-Royal to Saint-Cyr, where Mme. de Maintenon is awaiting her in a state of excited curiosity, eager to hear every detail of her visit to the rebellious House in the Fields, what we see brings us near, very near, to the incidents and personages of the past.

Sainte-Beuve delights in such details. He is happy to find even a note on the purchase of hay from Port-Royal by Le Camus, and, as another might describe a coronation or a royal progress, he devotes pages to the greeting of a new confessor or the reception of a party of nuns. These

little incidents are, indeed, the important events of his
theme, for it is not the material fact, but the spirit, that is
great. At the outset, Sainte-Beuve compares himself with
Gibbon meditating amid the ruins of Rome, and at the
end, he renews the comparison, this time with Gibbon, the
vast labor completed, pacing his moonlit garden at Lausanne; but in the contrast, his ruins, he recognizes, are
very modest ruins, and he completes his work in his room
on a Paris street with the morning light beating upon his
table. Here is no romance and no pretension. *Port-Royal*
is the work of a realist, but of a realist who repeats with
Pascal that thought is the true measure of all things. We
see the little happenings at the convent exactly as they
occurred, yet they are equated with great historic events;
the first *Provinciale* is like the four cannons at Fontenoy or
Kellermann's charge at Marengo; the nuns are on a par
with the heroes of Livy and Plutarch.

There are some details, it is true, that Sainte-Beuve
passes over rapidly, because they are distasteful to him.
The physical rigors of penance, the humiliating tasks and
menial occupations are matters he regrets. He cannot,
for one thing, get accustomed to men of brains knitting.
In another case, taste forbids quotation of certain passages
from Hamon's mystical writings, and reference is made to
remarks about Mme. de Longueville that no self-respecting
pen would transcribe. The Jansenism of the eighteenth
century—surprising vivacity for a sober critic—he would
not enter for all the gold in the world and all the promises
of heaven. He even regrets the miracles, as a humiliation
of the human mind. What he seeks is elevation of soul
and loftiness of sentiment shown by men of heart and
conscience, the moral beauty of the subject in its most
sublime expression. The question of the Formulary is
nothing; unlimited love of truth is everything. Yet mere
generalities are futile; "there is no life excepting in de-

tails," and, if we would seek to understand, we must look at things as closely as possible.

Hence Sainte-Beuve paints portraits and presents the whole of Christian doctrine embodied in an individual. Musty documents blossom into life and yield hidden secrets, for, as Vinet said, Sainte-Beuve confesses his authors. Even the rather remote Jansenius becomes a living personality and his ponderous book a sort of autobiography. In every case, the situation and the attitude of supporters and opponents add the elements of reality. In order to appreciate the force of certain calumnies, Sainte-Beuve puts himself in the place of the nuns, identifies himself with them, just as he would become an Athenian to understand Demosthenes, and for the moment, he adopts the delicacy of those buried souls. Even when he penetrates less deeply, he professes himself the friend of these *Messieurs,* an outside friend, like Mme. de Sévigné. This coalescence with the spirit of his subject is indicated in a subtle detail of composition: even intimates at Port-Royal addressed one another by the title *Monsieur*; throughout his book, except in the case of persons like Arnauld, Nicole or Pascal, persons so famous that the use of the title would be an affectation, Sainte-Beuve does the same.

He is a friend, but not a partisan, favorable, but just. He cannot always remain submissive. Love of his subject will not prevent him from exhibiting the weak and narrow side. For one thing, he recognizes that Port-Royal takes all the joyousness out of Christianity, and he admits that the editors of this school actually sought tediousness. He can furthermore be very severe on Nicole and even extort a compliment from a writer who likes to see the Arnaulds disparaged, a compliment which Sainte-Beuve disavows, since his purpose was not to belittle, but to present the whole truth. He realizes, nevertheless, that it was a weakness of the Arnauld family to think God's cause identical with themselves. His sense of fairness, as usual, leads him to present many facts highly discreditable to those he wishes us to admire, such as examples of obstinacy, disobedience, quibbling, together with subterfuges, suppressions and half-truths (Singlin, disguised as a physician, said that he was really a physician—of souls). Even Harlai's complaints are justified, as well as many others from hostile pens. The Jansenists were a party, and "all parties are venomous." The venom of the Jesuits, however, is found perfidious, excessive and continuous, and Father Rapin as an annalist comes in for many a vigorous castigation, though even to him some minor merits are allowed. When there is a contradiction in authorities on a matter of fact, Sainte-Beuve believes Lancelot, not from any prejudice, but because, through long intimacy, he knows his honesty and simplicity. Sometimes, on the other hand, antagonists are allowed to give an account of some episode, each from his own point of view, and when it comes to a dispute with a nineteenth century contemporary, an appendix may be inserted, printing in full an opponent's refutation of the author's own contentions.

Sainte-Beuve's essential moderation and many-sidedness are everywhere apparent. In Bossuet he admires the sovereign and perfect measure; he praises both Boileau and Pascal because they did not go to excess even in linguistic purism; and he himself always exhibits a sense of proportion and restraint in not pushing an opinion or an analysis as far as it could be forced to go. Commenting on de Maistre's arrogant declaration that every friend of the Jansenists is either wicked or a fool, he merely remarks: "That's rather hard." Why get irritated, when the manner of judging depends on the manner of feeling? "Let us be indulgent to one another," both as to fact and opinion. "The man who never makes a mistake is the man who never writes." "Every opinion is possible and comes forth at one time or another, as from a lottery, in this great human mass of contradictions.'' Such indulgence, however, does not stand in the way of strong convictions. Sainte-Beuve feels intense indignation against persecutors; he is thoroughly hostile to the Jesuits, in notes as well as text, and even when sympathizing with their relaxation of moral severity, his sympathy is impaired by the reflection that their common-sense and tolerance sprang from policy and self-interest. On the other hand, he does not hesitate to qualify as Jesuitical Pascal's statement, and his later explanation of this statement, that he was not of Port-Royal; and Pascal is the central hero of the history. When it is a literary judgment that is involved, neither affection nor antipathy has any influence: the enemy's merits are fully recognized, and a noble, pure soul, a de Saci, when he writes verses, is ''detestable.'' Indeed, Sainte-Beuve perceives that everything human is a mixture of good and bad.

Universal as his interests and sympathies were, Sainte-Beuve cherished decided personal preferences. Pascal and Racine are of course on the summits; their superior qualities could not be more highly exalted. In another category, Mme. de Sévigné and La Fontaine, full of ease, joy and charm, are ''divine.'' In the earlier volumes, and more or less in theory to the end, Sainte-Beuve is of the pure first generation of Port-Royal, though with much forcing of his disposition. Sometimes he tries to efface himself, and often his humble rôle in delicate Christian matters is limited to quoting. Saint-Cyran is honored as the dominant religious genius, admirable in force and constancy; but what a relief is felt when we find in this inflexible rigorist a tender love for children and a special affection for his little niece! Others, too, are repellent in their aloofness, however highly we must respect their virtues. Of the two kinds of Christian, the sweet, and the strong and ardent,

164

Sainte-Beuve prefers the sweet, admiring the other type, but with little real warmth. Lancelot, Feydeau, de Tillemont, on these humble souls he lavishes his sympathetic appreciation—Lamennais has faded before Gerbet.

Much of Sainte-Beuve's personality and much of his soul-history will, indeed, be found woven into his *Port-Royal*. Of personality as indicated in preferences, enthusiasms and dislikes, perhaps enough has been already said. Beyond this, a certain characteristic mobility is often disclosed in the way the style reflects the topic, severe with the severe, logical with the logical, eloquent with the eloquent, tedious (may we admit so crude a word?) with the tedious. Sainte-Beuve even condescends to present an analysis of Grace, for example, or of the progressive stages of Sister Angélique-de-Saint-Jean's soul-agony under systematic headings, according to the old sermonizing method. Very characteristic, too, is his appreciation of secondary natures, those who seek a master, subordinate and minor, indeed, yet more delicate and in some respects superior. "How they remain at the mercy of the strong and willfully tyrannical souls that possess them, exploit them and make them their prey! And what pains, what bitterness these misunderstandings of admiration bring sooner or later into the sensibility!" Whether the secondary natures continue attached or wrench themselves away, they are equal sufferers. Here is an unmistakable fragment of Sainte-Beuve's autobiography. His personal experience in religious effort, moreover, had given him insight in matters of conscience. He had felt to the depths the moral weakness of philosophy and the potential force of religion. He knew with certainty that sin is a simple choice, which leaves a mark on the soul, and he knew the paths of repentance, or at least of regret. Who, better than he, could assure us that the enemies of Christ are Priapus and Pan? Who, better than he, in appreciating Rancé's meditations at Veretz, could give warning against an agreeable retreat that may make us happy and wise, but can never produce the moral athlete, the great heart, burning and immolated? Every repentant soul has its Veretz, he adds, but to stop there usually means to redescend. In another place, he defines mysticism as a view of things· that turns the world into an enchanted forest where each object hides within itself another, which is truer and enshrouds a wonder. To this enchanted forest he had also paid a few fleeting visits, and memories of it were never quite obliterated.

"Young, restless, sick of heart, in love, and filled with eager curiosity to seek out every hidden flower," so we read in the *Epilogue,* Sainte-Beuve hoped at first to discover the secret poetry of these deep souls; but instead of poetry, he found a severe, rigorous, naked Christianity, a Christianity which he could by no means enter by way of acceptance and belief, but only to understand and expound. For the purpose of realizing for himself and others what was alien and peculiar, he draws upon his whole vast experience of both men and books, although thoroughly aware that, on account of inevitable disappearances, the past cannot be really made to live again. So far as we can go, however, analogy helps; the soul-sickness of Romanticism will throw light on the Christian soul-sickness of an old recluse, and the modern imaginative and artistic love of mystery closely resembles the vague shadows which in the olden time were purely religious. In the debates of the Sorbonne on Predestination and Grace, the author finds every trick and ruse recently practiced in the Assembly; Lamennais, Lacordaire and Gerbet often serve as terms of comparison, and now and then we even meet Ampère and de Rémusat; the literary parallels are naturally too numerous for mention, though Lamartine and Chateaubriand are frequent enough to attract particular notice. "Lélia is perhaps only Sister Anne-Eugénie out of the cloister," exemplifies an especially individual stroke. But in addition to contemporaries, all epochs are drawn upon for illustration, from the ancients to the French Revolution and Napoleon, often with the warning that due proportion must be observed. A favorite practice is to pursue a moral idea or attitude through a number of authors, perhaps through ages, noting identity of substance under variety of tone and expression. Sainte-Beuve is particularly fond of the ancients, both Latin and Greek: Demosthenes is easier to understand than these nuns and hermits, because more human, and Cicero, Virgil, Quintillian, the Younger Pliny, are always at hand to testify that, in all ages, man is man.

We would not convey the impression that the book is especially entertaining. To have attended the course at Lausanne three times a week, and between lectures to have looked up a bit of history or biography, or read a play, a sermon, a volume of letters, must have furnished a delightful and instructive pastime for any cultivated public; but to sit down and labor consecutively through the present six volumes is somewhat of a task. We appreciate and we admire, but we not infrequently look ahead to discover how many more pages the chapter contains. An unregenerate appetite might be satisfied with a smaller quantity of this very plain spiritual nutriment. One may even say that the portrayal is too lifelike, granted a certain drab uniformity and confessed tediousness in the objects portrayed. If the older Arnauld's eloquence is turgid, we must learn the fact by example; if Nicole or the Great Arnauld is as tedious as a king, we are not spared the demonstration. In many a lengthy passage, moreover, we are hammered with theological exposition and argument till we plead for mercy. In the case of present readers, we are at one time advised, possessed of the positive methods and knowledge of the nineteenth century, the first condition for entering these debates is to accept exorbitant hypotheses as the rules of the game; but a majority will have too little taste for the game to feel any live interest in the rules. Furthermore, however varied individuals may be, a certain sameness comes over them when they "get religion," particularly when this religious aspect is predominant. "In the things of Port-Royal," says Sainte-Beuve, "where nothing is brilliant, we deal with traits that have their full significance only when we go over them often"; and this full significance is impressed upon us by repetition without remorse. It is not that Sainte-Beuve gives the same episode a second time, though once or twice he does so through seeming forgetfulness, but these repetitions usually result from the fact that different men with identical beliefs will say or do about the same thing under similar circumstances, and in the limited life of the convent similar circumstances constantly recur. Without the digressions, the somber monotony of the theme would, for all but specialists, become intolerably oppressive. To linger in these pleasing by-ways is, in fact, agreeable and when, in the main march of the subject, we perceive a Pascal in the distance, we echo the author's cry: *Italiam! Italiam!*

The consideration of Pascal and of the schools, which formed the principal center and core of his subject, is concluded in the third volume, which was published in 1848. Eleven years intervened before the narrative was taken up anew and completed, years of intense labor—fourteen volumes of critical essays appeared—and of maturing experience that wrought important modifications in Sainte-Beuve's attitude toward his subject. The first volume (1840), which is dedicated to those who listened to the lectures at Lausanne, is, so far as may be judged from its adaptation to the audience and from the many indications still preserved of the spoken word, pretty close to the original form. In the second volume (1842), the author, in view of the favor shown by the public, has changed his idea and, instead of simply presenting what he had written for delivery, he has largely revised his lectures and added what closer study had revealed. Book III, of which seven chapters were included in this volume, was dedicated to his "excellent friend and confrère in Port-Royal and in Pascal, Dr. Hermann Reuchlin." Even more extensively revised is volume III (1848), though enough of the original matter is retained to preserve the general tone. The remainder of the work—books V and VI (1859)—has been entirely rewritten, and in a different attitude of mind. Some passages of the original have, as one might expect, been kept intact, these being occasionally pointed out to the reader in a footnote. Lausanne, however, is already ancient and the audience is wholly eliminated, the chapters lengthening at will. The arrangement, we are told, and this means only the general arrangement, has not been changed. "The architecture (if I may use this big word) is the same, only the rooms get more and more filled." The filling of the rooms, it must be added, is not the most important modification, for the whole coloring is altered. In earlier days, Sainte-Beuve had stood within Port-Royal; now he had come out. While he had, even in the first book, discussed such a matter as Grace for the rationalist, as well as for the believer, he had at that epoch generally written from the religious point of view and employed a religious terminology, at the same time sympathizing with the strictest and most austere application of Christian principles. Now he views the incidents with the natural eye, rather than with the eye of Faith. His own style has ceased to harmonize with his quotations from religious works. He is still on the best of terms with his characters, but intimacy has ceased; his heart no longer beats with theirs. It is clear, on the whole, that, in the first two books, Sainte-Beuve felt with his subjects, though not indeed sharing their beliefs; in the third book, he is carried on in somewhat the same spirit by his admiration for Pascal; the fourth book is a kind of intermezzo; and the last two are marked by a purely intellectual appreciation of an attitude of mind now wholly remote from his own. Beauty and elevation of character he continues to esteem, he is to the very last the friend of these religious devotees, but his enthusiasm for their doctrines and practices has cooled; instead of kneeling in the church, he examines it with a sort of affectionate interest and with a curiosity not much dulled through long and intimate acquaintance.

At the opening, then, we clearly perceive the lecturer at his desk, but as we proceed, the book becomes a series of chats, rather long and serious chats, it is true, but still distinctly chats. In the *Lundis,* as Sainte-Beuve confides to us, he was obliged to consider his public—a beneficent limitation, it may be added; in his book he can be entirely himself. We listen, generally with interest, always with respect, but sometimes half suppressing a yawn. We like him best when he is most discursive. He quotes Fontenelle on the subject of Malebranche, and he cannot forego an aside on Fontenelle's excellent style; he reads us a passage from Hamon on a tree failing to flourish in the shadow of other trees, and then reaches to his book-shelf for Virgil's *Georgics* and Lamennais' *Paroles d'un Croyant,* from each of which he reads a similar passage; or his subject suggests a page of Montaigne or Montesquieu or Pliny, and this, too, we must hear. As he talks, he tells us with a sigh that, between the thirty-first and thirty-sixth years, youth bids us adieu, that he has tasted the nausea of the world and become careless of externals; he slyly refers to anonymous publication that hides itself in order to be more in view; he likes to seize the first awakening of a vocation;

there are families of men, as of plants and beasts, and, when he takes himself seriously, he is a naturalist of minds; we know Pascal better by studying his sister, and anyway great sisters of great men are their superiors; the society of women is needed by the moralist to make him concise and lively; there is nothing equal to a portrait by a contemporary; he loves in every subject to establish extreme poles, opposite views that give thought all its play and all its openness; he suffers to find great men denouncing one another and would like to see them united in a sort of Elysian Fields. When the nuns describe a coach-ride by night, though they talk, not in the terms of Homer or Byron or Lamartine, but in terms of the Bible, he will permit himself a touch of the picturesque: Friends, he exclaims, there is no logic or philosophy that can be learned, for these are only made, and you will be fortunate if, understanding such things, you come to know better and do without them; in the olden time, there was a basis of reason in genius, but now lack of reason is the first quality; we have no longer the faith, but we have the Catholic attitude; though there are fine passages in recent plays, there is no great modern French drama; *Athalie* in the public theater is a profanation; Racine took great pains in minute correction and it were better had our great modern poets done the same. There was a time, he confesses, when it was hard to speak of Boileau, but now his incorruptible practical sense is recognized by all, and as to Racine, Sainte-Beuve lifts up his voice and recants the errors of his youth, for he had once made the mistake of comparing isolated passages of this poet's tragedies with passages of Hugo and Lamartine, thus finding more color in the moderns, whereas the true comparison is not of part with part, but of the whole with the whole. How delightful is study, which extends life beyond our narrow experience into a boundless past! Do you ask advice about your complainings? Write out your troubles; then put the paper away and forget it; this is not theory, but experience.

The comparisons, as usual with Sainte-Beuve, are apt, natural and effective: certain too liberal confessors are like physicians who allow the patient to overeat and at the end of the month administer a purge; M. and Mme. de Liancourt are Philemon and Baucis with an income of 100,000 pounds a year; a cloak of Saint-Bernard adored by the nuns is the *redingote grise* of the greatest spiritual conqueror of the Middle Ages; after Arnauld's death, Malebranche entertains himself by trying on the champion's armor; a pagan might pierce his heart with a sword on the grave of a friend, but here at Port-Royal Christian hearts break without a murmur. Somewhat akin to these comparisons is the way Sainte-Beuve notes by antithesis the seeds of the coming age, Nicole, for example, seeming almost to have a premonition of Rousseau's *Confessions*, and Saint-Cyran and his associates, by their insistence on the Fall of Man, confuting in advance the eighteenth century doctrine of the perfectability of human nature. Spiritual terrorism, which turns the world into a chamber of horrors, a den of serpents, is shown to lead by a natural reaction to the *God of good fellows*, and through a still more subtle filiation, the desecration of the graves at Port-Royal by Louis XIV is represented as repaid in kind by the Revolutionary violation of the royal tombs in Saint-Denis.

Such, in some of its aspects, is Sainte-Beuve's talk. Suppose some interesting suggestion has led to a digression. Suddenly the speaker recollects that he is expected to tell us about Port-Royal, and he hurries back to his topic, points out some landmark we are supposed to recall, and resumes his pilgrimage on the beaten track. Or, reaching a certain year which is decisive for some character, he proceeds in all leisure with a complete biography that begins perhaps long before and that carries us far in advance of the main narrative. Here, too, we need some vehicle of return to the point of departure, and as a result, the book is copiously supplied with summaries and other indications of location. Not infrequently, a chapter may open or close with a paragraph, much in the manner of Macaulay, telling us what the author is about to do, but rarely does Sainte-Beuve persist, like Macaulay, in a consecutive fulfillment of his prospectus. The side paths are too alluring for his truant disposition.

The reader, therefore, should never plunge ahead in an attempt to finish a volume at a sitting, but should allow time for impressions to mature. It might be advisable to intersperse the *Lundis* that deal with the seventeenth century so as to observe the author outside of Port-Royal, as well as within. After the first period of intense application, Sainte-Beuve was occupied with his subject at intervals over a stretch of thirty years. The difference in tone between the volume of 1840 and the two of 1859 has already been noted. At Lausanne he was speaking to Christians, and he himself without hypocrisy took a Christian attitude and talked of the Fall of Man, of the corruption of the human heart, of Grace and Salvation almost in the manner of a believer. Even in the partly rewritten second volume, we find a passage (on Montaigne and de Saci) like this:

If there is such a thing as truth, if all is not vanity (in which case the life of M. de Saci would be just as good as any other), if there is such a thing as morality—and I mean absolute morality—and if life leads to some purposeful end—which of these two men has accomplished the most and has most surely sowed good seed in his furrow on earth? At the hour when all shall be judged, which of the two will be found least trivial?

Later, instead of using such evangelical language, Sainte-Beuve is apt "to speak profanely"; to observe "from the standpoint of Mme. de Sévigné," though "we do not admire so much"; to say, "If you once admit the taste of Saint Augustine," or even, "Let us drop these wretched things." He is not really comfortable when the nuns open the Bible at random to find a guiding or a consoling text, or when they put a written prayer in the hand of a dead sister for greater assurance of its delivery. He can no longer completely sympathize with M. de Pomponne's aunt when she is glad for the sake of her nephew's soul that he has been disgraced by the king, and, while quotations still make it seem "as though we were present," we find, when we enter Arnauld's thought, that he is only "relatively right." Telling of the good omen drawn from a lightning-shattered oak that afterwards renewed its foliage, Sainte-Beuve remarks: "If the presage was trustworthy and if the sign expressed the reality, the tree must have revived very imperfectly." He finds that God is especially powerful when speaking through the king; he would have enjoyed the unctuous remarks of the licentious de Retz when he spoke in the convent church; what Du Guet calls "corruption of heart" is, to speak more justly, the inevitable foundation and motive of human action; and precepts given by a confessor to the converted Princess de Conti are called "Medieval cookery for souls." When the Prince in his zeal dismisses his troupe of actors, Sainte-Beuve exclaims: "Poor troupe of Molière! it pays the price of his penance."

For the earlier volumes, remarks of this sort are generally found in the footnotes, which were added to each new edition. These consist of reflections on the text, *obiter dicta,* additions, objections, recantations, applications to current affairs; the author discovers the identity of some obscure character, corrects a date, inserts an anecdote, adds particulars, recants his severity against the average morality, gives examples of refectory wit, appropriate to a character but a little below the dignity of history; or he presents a view of an incident or argument contrary to that originally given, discriminates between three or four persons of the same name who might easily be confounded, investigates every place visited by some exile, inserts a dig at Cousin, points a moral or expresses dissatisfaction with present political or social or literary conditions. It is particularly in these notes that we find the classical allusions, quotations from the Greek *Anthology*, the image of the veil falling from the eyes of Æneas, and all sorts of Roman and Homeric parallels.

What is too long for a note is transferred to an appendix. Here we find, at one time, an entertaining story; at another, an apology for some harsh judgment; or perhaps an essay on some bishop, or a republished *Lundi* on some topic that could not wait for the completion of the work. One appendix consists of a straightforward account of de Retz, written by a friend, and in striking contrast with the author's own colloquial and wandering method; in others are letters recently communicated from various archives, a list of the medical writings of a saintly physician, and an immense quantity of diverse biographical lore.

In all this Sainte-Beuve did not much disturb his text, once it was printed. As appears to have been his general habit, he allowed an original fault or uncertainty to stand, and simply added the new information. From the outset, he had striven to be as accurate and complete as his means at the time permitted. He always went to the source, the manuscript or the first edition; and to obtain such, he would follow a trace for years until he found and acquired what he sought. In this task he was aided by his friends, one of these, Magnin, being thanked for procuring some precious volumes. Sometimes, in quoting, he restores a reading mutilated in the printed texts, sometimes he restores only significant parts of the original, and there are cases where, contrary to the method of strict erudition, he prefers an edited form. In some of these procedures he may be pronounced unquestionably wrong, but it must be admitted that nothing he does is haphazard, that his learning is always controlled by good sense, and that every generalization is based on thorough study of detail. As a scholar, furthermore, he is perfectly honest and not only never deceives the reader, but gives him a straightforward account of his manner of dealing with his material. Having completed the work, he did not dismiss the subject, but kept a vigilant watch for anything that might be added, and continued to accumulate whatever came to him in printed texts or from manuscript collections.

Sainte-Beuve, indeed, is no professional scholar, but he is a very learned man, industrious, exact and minutely conscientious. Beyond and above this, he not only knew facts as facts; he had lived within his subject and knew it from personal intimacy. When M. Singlin is called Abbé Singlin by Cousin, Sainte-Beuve takes a somewhat malicious pleasure in pointing out that the blunder shows Cousin to be an outsider, since Port-Royal never called a priest Abbé unless he actually presided over an abbey, the fact being illustrated by an anecdote of Nicole, who, having been designated by courtesy as Abbé Nicole in the salon of Mme. de Longueville, complained humorously, after these visitors had been dispersed by the death of his protectress, that he had lost his abbey. The point is not really trivial, since it vividly indicates how deeply the nineteenth century skeptic had penetrated into the seventeenth century sanctuary chosen for his theme.

As in the case of contemporary movements and groups—Romanticism, Saint-Simonianism, Democratic Catholicism, and perhaps a dozen others—Sainte-Beuve was both inside of Port-Royal and outside. With all respect for these virtuous men and women, he could by no means become one of them, any more than he could identify himself with Lamennais or Enfantin. Had they revived, he would have gone to them a few times to verify his pictures, never to imitate, never to sacrifice his essential self. Having worked as a sincere, attentive, scrupulous observer, seeking to see men and things as they actually were, he feels, now that his task is finished, an inevitable distaste; he perceives himself to be, he says in the final words of the *Epilogue,* "nothing but one of the most fleeting illusions in the bosom of the infinite Illusion." Like a workman engaged in a deadly trade, the critic is here for the moment a victim of his own labors.

SUMMARY ANALYSIS OF PORT-ROYAL

Book I. Origin and Birth of Port-Royal (Twelve Chapters)

AFTER a sketch of the early history and legends of the Abbey, done in the manner of a professional historian, Sainte-Beuve takes up the Arnauld family, traces its qualities in certain warlike uncles, gives examples of the turgid eloquence of Angélique's father—"his character was better than his taste"—and then, reflecting that we find dishonesty in the best, relates the tricks and even falsehoods to which this good man resorted in order to get two daughters, aged five and seven respectively, appointed abbesses. It is well, remarks the author, to look at men and things as closely as possible. If you view them as a whole and from a distance, you are apt not to see them correctly. This mixture of good and bad is truly life; only a constant Christian thought can make one secure in justice. The soul history of Angélique follows, with a systematic analysis under five headings of the operation of Grace, invading and taking possession of the whole personality without reserve; the climax of the struggle being the exclusion of her father from the interior of the convent, known in the annals of the house as the "Day of the Wicket" (la Journée du Guichet). The unreason and religious fervor (the folly of the cross) which made such a scene possible made possible also the *Polyeucte* of Corneille; and here Sainte-Beuve devotes two chapters to an analysis of this drama and of its companion piece, the *Saint-Genest* of Routrou. Returning to the obscure day-by-day labors of Port-Royal, to the freshness of early years, a period of practice rather than doctrine, and finding here a graceful naïveté that recalls Perugino, Sainte-Beuve remarks: "It is by consecutive, reflective, almost contrite study that these must be approached, by study mingled with prayer, rather than by that kind of exposition, serious indeed, but external and too literary, in which imagination and curiosity have so large a part." At this point we meet Saint François de Sales, and the sweetness of Christian character. Then, by sudden contrast, we come upon one who prefers autumn to spring

178

and demands fruit rather than flowers, whose austere charity does not quiver before the doctrine of infant damnation, Saint-Cyran, imbued with the spirit of the martyrs, who, after years devoted to the study of Saint Augustine in company with Jansenius, becomes Director of Port-Royal. A debate with the Jesuits, a great debate on insignificant points, the repulse of Richelieu's advances, and a strong mastery exercised over the spirits of certain distinguished men (Singlin, Lancelot, de Saci, Le Maître) draw upon this Director the dislike of those in authority.

Book II. The Port-Royal of M. Saint-Cyran (Eighteen Chapters)

This book, with all its digressions, is dominated by the spirit of Saint-Cyran, the Christian Director, "a rigid and sure physician of souls." In fact, this spirit, modified by circumstances and individualities, is the essential spirit of Port-Royal, which endured, even if enfeebled, to the end. Saint-Cyran is distinguished from the Calvinists and Methodists by his belief in the Sacraments. He is no writer, but a speaker; he cares little for history or politics, only for souls; he has no distraction toward nature. Being ambitious, he particularly practiced humility, yet held the authority of the priest to be above that of temporal rulers. He never softened before great worldly ladies or feared the menaces of the powerful, being free from the weakness sometimes found in François de Sales, Bossuet, Fénelon and Massillon. He was consequently imprisoned for five years by Richelieu, who suppressed every form of independence. The hermits were also driven away from the neighborhood of the Convent in Paris, then from their refuge at Port-Royal in the Fields, to which, however, they soon returned.

The writings of Saint-Cyran, direct and vigorous, lead to a consideration of Balzac, the empty rhetorician, the man of letters, flat and vainglorious, absorbed in the dress and pomp of speech, who nevertheless gave rhythm to the French language, accomplishing the work of Malherbe in prose. Viewed from the heights of Port-Royal, his famous *Christian Socrates* is pure declamation. In contrast with a literary weighing of words is Saint-Cyran's judgment that such a process retards the movement of the Holy Spirit; in contrast with pride of authorship is the anonymity of Port-Royal; in contrast with the solitude of writers, the solitude even of Horace, Virgil, and Boileau—which to Saint-Cyran was silliness—is the solitude demanded by God.

The first recluse who sought this solitude of God at Port-Royal was the celebrated Parisian advocate, M. Le Maître, nephew of Mother Angélique, a great character, ardent, forceful, extreme. When in 1638 he gave up a brilliant career to live a life of penance in the vicinity of the convent, the public thought his renunciation an act of folly, which is, comments Sainte-Beuve, "the mark on the forehead of Christian heroism of every age." There follows the conversion of de Séricourt, who in a spirit of devotion occupied himself with copying the manuscript writings of others. To this story are added the lives of Lancelot and Singlin; Lancelot, author of naïve memoirs, who venerated Saint-Cyran, by whom he was assigned to teach Greek and mathematics in the "little schools," modest humanist, who remained a sub-deacon, considering himself unworthy of the priesthood, and who ended his life in exile as a Benedictine in 1695; Singlin, type of the real priest, uniting deep humility with authority, possessing no genius, but a sense of souls, a preacher without eloquence, but simple and effective from mere force of meaning, the oracle of Port-Royal and, though without wit or learning, the guide and leader of some of the best brains of his time. By these examples we come to know what it meant to be a penitent (La Maître), a teacher (Lancelot), and a priest (Singlin).

After the priest comes the doctor. We have first an extensive analysis of the *Augustinus* of Jansenius, a work published at Louvain in 1640, "the last monument of theology in Latin, a book which aroused in France a lengthy and interminable combat at the very dawn of the age of frivolity and incredulity." This analysis is, it must be confessed, not cheerful reading. It is hard for us to take much interest in the relative action of desire and will in Adam before and after the Fall, or in the intricacies of Grace, Predestination and Free Will. But, says Sainte-Beuve, if we take pleasure in the suburbs of our subject, let us acquire the right to do so by not shirking any serious point when we are at the center of it. The author brightens his somber task with a contrast between the Adam of Jansenius and the Adam of Milton and with a comparison between the fundamental theological doctrine of self-love as the essence of sin and the detached maxims of La Rochefoucauld. After the analysis, there is a glance at the quarrel in the Sorbonne, the Papal Bull and various opinions on the subject of Grace, Bossuet

180

being largely quoted because his expressions sum up the matter so completely that they cannot be supplanted.

Before returning to Port-Royal, Sainte-Beuve discusses the *Frequent Communion* (1643) of Arnauld, a book addressed to the general public and which wrought a revolution both in the practice of piety and in theological writing. The most effective religious volume since the *Introduction* of François de Sales, it is an answer to a Jesuit's letter that had "put cushions under the elbows of the penitent," Arnauld, on his part, demanding real repentance before absolution, inward purity before the Sacraments. The form is dogmatic, a series of propositions followed by demonstrations, as in geometry, and the rigorous style initiated a reform in theological writing parallel to that of Malherbe in poetry. The book, read by the fashionable world, by women and soldiers, gained additional popularity through the violent opposition of certain Jesuit preachers. Yet Arnauld's work has no real life. An original man, his personality does not enter his writings. "Truth must become *man* to touch man." Pascal and Bossuet were *themselves;* Arnauld was a great advocate in the Sorbonne, a lion, not primarily a writer, and in his forty-two quarto volumes there is not an expression that fixes the attention. Yet he was at once recognized as a general; we approach the *Provinciales.* Numerous quotations exhibit the spirit of the opposition and also the excellence of Arnauld's style, a style that surprised many at the time, but which d'Andilly, an elder brother, characterized as the way the Arnauld family talked at home. Arnauld, ordered to Rome to defend his doctrine, went into hiding instead, and for thirty-one years out of fifty he lived as a fugitive. Defended at Rome by another, the book was approved, not in the speculative matter of Grace, but in the practical matter of Penitence, and even Bourdaloue and other Jesuits were influenced and became more or less disciples of Arnauld.

We now return to Saint-Cyran, humble but stiff-necked, and follow his prayers to God, his consultation of holy men for guidance, his practice of exorcising the devil before opening a heretical book, and his attacks upon Protestantism, attacks which he perceived to be necessary to Port-Royal because of the accusations of Calvanistic doctrine. After his death (1643), M. de Bascle was cured of lameness by kissing his feet and miracles were operated at his tomb in Saint-Jacques-du-Haut-Pas, where his body lay, the heart, entrails and hands being interred in other places. After discussing Marie Gonzague, who became Queen of Poland, and Mme. de Sablé, an intelligent, but troublesome and nervous lady of society, who retired to a dwelling overlooking the court of the convent, and after then quoting from the correspondence between the Polish Queen and Mother Angélique to show that the real queen was the Holy Mother, Sainte-Beuve sums up the importance of Saint-Cyran in the history of Port-Royal. He is the founder, the restorer, the model for all those great characters. Others were more celebrated, but none was of such weight; and this preëminence, which other historians had not recognized, remains a thread of connection running through the whole of Sainte-Beuve's treatment of his subject. As a pendant to the life of Saint-Cyran, we find here inserted a biography of his nephew, de Barcos.

A chapter is now given to the recruits resulting from Arnauld's book; M. Pallu, a physician of whom it was said that it was almost a pleasure to be ill to enjoy his care; the whole family du Fossé, an example of the upper middle class that furnished the solid basis and the force of Port-Royal; and above all, the humble Fontaine, attached to de Saci as secretary, the real secretary lost in his master, whose *Memoirs* give the most lifelike idea of the recluses—we hear Pascal and de Saci talk, we see d'Andilly rise smiling and approach us through his blooming arbors—for this lovely old man found the secret of writing an inimitable book, Port-Royal's "historian and painter, its Froissart, only more naïve and wholly Christian." In 1646 there were not more than a dozen hermits, but hostile rumor greatly enlarged the numbers of the "Arnauldists," as they were called.

Now we come to d'Andilly, who retired from public office and court life at the age of fifty-seven and lived to be eighty-five. In contrast to Le Maître the terrible, he is the man of smiles. Vain and demonstrative, but polite, good and sincere, he brought a sort of grace into these austerities. Mlle. de Scudéry painted his portrait in *Clélie;* affable and well-dressed, he received and sometimes paid visits; he cultivated fruit-trees and sent baskets of choice peaches to the queen; he wrote poems and translations and coöperated in the work of Balzac toward purifying style. His *Josephus,* though inaccurate, reads like an original work; his *Fathers of the Desert* is delightful, presenting a charming asceticism, not repellant even to La Fontaine. D'Andilly's career is followed, not as in the case of the others, to the end, but only to the year 1664.

Let us return. "Our history (if history it be) is possible only with these perpetual undulations." We are in the epoch from the death of Saint-Cyran to the publication of the *Provinciales* (1643-1656). The *Memoirs* of the old soldier Pontis are discussed; Hamon, the physician, is reserved for his fine hour, which comes later; Baudri de Saint-Gilles, who became the agent for publication, has his place along with several others, each recluse retaining his distinct traits and temperament. The erection of new buildings, the migration of part of the nuns from Paris to the Fields, the institution of the Holy Sacrament and the change of garb, the accession of fashionable ladies, the numbers in the two houses, a register of deaths, the charities exercised during the wars of the Fronde—such are a few of the details of the chronicle. The Duchess de Luines, a soul "avid for Eternity," died in 1651, and her husband in his grief retired to Port-Royal and fortified it, building towers, each of which, according to the wish of Mother Angélique, was to be dedicated and to be surmounted with a cross to frighten away the demons. At this duke's house there were eager discussions of Descartes, a deviation and an inconsequence, but fertile and glorious from a literary point of view. A sister of Pascal is already at Port-Royal. Sainte-Beuve hastens to de Saci who, during a long period, holds the keys and who alone can conduct us to Pascal. As is appropriate, he imposes on us patience before we reach the *Provinciales* to which we aspire: *Italiam! Italiam!*

This patience, before we reach the Italy of our aspirations, takes us over two chapters devoted to the life of de Saci, younger brother of Le Maître (1613-1684). He is not a founder, but the chief successor of Saint-Cyran; he is the complete Director of Port-Royal, the soul and rule of its life, who conserved its unity; without brilliance or talent, he has prudence, moral beauty and the fear of God. M. Singlin, in view of providing a successor, insisted on his becoming a priest. Two incidents bring out the spirit of Port-Royal: M. Le Maître, who naturally resisted having his conscience directed by his younger brother, yielded instantly at a word from M. Singlin; de Saci, while conducting the funeral services of his mother and brother, did not shed a tear, but wept abundantly when alone. After an outline of the epochs of Port-Royal, we have the details of de Saci's arrest, examination, and imprisonment in the Bastile in 1666. His translation of the Bible, completed during his confinement, is discussed at length. No literary historian can guess its influence upon silent souls, but, compared with the biblical passages inserted by Bossuet in his sermons, Sainte-Beuve finds "the difference between Moses entering the cloud of fire on Sinai and the scrupulous Levite studying in the shadow of the walls of the Temple." Incidentally we learn that de Saci knew no Hebrew and that Port-Royal, while learned, was not deeply learned.

After such men as Le Maître and de Saci, we are prepared, when we come to Pascal, to observe a just proportion and not to be too greatly astonished. However superior he may appear, we are prepared to measure the glorious side of his genius without according it more than it deserves, and because the foundations are already known, we are prepared to admire the prominence of the relief. In a word, we are wholly prepared.

The book on Pascal is the center and culmination of the work. After this, not only does the spirit of Port-Royal decline, but Sainte-Beuve himself shows signs of fatigue. Here, however, he is in his native element.

Book III. Pascal (*Twenty-one Chapters*)

De Saci introduces us to Pascal, not to the author or even the penitent, but to the man. According to his usual method, the priest began with what most interested his patient, in this case with the philosopher; hence the Dialogue concerning Epictetus and Montaigne. Could art have invented a better episode for the introduction of Pascal to Port-Royal? Pascal, passing from philosophy to religion under the humble, keen, irrefragable de Saci, a true Christian Socrates, recalls the *Phaedrus*.

Two chapters are now devoted to Montaigne, his life, his works, his style; for, while there is much of Montaigne in Pascal, even to the use of borrowed phrases, Pascal's great object, in addition to fighting the Jesuits in the *Provinciales*, was to destroy Montaigne in the *Pensées*. Montaigne, with his maxims and anecdotes, perpetual truant, curious and amused at everything, indiscreet and eager to utter all he thought—is it after all of such consequence? It is only himself that he sets before us. No, it is ourselves, it is all men. He is not a skeptic, he is not a system, he is nature, nature complete, and without *Grace*. This is what Port-Royal hated by instinct. Three-quarters of Montaigne is harmless; the other quarter, where he places religion so high that it has no relation to man, is alarming. Pascal collects the scattered thoughts and shows their meaning, for there is, in each author who thinks, a combination, a spirit, a moral atmosphere, in which certain beliefs are divined or at least can live. The idea of conversion, a stroke of Grace, the essence of true Christianity, is inconceivable in Montaigne, and immortality is also lacking, as well as the perfecting of the soul. The *Apology for Sebond* is an ironical laugh at human infirmities, the nothingness of man and the futility of reason. All this Pascal remembers, but he crowns it with the Cross.

Sainte-Beuve now goes back and gives an account of the Pascal family. The early years of Jacqueline, her acting in a play before Richelieu and securing a pardon for her father, her winning of a prize in poetry publicly awarded by Corneille, her entering the convent against her brother's will and the consequent disputes over the division of the family property, all this is given in detail. At the same time, we get a full account of Pascal's studies and inventions, his relations with Descartes, his worldly life and his scientific writings, including his first dispute with the Jesuits on the subject of the vacuum. His conversion is recounted in quotations from his sister's letters—"our rôle is humble in this Christian matter and is limited to quoting"—and his aversion to the world, the reproaches of his conscience, his detachment, his austerities, his joy in the wilderness are shown to be the result, not of an upset brain, but of a soul that has been touched. His example was followed by his two chief friends, the Duke de Roannès and M. Domat, author of *Civil Laws,* a book that wrought a reform in jurisprudence. Each name evokes an account of the man.

Coming to the *Provinciales,* Sainte-Beuve gives a preliminary view of the disputes over Jansenism both at Rome and Paris, leading up to the condemnation of Arnauld by the Sorbonne. The cause, lost before the theologians, was carried to the general public, for the interest was extreme. Mazarin remarked that even the women talked of nothing else, though they understood the matter no more than he did himself. It was to this public that the *Provinciales* were addressed.

There follows a detailed and perfectly natural account of how Pascal came to write the first letter designed to show that the condemnation of Arnauld was mostly a question, not of real faith, but of words. Only five letters, however, deal with this affair, the other thirteen being on the moral ideas of the Jesuits, not defense, but attack.

The five—1, 2, 3, 17, 18—are studied first. "Let us read again

185

what we know so well. These fine familiar things seem very
different when taken in their framework." The tone of Pascal
is that of a man of the world; here is the first use of mockery in
such a subject; many things, now usual enough, are here found
for the first time. It is Pascal's début as a writer, for, though
his scientific writings had been good, solid and honest, he now
first thinks of style. A long analysis and discussion makes
Sainte-Beuve's points clear. The success of the letters, which
were anonymous, was immediate and immense—over 10,000 copies
being needed—and we are told of the arrest of the printer and
of the tricks resorted to in order to procure publication and
circulation, Pascal himself living at an inn under an assumed
name. The salons became a means of propaganda and Port-
Royal was brought into relations with the world. There follows
a long discussion of the attitude of the Port-Royal writers in
regard to one another and toward the Church.

Sainte-Beuve returns to the *Provinciales*. Letters 4–16, turned
against the Jesuits, save the series from being a mere ephemeral
pamphlet. These sprang from Pascal's indignation at reading
Escobar. He often spent three weeks over one letter, rewriting
it seven or eight times. At this point we have a remarkable
analysis of Pascal's intellectual and moral character and of the
way he came, from his sense of God, to hate Escobar. Though
the Jesuits had been attacked before, the battle had remained in
the schools, so that Pascal was the first who pilloried the guilty
before the world. The world, loving a fight, approved. Pascal
shows both dramatic power and eloquence. Up to the tenth letter,
we find the art of ironic dialogue, as Plato might have written
it; letters 11–16 are Philippics worthy of Demosthenes.

Pascal is a true Christian Socrates against the Sophists, the
Casuists. Jesuit critics have found exaggeration and inexact
quotations. The fault is admitted, for Pascal, like all men of
brains who quote, twists passages his own way, and passes over
subtle distinctions that do not exist for him. He also ascribes
doctrines to the Jesuits which are not exclusively theirs. All these
complaints are presented fairly, and the heroism of Jesuit mis-
sionaries is recognized. "I know all these things, yet I think
that Pascal has on the whole struck right." There are Jesuits
of learning and taste, lovable individuals, but it is the body and
its spirit that are detestable, the air breathed in the Society, the
Machiavellism in the shadow of the Cross. The contrast of
Jesuit and Port-Royal ambitions is embodied in Ignatius' order to

Xavier to conquer India and in Saint-Cyran's persistent siege of a single soul.

The eleventh letter, in defense of mockery in serious subjects, showing the extent of Arnauld's contributions, is copiously quoted to demonstrate its incomparable mastery. It might serve as a preface justifying *Tartufe*. Of the sixteenth letter Sainte-Beuve notes that Pascal made it longer than the others because he had not the leisure to abbreviate it, and here in connection with this open war we have an intermezzo dealing with Arnauld. His periods of concealment are enumerated and he is estimated to be, not the greatest genius of the age, as "our friends" thought, but a man of solid and attractive qualities, a heart of gold, in spite of his combative character. D'Andilly, on the other hand, was courteous and diplomatic, even in warfare. When every recluse was forced to leave Port-Royal in the Fields in 1638, he was back in a month, because the queen did not wish to separate him from his garden, saying that "it was to her advantage that he should not quit his trees, whose fruit he sent her." Angélique, who called Arnauld "poor little brother" and "father" in the same letter, believed that all ills coöperated for good. The buried life of the nuns is illustrated by the fact that they knew nothing of the order for the dispersal until the furniture of the expelled hermits was brought into the convent. At this dispersion, the schools were also broken up, and Racine, then sixteen, was sent away; but the history of the schools will be given later. Every detail of the visit of the lieutenant of police, who came to see that the order was enforced, is given, even to the tricks played on him. And all this to prepare for the cure of Pascal's niece by the miracle of the "Holy Thorne," which we come upon in the finest and strongest part of the *Provinciales*.

This miracle is told in the words of Mother Angélique. Sainte-Beuve gives a physiological explanation, but to Pascal it became a warrant for all miracles, even those of Christ. Marguerite, the object of this wonder cure, lived till 1733, and is the connecting link with new miracles, leading to the scandal of the Convulsions. Her dying confession brings in Massillon, of whom anecdotes are told illustrating his decline from holiness to worldliness. In the midst of this story of the "Holy Thorne," we have an account of Cardinal de Retz and his relations with Port-Royal.

The consequences of the *Provinciales* are then discussed. Tributes are quoted, particularly Boileau's judgment that this

was the one modern work equal to the ancients. The consequences are divided into (1) theological and (2) moral. To the
theological, two chapters are given. Nicole's Latin translation
went throughout Europe; there were admirers and opponents;
a copy was burnt by the executioner. It was both a victory and
a defeat: the doctrine of Grace lost, the idea of Penitence won.
All the later attacks on the Jesuits may be omitted; they are like
baggage wagons crossing the battlefield after victory, useful but
disgusting and tedious. The order of Jesuits is dead: the members "go, come, return, intrigue, injure, or even do good; they
do not live."

The Jesuit answers are flat, for a good writer could not be
found. The first worthy opponent was Father Daniel (1674),
but he merely caused renewed interest in the *Provinciales*.
Finally, in Joseph de Maistre, Pascal found a worthy foe. In
the discussion that follows, we get a good view of this distinguished writer, his arrogant, aristocratic spirit combined with
real elevation, his slap-dash methods mingled with profound
thinking. Sainte-Beuve would not press the advantage offered
by the temerity of a great mind, yet he notes that, in an account
of the death of Arnauld, Voltaire is more charitable, nay, more
Christian, than de Maistre.

The moral results of the *Provinciales,* including the abolition
of scholasticism in ethics and the destruction of casuism, a thing,
after all, very much a matter of bad taste, were not entirely
caused by the letters; the general march of progress would itself
have led to such results, but Pascal aided directly. What was
attained was not virtue, but a composite of good habits and
manners, procedures based on generosity and honorable examples,
a compromise, but useful, the *honnête homme* in opposition to
hypocritical devotion. Molière and La Bruyère are the heirs of
Pascal, though neither had any direct connection with Port-Royal.
There follows a long discussion of the personality and genius of
Molière, including a comparison with Montaigne and with Shakespeare. His sadness of heart and his feeling of the nothingness
of things, without the joy of penitence, leads to an imagined
dialogue between the comic dramatist and Pascal, in which Sainte-
Beuve becomes truly eloquent. The whole history of *Tartufe* is
given, and much criticism, though the author will not write a
feuilleton, but only deals with the points that touch his subject.
Pascal's mockery went further than he intended, passing from
the *Provinciales* through *Tartufe* to the *Marriage of Figaro*.

After much further discussion, partly repeating ideas already published in the *Portraits littéraires,* and including a consideration of incredulity in the seventeenth century, Sainte-Beuve declares the *Provinciales* finished and returns to the life of Pascal.

The conception of the *Pensées* is traced to the miracle of the "Holy Thorne." Much space is given to Pascal's sufferings, both from ill health and from self-imposed rigors, and it is noted that his use of geometry as a relief from toothache measures the power of his brain. To him sickness was a normal Christian state to be welcomed. He said to Pain, not only "Thou art not an evil" as the Stoics did, but "Thou art a benefit." A comparison of philosophic and Christian charity leads to an account of Pascal's insistence, as he lay dying, that, since he could not be taken to a hospital for the poor, he should at least have an indigent sick man brought into his own room. What is the use of these mortifications? They lead to a force of compassion, instead of mere passing pity, to a higher development of virtue and humanity, which would otherwise be inexplicable and without motive.

Pascal's skepticism and mysticism are in essence holiness, an habitual aspiration toward the infinite order, which is independent of belief, being found also in Confucius and Buddha. This aspiration is traced in Greece and Rome to its deeper, more contrite embodiment in Christianity, where suffering is an essential feature. Pascal is the last of the great saints. Can this tenderness ever be united with the good sense of Voltaire?

The persecution of 1661 takes us back to Port-Royal. Jacqueline signed the Order and died from regret; Pascal, in his unlimited love of truth, finding all his friends opposed to him in an argument on this subject, fainted: Fontenelle, Goethe, Tallyrand have no such fainting spells. The last brightness of Saint-Cyran shines in Pascal; in Arnauld this is mixed with other things, in Nicole all is softened. But is not Pascal a visionary, subject to hallucinations? A long discussion of the "abyss" which he perceived by his side disposes of this objection. Pascal died in 1662; his only love was for the Savior. Not only for believers, but for all who have a heart, here is something true that penetrates to the center.

A chapter is given to the first editing of the *Pensées* and the changes made, not for a literary, but for a religious end. Pascal was too strong for Arnauld and Nicole, but no other group could have done better; the only committee open-minded enough would have been Molière, La Rochefoucauld and La Fontaine, and La Fontaine would soon have gone to sleep. This first edition appeared in 1670; a list of contemporary literary works shows the greatness of the epoch.

The later editions down to 1835 are considered; all the editors forgot the original manuscripts. Since, in Pascal, reasoning is never separated from sentiment, the eighteenth century did not appreciate him; his moral superiority was felt by neither Voltaire nor Condorcet. The recent philological and literary work on Pascal has ruined the book in a certain sense; though Pascal gains, the purpose is lost. The ensuing chapter, written before these discoveries, is allowed to stand, for Sainte-Beuve's object is to present Pascal as known to his contemporaries, though restoring here and there certain words of the original text when they mark the thought. Pascal is imagined expounding his ideas in 1658, his reasons founded, not on metaphysics, but on moral and historical argument. Faith is "God felt in the heart." Man is an incomprehensible monster, the ego is corrupt (agreement with La Rochefoucauld and Hobbes); we must hate the root of our nature, as contrary to justice and truth—such is the first part of the book. Man, finding no answer within, seeks one in philosophy and finds this vain; then turns to religion, and finds only one, Christianity, in which the Fall of Man explains everything. This religion prophecies and miracles prove to be true. The argument leads to the love of Jesus. "Did Saint John, the apostle of love, ever show more tenderness than this Archimedes in tears at the foot of the Cross?" We can supply the unwritten parts of the book expounding the doctrines of Grace and Election, and Sainte-Beuve is glad that the work was not completed. The chapters on Pascal conclude with remarks on his style, the accord of words and truth, not the naïve style of Jesus, but that of a born writer, the first artistic writer of Port-Royal. In the *Pensées* we seize the expressions at their source. "Every great man who thinks is a great writer if his thought is seized at its birth. Richelieu must have been such in private; Napoleon certainly was, in his campaign dispatches. Pascal, admirable in his finished work, is superior here, where the labor was interrupted."

Book IV. The Schools of Port-Royal (Seven Chapters)

The schools, which were entirely suppressed in 1660, less than twenty years after their humble beginnings, are discussed rather systematically under methods of teaching, character of works produced, principal teachers and distinguished pupils, the crown and fruit of the institution.

The first idea came from the austere Saint-Cyran, who was devoted to children; the number of pupils grew from six at the outset to possibly fifty at the time of greatest activity. In Paris there were four teachers, each with six pupils, Nicole teaching philosophy and the humanities, Lancelot Greek and mathematics. The various changes of location and the dispersions are followed. The order of studies differed little from that of other schools; it was the spirit that counted. The child, offspring of fallen man, was not saved by baptism, but must be prepared for Grace in the age of reason. Teaching was a religious task, to be conducted with vigilance, patience and prayer. The pupils, children of the rich, were an élite and, though only nine or ten years old at entrance, were little gentlemen (*messieurs*) never addressed with *tu*. The school books, logic, language methods, translations printed with Latin text—expurgated, of course—were almost all published after the closing of the schools and were based on class experience. They contributed to the union of the solid and the polite which marked the reign of Louis XIV and were in harmony with the Academy. French was taught first, instead of Latin as was then the rule; there were reforms in spelling and an attempt was made to render learning agreeable. "These humble teachers, who subjected Will to Grace, and Reason to Faith, accorded to Reason its complete control over human branches." Previously "the unhappy children had always employed the unintelligible to direct them to the unknown." Here they read first translations from the Latin, then the teacher orally translated from the Latin text; only the necessary grammar was given.

The *General Grammar* and the *Logic* have the novelty of introducing good sense into these subjects, but rather by accident than design. Lancelot questioned Arnauld on the Art of Speech and got him to dictate his opinions, giving not only usage, but the reason for usage. The result is Descartes extended to grammar, language being considered a deliberate invention, which is, after all, a good enough practical supposition. Among Arnauld's disciples are de Tracy and his best successor, Silvestre de Sacy. The *Logic*, the most celebrated of the Port-Royal books, grew out of Arnauld's declaration that he could teach the subject in four or five days. The book is discussed and quoted, and Sainte-Beuve wishes that there were a new logic made on the same principles, but with modern examples.

From the books we pass to the teachers. Nicole will be studied when we come to 1669; but Lancelot's methods and his relations with Chapelain are given, as well as notices of a few of the less-known masters. Then follows a considerable list of distinguished pupils, including even the Duke of Monmouth. Stuart d'Aubigny furnishes an occasion for a pleasing digression on his friend Saint-Évremond. As for Racine, he was not so great a figure in Port-Royal itself, being hardly mentioned before the eighteenth century. The typical pupil is M. de Tillemont, whose biography is presented at length. Naturally a philosopher, and wholly devoted to ecclesiastical history, he studied prayerfully for himself and his friends with no idea of the public, fearing pride and desiring to escape the applause of the world. He was so humble that de Saci had to compel him to take upon himself the priesthood. Sainte-Beuve delights to dwell upon his goodness and affability, especially toward children and the poor, a sort of angelic beauty that kept him a "Christian child" for the whole sixty years of his life. The biographer delights to dwell upon a a childlike ingenuousness, not inconsistent with the spirit of criticism, upon de Tillemont's fear that his absorption in his work may be a sin, upon his submission to his father—even as an old man, he never did anything without asking this parent's permission—upon his beautiful thoughts on charity. (When a child of wealthy parents died, he urged that, since it now enjoyed so rich a heritage, they should give to the poor what they would have spent on its upbringing, a mark of parental affection the dead one had a right to expect.) De Tillemont softens and moderates what is too severe and antipathetic in Port-Royal, yet as an historian he would not yield the smallest point to the censor. His vast work is one of the authorities most used by Gibbon, who recognizes in him an exactitude almost amounting to genius. After citing both hostile and favorable comments, Sainte-Beuve remarks that this testimony of Gibbon dispenses with the need of all other.

A letter of de Tillemont to the Abbé of La Trappe furnishes an excuse for a biography of Rancé, the last of the great monks. Here we have also a long account of M. Le Roi and his abbey, of a debate with a Benedictine on monastic studies, and of the conflict, without bitterness, between the humble, yet firm de Tillemont and the rude and bitter Rancé, whose extremes serve to mark the temperance of Port-Royal. Besides Rancé, we come also to know Le Camus, an original figure in the Church of the seventeenth century, not of Port-Royal, but one of its best correspondents. Returning to de Tillemont, we see him till his death (1698) walking in the paths of sweetness and constant piety and reaching sublime heights unaware. He was the perfect pupil of Port-Royal.

The whole movement in studies is not appropriated to Port-Royal, but its schools were first in the march. Rollin introduced these methods in part into the University. Among contemporaries, Royer-Collard is a pupil, not of the schools and books, but of the spirit of Port-Royal. "From those men it came," said the old statesman, "that in my public life I never thought of myself." And Sainte-Beuve adds: "This man, who was a real monument, is no more; and we have fallen upon a time when no one has any longer the right to speak such words." [1]

Having finished a consideration of Pascal and of the schools, which formed the principal center and core of his subject, the author will now take up the narrative again and follow an easier current.

Book V. *The Second Generation of Port-Royal* (*Eleven Chapters*)

In 1660, because of a letter of de Retz which Arnauld was accused of writing, the king ordered the suppression of the Jansenists, their independent tendency being what he really wished to destroy. All the details of the hostile visits to Port-Royal, including tears, speeches, interrogations, are given, together with the biographies of a few of the novices who were sent away. The obstinacy of the nuns in refusing to sign the Formularies is traced to their fidelity to Jansenius as the friend of Saint-Cyran and their loyalty to the ideas of their associates, Arnauld, Nicole, Singlin, de Saci and others. As a study of the human heart, it is interesting to observe how these Directors and an Abbess could impress this force of cohesion on a body of women, so that out of more than a hundred, not over a dozen weakened. Miracles never failed Port-Royal in the hour of need. Catherine, daughter of the painter Philippe de Champaigne, was cured of lameness, subject of a celebrated painting, which is

---

[1] Royer-Collard died in 1845. These words therefore were not in the lecture, but were added in the volume, which appeared in 1848.

discussed. The death of Mother Angélique leads to a consideration of her justice and moderation, her anxiety lest the nuns should take pride in suffering, her feeling that affliction was more necessary than bread, her fear of the judgment of God as the end drew near. Her recommendation of humility and silence is contrasted with the later mania for telling everything, to which Arnauld so largely contributed. No one in the history of Port-Royal seems more truly great and royal; she is on the level of Saint-Cyran.

All attempts at conciliation were blocked by Arnauld, who would not even consent to silence. Mounted on his conscience, he renews open and declared war. The rather grotesque Péréfixe, Archbishop of Paris, is portrayed at full length, and his discomfiture in his conferences with the nuns, particularly with the rather pert Sister Briquet, is presented in lively fashion. (This sister was the delight of Royer-Collard.) After narrating in great detail the prohibition of the sacraments, the removal of selected nuns to other convents, all the conflicts between authority and Christian liberty (eternal antagonism; let each make his choice!), Sainte-Beuve turns to study the exiles, and particularly Mother Angélique de Saint-Jean, daughter of d'Andilly, whose early biography is followed by the complete story of her captivity, with all its heart-storms in methodical order. "If we, being profane and formerly a poet, who sought the poetical in everything and even (need it be said) in religion, if we sometimes meet such poetry in Port-Royal, it is here—Angélique's solitary prayers at midnight, Paris lying silent under the stars—and not elsewhere that it is found, a poetry without sunshine or bloom, nothing but what is inward and wholly in perfume." Then follow her return to Port-Royal, her verbal duels, disguised under courtly forms, with Archbishop Harlai, and a summary of her qualities. Though she dominated her talents in the continued presence of eternity, she had lofty thoughts and great accents, and no one but Pascal, in the second generation of Port-Royal, has as much genius as she.

The careers of some other sisters are also followed; and then, as this is the time of his greatest service, a complete portrait is presented of M. Hamon, the physician and mystical writer, with numerous quotations, much criticism and many digressions. Sainte-Marthe, the humble confessor, is also added. A life of Pavillon, Bishop of Aleth, is next given, since he was one of four who helped to save Port-Royal from annihilation; we get a glimpse of Mme. de Longueville, who sheltered Arnauld and Nicole, and there is an account of the reception by fashionable society of the New Testament of Mons, translated by Arnauld, de Saci and Le Maître. The Peace of the Church, which Sainte-Beuve feels sure that Jansenius, Saint-Cyran and Pascal would not have signed, shows a mitigated Jansenism, with no understanding of the primitive thought of Port-Royal. The lifting of the interdiction and the separation of the House in the Fields from the House of Paris introduce ten years of autumn, of sunset. This is the time of Mme. de Longueville and Mme. de Vertus, of the visits of Mme. de Sévigné, of the friendship of Boileau, of the publication of Pascal's *Pensées,* and of the attacks of Arnauld and Nicole on Calvinism.

This last fact introduces two long chapters on Nicole, who is differentiated from others, especially from Arnauld, who appropriated him as a second and with whom he is ordinarily inseparable. Pupil of Dr. Sainte-Beuve of the Sorbonne, school-teacher and indefatigable reader of all sorts of books, Nicole contributed materials to the *Provinciales,* translated these into Latin, and wrote Latin works defending Port-Royal on the ground that it agreed with the Pope. He enervated Jansenism and became a leader in the new direction, the inventor of the distinction between *fact* and *right.* His timidity and other failings are noted in order that we may get a personality more alive, though not of less stature, than the man of books alone. His controversies in the spirit of Pascal and those in the spirit of Arnauld exhibit his logic and good sense, but the *Moral Essays* and the *Letters,* written with a sort of smiling gravity, are more attractive. Sainte-Beuve, however, cannot echo the praise of Voltaire, "whose lightest word is authoritative in matters of taste," or that of Lamennais. It is not to be believed that either had just reread the pieces; both must have spoken from an old impression. Full of repetitions, commonplaces and useless developments, "Nicole may be pleasant to study, but he is decidedly wearisome to read." We cannot admire the essays as Mme. de Sévigné did, but we can seek to understand her admiration. We now follow Nicole's disguises, his hiding places, his painful yet friendly separation from Arnauld (the great, brave Arnauld; the good, gentle Nicole), his submission to the Archbishop, and his last pious, rather than penitent, days in Paris, where he died in 1695. A secondary nature, timorous yet firm, ingenuous yet sagacious, he is the most considerable in rank after Pascal and Arnauld.

Nicole has led us far from the subject; we must return to the years following the Peace of 1669.

It is like the days in September, summer still, but with winter in the air. When M. de Pomponne is made Secretary of State, his father d'Andilly goes to thank Louis XIV, his reception being recounted in his own words and in those of Mme. de Sévigné, who now has with Port-Royal frequent relations, though simply those of a friend like Boileau. She laughs at the extremes and prejudice of both parties and takes from Port-Royal, about as we do, the literature, the solid pleasure, the moral ideas, the useful and the charming part, with a little more of religion than it is given us to accept. How far we have traveled from Saint-Cyran! Cardinal de Retz also visited the convent. The patriarch, M. d'Andilly, died at the right moment (1678, aged 85). His funeral sermon, preached by his brother, Arnauld, has no color, but this is the character of Port-Royal.

As at this moment we meet all sorts of people, why not La Fontaine, who took his *Captivité de Saint-Malc* from d'Andilly's *Pères du Desert* and who edited a collection of Christian poems? He even proposed to dedicate one of his risky tales to Arnauld, but was dissuaded with much difficulty by Boileau and Racine. At any rate, we have run across La Fontaine, which was more than we could have hoped for in our narrow path.

We now encounter the biographies of four great ladies, protectors of Port-Royal, which are arranged in the order of their deaths; the Princess de Conti (1672), the Duchess de Liancourt (1674), Mme. de Sablé (1678) and Mme. de Longueville (1679).

When we come to Mme. de Sablé, we learn of her caprices, her ridiculous fear of disease, her desire to be important; the "cleverest of the incurables of Port-Royal," she kept one eye on the cloister and the other on the world. La Rochefoucauld consulted her, and "her salon was the great laboratory of the *Maxims.*" As she was important, she had often to be placated by the Mother Superior, a great soul engaged in pitiable affairs, who by a subterfuge of charity said, "She needs us."

We now make what Sainte-Beuve calls "a round of visits," in which we first meet the scholarly gentleman, painted by Bourdaloue, La Bruyère and Saint-Simon, M. de Tréville, too disdainful to print a book, but with a great contemporary reputation —"to be as clever as de Tréville" being a consecrated expression. No rigorist, but practicing the philosophy of Horace, he is a strange neighbor to Port-Royal. In contrast, are the true Penitents, M. de Sévigné, uncle of the letter-writer, an old warrior converted; Mlle. de Vertus, who, after serving Mme. de Longueville, became a sort of novice in the convent, patient in illness, bedridden for eleven years; Du Guet, the consoler, who helped Mme. de Lafayette to die, one who shows that the truest Christian solution lies in the intimate assemblage of all contradictions fused in a sort of living miracle by the flame of charity.

Finally we come to Mme. de Longueville, who has already often been mentioned. Indeed, the Peace of the Church was largely her work and it ended with her life. Her dominant passion was ambition to shine; it was this which involved her in the Fronde, it was this also which first led her to Port-Royal, where penance had most distinction and where, her beauty fading, she secured an inverse satisfaction, changing plus to minus. Not that she made this calculation; instinct made it for her. She refined in asceticism, as in gallantry, resolved, if she could not be first, to be absolutely the last. Sainte-Beuve would not analyze "the sacred folly," but refers to Saint Paul and the *Imitation*. This ardent love of the eternal Mme. de Longueville possessed. She was the organ of Port-Royal at court and there its adherents were known as her *friends*.

At this epoch, Port-Royal was regarded by many as a holy place and it was visited by pilgrims, often of high rank, an influx that interfered, it was suspected, with devotion to God.

Book VI. The Passing of Port-Royal (Thirteen Chapters)

Louis XIV, still determined to destroy Jansenism, orders Harlai, the political archbishop, to subjugate Port-Royal. This polite and almost amiable persecution is presented with all the details of visits and conversations to which we have become accustomed. To protests the king replied that Port-Royal was a center for gatherings and cabals. The recluses, the confessors, the novices and school-girls are all expelled. Arnauld leaves France for good (1679) and his nephew, M. de Pomponne, is disgraced (apparently for incompetence); reinstated in 1691, he is merely an honorary minister and merely an honorary Arnauld.

We now follow the life of the confessor, Le Tourneaux, his vogue as a preacher, his humility, his *Année Chrétienne,* prohibited because in it the mass is translated into French. In his case, we get a just idea of the frivolity and perfidy of the adversaries and of the moral elevation of the accused, of their habitual gravity and of the tone of their souls. How Voltaire must have laughed to see these quarrels!

The history of the gradual destruction of the convent from 1679 to 1711 is resumed and the decline in numbers noted. It is the history of a blockaded fortress. When an act of odious violence ended the resistance, there were only fifteen nuns, all over fifty years of age. Here come digressions on the Burgundian scholar, Bocquillot, and on the poet and wit, Santeul. Several deaths are recorded and also the burial within the convent of the hearts or bodies of outside friends, making Port-Royal a valley of tombs, a sacred necropolis. Among the deceased is M. Pontchâteau (1690), already known to us from many previous references, whose life-story is now told, including his frequent travels, his services in getting Elzevir to print the New Testament, and his labors as gardener at the farms. Ashamed of his noble ancestry, he is a little too rude even for Port-Royal. At his tomb miracles were performed and the populace forced the doors of the church to procure relics from his body.

The abbess, Mme. Racine, closes the convent against visits of noble ladies; we follow a procession in all its stations through the grounds; we assist at the prayers and ceremonies, and at the invocation of the patron, Saint Bernard, when it is feared the king will include the abbey in his hunting park; we learn of several deaths, including that of Archbishop Harlai, whose successor, M. de Noailles, is characterized; we learn how outside friends made trouble by publishing books.

Having conducted the community to this point in its decline, Sainte-Beuve arrives at the period when Racine frequently appears, inviting consideration from the standpoint of Port-Royal; but first the author must go back to accompany Arnauld in his exile and to narrate his last combats.

Though Arnauld wrote to the archbishop that he sought only retirement, he could not help making a disturbance, as well at a distance as near by. His letters reveal elevation, serenity, generous unction. When the matter touches your own interests, yield to authority, he says; when defense of truth is involved, fight to the death. His constant régime was one of prayer and study, as in a monastery. Though he is violent in controversy, abounding in such words as *calumny, lies, imposture,* quotations are offered to show his elevation. Every syllable is sincere and his character confirms and completes his eloquence.

Though Sainte-Beuve has to cut off more than one tempting

digression, he allows himself a considerable one on the life of
Arnauld's friend, Neercassel, Archbishop of Utrecht, including
an account of his own trip (1848) to Utrecht and Amersfoort
to work on the archives and to get the still living tradition of
Port-Royal from M. C. Karsten and his associates.

In controversy Arnauld committed every possible imprudence,
offending all. Violent and immoderate against the Protestants,
using his fists on those who extended the right hand, he approves
the revocation of the Edict of Nantes and the whole series of
repressive measures. Yet his words often reveal the man of
heart and conscience, the *grand Arnauld,* who steadfastly refused
to return to France so long as a single friend was in prison.
Among such friends was the Oratorian, Father de Breuil, imprisoned nearly fourteen years for receiving a package of
Arnauld's books, a saint, praying always for his enemies and
fearing lest he might become corrupted if the rigors of confinement were somewhat relaxed. Several, including Quesnel and
Du Guet, left the Oratory on account of its servility in this affair.

Touching the Oratory, we come upon Arnauld's great controversy with Malebranche. Of course, we find the biography of
Malebranche, followed by an account of his literary success and
an analysis of his chief doctrines. "I do not pretend to have
represented the whole of Malebranche in this sketched portrait,
but I am sure I have not disfigured him any more than he himself
disfigured Seneca and Montaigne in painting them." By quotation, summary and criticism, Sainte-Beuve follows the debate; he
discusses at length the notion of God working only by general
laws (Hegel in germ), the reduction of miracles to the lowest
terms, the insufficient ideas of Grace and of the function of
Jesus in salvation; yet, after all, what chiefly interests the historian is the weight and force of the blows delivered by the combatants; he sees the personal friendship of the antagonists and
even their politeness vanishing after the first attack (a lesson
for us); the prize is awarded to Arnauld, though he uses a club
on gossamer and requires a volume for what a satirist accom-
plishes in a single line; logic assails intuition and the heavy
fighter pulverizes a cloud, which incessantly rises again and forms
new shapes. Malebranche triumphs even in his defeat, and it is
only because of him that Arnauld's book is read. He gave proof
that great philosophical systems could be constructed in French,
without any departure from the best usage. The chapter concludes with several pages on the relations of Arnauld and Leibnitz,

including a good story and a contrast between the limited logician and the man of universal curiosity.

The literary friend of Port-Royal, Boileau, is now studied, among the topics being the public taste that he reformed in aggressive personal satires, his relations with Arnauld based on candor, truth and probity, the influence of Pascal on *Le Lutrin* and the influence of Port-Royal in general on the later satires, his friendship with both Jesuits and Jansenists, the pious devotion of his last years and the history of the twelfth satire. The aged Boileau saw nothing good in the new literature; had he lived, what would he have thought of one then a youth of seventeen, Voltaire?

We now find some anecdotes of Domat, a sincere Christian, author of *Civil Laws,* and his theory is judged from the standpoint of Pascal. Though he is not strictly of Port-Royal, two entire chapters are assigned to Du Guet, director of noble ladies, agreeable letter-writer, who gives advice on drinking tea as well as on matters of conscience and who pays compliments with a Christian turn, "spiritual madrigals," yet whose graceful playfulness did not weaken the severity of naked truth. In him consolation is drawn from the rigor itself, and the wretchedness of man only emphasizes the richness of the Cross. Lacking Atticism, he is less than Fénelon: he shuns originality and, in the true Christian spirit, would efface himself before the divine. Moreover, he lacks the good sense of Bossuet and, though not entering the final illusions of Jansenism, he did much to pave the way for them. Yet many who speak highly of Bossuet and Fénelon derive no benefit from them, while all who praise Du Guet profit from his works. This amiable and distinguished "cousin" of Port-Royal was unknown in the eighteenth century, except to his own party and to a few pious souls.

But let us come to the crown of Port-Royal, to the tender and brilliant genius, which, having mortified itself, awakened after fifteen years of silence, to produce two inspired masterpieces, *Esther* and *Athalie,* the last having no equal in beauty.

The Jansenist Necrology speaks of "M. Racine, poet, recluse of Port-Royal," and carefully forgets all but his sacred works. Not so Sainte-Beuve, whose two chapters on Racine offer a full biography and a compete criticism, recanting opinions of former years. The emphasis, nevertheless, is on the poet's relations with Port-Royal. Much space, for example, is given to his violent answer to Nicole, in which he makes a perfidious use of inside information, not sparing even Le Maître, who had been a second father to him. This, and the second letter, suppressed by Boileau, ought to be added to editions of the *Provinciales,* as a counter-type and a lesson. In a general consideration of Racine's tragedies, which serves as an introduction to the special study of *Esther* and *Athalie,* the perfection, unity and harmony of the whole are the qualities emphasized. Racine might have done anything he pleased in literature, epic, elegy, satire, but by vocation he was a great dramatist. In the repression of the Petrarch and Tasso within him, he was aided by Boileau, and also in the attainment of Greek beauty, pure, simple, perfect. From Port-Royal came Pascal, the perfection of French prose, and Racine, the perfection of French poetry.

Reconciled with Arnauld after *Phèdre,* the idea of fatality in the tragedy approaching Christian predestination, Racine became the solicitor of Port-Royal with the powerful. At Mme. de Maintenon's request for a drama without a love story, he produced *Esther,* a work of perfect and adorable fitness, and the prodigious success of this piece led to *Athalie,* a wonderful ensemble, in which everything contributes to the sovereign and infinite majesty. It is a drama that would survive even Christianity. This enthusiasm for Racine's masterpiece is followed by anecdotes of the poet's last years and an account of his death. The Jansenists living after 1700 were not of the first generation, nor indeed of the second; they were not even direct descendants.

The last two chapters recount in detail the proceedings leading to the destruction of Port-Royal. A score of nuns, obstinate, unreasonable, but inspiring respect, resisted every power in France; urged on by the king, the Archbishop of Paris resorted to all sorts of measures, legal and illegal. The story of the final catastrophe is presented in the words of a *Relation,* in order to give the impression made on the witnesses and victims, without introducing any modern and discordant note. We learn also of drunken boors digging up the bodies interred in the grounds, and, with a glance at the convulsions that followed, the work closes.

"All that has lived and shone here below is subject to corruption. What was flesh is subject to worms. What was greatness becomes matter of declamation, serves as a pretext for phrases, that other worm that inflates and devours. What, in the midst of persecution, was belief and faith, readily becomes in the long run hardness, narrowness, obstinacy, fanaticism, fetichism

There comes a time when the spirit that animated things and persons quits its corpse and ascends—let us follow this, and not lose sight of it for the cast clothes or the idol."

Except with a few, the spirit of Port-Royal did not survive in the Jansenism that followed.

The true, humble and great Christian spirit of Port-Royal Saint-Beuve has defined in principle, portrayed in living models and in original works, and followed to visible decadence. His history, beginning with the "Day of the Wicket," was enlarged with Saint-Cyran and reached its middle-point in Pascal; the end, varied with several singular figures, is sustained by the sole presence of Arnauld; it blooms ideally and is crowned in *Athalie.*

CHAPTER VII

1838—1840

On his return to Paris, Sainte-Beuve plunged into manifold labors and distractions. He renewed his connection with the *Revue des deux Mondes,* contributing at least an article a month and often two, besides notices in the literary *Chronique.* When he found time, he prepared his lectures on Port-Royal for publication. Meanwhile he edited the writings of Fontanes in two volumes, a work which appeared early in 1839, and shortly afterward he published two further volumes of his *Critiques et Portraits littéraires.* With the money thus obtained, he made a flying trip to Italy in May and June, dividing a month between Naples and Rome, and spending another month at Lausanne on his way home. Some poems resulting from the trip appeared in the *Revue de Paris* shortly after his return. A slashing article in the *Revue des deux Mondes* on "La Littérature industrielle" (Sept. 1) excited much talk and wrath. Two essays of 1840, that on La Rochefoucauld (Jan. 15) and one entitled "Dix ans après en Littérature," mark a decided change in Sainte-Beuve's mental attitude, a change that had been long maturing. In April, 1840, was published the first volume of *Port-Royal,* which had considerable success. A collected edition of the poems also appeared this year, constituting in a certain way Sainte-Beuve's farewell to the Muse. In August he was appointed one of the Keepers of the Mazarine Library, a post which gave him a fixed income and a fitting habitation, though he did not receive his living quarters for several months. A proposal of marriage made to a young lady was rejected, and Sainte-Beuve became a settled old bachelor. In 1840 he thus entered a phase of his career that lasted till the Revolution of 1848.

The manifold occupations of Sainte-Beuve on his return to Paris are set forth in his letters to the Oliviers. He is much fatigued and even rheumatic but, after freshening up at his rooms in the Cour de Commerce, which he has retained, he first pays his respects to his mother, who grows more and more maliciously witty as she grows older. Ampère calls and reports all the gossip of the Abbaye-au-Bois, a salon which Sainte-Beuve himself immediately revisits, soon to spend his Sunday afternoons there listening to installments of Chateaubriand's *Memoirs* read week by week as they were composed. Mme. Valmore is sought out in her apartment in the Palais-Royal, enjoying a moment of calm in her hunted existence; only a moment, however, for her husband soon lost his position and the family is off for a disastrous theatrical engagement in Italy. Sainte-Beuve also sees Mme. de Castries, Mme. de Tascher and others. One of his earliest visits is to Buloz and the *Revue*, where he is received more as a friend than as a mere utility. He presents himself to Mme. de Fontanes, one of his great affairs being an edition of her father's works in two volumes. Meanwhile, he resumes his seat at Ampère's lectures. Early in July he has already given the printer copy for the first sheets of *Port-Royal*, and in August he is reading proofs, but the printing proceeds at a snail's pace, for "at the aspect of the proofs," he says, "I fall into infinite scruples; I want to verify everything, annotate everything, consult every authority over again." He talks with Reuchlin, who is bringing out a German history of Port-Royal, as well as a book on Pascal, and profits from his theological learning, giving in exchange literary taste and knowledge. In addition to the *Revue*, *Port-Royal* and Fontanes, two new volumes of *Portraits* are being gathered from his magazine articles. In the midst of this rush of occupations, Marmier returns and "debauches" him, leading him to pass his life "dining in restaurants," a piece of news that excites apprehension in the somewhat strait-laced heart of Mme. Olivier, an apprehension which he seeks to allay by saying good things about his friend. Having lost his voice from "vociferating" his Lausanne lectures, he has to be careful even of drawing-room talk. Yet there are social duties, dining out, evening parties, "a life of fatigue and dispersion without domestic joys." On the other hand, if an important article has to be prepared, he concentrates on his work for a week or a fortnight, allowing no distraction; and finally he writes in view of *Port-Royal*: "I am going to pen myself up, letting it be thought that I am in the country, dining in my room, and emerging only at night with my nose buried in my cloak."

Sainte-Beuve's letters overflow with literary gossip, for he loves the personal tattle of the present quite as much as that of the past. He is equally eager for news from Lausanne. The little Swiss city had become a second country to him, sharing with Boulogne and Lyons his strong local attachment. He thanks for a watch presented by his auditors, noting a special mark between the figures three and four, the hour of his lecture. To a multitude of friends he incessantly sends remembrances. The French bullying of Switzerland on account of the asylum given to Louis Napoleon after Strassbourg excites his indignation and leads him to ask for accurate information to lay before his friends in the government. Military demonstrations are, he says, equivalent to bombastic phrases. "Don't worry," he writes, "conflagrations always go out." He also undertakes in a published letter a valiant defense of Monnard, member of the Council of Lausanne, who has been calumniated in the *Débats*. From Olivier he urges an article for the *Revue*, and he interests himself actively in the appointment of the Polish poet Mickiewicz to a professorship in the Lausanne Academy.

Such is a summary sketch of Sainte-Beuve's first seven months after his return to Paris. It soon becomes evident that, besides a wrecked voice, a lame back and many new and firm friendships, he brought back from Switzerland

certain important moral results, due partly to his association with a serious society, and with Vinet in particular,
but chiefly to his intimacy with the grave recluses of the
seventeenth century, whom he had studied so intensely
that a new stability was transmitted to him from their
example, not their own rigid stability indeed, but a kind
transformed by his personality and adapted to the positivist conceptions of a scientific age. Coinciding in time
with his physical maturity, this was the last important
formative influence in his life.

It is only gradually and piecemeal that the indications
of such change emerge, the superficial and temporary
effects being at first the most obvious. He feels himself
almost a citizen of Vaud, longs to return and dreams often
of a permanent retreat amid those quiet surroundings.
"After a sweet and captivating sojourn with happy friends,
one feels altered, converted to their virtuous felicity and
desirous of meriting it." The sentence is from a book
review, Sainte-Beuve as usual putting himself into even
his most insignificant writings. He welcomes Mme.
Olivier's sermonizing about Faith, although he himself has
only desire and regret. Just as he entered into various
kinds of characters and thoughts, so he entered into and
appreciated various kinds of life, and he longed in turn for
each, excepting of course the kind he was at the time living.
Now he longs for marriage and a home in the country, but
does not consider himself fit for the tranquil happiness to
which he aspires; and he does not conceal either from
himself or from his friends that this incapacity is his own
fault. At Lausanne the name of Sainte-Beuve had been
coupled with that of a wealthy young woman, but he looked
on marriage for money with abhorrence and contempt. If
a Swiss girl should consent to become his wife, he said, she
would do so only because she wanted to get to Paris. A
Parisian courtship undertaken while in this mood resulted

in a refusal and, though later he once again caressed the idea of a domestic life, he did not venture any effort to realize it.

Meanwhile he returned to his work on the *Revue des deux Mondes*. After the article of Planche on *Pensées d'Août,* in which Sainte-Beuve felt that he had been lectured in a tone of superiority and otherwise treated without consideration, he had "sulked a little," just to show that he amounted to something. His wound was salved, however, when his friend Charles Labitte inserted an article in defense of the author of these abused poems, decrying detraction and ridicule, and allowing the poet-critic "elevation of sentiment, fervent devotion to art, lofty critical probity, purity of literary taste, disinterestedness and independence" (November 1, 1837). Other conciliatory efforts were also made. When the *Revue* published Sainte-Beuve's *Inaugural Lecture,* this was introduced by a note which applauded the success of his course, deeply regretted that it was not given nearer by, and spoke of *Port-Royal* as a work long announced and eagerly wished for. Furthermore, just at the moment of Sainte-Beuve's return, another note was inserted in the *Chronique* (June 1): "The course of M. Sainte-Beuve at the Academy of Lausanne is entirely finished and has obtained all the success that could have been predicted. . . . We are happy to announce to our readers the return of a collaborator whose works are as precious to us as his friendship is dear."

Sainte-Beuve's first article on resuming his connection with the *Revue,* an article that he had refused to write before starting for Lausanne—"We are late in our mention of this book," he begins—was on the *Memoirs* of Lafayette (July 15, August 1), a beautiful essay which towers above the mere book reviews that were to make up most of his work for three months. Here we find a tribute to Washington and a long analysis of Lafayette's motives, of which even the less admirable are traced to the essential chivalry of his nature. In this analysis, emphasis is laid upon the ruling passion, the central quality, an idea matured in the study of Port-Royal. As regards the theory of historical fatalism and the opposing theory of the unlimited action of great men, Sainte-Beuve accepts neither system, but admits the force of the current at the moment of its real supremacy and also the direction of the great man when such a one has made a decisive appearance. No formula can restrict life. Principles, he says in another book review, wherein he finds the system of humanitarianism a natural reaction from the system of Romanticism, principles are of value only for the particulars put into them and with a perpetual corrective in the application.

In literary criticism Sainte-Beuve's recoil is shown both in an essay on Fontanes (December 1, 15), undertaken in connection with the edition he was preparing, and also in an essay on Joubert (December 1), whose *Pensées* had just been privately printed. The Fontanes article, he wrote Olivier, was his "classic masterwork." Even in portraying Lafayette, Sainte-Beuve had paused suddenly to apply political terminology to literature, distinguishing the men of '89 from the Girondins and the Jacobins, not for their ideas, but as families of minds. The men of '89 had audacity and made innovations, but they did so with circumspection and within limits, the type in poetry being André Chénier. The Girondins, more audacious, more narrow, go at first to extremes; they go for a time with the Jacobins, but instead of proceeding, as these, from audacity to audacity, they at a certain moment draw back, saved by their probity of taste and sentiment. Happy those of '89, he exclaims; happy, too, the Girondins, returning honorably with amendment and with judicious inconsequence; but the Jacobins, but '93, never! In literature, as in politics, Sainte-Beuve was the Girondin. He realizes, indeed, that he had gone far and that one does not pass through systems without taking a mark, a shade, an impression, a twist, but his good sense had never capitulated and the injury, if injury there had been, was after all slight. He sympathizes with the Atticism, delicacy and serenity of Joubert. He constantly asks himself, what would So-and-so have done in the age of Louis XIV? in the eighteenth century? In his liberty of intelligence, he had always had a taste, inconsistent if you will, for Fontanes, one of the family of Racine. Though Romanticism had, he admits, been a real advance, it was false as a system; from excess of reason, poetry had gone to the opposite excess of image, thus falling into the exaggerated and the emphatic. He had praised, indeed, but his praise had often been "only sugar-coated advice." Now the advice ceases to be sugar-coated, and in reviewing Gautier's *Comédie de la Mort*, he roundly chastises the poet for expression turned exclusively to color and image and for the neglect of ensemble. The grumbling "uncle" was later pardoned by the "nephew," says a note; and in a laudatory essay on Gautier (1863), we read: "I think I remember having pointed out some errors." At this time, after reading a vague humanitarian poem, the critic hastens to Petrarch with his drop of crystal and pearl of art; after Gautier's sparkling miniatures, he turns with relish to the naïve and flowing verses of good old La Fontaine.

Sainte-Beuve has almost ceased to visit Lamartine, fearing to come again under his charm. His discontent with the poet had reached such a degree that he regrets the necessity of expressing it, but he has either to speak or abdicate. Another talent has broken its unity; the ideal poet has gone into politics and denied and slighted his poetic gift, calling it but a twelfth of his life and treating it with disdain. But God will demand an account of the special talent confided to each. "If there is diversity of gifts among men, there may readily be diversity of ministries, and this view seems especially plausible when the mark is as glorious and as obvious as in the case of M. de Lamartine.'' Not that he can be really blamed for going into politics, though his ministry seemed rather in song than in parliamentary debate, but he must be reproved for disparaging his poetic gift and holding it cheap. ''Art, for the artist, is a matter of conscience''; he must do his best, such striving being identical with the effort of morality to attain virtue. ''In the poetic, as in the moral order, the price of grandeur is effort, battle, constancy.'' How distressing to find this poet playing on his precious lyre, not only with his fingers, but with a stick, with his arms and his elbows, drawing forth clangorous noises, but no harmony, no melody! What can be pardoned in Hugo (a great poet), because more or less consistent with his other qualities, cannot be pardoned in Lamartine. Sainte-Beuve's criticism of his contemporaries, it has often been maintained, was inspired by envy, but assuredly it is the very opposite of envy that here inspires his plaints. That these friends did not proceed to ever new heights of achievement is a grievous disappointment. Their ruin, he laments, is his own, as their triumph, so often predicted, would if it should come to pass, be his pride and his joy. ''The sagacity of the critic is bound to their destiny of faithful poets and revered authors; the best of our capital was embarked on their renown and the greater part of us will perish in their shipwreck.''

This article (April, 1839) was a review of the *Recueillements Poétiques*. Other essays owed their subjects to various occasions, and while Sainte-Beuve is largely journalistic, both in subject-matter and in appeal to the interest of the hour, he rarely fails to embody his own personality, together with reflections of permanent vitality. Securing access to the papers of André Chénier, he published (February 1) selections from these, with comments which emphasize the Greek inspiration of the poet and show the critic's strong classical tendency. The Romantic movement is spent; the theories, so far as they were true, have triumphed, while so far as they were contestable, they have been defeated.

When Xavier de Maistre, a charming old man, visited Paris for the first time at the age of seventy-six, Buloz demanded an article (May 1), which was hastily prepared, personal information being obtained from the subject himself. De Maistre was much offended by what he considered a violation of confidence and what was, at least, an indiscretion, a passage hinting that, as a young officer, he had met his mistress in the leper's garden of one of his tales. Here the old gentleman's notions of propriety differed from those of the journalist. The ground tone of Sainte-Beuve's criticism rests on the idea that touching simplicity gains its adherents without noise, a method opposed to the practice of the day. An interesting aside tells us that de Maistre himself could not understand the value of so much talk in the Chamber. "And I confess," adds Sainte-Beuve, "it would have been rather hard to explain it to him just then."

If a journalistic necessity brought forth the essay on the Savoyard story-teller, it was a long-standing curiosity at length satisfied to which we owe the essay on the Dutch-Swiss novelist, Mme. Charrière (March 15). As a boy Sainte-Beuve had read her *Lettres de Lausanne,* and once he got to Switzerland, he took pains to unearth information about the lady. While the essay is pleasing enough, the really significant part is the introduction. Here he puts the query: Is it criticism he is doing in these portraits? And he answers that they are rather an indirect way of expressing his views of life and exhaling a certain latent poetry, bordering indeed on the history of literature, but not actually within its bounds. It is an outcome, rather, of the same taste that causes others to produce novels, for he deals with characters that are not invented, it is true, but rediscovered, and in a sense created, with something in them of the author's self.

Throughout these months, as usual, he is short of money, yet at the same time he has too many things to do. He fears the *Revue* will go to pieces, first because Buloz is seeking a position from the government—he was made Royal Commissioner of the Comédie Française in 1838— and then because the hostile ministers after the fall of Molé threatened to start a rival magazine, if political support were denied them. Sainte-Beuve nevertheless refuses a provincial professorship, though he has a choice of either Marseilles or Lyons. Even the opportunity to supply the place of Ampère in Paris is renounced on account of his weakness of voice. In order to get some money he obtains Renduel's consent to a plan to detach a dozen *Revue* articles from *Port-Royal*. If possible, he would go to some country place to work consecutively on his history, but the need of libraries keeps him in Paris.

Meanwhile, besides the magazine articles, there were the published volumes. Early in 1839 appeared the works of Louis de Fontanes, which had demanded infinite patience, including a multitude of visits and an extensive correspondence. Mlle. de Fontanes appears a trifle fussy, owing to that ancestor-worship which is so grateful to the children of a distinguished parent and so insipid to outsiders. Sainte-Beuve skillfully humored her sensibilities, but refused to change a word of his essay in the *Revue,* omitting a passage, however, when it was used as an introduction to the works. This essay he read at Mme. Récamier's to Chateaubriand and a few others. Half-way through, his voice gave out, and the task was deferred to another afternoon. His eyes were also weak, and he had a M. Dourdain

212

to read to him and to copy manuscript, the first of his secretaries. Very surprising is the fact that Sainte-Beuve tampered with the text of Fontane's verses, correcting inelegancies and even adding lines of his own. He was not what we should call an exact editor. In May appeared the fourth and fifth volumes of his *Critiques et Portraits littéraires,* to the proofs of which, as was his custom, he had devoted much time and labor. The trouble was worth while, however, not only for accuracy of text, but because the impecunious critic received a small sum of money which enabled him to make a trip to Italy, through the northern part of which he had previously taken a week's tour during one of his Lausanne holidays.

He had planned to spend a long vacation at Lausanne, but an obstinate bronchitis necessitated the south. Provided with directions—*guide-âne*—prepared by Stendhal, he went by coach to Châlons, passed down the Rhône in a steamer, and then by sea from Marseilles to Naples, stopping briefly at Genoa and Pisa. After a fortnight at Naples, he proceeded again by sea to Rome for another fortnight, and thence (June 18) took ship for Marseilles, becoming acquainted with Gogol during the return voyage. The trip was, as he said, nothing but a "raid," in which he might get a first view that would enable him to recognize places. Under such circumstances, no decisive influence could be expected, nor was Sainte-Beuve's nature of a sort calculated to be molded by the charm that has transformed so many men of distinction. He apparently enjoyed beautiful objects of art, and at times appreciated even music, both, however, from a literary standpoint, the subject being more than the expression and the words of the song more than the melody. If he took this trip, as he proposed, in order that he might reflect on his situation at the moment of passing from youth to the succeeding age, he could have had little leisure for such meditation.

The only traces of Italy that remain are a handful of poems and some infrequent allusions scattered through his essays.

At Genoa he rushed through palaces and churches, not seeing "Mme. Dudevant" on any balcony, though informed of her presence in the city. The name implies that this was one of the intervals when he did "not love her any more." The beauty of Naples he admired, but not always those features which had been most highly vaunted. The general enthusiasm is nothing but phrases, and travelers are mere sheep. He, however, is unwilling to be a dupe. In this case he has Lamartine on his mind. The literary reflection is never long absent. The marbles in the Museum recall André Chénier; from Capri lowers the figure of Tiberius; the Neapolitan populace realizes the life portrayed in *Gil Blas*.

His first impression of Rome was of ineffable beauty. Then he perceives that this is the city of the dead, the best place in which to cultivate a fixed idea, a devotion, a devotion to Raphael, it may be, or to the antique, to Apollo, to some saint or martyr, to early Christian art, to medals and coins, to papal benedictions and the telling of one's beads—each devotee wholly absorbed, oblivious of all else and entirely contented.

Sainte-Beuve himself saw and appreciated many beautiful things, the Vatican, the view on descending Vesuvius, a sunset at Tivoli, Sorrento, which he finds divine. At Naples a banker friend introduced him to two charming ladies; at Rome he saw Gerbet in a cloister, as well as Overbeck, Ingres and other artists—"I prefer these workers to a few stones"—also Mme. d'Agoult and Liszt, whom he found charming and to whom he addressed some verses. In the midst of all his experiences, he was always eager for news from Paris and especially for news about the *Revue*.

From Marseilles he went to Lyons to pass three talkative days with Collombet, meeting Laprade for the first time; and then to Lausanne, where he stayed with the Oliviers for a month. Going to hear Vinet lecture, he was much struck with his simple spirituality in contrast with the pomp of Rome. He hopes to pass all of his summers in Switzerland, but by one of life's ironies, this was his last visit. Obliged by a delay to pass a day at Besançon, he sacked the library in the morning, finding a roomful of old literary journals from which he took notes, and he passed the afternoon in lively talk with some friends captained by "the learned Weiss, *genius loci*," a friend of Nodier's boyhood.

The second week in August Sainte-Beuve is back again in Paris, and again we get a picture of the same unquiet life, visits, studies, work on *Port-Royal*—he finds every one plunging into the seventeenth century—work for the *Revue*. No wonder his brain is distracted; yet we feel that nothing but an active participation in the agitated life of Paris, combined with those fevered periods of production and those other long hours of secluded study, could have produced the incomparable portraitist. "Provincial life," he remarks in a little read essay, "has its many gifts of study, sensibility and virtue; but taste, it must be confessed, is rarer and more out of view than in Paris, where, after all, it is dearly bought."

Plant Sainte-Beuve ten years in Lausanne, and your fruit will have a different flavor. He spends a week in Mme. de Tascher's country place, first exploring the library, then taking long walks, introduced to an eccentric curé, laughing as he never laughs anywhere else. Back in Paris, he is diligently gathering material on Joseph de Maistre and is still at *Port-Royal*, though his "poor cloister has many windows." Saturdays in November he reads chapters of his book to Chateaubriand at Mme. Récamier's, continuing even into the new year. In this salon, too, he is present at a scene which he recalls in 1862, M. Delécluze reading his *Memoirs* to a select gathering of aristocratic ladies and gentlemen, plunging ahead through a vivid description of filth in the old Louvre, not sparing private places unmentioned by the polite; then, feeling a trifle uneasy on this score, trying to skip a few pages, and disconcerted at the lack of connection, resolutely turning back again to begin the obnoxious passage anew and emphasize it by repetition. Meanwhile, Sainte-Beuve (September 10) has had a quarrel with Villemain, to whom he writes a long letter, polite enough in form, which may be rather brutally summarized as follows: Sainte-Beuve has heard that Villemain has complained in various companies of references to him in the notes to Fontane's poems. Sainte-Beuve thereupon accuses Villemain of excessive avidity for praise, declares his own independence, will always recognize the charming and accomplished writer, but will get along without his friendship. This is a characteristic unreasonable outburst, of a sort that scarcely any of Sainte-Beuve's friends escaped. But the wrath is often of short duration. Villemain seems to have paid little attention to the explosion, and by November Sainte-Beuve himself is ready for a reconciliation. A point to note is that an accusation of self-seeking can hardly be lodged against a critic who, with scarcely a livelihood, thus lets out his bile upon the Minister of Public Instruction and Perpetual Secretary of the Academy.

The poems inspired by the hasty Italian trip were written at Lausanne. In the *Revue des deux Mondes* (September 15) was published the *Eglogue Napolitaine,* a versified version of Sainte-Beuve's reflections on the paganism surviving in Neapolitan Christianity. This piece was not only anonymous, but pretended to have been written by "a poet who had traveled in Italy some years ago." The rest of the pieces appeared in the *Revue de Paris* (August) as *Notes et Sonnets,* translated, rendered or imitated as a relaxation from *Port-Royal.* Youth is past; he seeks not art or nature so much as "still the dream when hope is lost"; mountains are too high for him to climb, better adapted to his nature being the little hill, whence he can hear the sacred tones from aloft; in Swiss scenes, "the truest aspect is the most hidden." To Olivier he sings of Switzerland; to Liszt he reflects on human feelings and friendships in connection with a sunset at the Villa Adriana; to Latour he complains that *Port-Royal* is a "sterile occupation if the heart is not changed . . . always touching the altar without embracing it"; to Brizeux he addresses a picture of the beggars at Salerno, a piece later bearing the name of George Sand, thus indicating two quarrels and one reconciliation. Another group of poems had been previously published in the *Revue de Paris* (January, 1839), a sort of appendix to *Pensées d'Août,* where indeed all these pieces, together with a few others, are collected. Far better than the verse, however, is a bit of emotional prose written at Aigues Mortes near Marseilles: "My soul is like these shores where they say Saint Louis once embarked; both the sea and my faith, alas! have long since withdrawn, and it is much if, from time to time, amid the sand, under the arid heat or the chilling mistral, I can seat myself for a passing moment in the shadow of a lonely tamarind."

To the sentimental and poetic production of these months belongs also *Cristel* (November 15), a little story of a consumptive girl, or rather an analysis of her sensibilities in a few scenes. But, on the other hand, sensing himself as "the indefatigable critical pirate in Paris, yet as equitable as possible," Sainte-Beuve entered a warfare long meditated, striking, as he says, right and left, his right commonly landing on Balzac and his left distributing blows upon unnamed persons among whom Girardin, at least, was expected to recognize himself. This polemic, a real fulmination, *De la Littérature industrielle* (*Revue des deux Mondes,* September 1, 1839), pointed out symptoms of inward degeneration—emulation, self-esteem, charlatanism, log-rolling, intimidation, avidity for popularity and gold— and assailed the abuses and the mercantile organization of the press. Its venal subservience to advertisers is strongly condemned, particularly publishers' puffs printed as reading matter, the critics being bound by these puffs. The procedure is ruinous also to the publishers themselves, because the public, so often fooled, refuses to buy books written to furnish the largest number of pages at the expense of the fewest possible ideas, the cupidity of each bringing ruin on the whole. Balzac is several times mentioned by name and he is ridiculed for proclaiming himself the first of "the twelve literary marshals of France." Resentment was general, and Balzac even brought suit against the *Revue,* a suit that is mocked in a note, evidently by Sainte-Beuve, which concludes: "He will find that we never in the least dreamed of contesting the *intrepidity* of his bad taste."

This sort of thing, however, many another could do, perhaps not quite so neatly as Sainte-Beuve, but sufficiently well. His next article, which treats of some minor poets of the age of Louis XIV, and particularly Mme. des Houlières (October 15), begins, as all contemporary readers must have been relieved to observe: "*Revenons à nos moutons.* . . . I take again my shepherd's crook and quiet my dog." Here we have a real chat, gleanings from a row of little volumes the critic had been glancing over, the works of a school of seventeenth century poets for whom the age of Louis XIV did not exist, but who continued the sixteenth century, on the one hand, and looked forward to the eighteenth century, on the other. "For the amenity

of life," the critic reflects when he finds a gem in some
forgotten lyrics, "it is not necessary to have relations only
with the immortals."

The last essay of this year, a review of Le Clerc's *Les
Journaux chez les Romains* (December 15), is especially
interesting, not only for maintaining that the history of
journalism is essential to the history of literature, the peaks
being understood only in relation to the lower lands around
—a principle consistently applied by Sainte-Beuve in his
own work—but chiefly as illustrating his attitude toward
erudition, an attitude which is both appreciative and sarcastic. The learned are respected: "A certain circle of
tediousness protects them and raises a fog between them
and the public." "The fine moment for the academic
reconstruction of a civilization is when this civilization has
left nothing behind but one undecipherable piece of writing
or some broken pots." But such mockery is only one phase
of the matter. Among scholars, Sainte-Beuve seeks the rare
man of ideas. Judging "only as one of the ignorant and
as a mere amateur" (O, for an army of such amateurs!),
he defends Niebuhr against the strictures of Le Clerc,
Niebuhr whose results remain precious, not perhaps in
detail, but as a way of conceiving Roman history. At one
moment, the whole labor seems futile—"Man is always
forgetting, and doing the same thing over again"—yet,
though nothing is left but works uncompleted or in ruins,
each of us should labor valiantly in his time, as if everything were to last and to be perfected.

Man flatters himself when he believes that at least all positive
results remain intact, and that science never forgets. For each
generation there is a shipwreck of living ideas; a sort of ignorance begins again; a good part of the knowledge and thought
of each year perishes with the year itself; another portion is
heaped up in learned storehouses, and is drawn out only to be
distributed among a few heads more and more exceptional.

Such impressions come, we may be sure, from the vain attempt in *Port-Royal* to enter completely into the life of Pascal and to appreciate every stroke of Molière and Boileau. Sainte-Beuve, indeed, is saturated with his Port-Royal studies, as is evidenced in every essay now coming from his pen, not a single one being without allusions to the persons who had become his familiars. Often he even talks to the public about his book, as when he here quotes Hermann Reuchlin, "who is writing a history of Port-Royal which will, I fear, appear ahead of mine."

The background of Port-Royal is unusually conspicuous in a review of Ampère's lectures on French literature before the twelfth century (February 15, 1840), an essay in which are also found further reflections on erudition. Having asked friendship to pardon the analyst, Sainte-Beuve judges, not only the published book, but the succeeding lectures which he has attended as a pupil, thus getting his perspective and perceiving each period as a link in the general law of development. From his father, Ampère inherited the scientific spirit which he now applies to literature, but to this inheritance many and varied inspirations were added, Chateaubriand, Goethe, Lamartine, Cousin, Fauriel, and—what need to name Mme. Récamier? —"those other incomparable influences, not to be measured, a fitting appellation for which must be craved of the Muses." With such advantages, a scholar is more than merely erudite. Poetry pervades his criticism, not in the flowery phrase, which is empty rhetoric, but in a certain light shining through the analysis, a life and reality in the things treated, divination based upon learning. The chief peril lies in the attempt to bring everything under some principle. "Every method, even the most natural and true, is nothing but a method, and has its limits. In the history of human thought, we meet a number of accidents to be dealt with perhaps only with the laugh of a Voltaire or the headshake of a Montaigne. In seeking everywhere a law, do we not run the risk of forcing its application and indeed even of making it up ourselves?''

We are thus introduced into the year 1840, a year that is not to be considered as decisive in Sainte-Beuve's biography, but which marks by a series of external signs and incidents the culmination and completion of a change long prepared and gradually matured. It is the dividing line between preparation and maturity, so definitely drawn that it cannot be obliterated by the flow of continuity, by any perpetuation or recurrence of earlier features or by any anticipation of subsequent characteristics.

A continuation of what had been partly outlived is manifested in the first volume of *Port-Royal,* published in April, and this mental attitude is extended to the second volume, which appeared two years later, indicating that this subject attracted to itself a mood quite at variance with that in which work on other topics was being done. At the same time, by reaction, Port-Royal fed Sainte-Beuve's skepticism; yet, however skeptical he might become in theory, he perceived that in practice some sort of faith is essential to productivity. Such a notion may be found in the essay on Ampère already discussed:

If a certain amount of folly is not alien to man, even to man taken in the mass, it is vain to argue for the necessary truth of an idea or for its triumph in any given epoch. Since, indeed, something must triumph, there is just as good a chance that it may be something foolish. Now, while the historian in quest of laws chiefly concerns himself with distinguishing and often introducing reason beneath every error, the share of madness gets glozed over and diminished under his pen.

But these reflections, I really feel, ought to be held back, for even if true, they are not fertile. Such sad dregs of ironical experience do not deserve even the name of results; still less are they fit for instruction and for use as a spur. No human monument is ever raised but by means of certain views in which greatness and order rule, and which on many points bear the impress of the mind of the architect.

In a note dated 1869 Sainte-Beuve indicates his essay on La Rochefoucauld (January 15, 1840) as marking his return from a deviation to saner ideas, and, while some critics have seen no unusual significance in this piece, it is well, even at the risk of what in respect to another might seem oversubtle interpretation, to follow the warning and read between the lines. Taking the hint, therefore, we find many personal analogies between La Rochefoucauld and his portraitist. In youth the young nobleman had cherished a romantic devotion; at the age of thirty-three— Sainte-Beuve was now thirty-six, and it was three years since his break with Mme. Hugo—"ill-paid for his first devotion, he promised himself not to be caught again." A maxim is quoted: "When weary of a love affair, we are glad the object is faithless, so as to release us from our own fidelity." Yet there are returns of bitterness. "Jealousy is born with love, but does not always die with it," says La Rochefoucauld, and Sainte-Beuve writes of Mme. Hugo in his note-book, "I hate her." La Rochefoucauld's vengeance, however, is called a dirty act, for which he was punished, a plain indication that nothing of the sort was meditated by Sainte-Beuve. The *Livre d'Amour* was not a vengeance. A further analogy is furnished by La Rochefoucauld's timidity in society. He could not speak in public. Under a constitutional government, where it is necessary to laud oneself and to flatter the audience, too, he could have been nothing but what in his own day he was, a moralist. This is almost a substitution of one for the other. When Sainte-Beuve laid siege to Mme. d'Arbouville (April, 1841), did he not have in mind a literary liaison, such as that between La Rochefoucauld and Mme. de Lafayette? His life is not free from such imitations.

In addition to biographical allusions, the essay contains a statement of a changed attitude of mind. The mature critic has seen the under side of things. One comes to mock the heroics of youth and "from that day there is no further tragedy or serious transaction; one has entered the region of profound irony." Elvire and Lamartine have yielded place to the *Maxims,* which entertain us because they are dismal, like ourselves. Yet absolute faith in these maxims can be no greater than faith in romance. There is a folly of thirty-five, as there was a folly of twenty; "Alceste after Werther." "If you live long enough, you will see everything, and also the reverse of everything." You become entirely disinterested; good sense, having nothing to do but judge those who lack it, attains its culmination. "What seemed the débris gathered by experience after shipwreck, composes the true center—found at last—of life." Taste, too, returns to the simple, becomes pure Louis XIV. "In youth," adds Sainte-Beuve, "thoughts came to me in sonnets, now in maxims"; and of these he appends several pages somewhat in the disillusioned spirit of his model. "If any one of the foregoing maxims offends you," he concludes, "I promise without delay to refute it."

The poet in Sainte-Beuve is, if not extinct, at least reduced to embers glowing under the ashes. To what extent *Port-Royal* contributes to this result, it would be hazardous to specify, but, in the transformation "from him who sings to him who analyzes," the influence of these rigidly plain Christians was unquestionably important, for their society was quite as much an experience of reality as the contemporary society of the salon, the boulevard and the editorial office. Here again, the effect was not immediate. In one of Sainte-Beuve's letters, we have a picture of an evening in January, 1839, at Marmier's where friends drank punch and recited verses to one another, Brizeux violently antagonistic to the poetry of the

north, answered by Marmier and Tourgeneff, and finally
disarmed by Sainte-Beuve's reading of Olivier's poem on
a fir tree. There existed, however, no further active impulse to fresh production, while at the same time his own
critical faculty became a deterrent, which could not be
quieted by a little friendly praise, such as he received, for
example, from Chaudes-Aigues in the *Revue de Paris*.
When Sainte-Beuve completes a poem of André Chénier
with a line of his own, the only thing of which we are perfectly sure is that the line was not the one Chénier would
have written. Nor could the critic's taste be really deceived
in the matter of his own limitations. In the same month
with *Port-Royal* were published the collected poems of
Sainte-Beuve with a preface in which he practically bade
farewell to the Muse, not entirely renouncing poetry indeed,
but reducing it to the strict necessities of the heart, since
there would be henceforth little that was new to present
to the public. He hopes, however, that, although *Les Consolations* alone had so far been received with any favor,
some little attention would be paid to the other parts as
serious and frank studies and as attempts to apply severe
art within a limited compass. Sainte-Beuve cannot be
called altogether unsuccessful as a poet, since new editions
were called for in 1844 and 1860, and Banville, Coppée
and Baudelaire are generally recognized as his offspring.
He has also given some phrases to literature, one of which,
de Vigny's "ivory tower," belongs as much to English
speech as to French. Late in life he wrote in connection
with de Vigny:

I have just reread a dozen of his letters belonging to that
year (1829) and those following, and I have found in them a
complete image of those days of lively ardor and mutual sympathy, precious testimony of an expansion which was later too
much repressed and opposed. Why, I have often asked myself,
why am I a critic? Why did I not remain the official servitor

and devoted defender of the same glorious reputations? Why this need to analyze, to examine what lay inside and behind men's hearts, for which de Vigny reproved me on the occasion of my preface to *Consolations,* and which, to my sorrow and as a penalty for my sins, I have applied to the minute and intimate scrutiny of talents? But why is it that these beloved talents themselves, these chosen poets, why have even the most faithful among them also changed and varied with the seasons? Why does mind obey its inclination? Why has life its irresistible current? Why, after you have come out but an instant, do you find it impossible to enter the stream at the same spot on the shore and amid the same waves?

Although again and again in subsequent years Sainte-Beuve cries out that poetry is the only vocation he really loves, he yet from now on becomes fairly contented with what he clearly perceives must be his literary career. "Ten Years After in Literature" (*Revue des deux Mondes,* March 1, 1840) is quite as much a review of a personal change as of a change in surrounding conditions. Speaking of criticism, he says: "In youth it hides under art, under poetry, or, if masquerading by itself, poetry and exaltation are intermingled with it and trouble it. It is only when poetry gets a little dissipated and enlightened that the second phase is truly disclosed and that criticism slips in and infiltrates itself from all sides into the talent. Sometimes it is limited to tempering the talent, oftener it transforms it and makes it different." Fontanelle, from an insipid poet, became a consummate critic and the patriarch of his century. "Thus, at the bottom of most talents lurks a makeshift which is honorable enough, if not despised and if regarded as a sort of progress. To this evolution we must, sooner or later, submit, whether we will or no; and criticism in the long run falls heir to our other more stately or more naïve qualities, to our errors, our fondled successes, our reverses rightly interpreted." To conduct criticism as thus conceived in a large historical

spirit and as a moralist, yet without dogmatism, is to
render a public and even a social service.

The definite purpose of this essay was to rally to the
Revue a group of writers, particularly those of the old
Globe. The general ideas are such as Sainte-Beuve had
often expressed; the Revolution of 1830 had broken up all
literary association, the *Globe* editors abandoning authorship for politics, and the Cénacle dispersing as isolated
individuals. Yet only by work in common is there hope
for disinterestedness; casual meetings at social gatherings
will not do. Now that ardor has been displaced by experience, it would be possible with a little mutual tolerance
to meet on neutral ground, each with his own reservations,
but ready to form a community and to support one another. For such community the first condition is moral
equality, allowing what you please to superiority of talent.
The reign of the demigods is past. This is an appeal to
Hugo. Leroux and his associates are advised to be less
exclusive, less absolute and rigorous. Almost all the principal writers are named and urged to make common cause.
Balzac, however, is considered hopeless, and Lamartine
and Lamennais are reproached for having broken the unity
of their lives. The aim of the essay was laudable enough,
but the project was obviously chimerical.

There was, indeed, already a sort of unity among the
contributors to the *Revue*. While Buloz allowed a wide
diversity of individual judgment, the critical writers of
the staff naturally came to feel and think more or less
alike. In truth, to this common stock belong many of the
opinions falsely ascribed to Sainte-Beuve's malignity. If
Sainte-Beuve wrote in a private letter that *Ruy Blas* was
"an omelette beaten up by Polyphemus," Planche, who was
assuredly independent, went much further in a published
review (December 1, 1838). "The whole piece is a puerile
heaping up of impossible scenes": "He snatches words

from the vocabulary as from the wheel of a lottery": "He makes verbosity the first law of style": "His mind is nothing but a gloomy chaos where words dance about whose meaning he has forgotten": such are a few of his violences. Hugo's conceit is also ridiculed: "Shakespeare, says Mr. Hugo, gives his left hand to Corneille and his right to Molière. The author of *Ruy Blas* would naturally be called upon to take the place of Shakespeare, if he were not himself Shakespeare, Corneille and Molière." Consistently, since 1832, Planche had maintained that Hugo, while a great lyric poet, was out of place in the theater, *Lucrézia Borgia* and *Marie Tudor* being both severely condemned. In the *Revue de Paris,* now under the same management, Nisard, after much disparagement, calls Hugo a man of second rank, and Jules Sandeau reviews *Ruy Blas* most unfavorably as drama, while praising some passages as poetry. Yet all unite in urging over and over again Hugo's election to the Academy, and disappointment almost amounting to indignation is expressed when he is defeated. In this matter, too, though Sainte-Beuve has been accused of favoring Hugo for no other reason than that his own election would otherwise be impossible, he was in reality merely one of a chorus. He knew and said that Hugo carried with him the academic future of all his former friends, but independently of any personal incentive, the fitness of such an election and the incongruity of Hugo's exclusion from the Academy constituted a sufficient motive.

In the case of Balzac, also, the two Reviews, to both of which he had been a contributor, were quite as hostile as Sainte-Beuve, and for cause. In May, 1835, the *Revue de Paris* published a bitter complaint against the novelist on account of stories paid for and not delivered, as well as others in course of serial publication which were never completed. Chaudes-Aigues in 1839 found fault with one of his stories and Janin calls another vulgar, fantastic, fabulous and not worth reading. Buloz, therefore, came in for his share of brutal abuse when Balzac took his revenge in his *Revue Parisienne*. As to Sainte-Beuve, the wrathful "literary marshal" congratulates de Rémusat on having given a literary post (at the library) to a man "who occupies himself little or not at all with literature," and whose Muse, the Muse of bats, "seeks darkness like a jackal." Sainte-Beuve's intelligence is superior to that of his foe. He deftly taps the tenderest spot, while Balzac blindly and confusedly beats the air, often landing blows where his opponent is invulnerable. No better example can be found than his clumsy assault on *Port-Royal*, partly preserved in the appendix to the first volume. To print this piece with a malicious commentary was itself a squelching reply. As Sainte-Beuve in later years remarked: "Such judgments injure only those who express them."

The violence, as well as the frequency of these literary quarrels, is rather amusing. That they should be fought out angrily almost a century later, the champion of one opponent railing against the misdeeds of all the others, is surely more creditable to the spirit than to the good sense of the belated combatants of our generation. It was a thin-skinned epoch, and Sainte-Beuve was by no means alone in being irritable, suspicious and susceptible. De Vigny, for example, challenged Hugo to a duel on hearing reports of certain contumelious words spoken to Buloz, the affair being dragged along by Renduel till anger cooled. Almost all the leading writers were at one time or another at swords' points, the exceptions being Mérimée, Lamartine and de Musset, Mérimée because of his aloofness, de Musset because such things were not worth caring about, and Lamartine because he was really above them. In the number of feuds, probably no one, not even Hugo, surpassed Sainte-Beuve. A fastidious censoriousness, a tendency to carp and cavil—de Musset called him Mme. Pernelle—was

constantly giving offense. Add to this his habit of making
and repeating disparaging remarks, his further habit of
revolting and freeing himself from parties and associations after making them feel that he was entirely theirs,
and his almost demonic skill in finding in correspondence
put into his hands compromising matter that relatives and
friends did not realize was there until seen in print, and
we can find reason enough for the frequent and bitter animosities that have tended to obscure his real impartiality.
No one, moreover, was more quick, on unexpected occasions,
to take, as well as to give offense. It is his own case upon
which he comments in explaining Bernardin de Saint-
Pierre's hard and violent sayings as "Human infirmity and
the old leaven always ready to burst out—nothing more."
Sensitive natures, we are told, feel greater irritation from
stings, and it is the utmost tenderness that gets most bitter.
Sensibility penetrates concealed motives, bad roots of acts,
seizes the thought under the accent, the falsity behind the
smile, scents the faults of others better than they themselves, and is promptly distressed. Moreover, "every one
is at bottom a little like the peasant of Aristides." If the
"statue" is too irreproachable, let us muss it up a bit and
bring out a stain here and there to make it more natural.
It is to Sainte-Beuve's credit that he remained fundamentally tolerant and fair, and that he never permitted
himself any of the violence of expression then so common.
Angry as he once was with Latouche, he had too just a
sense of propriety ever to have written such an article as
La Haine littéraire (Gustave Planche, *Revue des deux
Mondes,* December 15, 1831) wherein that author is assailed
with almost incredible bitterness.

In the case of George Sand, though Sainte-Beuve's
periods of sulks were entirely personal, yet they as a rule
synchronized with "Mme. Dudevant's" alienation from
the *Revue*. In 1838 she had been so severe on him in an

essay on Lamennais that Buloz not only inserted a note expressing his regret, but also wrote her that he could not allow such ill-treatment of a friend to whom he owed so much. There was a reconciliation in 1839 and Sainte-Beuve's letters speak of frequent friendly meetings. He even wrote for her a dissertation on the Greek spirit in French literature which she inserted in her essay on Maurice de Guérin (1840). But soon her socialism got too rabid both for Sainte-Beuve and for the *Revue*. The reproaches of Buloz she answered with an irritating air of magnanimous injured innocence, at the same time stabbing him and calling all those who rejected her extreme radicalism reactionaries and ministerialists. This was her least amiable period. To Sainte-Beuve, who refused to visit her on account of "those persons" whom he had to meet, she replied that it was he himself who had introduced Leroux and Lamennais to her, that he, not they, had changed, and that she still considered him together with them to have been the chief influences in her intellectual life. It was many years before she made up with the *Revue,* and it was not until 1850 that she was again on entirely friendly terms with Sainte-Beuve.

The revulsion from humanitarian cant and radical republicanism, which made George Sand's circle so obnoxious to Sainte-Beuve, was no novelty. Even in 1835 when he reviews *Democracy in America*, there appears no advocacy of popular government. While sympathy with poverty and labor continues, and a belief in very slow social improvement, there is not a trace of revolutionary ardor, and demagogy has become an object of utter aversion. Enthusiasm and idealism are past. The realization of an order one has dreamed is always inferior to the ideal, even the most moderate ideal; the imperfections and insufficiencies, not only of men, but of principles, are felt; no human result answers the promise. Society, finding conditions endurable, now directs its energies toward material interests. There was, however, an occasional twinge of regret. Discussing certain of Lafayette's temerities, Sainte-Beuve says: "Our old ardor accords with his too well to allow our drab impartiality of to-day to be exigent."

Here, too, Sainte-Beuve was largely in harmony with the *Revue*. Buloz had opposed Thiers and Guizot and consistently supported Molé. In the *Chronique* the Coalition of 1838, a union of incoherent parties to overthrow the ministry, is a "miserable intrigue," and it is a "miserable intrigue" in Sainte-Beuve's letters. Yet partisan prejudice cannot blind him to talent, and Thiers is to him the brilliant prince of Athenian oratory. Many letters abound in expressions of distress and disgust over the political situation, the sad state of society, democracy, vulgarity, universal corruption and self-interest. He has visions of a dark future. If a republic comes, he will bury himself in some Swiss canton. At other times he simply amuses himself, being interested, but without political passion. He is so much in the thick of affairs at dinners and other reunions that he thinks of writing a novel, *Ambition*, as a pendant to *Volupté*. At the *Revue*, too, he found himself at a center of political gossip and, though he never contributed to the political *Chroniques*, he allows traces of his feelings to appear from time to time in his literary essays. Under representative government, he thinks, which is so good for guarantees and interests, taste suffers and delicate souls are unhappy. In 1841 he even writes his publisher Renduel that, in aging, one returns to absolute power pure and simple.

With Molé and Salvandy Sainte-Beuve was on good terms, though he could not profit from their favor, possibly owing to some former revolutionary engagement. Yet from the next ministry, or rather from his friends, de Rémusat, Minister of the Interior, and Cousin, Minister of

Public Instruction, he accepted the post of Keeper in the Mazarine Library. His situation had been anomalous, one of the foremost literary talents of the day struggling for a bare subsistence. Every one but Sainte-Beuve seems to have been cared for, even Quinet and Charles getting chairs at the Collège de France in 1841, while Labitte, his chief assistant, had already been well placed at Nantes. The post at the library carried a salary of 4,000 francs, with a lodging in the buildings of the Institut and a month's vacation in September. Sainte-Beuve was one of five Keepers, under the Director, M. de Feletz, a former editor of the *Débats,* who gave delightful and long-remembered dinners, the other four being the Abbé Guillon, who was past eighty and never put in an appearance, Sacy of the *Débats,* Charles and a M. Pignollet. Every third day Sainte-Beuve had to be in attendance from 10 A. M. to 3 P. M. "What a nuisance!" he exclaims, "and the national guard!" for he could now be called upon for the service so long avoided in his retreat, Cour de Commerce. Indeed, his mother was the only one who was really happy about the position.

One of Sainte-Beuve's reasons for taking this post was his desire to marry a daughter of General Pelletier. Her refusal caused some sharp pangs and practically ended his hopes of matrimony, though later he dallied with the idea of a union with Ondine Valmore, an idea finally rejected. At the present time, he attempted to keep up his relations with the Pelletiers, but finding his visits too painful, he renounced them in a frank and manly letter to the General.

When he entered the Mazarine Library, Sainte-Beuve stood high in public estimation. The first volume of *Port-Royal* had been a great success. Royer-Collard gave the tone by speaking most favorably of the work, and even Bertin and Janin of the hostile *Débats* joined in the general praise. Society itself, Sainte-Beuve reports, was talking of Mother Angélique. Far more satisfactory was the favorable comment of Vinet in *le Semeur,* which completely obliterated the discordant note uttered by Balzac. De Sacy, too (*Débats,* May 1, 1841), spoke of Sainte-Beuve as predestined to write the history of Port-Royal, and could not have believed that any man of the day would have been able to enter so deeply into the subject. He was impatient for the second volume.[1] In the *Revue,* Lerminier began his article with the words: "Here at last is a book that consoles us for the sad state into which letters have fallen for some years past." From beginnings that merely announced a brilliant pen, Sainte-Beuve had grown till he had "taken rank among the first prose writers of our epoch." "There is in M. Sainte-Beuve," he adds, "a half skepticism that permits him to seize every point with sagacity and to render it persuasively, he is penetrating and lucid, because his mind is always free and disengaged." That wherein he particularly excels is in applying his imagination to the ordering of reality, so that we become contemporaries of his personages, actually present in the epoch of which he treats.

Of the essays, too, one of the qualities most noted by contemporary critics is this use of imagination, a feature which Sainte-Beuve himself praises in his friend Ampère. As early as 1834, Gustave Planche had said that it was Sainte-Beuve's honor to have put poetry into criticism, to have been the first to make of the analysis of literary works something living and animated, capable of interesting even outside of the book that served as the point of departure. "Here is a new manner in literary criticism," said Louandre in the *Revue de Paris* (June, 1839), adding that the

---

[1] In December, 1842, he found this second volume superior to the first. There was nothing less Jansenist than the style, but the author had found and exhibited the soul of Port-Royal and produced "a book exciting to mere curiosity, serious, and profound from a philosophic point of view."

critic seemed to have second sight; and a note in another issue of the same periodical pointed out the fact that Sainte-Beuve had joined art to literary criticism, giving his portraits creative value. Chaudes-Aigues, a rather formal mind—he wanted Hugo to abandon the lyric and write a long philosophical poem—had objected that the purpose of the *Critiques et Portraits* was less to judge than to paint and that criticism was sacrificed to the portrait. Thanking for this article, Sainte-Beuve agrees that his book is of the elegiac and romantic part of his nature, rather than expressly critical.

Another point made by Planche is expressed about as follows: In Sainte-Beuve there is a happy mingling of enthusiasm and curiosity, always renewed. Although he has cultivated many passing friendships, believing them lasting, he does not, thank Heaven! shrink from any ingratitude. He speaks the truth for the pleasure of speaking it. His perpetual mobility is only a constant good faith. He believes in Chateaubriand and Lamennais, but with him believing is merely a way of understanding.

If we study the views of an author's contemporaries, Sainte-Beuve had remarked in his essay on Delille, we find that everything has been said.

"We can wholly count on him," wrote Enfantin (November 5, 1830). And many others were equally deceived. Of persons herein like himself, Sainte-Beuve wrote: "You believe them to be at a certain point, and they are already at the opposite pole. They are like generals who set fires on the hills behind which they are believed to be encamped, while they are already leagues away ready to attack you on the flank." "Parties hate those who pass through them and do not join them irrevocably," he adds in one of his notes; "I gave no one the right to say: 'He is ours.'" The parties, whether right or wrong, thought otherwise. "I have indeed my vices and weaknesses," we read in the

Cahiers, "but it is for what is good in me, for my taste for uprightness and truth and for my independence of judgment that I have irritated so many and provoked so much anger."

Revolutionary ardor, Saint-Simonianism, Romanticism, have been left behind. "I have been an advocate long enough; let me now be a judge." "Most men, youth being past, come back to an exact appreciation of things." Misanthropy, ripeness and prudence take the place of passion and illusion. Yet passion and illusion have their value as elements in growth. If Sainte-Beuve had gone on in the rather dry spirit of the *Globe,* he would have lacked much of his sensibility and a whole side of sympathetic adaptability to certain movements. If not a better critic, he was at least a more delightful critical writer, because he had experienced the disturbances of equilibrium resulting from Romanticism, from his love affair, from his violent political partisanship and from his long attempt to attain religious faith. No man this side of the Middle Ages can be an exact successor of the ancients. The sight, hearing and vocal organs of humanity have been modified. In somewhat the same way, Sainte-Beuve's moral constitution, having passed through his epoch of mysticism, came back to a positive outlook with all the sharp edges softened. He was a materialist, somehow trailing clouds of glory.

CHAPTER VIII

1840—1849

AFTER receiving his appointment at the Mazarine Library, Sainte-Beuve continued to contribute an undiminished number of articles to the *Revue des deux Mondes,* and he also wrote a few for the *Débats* and the *Revue de Paris.* He did not secure his apartment at the Institut for over a year (Oct., 1841), and then, at last, he had space enough to enable him to view his books on the shelves. The richness of the Mazarine collection in Renaissance literature incited him to review the sixteenth century, the result being a group of essays on the subject and a new edition of his *Tableau* (1842) with these added and with many fresh notes. In this same year appeared the second volume of *Port-Royal.* In memory of his course, Sainte-Beuve was made honorary professor at Lausanne (1841). To his friend Olivier, who edited the *Revue Suisse,* he sent a series of letters (1843-1845) on the literary and other gossip of Paris, which Olivier used for his department called *Chronique Parisienne.* Once established at the Library, Sainte-Beuve began to relearn Greek, being aided by a native of Epirus, Pantasides, and as a consequence, we have, not only numerous allusions in the essays, but also a separate treatment of Homer, Theocritus and others. Elected to the Academy, March 14, 1844, in place of Delavigne, he was received, Feb. 27, 1845, by Victor Hugo, the occasion exciting widespread curiosity. In 1843 Sainte-Beuve privately printed the poems he had written to Mme. Hugo from 1831 to 1837, intending to reserve all copies till after the death of the three persons concerned. A journalist, however, secured some proofs in 1845, and advertised the matter in such a way as to create a scandal, though refraining from mentioning actual names. From 1841 on, Sainte-Beuve had several love affairs, not all of which have been disclosed. His passion for Mme. d'Arbouville was the most deeply felt, though reciprocated only with a sort of affectionate amity. Mme. Allart, with whom he had intimate relations for a moment, continued an assiduous correspondence for many years. Toward the close of this period, he thought of marriage with Ondine Valmore, but withdrew before making a final engagement.

It was not until October, 1841, that Sainte-Beuve was able to take possession of his apartment, a dark and inelegant apartment, at the Institut and at length spread out his books so that he could view them and really know what he possessed; but meanwhile, prompted by the rich collection of rare Renaissance texts now at his disposal in the Mazarine, he resumed his sixteenth century studies, producing a series of five essays on "Old French Poets"— Du Bellay, Bertaut, Du Bartas, Des Portes and the imitators of Anacreon—which appeared in the *Revue des deux Mondes* (1841-1842), and in the last of which he bade farewell for a long time to this literary period, having reached the bottom of his basket. These essays, with two other pieces, form the supplement of the new edition of the *Tableau,* published in May, 1842, and dedicated to Dubois, whom he had urged, in "Ten Years After," to resume his pen. By publicly associating such a type of moderation and reason with what had been looked on as a polemical work, the critic marks his renunciation of his early partisanship both in literature and politics, and we cannot wonder that Mme. Girardin (Sophie Gay of the Cénacle) called him a renegade. No longer an advocate for the Romantic School, Sainte-Beuve now writes, as he says, with the sun not in his eyes, but behind his back, the result, however, being, at bottom, not very different, though differently expressed, with no exaggeration or sound of the heroic trumpet. He even perceives between the poetry of the sixteenth and the nineteenth centuries a likeness in the fact that both produced more blossoms than fruit.

Of poets, remarks Sainte-Beuve, in one of these essays, the beauties are remembered; of critics, only the faults.

"Who but scolds at La Harpe and Marmontel, men who, in attainments and taste, were all that their age demanded? I did so myself as a beginner, and the same thing will, in time, happen to me." In this passage a change of tone and a change of attitude are illustrated, the tone having become conversational and the attitude tolerant. Yet the critic's taste is even more rigorous than before. Poetry is not relative: what is once beautiful does not cease to be so, and, on the other hand, the clumsy cannot become graceful merely because it is old. The standard of comparison is now constantly Greek, not an essay being without quotations from Homer, Theocritus and the Greek Anthology. Traces of his return to Homer are, indeed, to be noticed as early as 1837, and Theocritus he had begun spelling out for himself in 1841; but once settled in a permanent position, he secured the services of Pantasides,[1] a native of Epirus, and for the rest of his life he read and reread Homer and the Anthology with a man who lived less in modern Paris than in the Athens of Pericles. Dispense with the classics, if you please, in the education of your men of affairs; for the critic they are a necessity.

Being a spirit akin to Horace, Sainte-Beuve had, from the first, more or less chatted with the readers of his essays, but after Lausanne this tendency becomes more pronounced, possibly from the habit there acquired of actually talking in the presence of an audience, departing occasionally from the written lecture and indeed always doing the writing itself with his hearers before his mind's eye. Being really about a decade older than his years, he now usually takes the conversational tone of a man past fifty, approaching more and more the ease and authority of the *Lundis*. The reader is treated as a friend and, to speak

---

[1] He paid Pantasides fifty francs for ten lessons. This fee has its interest when we remember that Sainte-Beuve's salary was only 4,000 francs.

the truth, as a highly cultivated friend, who is possessed of a vast deal of literature and who may be asked to reread some book with which, in sad reality, his acquaintance is, it is most likely, confined to the title, or at most to a few extracts. The writer, on the other hand, has himself slight pretensions to learning, being purely a literary critic. He fears to approach some question of erudition, confesses his insufficiency, really only applies common-sense, and would like specialists to judge. Finding at the Library a little leisure and having access to a collection of Renaissance Latin poetry brought from Italy by Naudé, he will talk a bit further on Du Bellay, particularly since he and some friends have recently had a dispute on the subject. On another topic, he wants to have his say before Ampère has closed the debate. Mlle. Bertin's poems recall the circumstances of a visit to her father's country place, Les Roches. Personally, he tells us, he has a weakness for writers who never dreamed of authorship. Des Portes tempts him to relate several pages of anecdotes, gleaned from old retailers of gossip, but having told these, he offers a few lines of de Musset's verse, feeling the need of counteracting so much barren worldliness by the perfume of real poetry. After all, the critic is no very momentous creature. "You take a book, plunge into it, and forget yourself; you meditate upon it, muse over it and take pleasure in your musings; then a thought presents itself half unconsciously, an idea seems worth while, you wish to expand it, to complete it; your pen begins to run along, you grow at last industrious in pursuit of your ingenious deduction."

Such an attitude of itself engenders tolerance. When you converse with people, you are no longer at liberty to insist too dogmatically upon your point. They are perhaps enthusiastic over some recent poem; the critic replies that, "nourished if you choose on other faults," he cannot so greatly admire the passage. The praise once showered on

Du Bartas becomes for him a lesson in humility. Even when he condemns severely, he admits excellence. Although Sainte-Beuve's preference is always for the Attic, he could appreciate what was good in the Bœotians; no offense, for example, of Balzac, literary or personal, prevents the recognition of his talent. In literature, as in morals, it is enough that there be at least something in each person, individuals with sins but with virtues as well, being better than the merely neutral. Nor does Sainte-Beuve overestimate himself. To Mme. Olivier he writes, after much disparagement of contemporaries: "They have strength, but abuse it; I have none, hence am clear-sighted and sober." Even in his note-book, a long portrayal of the hypocrisy of Flourens concludes with the words: "Nevertheless, the merits of the learned scholar and of his works subsist." Does youth despise its elders? "Always and everywhere the old story of Saturn and Jupiter; the different generations, the closer they touch, the more inexorable they are and the more eager to deny, when they cannot devour one another. Being warned, let us at least make an effort not to act in this way." He was not a critic who aimed to overthrow the judgments of his predecessors.

"Our desires grow gray with our hair," is the epigraph to the essay "Ten Years After." The quotation, however, does not imply exhaustion, but maturity. Assailed by universal doubt, Sainte-Beuve answers with an unmistakable affirmation. "Art, like morality, like all kinds of truth, exists independently of success itself." Magnin is reproached because he does not definitely enough pronounce works either good or bad, and Dr. Samuel Johnson is praised for his good sense and particularly for his authority. To many, such praise seems strange, but we must remember that, in spite of his habit of qualification and insinuation, Sainte-Beuve really possessed authority. As early as 1835 de Tocqueville had written: "You are one of those the public likes to have before it to mark out the path for opinion to follow." Sainte-Beuve is continually pronouncing judgments, although these are not always, or even generally, handed down in the form of rigid decisions from which no appeal may be taken. His literary conscience was revolted by anyone who "diminishes or upsets distances" between estimable mediocrities and the truly great. A critical remark out of measure and proportion, the banal repetition of consecrated cant, any unreal and insincere appreciation irritated and pained him as a false note pains a musician. Without general theory, system or method, but guided by curiosity to observe things as they really are, he studied men and books according to their spirit. If he found a dominant point of view, so much the better; if none was offered, he did not construct an artificial outlook, but sought the personality, however varied and even inconsistent this might be.

Many would make every writer of critical essays a mere bundle of doctrines and processes, as though procedure and system had ever made a critic. Classification, in truth, is a mere matter of convenience; if it does not lie in the nature of things, it is not to be forced. What really constitutes the critic is the attitude of mind, reinforced by an immense literary experience; it is taste, "a lively, delicate, mobile sense that at every point raises a doubt anew and has no absolute belief in the results of logic." The first requisite is to have no program, but to follow practice instead. Sainte-Beuve is opposed to the spirit of system, whether liberal or reactionary. He is averse to catchwords and slogans: Romantic School—"I use this wretched expression merely for brevity." We realize, indeed, that he had a method, but it was a method of study, never a method of criticism.

As a case in point, take his attitude toward history, "the

clearest gain in our modern conquest.'' History, he asserts, is not a complete mirror or facsimile of past reality; it is an art, for, after all, every historian somewhat makes up and arranges his account of facts. Let the various schools live together in peace, for one type does not exclude all others. "Above all," he says, "I love the method of a strict, positive, inexorable mind, that enumerates and fixes the facts, the precise points, and says, 'Not a step further.' I know then what to abide by, and if I allow myself to speculate, I am aware that it is conjecture. I love also (reserving judgment) the method of an ingenious, bold, skillful, vivacious mind that ventures upon divination and reconstruction and makes me an associate in its fearless and learned adventures.''

A few quotations from notes, apparently belonging to this period, though published later, will indicate the character of Sainte-Beuve's theoretical reflections:

Let us be philosophers and even have a philosophy, but let us not insist on any particular philosophy.

How good it would be to introduce a bit of moderation, a corner of good sense and truth.

Beware of irony in pronouncing judgment. Of all dispositions of mind, irony is the least intelligent.

About criticism, I have two thoughts that seem, but are not, contradictory:
(1) The critic is nothing but a man *who can read and who teaches others to read.*
(2) Criticism, such as I understand it, and wish to practice it, is perpetual *invention* and *creation.*

What I have desired to do in criticism has been to introduce a sort of *charm* and, at the same time, more *reality* than had formerly been put into it, in a word, *poetry* and, with this, a bit of *physiology.*

I have only one pleasure left; I analyze, herborize, I am a naturalist of the mind. What I seek to build up is a *literary natural history*.

More than ever there is room for judgment based upon good taste, but no longer for rhetorical judgments. To-day literary history is made up like natural history by observation and by collecting specimens.

The existence of the *Revue* suggested the idea of portraits of contemporaries, which appeared as "Poets and Novelists of France," to which were afterward added "Critics and Moralists," "Critics and Writers of Literary History," "Modern Historians," etc. To these series Sainte-Beuve was merely one of the contributors, though by far the most prolific. Gaps in the picture of his own age are thus explained, for he never attempted a complete view. The great figures, the glorious monuments, up to his trip to Lausanne, are, however, all there, and many very subordinate figures are also found. Is this a fault? If so, it was intentional. "I am not one of those," says the preface of the second volume of *Criticisms and Portraits*, "who concern themselves only with the great; in many cases secondary men and works have for me a singular interest." They enable us to penetrate into obscure parts of the past, where, blinded by the great, we could not find our way.

In these portraits, both of contemporaries and of men and women of the past, the subject is never alone, but in the world, acting upon others and acted upon by them, carried in the stream of time and in the main flood of general humanity. Behind the personage is a background of innumerable details, never mentioned perhaps, but which color every statement or reflection. The facts presented are felt to be a mere selection. Contradictions there are, but such as do not falsify the general view, and this view is not a mere assemblage of fragments, but a composition, a product of intuition exercising its magic upon facts.

Underneath every essay, moreover, after 1835, stands the solid basis of *Port-Royal,* a subject now so continuously in Sainte-Beuve's mind that not an article escapes some contact with it, and in many it becomes dominant. The studies for each essay, too, leave a residue that is apt to come forth in some succeeding piece. Read a year's production in chronological order, and you can see how each study adds to the author's wealth, fragments of which get revived as occasion suggests. If George Sand has been the main subject today, she reappears tomorrow in a discussion of Mme. de Staël; Mme. Swetchine reappears in a talk on Lamennais; the Troubadours and Trouvères in that on Jasmin or on Bernardin de Saint-Pierre. Bayle shows himself so frequently and for so many years that we cannot doubt his vast influence on Sainte-Beuve, and La Rochefoucauld is hardly less persistent.

There was, furthermore, no barrier separating his social experience from his experience in books, and the one was no more vivid than the other. He sees de Maistre and Benjamin Constant in their letters that he took such pains to unearth, just as clearly as he sees Fauriel or Daunou or Nodier, with whom he had been personally associated. No source of information was left untapped. For de Barante, for Ségur, for Mme. de Rémusat, he had access to family papers; for de Maistre and Fauriel he supplicated Collombet to supply forgotten facts; for Daunou and Nodier, he drew upon his own familiar intercourse with his subjects. In his own opinion, whatever he did, whether consecutive investigations or scattered studies, whether hours given to society or to the street, to bores, beggars or secret appointments, he was reading but one book, the book of the world and of life.

Not infrequently he used his information in a way that

244

caused discomfort. He had an uncanny gift of finding in some obscure pamphlet or newspaper article, in some forgotten letter or conversation, hints that give significance to passages conveying to others no message. Even the family and intimate friends might be surprised and angered by his revelations. Full of curiosity, holding nothing back, seeking truth rather than adulation, Sainte-Beuve was a portrait painter who did not please sitters wishing to be represented with conventionalized dignity or beauty. The sitter, too, was often an involuntary accomplice. A distinguished friend might any morning experience the painful surprise of finding in the *Revue des deux Mondes* an unflattering, though rarely unjust, estimate of himself, wherein appeared traits that he had done his best to conceal, together with anecdotes, often enough exchanged in private talk, but, if written, generally reserved for posterity. We like our idols perfect, and get wrathful when defects are pointed out, the more wrathful the more undeniable the defect. An outcry would at once burst out against the *malignant* critic, if not from the subject himself, surely from family, disciples and camp followers, the rage being prolonged for half a century or more by eager partisans. Such frankness about contemporaries may be of questionable taste, but it is far different from malignity. Very often Sainte-Beuve strove to mitigate the unpleasant effect. Of his article on Nodier (1840), he wrote Labitte: "May it seem exact to others, without displeasing him." In many other cases he had less heed for susceptibilities and portrayed for "minds capable of bearing the whole truth without taking it the wrong way or turning it to abuse." What he called *oral criticism,* the free talk of contemporary society, seemed to him more real than the factitious elevation of academic eulogists. Under his very eyes he had seen the men of his age brightened up, denatured or transfigured for the benefit of posterity. Knowing these men well, he saw that they did queer things and mean things, and yet were possessed of wonderful talents and even of greatness of character. Aware that such is the way of the world, he examined and reported the facts, without much anger or prejudice. Doubtless he accumulates disparaging anecdotes around persons whom he dislikes, but when there is occasion for praise or compliment, he never lets it slip. When, in a portrait or criticism, the bad characteristics alone are noted, or when these are so overweighted as to distort the impression, we may say that malignity has been at work; but not a single such case can be found in any complete essay of Sainte-Beuve. If he adds many disparaging remarks to his portraits of Lamartine, de Vigny, Hugo and de Musset, he still writes: *"Le Lac, Moïse, Ce qu'on entend sur la Montagne, La Nuit de Mai*—it is thus from afar, I imagine, that Posterity, the great shepherd with the summary glance, who sees naught but the peaks, will enumerate the princes of poetry in our day.''

Occasionally Sainte-Beuve undertook a definitely polemical article, but in such work his talent was less engaged than his passions, and we feel that others could easily have done as well or perhaps even better. ''I care little for satire,'' he once wrote. ''Certain Truths on the Literary Situation'' (July 1, 1843) continues the expression of dissatisfaction already noted, complaint of the general lassitude, the retreat of critical groups to politics with consequent anarchy in literary judgment, the exaggerations of imaginative writing, and the cupidity of industrialism resulting in immoral and depraved fiction. ''I have never said so much of what I have thought,'' wrote Sainte-Beuve to Olivier, indicating further that Lamartine and Balzac had been in his mind, though unnamed; but the article apparently made no noise, the plaint having been too often iterated. Indeed, almost all the regular critics of the

Revue utter, in one way or another, these same reproaches. Far more vigorous is the refutation of Fremy's disparagement of André Chénier, an attack which Sainte-Beuve seems to take almost as a personal affront, the judicial critic for the moment forgetting himself in his irritation. A few months later (February, 1845), he is so aroused and revolted by the fanaticism of a biographer of Victorin Fabre that he pronounces the writer's judgment a literary enormity. Though willing enough to allow a moderate quantity of illusion to personal friendship, Sainte-Beuve, who had followed Fabre's course at the Athénée in 1822, cannot pass over this worshiper's exaggeration in praise of the idol and in condemnation of Villemain and other competitors. What he says in this case, however, is strictly within the limits of just, if perfectly outspoken and a little overheated, criticism.

In January, 1843, Olivier became proprietor of the *Revue Suisse,* published at Lausanne, and from February of that year to July, 1845, Sainte-Beuve sent his friend a fortnightly letter, or group of letters, sometimes to be published without modification, and sometimes to be edited before appearance, retailing the literary, theatrical, political and religious gossip of Paris, the subjects that all Paris talked about, the *dada,* as Sainte-Beuve calls his news. Here we have the observer's oral criticism in the form of free talk, so free, indeed, that he often dispatched a second letter modifying some exceedingly frank statement, and at other times he indicated that the matter was for his friend's confidential information and not for publication. Once or twice Olivier's judgment concerning what he gave out was at fault, and he then received a sharp reproof, followed almost immediately by an apologetic explanation.

To Sainte-Beuve distance in space was somewhat equivalent to distance in time, and foreigners were a sort of present posterity, so that what might shock the proprieties in Paris might perfectly well be published at Lausanne or at Liège. That his own convenience, that is, avoiding offense to people he had to meet or who might be useful to him, entered into the calculation is not to be doubted, but it was not often the main point, this being rather a question of what seemed to him good manners. When in the humor, he gave offense right and left, regardless of intimacy, rank or station, but when he took time to reflect, he always preferred the mode of courtesy, even with enemies.

Distance from Paris, then, seemed to Sainte-Beuve as did distance in time, to allow a freedom of speech that propriety forbade to one likely to meet his subjects every day. What was false he could call false, what was puerile puerile, without circumlocution or compliment, even were the perpetrator Chateaubriand himself. As a matter of fact, Paris being sufficient unto itself, no one in the capital read the *Revue Suisse* or knew of its existence, excepting when, now and then, Sainte-Beuve quoted from it his own words as the opinion of a well-informed foreigner. The subject-matter of his communications ranges from the interminable debates on the freedom of teaching to the cat that appeared on the stage to spoil a scene in *Judith,* from Lamartine's political vagaries to Mme. Dorval's remark to the undemonstrative Ponsard: "You are like a hen that has laid an eagle's egg." Here, as in his acknowledged essays, Sainte-Beuve never forgets the merits of distinguished men when pointing out their faults. He discusses literary quarrels, a row in the Chamber, the pilgrimage of a body of legitimists to London, the big pay given to Thiers and Sue as an example of the commercializing of literature. The competitions for the Academy are the Parisian equivalent for Spanish bull-fights. When he himself is elected, he chronicles the fact and, on the occasion of his reception, he sends Mme. Girardin's uncomplimentary article and then, while trying to be equitable, he appreciates M. Sainte-Beuve's speech more highly than Victor Hugo's. Yet Hugo's eulogy at the burial of Delavigne a year or so earlier is lauded without restriction: he was "never better." In this undress, we certainly have an indisputably sincere Sainte-Beuve.

One of the topics prominent in these *Chroniques Parisiennes* is the revolution in public taste indicated by the failure of Hugo's *Burgraves* and the success of Ponsard's *Lucrèce*. Almost at the same time Rachel's genius had put new life into Racine, leading de Musset, for it was he who celebrated her triumphs in the *Revue,* to suggest the revival in translation of the actual tragedies of ancient Athens. As we have seen, Sainte-Beuve had already gone back in good earnest to his Homer. Virgil, Horace, Cicero, Quintillian and Pliny the Younger had never ceased to be his daily companions; now he added to the treasures of Rome the treasures of Hellas, and particularly the epics of the Father of Poetry, Homer, whom he is never weary of citing. Far removed from the faded classic allusion of convention, here the heroic myth or the ancient maxim is summoned forth with such freshness and imaginative appropriateness that each becomes in effect as original and novel as though the dew still lingered in the petals of some unplucked and untrampled flower.

Ampère, making a trip to Asia Minor in company with Mérimée, sent to the *Revue des deux Mondes* (January 15, 1842) a descriptive article in the form of a letter to Sainte-Beuve. Here, in the course of a profession of faith in beauty as understood and rendered by the Greeks, he said:

You, a critic so delicately inspired, you who, with a stroke so rapid and so luminous, penetrate every conception of the mind, all the secrets of sensibility, all the by-ways of the imagination and the heart, you I have seen ever more and more taken by Greek beauty, rising to Homer through Ronsard and André Chénier, poets who, after all, are of the same family. Proceed, my dear friend. This antiquity, so often burdened and travestied by false interpretations, will deliver into your ingenious and dextrous hands her most hidden riches, her most exquisite pearls.

Biographers of Sainte-Beuve are apt to speak as though he alone had changed, while the other members of the Cénacle had stood unmoved under the same banner; but such a view is obviously distorted. In many cases the poets proceeded to exaggerate, instead of correcting, their faults, and the new recruits, who are most favorably represented by Gautier, exceed all bounds of reason and common sense in their audacity and contempt for precedent. They "act as though everything were born with them and they were to inaugurate the future." Gautier himself likes to upset received opinions and make people stare at his irreverence, but a writer with such brains ought to get along without tricks of this sort. Tradition is "a thing essential and truly sacred in literature." It thus becomes the duty of sane criticism to call a halt. The old excess had been conservative; the new excess was reckless innovation.

As a result, the public had grown weary. Glutted with repulsive episodes from medieval chronicles, it craved another kind of novelty, and this craving was gratified by a return to abandoned fields, by dramas taken from Livy, and by a revival of Racine so marvelously interpreted by Rachel. The classic reaction was thus legitimate, but a just observer will refuse to see in it more than is actually there. Sainte-Beuve does not overestimate Ponsard's *Lucrèce,* whose author was scarcely emancipated from school. The play, indeed, is not classic, but a sort of application of André Chénier to the stage. As for the Romantics, their greatest failure had been their assault on the theater, where they had produced nothing worth while but *Hernani*. In this piece there had been at least movement, hope, poetry, replaced in later efforts by the gigantic, by false history, and by excess in sentiment and passion. *Ruy Blas* was "an omelette stirred by Polyphemus"; the *Burgraves* "are marionettes from the isle of the Cyclops." Sainte-Beuve had looked for a drama to rival that of the age of Louis XIV, and he had been keenly disappointed. The critics had built a bridge for the innovators of 1829, but those who crossed over were not a civilized army, but a horde of barbarians. To discover what good taste could do with medieval dramatic subjects, we must go to Manzoni.

The foregoing are "oral" judgments from Sainte-Beuve's *Chroniques Parisiennes*, representing a sort of irritated revulsion, such as seized upon him in the presence of anything false and stilted, whether Classically formalized or Romantically monstrous. Such revulsion, indeed, was but one form of a general contrariety of disposition, which needed some scandalous book ready on the table as an antidote to an overdose of elevation.

When I have read something very lyrical, he says, or heard and applauded something very academic, when I have been present at one of those parliamentary triumphs in which the factious orator has laid his hand on his heart, in which the self-interested and versatile politician has been prodigal of the words loyalty and country, and when each has made his magnificent bow to the lofty lights of the epoch and the conscience of the human race, I open, on coming home, my Grosley, or some book like it, my *Journal de Collé*, my *Margrave de Bareith*, and after having read a few pages, I find a foothold on the earth fit for our humble nature, saying under my breath to the honorable, eloquent, illustrious speaker: "You lie."

When Romantic hyperbole, losing its freshness, became as conventional in its way as the old stilted Classicism at its worst, Sainte-Beuve's taste turned to simplicity and

251

order. In matters of style, the "Asiatic," always obnoxious, became more and more unendurable, and the only pleasing type was at last the pure "Attic," urbanity even in rusticity. The power of the French seventeenth century grows upon Sainte-Beuve. A writer abandoning himself to his tendency does not attain the supreme work of which he is capable; he needs a rigorous sense of duty; Boileau is realized to have been the literary conscience of his age. The unmatched masters of perfection, however, are the ancients. "That phrase of Pindar," he writes in a notebook, "over two thousand years old, is as fresh as on the first day: Truth and freshness."

How deeply Sainte-Beuve meditated his classics is shown in the frequent quotations and references in the essays—text as well as notes—quotations that often not only embellish and interpret the subject, but flood light over the original itself. Napoleon, for example, working on Daunou's anti-Roman prejudice to induce him to write an ungenerous attack on the captive Pope, an attack which place or money could not have purchased, gives occasion to this reflection:

Many honest people are like Sleep in the fourteenth book of the *Iliad;* when Juno tries to seduce him to sink Jupiter in slumber, she offers him a fine golden throne, and he refuses; she then offers Pasithea, with whom he is in love, and he forgets all, he yields.

Does not Homer at once become for us an unexhausted mine of priceless and radiant gems?

When a translation of the *Iliad* appears, Sainte-Beuve, in an article in the *Débats,* makes the book "a pretext to stop and bow down before the great figure of Homer." "Antiquity alone," he says, "gives to criticism the true law of taste, gives to the writer the true secrets of style, the sane and severe procedures that serve as a guarantee even for innovation and audacity." Shakespeare and Dante are not wholly free from rust; Corneille and Racine are too close by. "Antiquity alone gives in a certain sort the proper distance and the breadth of angle necessary to measure elevations correctly, and to guide us by the stars." Yet Sainte-Beuve, the literary man, and by no means a philologist, defends Aristarchus for tampering with Homer's text, on the ground that the voice of taste must always be heard. On the other hand, he looks at the heroic age directly and as something wholly real; on the authority of a practical expert, the greatest of his kind, Napoleon, he is assured that Homer had actually taken part in war, erudition in this case weighing less than a feather against the judgment of a soldier. Both these procedures, the appeal to taste and the appeal to experience, are combined in almost every essay written by Sainte-Beuve in this post-Romantic period, and an ancient poet or orator is for him as full of life as the man across the street.

Both taste and a sense of reality are apparent in the recognition of gradations in merit among writers and periods of antiquity. Sainte-Beuve feels his perfect insufficiency to discuss the authenticity of the odes of Anacreon, but accepting the judgment of competent scholars, he perceives the difference between an original and the imitations, the relation being akin to that between a statue and its replica. The imitators of Anacreon represent a sort of Greek Eighteenth Century. Fully recognizing the superiority of the highest genius, Sainte-Beuve also takes much pleasure in smaller men and forms. Homer stands unrivaled, and there are fairly numerous references to Sophocles and Euripides, but affection lingers on Theocritus and the Anthology. No poet is a greater favorite than Virgil, although the appeal of Horace is more intimate, more personal, more companionable. Among prose writers, while Cicero is declared the greatest of all men of letters,

Pliny the Younger supplies quite as many passages for quotation.

The classic comparisons are generally delightful. Fauriel's exclusive preference for the primitive in poetry is a little like the love of Ulysses for his *rocky Ithaca*. The vendetta in *Colomba* is equated with the antique Nemesis, and Colomba herself is found more truly classic than all the Electras of modern tragedy. When the critic answers the query why he should always be seeking something new, he finds the most appropriate phrase in the words of Ulysses to Alcinoüs: "I cannot bear to repeat to-day what was well said yesterday." Examples such as these might be indefinitely multiplied.

Articles devoted to classical subjects were at first intended for the *Débats,* which was especially the organ of the University; but two, those on Meleager and on the *Medea* of Apollonius (both 1845), formed part of a series of "Studies on Antiquity" appearing in the *Revue des deux Mondes.* In the first, we are taught to admire the grace, freshness and ingenious subtlety of the Anthology, of poets who wrote with an eye on the subject, who presented, not an ideal, but what they saw, something distinct, instead of vague and conventional. Sainte-Beuve, indeed, was fond of recalling that the Greek *I have seen* was equivalent to *I know.* With him, as with all genius, the basis is what Carlyle insists upon, the seeing eye; he perceives with sure intelligence the essential point, and also behind the written word, he discerns the human being. It is a power of vision based upon exact and extensive knowledge, as well as upon special talent. Just as Rembrandt's view of a countenance or Wagner's view of a Beethoven symphony surpass what can be seen by Smith and Jones, so in its more humble sphere did Sainte-Beuve's perception of an historical character or of a literary work.

The second of these classical pieces in the *Revue,* an

analysis with translations of a portion of a poem not too familiar, is, as a study of one of Virgil's sources, a sort of forerunner of the later lectures. For the *Débats* were written a review (1847) of a book on the Eclogue (with special reference to Virgil), and an article on the French School at Athens, praising the project and indicating its advantages, the original suggestion of such a school being elsewhere claimed by Sainte-Beuve as his own.

But far more attractive than all of these was the essay on Theocritus (*Débats,* November 11, December 2, 16, 1846). Think of opening your Wednesday morning newspaper and finding this masterpiece of literary charm! The tone is given in the first sentence: "Greek poetry, beginning with Homer and opening with him a long period of glory, seems to bring its course to a close with Theocritus; it is thus enclosed between grandeur and grace, and this grace, though doing the honors of the leave-taking, has lost not a whit of its entire and supreme freshness." Sainte-Beuve points out, translates and comments on the passages he particularly loves, as indeed he had done for Meleager and for what was significant in Apollonius, the translations being in effective rhythmical prose, and the comments not only associating most diverse literary periods —*Medea* and the *Princesse de Clèves,* for example—but detaching and illuminating the trait that gives character and distinction. Here is no pedagogue, but a genius, a genius in imaginative reading, who talks to us about his favorite Greek poems and invests us bountifully with his own appreciation.

"A fine day," reads a jotting in one of the notebooks. "I read Homer this morning and saw Mme. —— at four." Such days were, indeed, not unusual. Sainte-Beuve continued to read enormously, though often unsystematically and without definite object. He could not otherwise have attained his universality of taste and knowledge. In a late essay he says that de Tocqueville had not read enough at hazard and in the way of foraging; adding, "It is the good method." There were times, too, when Sainte-Beuve went much into society, accepting every invitation from four in the afternoon to midnight. Now he is absorbed in a volume of *Port-Royal* that he is finishing; now he is enjoying aristocratic social life at some château; now he is plunged in work on purpose to quiet gnawings at his heart. He has fits of discouragement, sulkiness, peevishness; he stays "like a rat" in his corner of the Institut, sees nobody, and is silent to all his friends, even the best. "The shameful wrongs committed against them he can no longer count; it is a sort of universal bankruptcy." In another mood he dines with George Sand and drives with her and Chopin in the Bois; a few months later he avoids her in order to prevent a break over communism and Leroux; less than a year passes, and he is again very fond of her and sees her often. There are also periods when he plunges into study as others take to drink, and during these short and frequent fevers, nothing else exists for him. He is always behind in his work, with more begun than he can accomplish. He wants six or eight months to complete *Port-Royal*. Over and over again, he complains of the distractions of Paris, cursed Paris, that grips one so, a life cut to pieces, drifting by chance, commanded by a thousand nothings. In Vaud are his regrets and his desires. Yet, however frequently he contemplates retirement to Lausanne, he cannot be lured away. There is, he says, a sort of poison about Paris that makes living elsewhere insupportable, though we imagine for an evening that some other place may be better. He has become sedentary, and has no desire for travel. Meanwhile, the same labor, the same distractions fill his days.

In accepting so many invitations, Sainte-Beuve met almost every prominent personage of his day, an indis-

pensable experience. He dined out a great deal; he heard
Rachel recite at private receptions; he was on familiar
terms with aristocrats like the Chancellor Pasquier, the
Countess de Boigne and the de Broglies; he visited cabinet
ministers, authors, priests, pastors, and scholars, as well
as persons of no social or intellectual pretensions. Of the
old *Globe* group, he continued to see Magnin, Ampère and
de Rémusat; though on less pleasant terms with his former
Romantic associates, he met them all, even Hugo, at various
gatherings, and one day he hunted up Émile Deschamps,
whom he had not seen for years; Mme. Récamier's salon
he still attended, though not assiduously, offense having
been given by the essay on Benjamin Constant and petty
disagreements having arisen with Chateaubriand. Sainte-
Beuve's notebooks give evidence in 1847 that he was a frequent guest, along with the eloquent Cousin and the loud-
spoken Royer-Collard, at the Sunday dinners of Thiers,
where everything was discussed but politics, and he has
preserved a number of remarks made on these occasions.[2]
But his most important social relations were with Molé and
his circle, Sainte-Beuve often visiting one or another of
the Count's country seats, particularly Champlatreux and
le Marais. The latter furnishes the setting of the *Fontaine
de Boileau,* and in the essays there are abundant recollections of incidents and conversations which took place in the
gracious and distinguished society that frequented these
houses. Like Horace, Sainte-Beuve was not averse to alluding to friends of whom he might be justly proud.[3]

---

[2] The first mention of these dinners is in a letter to Olivier,
May 27, 1840, but the dated notes in *Cahiers* and *Lundis* xi are all
for Sundays of 1847.

[3] A few scattered notes will give some notion of these social relations. After 1840 Sainte-Beuve met at dinners Mme. de Girardin
(Delphine Gay), whom he had not known in the Cénacle; in 1841,
he was at the house of Augustin Thierry to hear Jasmin read
l'Aveugle de Castel-Cuillé; in August, 1843, he spent ten days at
Molé's Château du Marais; in July, 1844, Pasquier, after presiding

It was Molé and his circle that chiefly supported Sainte-Beuve for the Academy. There was, as usual, much negotiation and intrigue. Théodore Pavie, who saw the critic making the customary calls to solicit votes, was so amused at his abnormal appearance as to write: "When he is dressed up, he looks like a schoolmaster or a country notary." After Hugo's election in 1841, Sainte-Beuve had looked forward to his own as likely in three or four years. There were moments when he ardently desired the honor; others when it was utterly indifferent to him; and there were even times when the annual stipend of fifteen hundred francs seemed the most attractive feature. In 1844, the chairs of both Nodier and Delavigne had become vacant, Mérimée contesting the first and Sainte-Beuve the second. The two joined forces and made a deal, offering in exchange for present votes for themselves enough future votes to assure the election of de Vigny to fill the next vacancy. Sainte-Beuve had much powerful support in the salons of Mmes. Récamier, de Broglie and de Boigne, his chief competitor being Vatout, royal librarian, with de Vigny a hopeless third, but holding enough votes to prevent a majority for either of the leaders. Hugo being antagonistic, Saint-Priest visited him to prepare the ground; then Sainte-Beuve spent an afternoon trying to win over both Hugo and de Vigny, with success, as he thought; and in the evening, Molé added his persuasion. The effort eliminated de Vigny, but did not win Hugo, who throughout voted a blank. On the first ballot in February, Sainte-Beuve received seventeen votes to Vatout's sixteen, with three blanks, and, as there was no majority, the election was put off for a month.

---

over the House of Peers, took him in his carriage to dine at Châtenay with Mme. de Boigne, and in September Sainte-Beuve spent some days with these two at Châtenay. A selection of such incidents gives us an impression of the intimacy of these relations, such as enables us to appreciate the wrench of the separation when it came.

As always in cases of practical unsuccess, Sainte-Beuve felt like giving up, but it was not easy to back out of such a situation. "While ambition is not in my nature," he wrote, "I got somewhat inoculated with it in connection with my candidacy for the Academy, enough at least to understand and feel it on a small scale." After further negotiations, de Vigny continuing to hold his three blank-vote supporters to the end, Sainte-Beuve was elected, March 14, by twenty-one against fifteen for the other two.[4] He writes Labitte that his mother is very happy and that he is happy himself; yet there came, as usual, a disturbing incident. The cross of the Legion of Honor, which he had refused in 1841, was again conferred upon him by Ville-main, and again rejected. When acceptance was urgently insisted upon, Sainte-Beuve, growing more and more obstinate, resigned his post as librarian (April 30) rather than "contradict himself publicly," as he said, but, as we suspect, rather than break a secret pledge. The affair was quickly adjusted; Sainte-Beuve remained at the library and received no cross, though the mark indicating this distinction was regularly appended to his name in the published Annual of the Institut. In later years he condemned such conduct, remarking in a footnote (*N. Lundis,* viii, 180) that it would be puerile for a man to refuse a title that had become an almost obligatory accompaniment of an official position.

As Hugo was Director of the Academy at the time of the election, it became his duty to receive his former friend. When, on account of delays on his part, the reception was postponed till February 27, 1845, there was no diminution of public expectation. Labitte, who reported the affair in

---

[4] Mérimée was elected at the same sitting and he came to Sainte-Beuve's lodgings to receive the news. In announcing this double choice, the *Revue des deux Mondes* (March 15, 1844) hopes that de Vigny, with his "glorious and incontestable title," will enter at the first vacancy.

the *Revue des deux Mondes* (March 1), described the séance as the most brilliant he had attended. In the first place, there was a certain spiciness in the circumstance that both Hugo and Sainte-Beuve would be obliged by academic precedent to praise Delavigne, whose writings were not exactly to the taste of either; and in the second place, Sainte-Beuve's defection from Hugo, both personally and in critical judgment, was notorious, though Mme. Hugo's part in the matter had not been divulged. There was consequently a lively public curiosity and a fashionable and distinguished audience crowded the hall of the Institut. If the hearers expected a battle, they were disappointed, for everything proceeded with the utmost decorum. What they actually received was an intellectual treat, both speakers being at their best for substance and handling risky topics with the utmost skill, while the rotund and vibrant organ of Hugo heard after the rather feeble delivery of Sainte-Beuve furnished such contrast as kept alive attention and satisfied the ear.

After the customary phrases of appreciation, the newcomer devoted himself wholly to Delavigne, a delicate task delicately executed. When he would express his wish that Delavigne, instead of yielding partly to the Romantic current had remained inalterably classic, he puts it as a query: What would have happened? Would not a rising tide have lifted him aloft? (Rachel and Ponsard were fresh in the minds of the hearers.) The critic's own view that the language of Racine will suffice, he ascribes to Delavigne, and without making a choice, he insinuates his belief by almost imperceptible turns of phrase. At another point, he lauds Delavigne for remaining a poet, and not spending his gift on politics (before the speaker sat Chateaubriand, Lamartine and Hugo), at the same time using terms implying admiration for the men of action. Sainte-Beuve's real view is then confirmed by a quotation from Horace:

"The one whom thou, O Melpomene, hast looked upon, will never be a victor in the games or celebrate a triumph on the Capitol, but he will win glory by verse born in the shade of a grove." Concluding with a beautiful tribute and with an account of the poet's funeral, at which Hugo had spoken for the Academy, Sainte-Beuve gracefully gives place "to that grave and eloquent voice, which represented you then, as it still does to-day, and to which the moment has come for me to yield."

Hugo, in turn, opens with a compliment—"it is dangerous to speak of Delavigne after you"—and then most adroitly proceeds, for almost half an hour, to evade his difficulty by praising the poet, not as poet, but as man: "His life was better than that of a philosopher, it was the life of a sage"; "he dedicated his intelligence wholly to his country, his soul wholly to his family"; antithesis, as usual, getting the better of the orator's conception. Coming to the ten minutes' praise of Sainte-Beuve, there is still excess: "Poet, in this age when poetry is so lofty, so powerful and so rich, between the epic Messenian and the lyric elegy, between Cassimir Delavigne, who is so noble, and Lamartine, who is so great, you have been able in a half-light to discover a path which is your own and to create an elegy that is your very self. You have given to certain effusions of the soul a new accent." As a biographer, Sainte-Beuve unites charm and erudition. "As philosopher, you have faced every system; as critic, you have studied every literature." Hugo speaks of a "mingling of erudition and imagination, whereby in you the poet never entirely disappears beneath the critic and the critic never despoils himself of the poet"; adding that Sainte-Beuve recalls Nodier. For the next twenty minutes, *Port-Royal* gives Hugo his great opportunity, his knowledge of the subject coming, as he confesses, from Sainte-Beuve's book. After this eloquent summary, the orator concludes with a glori-

fication of patriotism, which he attaches to one of Delavigne's poems.

It is doubtful if two opposite types of mind had ever
been so perfectly contrasted in any afternoon at the Academy. Sainte-Beuve's letter of thanks [5] to Hugo abounded,
as was fitting, in compliments, and Hugo replied that he
was moved and touched by the expressions. To his fellow-
expert, Reuchlin, Sainte-Beuve remarks that Hugo spoke
wonderfully of *Port-Royal* for one who had just learned
about it, though the recluses who read the Bible did not
really pay much attention to the sun and to nature.[6]
"But," he adds, "that is a Port-Royal adapted to the
Academy, *ad usum saeculi,* and it was a success."

In his account of the reception, Labitte naturally favored
his friend somewhat at Hugo's expense, emphasizing his
grace, delicacy and seduction, his amenity, measure and
good-taste. There was nothing commonplace in the speech;
it was one of the most charming ever pronounced at the
Academy and it evoked hearty applause. No fault is
found, excepting on one point: "If Sainte-Beuve refined
his thought too much, Hugo inflated his." From the
abundant testimony to the effectiveness of the new academician on this occasion, it will be sufficient to quote a
letter of Mme. Buloz: "His success was complete. Everything ingenious and brilliant in his charming speech was
deeply felt by an audience which, it must be said, was well-
disposed and prejudiced in favor of the newcomer."

During the early forties, Sainte-Beuve was constantly
complaining of ill-health. Doubtless he was really ailing,
but his chief trouble seems to have been hypochondria,
"organized decadence," as he called it. Thinking himself

---

[5] Hugo pinned this letter to a printed copy of Sainte-Beuve's
speech given to his wife.

[6] Hugo's phrase reads: They "meditated the sacred books and
eternal nature, the Bible open in the church and the sun abroad in
the heavens."

on the verge of death, he made his will (December, 1843) and began to put his literary affairs in order, a procedure which consisted in publishing a new edition of his collected poems (1844), in regrouping his essays into *Literary Portraits, Contemporary Portraits* and *Portraits of Women* (1844-1846), and in privately printing his *Livre d'Amour* (November, 1843). As indicating his feeling toward his work, it is to be noted that his first attention was given to his poems, which now at length were complete in the four parts, though one part was withheld from the public.

In 1829 Guttinguer had printed and privately distributed a volume of poems addressed to Rosalie and giving the history of their love, "true ideal of an imprint," says Sainte-Beuve (1836), "such as every amorous, delicate and disdainful poet would wish for his *Arcana cordis*." Another book which probably had some influence was Hazlitt's *Liber Amoris*. The English critic had been a personal friend of Stendhal. His works are often mentioned by Sainte-Beuve, who in 1831, it will be remembered, announced his forthcoming essays for the *Revue* as in the manner of Hazlitt, and who even fathered upon this prose writer one of his own sonnets as a translation. In form, the dialogues and letters of the *Liber Amoris* are utterly unlike Sainte-Beuve's verses, and the situations also resemble one another in no respect; but in both works there is presented, without a trace of reticence and with the actual localities and undisguised proper names, an irresistible, absorbing and fatal passion, subtilized at times into a sort of adoration.

The *Livre d'Amour* recounts in verse every important phase of Sainte-Beuve's relations with Mme. Hugo. At first, wholly absorbed in the great poet, he paid little attention to the wife; gradually the charm grew upon him, unperceived by her, and bringing forth on his part a resolve

of renunciation; finally, Hugo leaving the two alone together one afternoon, she let down her hair in her lover's
presence and his passion became so overwhelming that it
led to an avowal (VIII). Then followed mutual love, but
within the permitted limits of happiness. He wants of her
nothing but her heart (IV). What she loved was not his
real self, but a thought, her idea of him (XV). Kept pris-
oner by her jealous husband (a trait which gains credence
from Hugo's known treatment of Juliette), she laments the
necessity of burning her lover's letters (VII). The two
hold clandestine meetings in the woods at Les Roches, in
a church, on a bridge, one of these meetings being almost
prevented by Ballanche who insists on resolutely attaching
himself to the lover and talking endlessly about his social
philosophy. After Hugo's infatuation for Juliette, they
have more liberty (VIII) and even meet in a room (bou-
doir) in the old building of Saint-Paul (XXXIII) or walk
openly in the suburbs. At length the rupture is indicated
in an appendix of four pieces.

Sainte-Beuve speaks of caresses and kisses, but only two
pieces (XXXI, in a cab; XXXIII, in a room), neither of
which can be earlier than 1833, represent meetings anywhere but out of doors or in public places. In XI Sainte-
Beuve says: "Even when we most forget ourselves, you
have never known a caress or a word that has not respected
every point (*tout*); I from your love have never drawn
either vanity or pleasure of the senses (*volupté*)." XVI
(*à la petite Ad.*) has been often misinterpreted as claiming
for Sainte-Beuve the actual parentage of his godchild, but
he does nothing of the sort. The adultery of which she is
the fruit is mystical and the subtlety is clearly explained;
because the mother at the time of Adèle's conception carried the lover in her thoughts, the child had in her some
part of him, whereas her sister Léopoldine had not, being
all Hugo. However tenuous the idea, the statement in the

poem is plain, and there is no word against the legitimacy
of the babe. Judging from Mme. Hugo's physical condition after 1832, we may well consider not only this incident,
but the whole affair, a case of "spiritual adultery," in
harmony with the hair-splitting and mystical emotionalism
of *Volupté* and a few other autobiographical productions.
Morally, indeed, the question is idle, intention, even when
not tested by the Christ ideal, being here little less than
act; but psychologically there is interest in the reactions of
absolute, or nearly absolute sentiment and thought in the
heart of one who, by his own confession, had been "as
sensual as the brutish sting itself." [7]

Sainte-Beuve, indeed, scorched himself in the vulgar
blaze, and it made him suffer, but his idea of love was on
another plane. He blames Bayle for confounding libertinage and passion, and of a poem by Leopardi he says:

---

[7] Of the *Livre d'Amour* a number of pieces were published before
the book itself was put together: III, *Oh! que son jeune coeur*, appeared in the *Revue des deux Mondes* Jan. 1, 1830, with music by
Mme. Jules Menessier-Nodier; XXXVII, a version of Gray's *Eton
College Ode*, was inserted in the article on Mme. Guizot, May 15,
1836; XXIII, *Moi qui rêvais la vie*, formed a footnote to the article
on Du Bellay, Oct. 15, 1840, introduced by the words: "A modern
elegiac poet, an imitator of Du Bellay in writing sonnets, has curiously marked the difference between these two *ennuis* (i.e., *l'ennui
enchanté* and *l'ennui tracassé*), but at a time when he himself had
a Faustine to console him" (Faustine being the name of Du Bellay's
Roman sweetheart).

Of the other pieces, several formed part of groups published in
the *Revue de Paris* as follows: Oct., 1841, *Par un ciel étoilé*
(XVIII); Dec., 1841, *Si quelque blâme* (XXV); May, 1842,
Volupté, Volupté (XXII), *Que vient elle me dire* (VI), *Laisse ta
tête, Amie* (XXXI)—the piece quoted by Karr in *les Guêpes;* May,
1843, *Jeune, avide, inconnu* (XIV), *Oh! ne les pleure pas* (VII),
Triste, loin de l'amie (XXXIX), *Attendre, attendre, encore* (XVII),
Je ne connais (XIX), *Ode au soir*, Collins (XX). For VIII, the
first part of which belongs to 1831 and the last part to a later date,
Sainte-Beuve quotes in a footnote some verses from Molière, which
he had used in his essay of 1835. As XXXII, in which there is talk
of Hugo's infidelity, cannot be earlier than 1833, and as XXXVI
represents Sainte-Beuve as secretary of the Historical Commission
(1836), it is easy to assign an approximate date to nearly all the
poems.

"The flame of passionate desire reflected so vividly in the piece to Aspasia does not deserve the name of love." His relations with Mme. Hugo and later with Mme. d'Arbouville must therefore be distinguished from his relations with other women. In the essay on Leopardi just referred to, there is a significant passage on friendship. Those, it is said, who put themselves in relation with the great soul of the world by belief and prayer find peace and support. If, however, a human being cannot believe and hope, he is punished by aridity and desolation. But the noble and generous find a bitter consolation in the struggle itself and in their stoic resistance. If tender, they seek equivalents. What comforted Leopardi was faith in friendship. May we not add that Sainte-Beuve attempted to put his faith in love, finding happiness when he felt a full response, and consumed with bitterness when the response was diminished or denied?

As to his thought about the morality of the alliances he sought, a quotation from the essay on Fauriel (1845) will enlighten us:

Let us not forget that the standard of morality varies singularly according to epoch and country; and that the imagination of poets has always been apt to pervert this standard. It often happens that a poet grows so fond of his past, even of a painful, a lawless and a culpable past, that he becomes more and more attached to it in aging, that he cherishes it in remembrance, that at the risk of losing his reputation, he feels a passionate desire to transmit it, and has the weakness to sacrifice everything to this end. I recommend these considerations to those who have fathomed in some of its secret depths the moral nature of poets.

Many years later, in reviewing Fromentin's *Dominique*, Sainte-Beuve maintained that passion which has reached a certain paroxysm has no scruple, no present remorse. This regret may arise subsequently in certain souls, but at the moment of inward conflagration, it is smothered and counts for nothing.

Whatever opinion may be held concerning the ideas here expressed, we at least need seek no further for the motive that caused Sainte-Beuve to print his *Livre d'Amour*. Every indication contradicts the notion that the book was a malignant vengeance designed to disgrace Mme. Hugo. "To have been loved and sung by a true poet" was, on the contrary, an honor to any woman. Chateaubriand is even blamed for not naming in his *Memoirs* his mistress of 1829, Hortense Allart. As a human document, even apart from poetic value, Sainte-Beuve would prize the portrayal of a love in which there was conflict between what was "antique, fatal, violent," and what was "Christian, mystical and ideal." In his will, after carefully enumerating the copies in his possession, he leaves them all to Olivier with the express wish that the work be divulged after the deaths of Hugo, Mme. Hugo and himself. In spite of all his care, however, someone printed in 1843 thirteen clandestine copies for bibliophiles, and some stolen proofs also fell into the hands of a scandal-monger by whom Paris was treated to a sensation, all the more alluring because there was no open mention of names.

Alphonse Karr, author of a number of stories, one being a serial contributed to the *Revue* itself, was engaged in publishing from 1839 to 1849 a monthly periodical of some thirty pages made up of gossipy items entirely written by himself. This little periodical was called *Les Guêpes,* each item being preceded in the indention by the image of a tiny wasp, which indicated both the scattered nature of the subject-matter and its usual stinging quality. "We shall find amusement in measuring the pettiness of great men and of great things," said the first issue. The satirist, as usual, takes a lofty tone, but also, as usual, makes it a point to be disagreeable, indulges in obnoxious personal-

ities, mocks and insults his victims, and makes a constant
effort at smartness, which is, in the long run, tedious, particularly since most of the matters treated are of purely
ephemeral appeal. Alphonse Karr, moreover, does not pretend to the slightest modesty.[8] It must be confessed that
he is not personally as interesting as he seems to have been
to the author of *Les Guêpes*. In the main, the point of
view is sensible enough, and now and then a good anecdote
relieves the dullness. The press is a special field for mockery, both for its normal bad or dishonest writing and for
unintentional absurdities, such as Renduel's announcement
of Hugo's *Chats du Crépuscule*. Politicians, who occupy
the largest space, generally fare badly. Lamennais and
Cousin are despicably ill-treated, while Hugo is commonly
exalted, though he, too, receives warnings. As to Sainte-
Beuve, there is favorable comment on his appointment to
the library in 1840,[9] and there is harmless, if discourteous,
ridicule of his dress and personal appearance on the day of
his reception at the Academy. Reading the *Chronique
Parisienne*, one becomes subject to the illusion that Paris
was chiefly interested in the things of the mind; reading
Les Guêpes, one realizes that the salon may be merely a
glorified village sociable and the Boulevard but a pro-
longation of Main Street.

In May and June, 1840, there is in *Les Guêpes* much
abusive talk about Cousin, especially about the cheap din-

---

[8] When Karr wanted to join the staff of the *Constitutionnel*,
Véron refused him on the ground that he lacked the sentiment of
hierarchy; and Karr replied that he possessed this sentiment so
strongly that, whenever he and Véron might meet, he would feel
himself the superior. The authority for this story is Karr himself.

[9] In the *Livre de Bord*, where Karr vents all his bile, he tells of
a visit by Sainte-Beuve—June 18, 1840—in behalf of Cousin, to in-
vestigate the Colet affair, adding that Sainte-Beuve reported the
interview falsely to his own advantage and thus received his appointment to the library. Karr's lies are often so transparent that
they should deceive nobody. His unsubstantiated testimony is
worthless.

ners he gives as minister. The climax is reached in portraying his attitude in one case, that of "Madame C., née R., who has won a prize for poetry at the Academy."

Mlle. R., continues the backbiter, after a union of several years with Mons. C., has at length seen heaven bless her marriage;—she is about to give the world something different from an Alexandrine.—When the venerable minister of public instruction learned this fact, he nobly conceived his duties toward literature.—He did for Mme. C. what he will doubtless do for any other woman of letters in her situation.—He invested her with care and attention—he did not permit her to use any other carriage than his own. . . . He himself went to Nanterre to secure a nurse for the child of letters soon to see the light—and it is hoped he will not refuse to be its godfather.

When Louise Colet attacked Karr with a carving knife in front of his house, he affected surprise, since her name had not been mentioned in the article. It was the danger of just such excess of which Sainte-Beuve had given warning in his appreciation of the first issues of *Les Guêpes,* and the warning had been repeated by other writers in the *Revue.* No advice, however, had any effect on Karr. "One of those who listen at key-holes," the characterization in the *Chroniques Parisiennes* (May, 1844), well fits his disclosure of the *Livre d'Amour.*

A dishonest printer brought the editor some stolen proofs, presumably for pay. The same bait was offered, a few weeks later, to another editor, Arsène Houssaye, who received Sainte-Beuve's authorization (July 14) to make a thorough investigation and to get possession of as much of the material as possible. When, in the *Livre de Bord,* Karr gives his version of the affair, he unwittingly convicts himself of lying. The printer, he says, begged him to prevent the publication of a book that had, in fact, been in existence for eighteen months. This falsehood is followed by an account of a visit from Mme. Hugo, which is so preposterous as to do little credit to the author's talent as a romancer.

What was published in *Les Guêpes* was scandal, pure and simple, put in such form as to arouse curiosity and invite the violation of secrecy. "An infamy is preparing in darkness by a sanctimonious poet, a dreadfully ugly poet, who once in his life dreamed he was the lover of a beautiful and charming woman. To those who know the two, the thing, even if true, seems impossible. This frightful and self-complacent person, not content with the favors falling to him through some act of folly or despair, wants not only to possess a beautiful woman, but to dishonor her." The volume is described with enough inaccuracy to make it doubtful that Karr had seen all the proofs, and one poem (XXXI) is quoted.[10] After stating that the book was to be distributed only after the author's death, Karr concludes: "I hope that those who then read this dastardly work will find the man who wrote it even uglier than he was when alive. This book of hate is called by its author *Livre d'Amour.*"

No public notice could, of course, be taken of such an attack. Victor Hugo, in a rage, wrote a violent sonnet, which was found among his papers after his death. In a letter on this occasion to Mme. Hugo, Sainte-Beuve suggested that she might say: "All that is in the book I know, and I have long known it; it was written years ago; in a distant future, it can have no impropriety; but at the present, there is danger, and you, who are my friends, are the ones who make this danger." Obviously, then, the *Livre d'Amour* was no secret to the person most concerned and had met with no objection from her. She resumed friendly relations with Sainte-Beuve in 1849 and she never

---

[10] If Karr had seen a galley containing this piece and the following one, he could, with a little help from the printer, have gained all the information his article contains.

came to Paris from her Guernsey exile without seeing him. The one effect of Karr's vicious article seems to have been to diminish Sainte-Beuve's precaution about absolute secrecy. He distributed a few copies of these poems among trusted friends, the known recipients being the Duchess de Rauzan, Mme. Allart and Paul Chéron, though the date is uncertain. Had not the episode made so much inane noise in the world, and had not so many biographers accepted Karr's virulence for truth, the matter would be worthy of no more than a passing mention. One valuable result, however, is the confirmation by a contemporary letter of the truthfulness of Sainte-Beuve's statement that the *Livre d'Amour* was known and approved by Mme. Hugo. There seems, therefore, little reason for posterity to grow abusive on the subject. On the other hand, Sainte-Beuve's high esteem for these pieces remains one of his few aberrations of literary taste, though he does remark that they manifest "lack of open air and sunlight."

His numerous relations with women during the forties could not be disentangled, even were the task worth while. Two or three objects of his inclination, however, must be mentioned.

In January, 1841, George Sand invited Sainte-Beuve to dine or spend the evening with her, for he would there find Mme. Allart, "overflowing with wit, erudition and life." This lady, Hortense Allart de Meritens, had been the mistress of several distinguished men, including Chateaubriand and Lytton. For a few months, in 1843, she also experimented with marriage, but found a husband an unendurable despot, and gave it up. A wide reader in Latin, English, Italian and French, she wrote a shelf full of books on philosophy, history, religion and politics, as well as some novels, and she met and corresponded with an extensive circle of literary men and political leaders. Her affection for Sainte-Beuve seems to have been earnest

271

and self-sacrificing. In her letters, she makes love to him, flatters him, scolds him; is in turn tender, serious, mocking, coquettishly jealous of the blond Marie d'Agoult and of unnamed others; sometimes she is full of admiration for his writings, and again she will raise lively objections and heap blame upon something that displeases her. In this vivacious chatter every sort of idea and argument on books and affairs is flung forth helter-skelter; she is clever, positive, stimulating, often sensible, and even at times a good critic. She characterizes Sainte-Beuve as the "Plutarch of men of letters," complains of his secrecy about his inner self, calls him interesting, amiable, melancholy, seductive, disinterested and sincere, speaks of his sweetness followed by sudden coldness, fears the vivacity of his feelings, and remarks: "It takes little to irritate you." If she had not destroyed Sainte-Beuve's replies, we might, from this correspondence, have obtained a fairly complete portrait of him. Obviously, however, he was not moved to the depths. One fact gleaned is of special interest. When, in the course of the essay on de Maistre, we are astonished, in spite of his disclaimer, at Sainte-Beuve's exact knowledge of Bacon, a glance at the letters of Hortense shows that he had just been reading the English philosopher with her at Herblay. Inevitably literary, he seeks his honey from every flower, and even love-making becomes a handmaid of the critical pen.

Sainte-Beuve's passion for Mme. d'Arbouville, niece of Molé, was more absorbing, for, though this affair seems to be pervaded by a literary reminiscence, the relation of La Rochefoucauld and Mme. de Lafayette, it is not for that reason less deeply felt. Here we find the spirit of René, what he did not have appearing more desirable than any actual possession, the unattainable furnishing an invincible attraction. In the few letters preserved, Sainte-Beuve speaks of his ardent, sick, weary heart, complains of the limitation of the lady's affection, a feeling without abandon; reason, always reason; not a cry, not a thoughtless, unrestrained word; nothing but flowers to one who longs for fruit. These complaints are found in the unfinished *Clou d'Or*, the *Golden Nail of Affection*, a title whose meaning is explained elsewhere as "to possess, toward the age of thirty-five or forty, if it be but once, a woman one has long known and loved." Mme. d'Arbouville's letters are sensible and affectionate, but unyielding. Sainte-Beuve breaks off the relation, caresses solitude and sadness, sinks into lassitude, but always comes back. It is a real feeling, but, as usual, he stands aside and studies it, giving the impression of something artificial, sentimental and diseased. At one point, he ascribes the lady's reserve entirely to selfishness, to a desire to be passionately loved and still to preserve her good fame before the world. "Mme. Récamier, Mme. de Maintenon were of that wretched race; I have always hated them": a phrase recalling the note on Mme. Hugo, "I hate her." This is a bitterness and irritability, however, that does not last. The love for Mme. d'Arbouville, indeed, was, in depth of feeling, second only to that for Mme. Hugo, and there was never a third of this kind. Here again there was some mingling of religion, the lady being designated in Sainte-Beuve's will to receive his favorite and much-read copy of the *Imitation of Christ*. For her, too, were probably destined two pamphlets of poems that he printed at this time. Though mysticism was dissipated and youth was past, Sainte-Beuve still, when his emotional nature was disturbed, clung to expression in verse. In this case, there was no permanent breach. During an interval between the Liège lectures, Sainte-Beuve hurried down to Lyons for a last visit to Mme. d'Arbouville, who was slowly dying there of cancer.

One further affair of the heart will conclude, if not exhaust, the list for this period. At one time, Sainte-Beuve was tempted to offer himself in marriage to the fragile, almost angelic Ondine Valmore, who was teaching in a private establishment near Paris. We have pleasant pictures of the great critic playing rhyming games with the little schoolmistresses, helping them with their Latin, or enjoying Ondine's translations from English poets.[11] Disproportion of age, combined with his own unfitness, doubtless led to the relinquishment of this project. Ondine married a lawyer and deputy in 1851, and died of tuberculosis two years later. Sainte-Beuve's letter to the bereaved mother is one of those expressions of tenderness and sympathy whose perfume does not evaporate with time. He had always loved and admired Mme. Desbordes-Valmore, his introduction to her *Poésies Choisies* is one of his most exquisite essays, and she, in her turn, wrote of Sainte-Beuve's kindness toward her and of his generosity and compassion toward the poor and suffering: "I do not believe that anyone performs greater services than he, or more nobly forgets them. . . . I have twenty letters blessing him, from unfortunates whom I have asked him to help . . . and, in addition, giving, always giving." Such words, like the tear of Stern's angel, tend to efface the record which justice feels obliged to make of Sainte-Beuve's manifold and often humiliating faults and weaknesses.

[11] Her translation of Cowper's hymn, "God moves in a mysterious way," is a fine rendering.

CHAPTER IX

1840—1849

SAINTE-BEUVE was at this time on rather close terms with Cousin, though there were disagreements and antagonisms. Lamartine's political activities he found highly objectionable, in spite of his constant admiration for the poet. With Chateaubriand he continued his amical relations, yet the strain is at times visible, and there was a sort of polite quarrel with Mme. Récamier over an article on Benjamin Constant. Labitte, a very close friend and willing helper, died suddenly in 1845. When the Oliviers came to live in Paris, there arose some irritations, but the friendship was not broken, though gradually cooling in later years through diversity of interest. As to his mother, Sainte-Beuve's affection was normal and practical, but not effusive. The essays in the *Revue des deux Mondes* continue, Sainte-Beuve being the most copious contributor to that periodical. Among the notable portraits are those of Joseph de Maistre, Benjamin Constant, Daunou, Fauriel, Naudé, Leopardi, Thiers and Mignet. Much of this work, even of the highest type, was occasional, and not on subjects selected by free choice. Some groups of poems, mostly of earlier composition, were published in the two *Revues* from 1841 to 1843, the last piece of importance being *La Fontaine de Boileau*. Though Sainte-Beuve now practically ceased writing verse, he yet retained in his prose many of the characteristics of the poet, a feature which lends vivacity and nobility to his writings.

The academic votes promised de Vigny were delivered according to contract; he was elected in 1845 and received in January, 1846. His speech of reception was intolerably long-winded [1] and empty, and Molé's reply took the form

---

[1] In the collection of *Discours*, it runs to thirty-six pages, the average for these years, 1840-1849, being from twenty to twenty-five. De Rémusat's, however, on Royer-Collard, extends to forty.

of a contradiction and refutation, severe enough in print and rendered still more severe by the manner of delivery. The reporter for the *Revue des deux Mondes* was Sainte-Beuve, his article being a masterly example of that intermingling of roguishness and serious intention which the French call *malice*. In order to counter a previous jejune article by de Molènes, which will be discussed further on, he opens with a review of the history of academic receptions, alluding, as though unintentionally, to the fact that the eighteenth century speeches lasted but a half-hour. He then praises de Vigny prodigally, at the same time insinuating in unmistakable manner that the poet has completely misrepresented his subject, M. Étienne. A portrait of this writer follows, as a corrective to de Vigny's exaggerations; and Molé's speech, incidentally called a half-hour speech, is praised in almost every particular. While generous in acknowledgment of de Vigny's lofty and truly poetic nature, Sainte-Beuve indicates how a poet may avoid the world's accusation of extravagant dreaming, this being the critic's usual mode of hinting a weakness. The only direct objection, indeed, is that the new academician had remained in a rut, producing works ''in which he has not ceased to represent, under one form or another, the thought that preoccupies him, the fixed idea of discord and conflict between the artist and society.''

We, upon whom that speech was not inflicted, can readily preserve our serenity, and the devotees of de Vigny may hotly accuse Sainte-Beuve of malignity, but to contemporary sufferers it must have seemed that the critic had administered a delicately sugar-coated pill and that a perfectly natural impatience had been, not only tempered, but made the servant of uncommon suavity and wit. Several footnotes, published subsequently, emphasize de Vigny's self-esteem and tediousness, qualities which grew upon him with years, but such personal peculiarities are never allowed even in the slightest degree to diminish appreciation of his poetic gifts.

In Sainte-Beuve's treatment of distinguished men, most of whom had at one time or another been his personal friends, we must distinguish between the essays as originally published and the notes added to these essays or printed in separate collections, the essays being official and ceremonious, the notes being "oral" literature, of which the critic was so fond. However the sensitive might squirm, he seems in the essays to have kept within the limits of propriety, the one exception being his review of Hugo's *Chants du Crépuscule;* in the notes he allows himself almost as much freedom as though he were talking in private. Personal animosity is not usually the motive for the revelations, for he is just as free in dealing with authors of the past, always enjoying a discreditable incident that gives life and reality to the portrait. At the present day, we have got so used to intimate disclosures that those of Sainte-Beuve seem mild in comparison. They certainly are interesting, and often a little anecdote is told with a skill that even Thackeray might be glad to match.

This period (1840-1848) was the time of Sainte-Beuve's closest intimacy with Cousin, Minister of Public Instruction in the cabinet of Thiers and, till the Revolution, Grand Master of the University. Such disproportion in official station led Karr to call Sainte-Beuve Cousin's lackey, but the accusation is a libel. The deference of the more humbly placed man was perfectly normal, and his public compliments to the "eloquent" and "charming" writer were repeated in the *Chroniques Parisiennes* and in private notes. At the same time, Cousin's faults of character were not passed over, and on one occasion at least (July 12, 1842) independence was vigorously asserted. The outburst, for which Sainte-Beuve had perfectly just cause, was occasioned by the publication in Cousin's volume of miscellanies of the *Pensées* of Domat and the letters of Mme. de Longueville, both of which Cousin knew Sainte-Beuve was about to use in his *Port-Royal*. The letters, indeed, had come to Cousin from Sainte-Beuve himself. "Poaching on my preserve and killing my game without remorse," is the phrase used to Olivier. With perfect measure, but with biting severity, Sainte-Beuve writes Cousin a statement of the wrong committed against him, a wrong of which he himself would never be guilty, even if he had the power. "When I say that man is not free," he adds, "and that I do not believe in freedom of will, it is because I know well enough that you are not free not to do these things and to resist the force of your appetite. Although I have put myself under obligations to you in an important matter, durable in its consequences and impossible to forget, I need not for that reason bear this lack of regard, this unfair procedure which, in your eagerness, will doubtless not stop here; I wish at least, man to man, to utter my complaint and tell you that I resent your action." Some compliments at the close cannot mitigate the rigor of the reproof. No jotting in the notebooks is more outspoken and severe.

If we remember that Cousin was not only all-powerful in the University, but that his veto meant exclusion from the Academy, we can appreciate Sainte-Beuve's heedlessness in the face of what he considered an affront. For many persons, great and lowly, he performed services, but he was never a lackey and never much of a schemer. Cousin, on his part, does not seem to have taken offense. He once replied, Sainte-Beuve reports, to some complaint of ill-treatment: "I think I am at bottom as delicate as another, but I confess that I am a bit gross in form." At any rate, the two remained for some years close friends, although their relations grew less courteous after 1852. The notes added to *Port-Royal*, while invariably deferring

to Cousin's talents, are often disparaging, either directly
or with a happy touch of malice. One of these accompanying a passage on Mme. de Longueville's lost beauty,
refers to Cousin's sentimentalism over the matter as
"these regrets of a smitten swain"; but perhaps the neat-
est stroke is the following: "Mme. de Sablé has been the
subject of a brilliant study by M. Cousin; my humble
medallion can therefore have only one merit, to be exact
and drawn from the original."

Another defiance of authority which we cannot help
applauding occurred in 1846. The publication of a manuscript on the death of Louis XV, prepared by Sainte-
Beuve for the *Revue des deux Mondes,* was prohibited by
Salvandy. The critic printed it privately and sent a
copy to the minister, with a letter, in which he inflexibly
defended his rights and his dignity as an author. The piece
was included in the *Portraits littéraires* (1849) after the
censor had fallen.

In one of his essays, Sainte-Beuve distinguishes between
the men who gain in reputation through politics, Guizot,
for example, and those who decline, such as Cousin and
Villemain. In the first case the political career is a complement to the natural exercise of a talent; in the second,
it is a diminution and dissipation. Such loss was especially prominent in poetical talents like Lamartine and
Chateaubriand. Once, after quoting the complaint of
Duplessis-Mornay about the degradation of his talent in
affairs, the critic remarks: "Eternal complaint of all men
of letters involved in politics, which nevertheless does not
hinder them from doing everything in the world to get
ahead; and once involved, they never get out."

Sainte-Beuve's regrets over Lamartine's abandonment of
poetry for politics are unceasing. Considering him, moreover, an agitator without fixed principles, he even writes
Olivier (1843) that he is crazy, as well as a bit ambitious.

In jottings of 1848, the opinion is expressed that Lamartine provoked the Revolution so that he might shine as a hero; the whole movement showed history imitating literature; and an instinctive motive was talent seeking its field of action. "Whatever his faults," adds the commentator, "he condoned them all by his conduct in a moment of peril: he had then a moment that was sublime, heroic, immortal." The subsequent failure of the great leader is seen as a complete loss of prestige. "If he could only have vanished like Romulus on the evening of his triumph, what a historic and legendary figure!" Sainte-Beuve certainly "sought nothing in Lamartine but the poet"; there must be in his essays something like a hundred expressions of admiration for the elegiac genius, as well as a score in which he regrets the abandonment of the precious gift.

With Chateaubriand and Mme. Récamier Sainte-Beuve's relations were so continuous that he was under considerable constraint as a critic and, in spite of great caution, there were occasional disagreeable episodes. In the essay on Mme. de Rémusat (1842), a quotation from this lady's autograph-book brought forth a denial from Chateaubriand that he had ever written the passage, in spite of the fact that Sainte-Beuve possessed the signed document and had taken pains to compliment the distinguished author, who "introduces grandeur even in the midst of his grace." A more serious matter was the publication of the correspondence of Benjamin Constant with Mme. Charrière (April 15, 1844), which led Mme. Récamier to instigate Loménie to refute Sainte-Beuve's estimate of Constant's character, a refutation which was in turn answered politely enough but with resolute firmness (1845). The dispute was continued in later years by Louise Colet, to whom Mme. Récamier had bequeathed her papers, and, in a lawsuit over these, an uninformed advocate declaimed conventionally in court about Constant, much to the irritation of the critic. When Chateaubriand published his *Life of Rancé*, Sainte-Beuve, who had to write of it in the *Revue des deux Mondes* (May 15, 1844), abounds in admiration for the veteran who had stood for half a century at the head of the literature of the age and from whom everything in the imaginative vein had proceeded; but when he comes to the book itself, he renounces his task as critic to gather flowers along the way, and then treats the life of Rancé independently, here and there quoting Chateaubriand. Of these quotations, the most important, a passage dealing with letters, particularly an imagined series of love-letters, makes it clear that Chateaubriand embroiders upon his austere subject, emptying every sort of emotion into what should be simple and serious. By this means the critic allows the reader to judge what he himself could not venture to condemn. Anonymously in the *Chronique Parisienne,* Sainte-Beuve calls the work a piece of *bric-a-brac* and notes that the author's lament for his lost youth betrays a "lack of positive moral inspiration and faith." It is as though La Trappe opened on the green-room of the Opera. He can here also speak directly of negligence, while in the *Revue* a gross blunder is referred to as an inadvertence.

Sainte-Beuve never lost his admiration for the genius of the author of *René,* but his study of the sober writers of Port-Royal tarnished a good deal of Chateaubriand's glamour, and made his Christianity seem but superficial glitter alongside of so stern a faith and so rigorous a practice. After the sonorous phrase, objections still survive. The picturesqueness of a mass recited on the deck of a ship or in the ruins of a temple, the vague emotions in a Gothic cathedral are not of the same religion as the austerity of a Saint-Cyran. It is at bottom this contrast which leads Sainte-Beuve to doubt the reality of Chateaubriand's religious faith, so that this much-discussed view is, like almost all the fundamental tendencies of this period, to be directly ascribed to the study of Port-Royal. Even in the essay on de Maistre (1843), Sainte-Beuve had already maintained that Chateaubriand had remained to the end the man of his first book, the *Essai sur les Révolutions.*

Certain external variations in the relations of the two may be traced in letters to Olivier and Collombet. In 1838, Sainte-Beuve says: "The quality of his talk is good sense, but when he writes, some demon gets in and causes an explosion. I have heard him say so himself." A few days later, the critic speaks of a flattering mention of himself by Chateaubriand in his essay on Fontanes, a favor which binds him to the adroit man "with a silken knot and a golden collar," but he adds: "I am not used to living and moving in shackles." In 1843, he reports that Chateaubriand has returned from a visit to the ex-king in London an *ultra,* not only because he had been flattered, but because he had received a large sum of money. "Horrors! let us know the fact, and bury it." In 1844, he has to speak of *Rancé* "even in the very mouth of the lion, but the lion has no longer any teeth." His meaning he will make clear without failing in respect to his Majesty. In 1845, Chateaubriand has returned from Venice in wonderful condition, but the next year he fell while stepping into his carriage, and in 1847, he is mute and dreaming, he smiles and weeps, the broad forehead in repose. "What is in it and beneath it? Is there anything?" This abstraction continued in 1848, yet Chateaubriand said to Béranger: "Well, you have your republic"; to which Béranger replied: "Yes, but I had rather dream of it than see it." There has been so much objection to Sainte-Beuve's statements about Chateaubriand's mental decline that the testimony of Mme. Lenormant may be welcome. She says that Mme. Chateaubriand got her husband to sign anything she wanted, for, "as his memory was gone, he did not know what he was doing." He, however, recognized Mme. Récamier (July 1 and 3, 1848), and after the last sacraments (July 6), he did not speak another word.[2] In this case as in others, Sainte-Beuve's statements are at any rate not gratuitous. It is safe to say that he never invented a fact or made a totally unfounded assertion.

To make an approximately complete mention of Sainte-Beuve's friendships, even of those that were comparatively intimate, would exceed all reasonable limits. Some attention, however, must be paid to Labitte and to the Oliviers.

Labitte's devotion to Sainte-Beuve is sufficiently shown in an account of his friend's academic reception and in a laudatory review of the new edition of the *Tableau* (*Revue des deux Mondes*, September 15, 1843), signed Lagenvais. A graceful writer from the age of sixteen, he began at twenty to insert critical and learned articles in the *Revue;* he acted for some years as professor of foreign literatures at Rennes, then supplied the place of Tissot as professor of Latin poetry at the Collège de France, and died of lassitude, apparently worn out by study, at the age of twenty-nine. In spite of difference in age, Sainte-Beuve found in this youth a kindred and a helpful spirit. He asks him to note the blunders in the *Tableau* in view of the new edition; from Lausanne he requests of him numerous researches in Paris for the lectures; and he freely acknowledges his debt to him for helping the erudition at the foot of the pages of *Port-Royal*. The two were in frequent correspondence, and on Labitte's death (September 19, 1845), Sainte-Beuve pronounced a eulogy over his tomb and prepared a portrait for the *Revue* (May 1, 1846), which opens and closes with the heartfelt expression of affectionate admiration and regret.

---

[2] *Memoirs of the Countess de Boigne*, vol. iv, appendix.

The friendship with the Oliviers, ardent as it was at first, became subject to fluctuations, and at the end simmered down into that sort of half indifference which is induced by diverse occupations and interests in a metropolis. In 1842 Mme. Olivier came to Paris with literary aspirations. She seems to have believed, as others did, that Sainte-Beuve had only to speak a word to get her stories and poems accepted by the *Revue*. He did his best, but Bonnaire and Buloz, the proprietors, rejected the offering, and the lady returned to Lausanne in a state of discontent. An article by her husband, on "The Intellectual Movement in Switzerland," was finally published (May 15, 1844), but it is undeniably dull and of inordinate length. Olivier, good, earnest provincial, convinced of the importance of his subject, had not the Parisian touch, and could not acquire it from his friend's admonitions. The revolution in Vaud (February 14, 1845), which Sainte-Beuve called "a brutal triumph of force and gross cupidity over intelligence, justice and liberty," drove the Oliviers to Paris, at the same time that it demolished the critic's dream of an idyllic retreat on the Lake of Geneva. Very soon Mme. Olivier flared up at some hasty remark of Sainte-Beuve about her husband's incapacity, but the irritation was soon assuaged by Olivier's good sense and forbearance. It was while on his return from reading a chapter of *Port-Royal* to these friends, that Sainte-Beuve accidentally met Lamartine after his great speech at the Hotel de Ville (April 16, 1848). Lack of identical interests caused them later to drift apart, but to the end they corresponded at rare intervals and were glad to meet when occasion offered.

Sainte-Beuve's affection for his mother, while not demonstrative, was real and sufficiently dutiful. That she is absent from so much of the published correspondence is not surprising, considering the persons addressed; in the letters to Collombet, Labitte, the Oliviers, and of course Barbe, references to her are frequent and show filial feeling. To the reasons already given for the son's living in an apartment by himself—a possible political conspiracy and the desire to escape service in the national guard—may be added the necessity for uninterrupted concentration on literary work. As Mme. Sainte-Beuve rented her unoccupied rooms, such seclusion would have been at least difficult in the home. In 1857 the son wrote:

I was never a happy child. . . . My mother loved me as much as any mother could, and out of her pitiful income [3] she made all possible sacrifices for my education. I responded as best I could. . . . I did not live with her; she loved me in such a way that we could not get along together; she wanted to absorb me too much; and I was independent and rebellious. I went to see her almost every day and dined often with her, and she visited me in spite of her advanced age. She never flattered me to my face, but liked to talk about me with others and to hear me praised. In short, our relations were as happy as our characters would permit.

The mother was proud of the son, and, as it was her ambition to see him in a fixed position, she was delighted at his appointment to the library and his election to the Academy. When Sainte-Beuve was inclined to resign his post at the Mazarine, where he was bothered by customers "like a retail grocer behind his counter," the thought of his mother's impatience intimidated him. It was largely on her account that he did not seek refuge in America in 1848; from Liège he journeyed to Paris several times to see her; in her last illness, he cared for her both as son and nurse; and at her death (November 17, 1850, aged eighty-six), he felt absolutely solitary and without any real tie in the world.

---

[3] 4,000 francs.

Of all the members of the Academy, Sainte-Beuve was probably the most meagerly provided for, and, though of economical habits, he appears to have been chronically short of funds. It was partly to supply this deficiency that he wrote so prodigiously for the *Revue des deux Mondes*. In the table of contents published in 1848, the titles of his contributions for the preceding eighteen years fill two closely printed columns of small type. No other writer is within measurable distance of him, the nearest being Ampère, Blaze, Charles and Lerminier, each with about half the quantity. We are rather surprised, therefore, to read in Sainte-Beuve's letters his not infrequent self-reproach of idleness. He seems, indeed, to have practiced the well-known journalistic maxim, never do to-day what you can put off till to-morrow. His article on de Vigny's reception was published within five days of the event, unprecedented rapidity for a magazine of that time, and most of his essays were completed within a fortnight, often within a week, though in a few cases they had been meditated for years. We can well understand, therefore, that overwhelmed at times by fatigue, he almost succumbs under the pressure of his occupations.

The combination of rapidity of execution with ripeness of meditation gives a peculiar freshness to these products of a well furnished mind. Complaining to Lebrun in 1867 about delays in sending proofs from the Imprimerie Impériale, he writes: "How can I put any warmth into completing an article from which I have been separated for a fortnight and which has got well cooled off?" Sainte-Beuve, moreover, had already acquired excellent journalistic sagacity in discerning and seizing every aspect of novelty and current interest that his subjects might offer. This appeal being essential to success, he was never absolutely free in choice of topic, for, though whatever he might write was assured of publication, he held this privilege only on condition of not abusing it. His productions, therefore, are as unsystematic as his studies, the subjects being suggested occasionally by his own desire, but more often by circumstances, a book to review, the acquisition of interesting unpublished papers, or the appearance of some volume that needed a biographical introduction. "Mornings, I study well enough," he writes, "I have always had so little freedom of choice that it makes little difference what article I write, provided I do it well." In fact, there is no criticism of the incompleteness and disproportion of his work that Sainte-Beuve has not himself made.

The *Revue* had a practice of publishing series of essays, the most persistent of which was that on "Poets and Novelists of France." To this series Sainte-Beuve had contributed extensively, and it is here that we find his studies on the Romantic group, youthful portraits painted by a youth. In 1843, he said: "The time has come to do over what has aged, to take up again what has changed, to show decidedly the grimace and the wrinkle, where only the smile was once perceived, to judge at length without flattery, without depreciation, too, and after the decisive experience of a second phase." The new series thus announced was begun by Lerminier with essays on Mme. Sand (1844) and Victor Hugo (1845), and these bore the sub-title proposed, *Second Phase,* but Sainte-Beuve himself never fulfilled any part of his promise. He tranquilly continued the old group, adding No. L, *Parny* (1844) and No. LI, *Desaugiers* (1845).

This final piece is charming. The praise of wine and revelry, the history of gay dinners from the days of Marot to the Caveau, the love of hilarious song, these things seem to proceed from a veritable bacchanalian. When the expression *in a literary sense* escapes the critic, he exclaims: "Sober, profane, academic word, I cannot sufficiently beg pardon for it in such a subject." Incidentally Béranger is generously praised, though it is noted that he used his high spirits for a purpose. Above all, the sweet character of Desaugiers, the last representative of French gayety, is portrayed with loving touches. Though the jovial singer has fallen into the hands of one who least of all has the happiness of resembling him, this serious student will yet pour "milk and honey, and even a little wine, upon his tomb." Thus a series, begun in youthful Romantic ardor, closes with an appreciation of Epicurean levity, the former enthusiast having cooled down into an observer who appreciates even those phenomena which are most alien to his own disposition and habit of life.

Without much regard to the several labels, "Critics and Moralists," "Critics and Historians," etc., which indeed often get mixed in their numbering and have to be straightened out in footnotes, we might group a few of the more important essays according to epoch treated and occasion for writing. One collection, which by itself would form a fair-sized volume, deals with the transition from the eighteenth century to the nineteenth, these essays being on Joseph de Maistre (1843), Benjamin Constant (1844, 1845), Daunou (1844), and Fauriel (1845).

Fulfilling a promise publicly made in 1837, the essay on Joseph de Maistre (July 15, August 1, 1843) had been meditated for over seven years. The delay was caused by persistent efforts to secure from Collombet and his associates personal information and the possession of rare early works. By means of such material, Sainte-Beuve is enabled to explain the apparent suddenness of de Maistre's appearance as a thinker, to substantiate his connection with the eighteenth century, to show the effect upon him of local experience of the French Revolution, and to accumulate intimate touches that bring out his physiognomy. In some respects the "theocratic theorist," the "aristocrat-magistrate," positive, intolerant, averse to revery, perform-

ing incredible exploits of reasoning and constantly shocking historical exactitude and impartiality, cannot be a
sympathetic figure to the critic, yet de Maistre was always
magnificent, a great writer, a master of style, and, apart
from his books, socially amiable and charming. Much of
his severity is ascribed to his fourteen years of isolation
at Saint Petersburg. "In his habitual desert, he did not
know how loud and piercing his voice was, for there were
no echoes to reply."

When de Maistre's correspondence was published in
1851, Sainte-Beuve returned to the subject, and though
his treatment manifests the stride he had taken from these
portraits, already so exceptional, to the easy mastery of
the *Lundis,* the new material does not substantially modify
his judgment. The haughty writer, systematic, pitiless,
intolerant, provoking anger, is, on the other hand, sincere,
cordial and humane, a superior and charming personality.
Again, in 1860, after praising Schérer's vigorous refutation of this author's political and philosophical doctrines,
Sainte-Beuve, with a confession that he is always doubting
and repenting, comes back at last to the note of admiration
for de Maistre.

It is true that his own treatment of this author in *Port-
Royal* had been severe, almost rough. The difference of
procedure is, however, explained in this essay of 1843:

When I make a portrait of some personage, and just as long
as I am making it, I consider myself somewhat as a visitor in his
home; I try not to flatter him, but at times to humor him a
little; I envelop him with attentions and pay him a sort of deference, so as to make him talk, to understand him, to allow him
that indulgent justice which generally arises only from close contact. Once this task is accomplished, I find myself again out of
doors; I am in a position to express myself more freely, remembering always, if possible, what I have already said and what my
previous judgment has been, but I speak louder, if necessary,
and in whatever tone the fresh encounter may inspire.

Here we surprise the secret of certain contradictions between one essay and another, or between text and notes, such contradictions resulting simply from a literary etiquette which Sainte-Beuve had devised for his own guidance.

The essay, "Benjamin Constant and Mme. de Charrière," signed in the *Revue* with a row of stars, was occasioned by the acquisition of some correspondence, and in the table of contents the letters were said to have been "communicated and annotated by E. H. Gaullieur." Sainte-Beuve was not by this means trying to hide his share in the transaction, which, indeed, no one acquainted with him could fail to recognize, but he actually considered his part in the publication merely that of editor and arranger. He, as a matter of fact, put so much confidence in Gaullieur's notes that a number of errors crept in. The tone, however, is all his own. Observe the ominous opening reflection, that it is "instructive to contemplate the man in undress and before he became a personage, to discover the secret and original fibers . . . to study the character in its very nature on the verge of the rôle." The judgment on these beginnings of Constant's qualities in literature and politics, emphasizing the mockery under his seriousness and the aridity under his sentiment, gave offense, as has been seen, to Mme. Récamier, of whom Constant had been an adorer, and she inspired answers to the article. But Sainte-Beuve was a dangerous man to attack. It was a principle with him that a writer must know more about his subject than he is willing to print, so as not to be led into deceptive statements, and in this case, he himself knew much about Constant which he had withheld until provoked to publish it. As we find from his letters, he had throughout suppressed Constant's indecencies. Now that Loménie has made him an adversary, he will not seem beaten. In "A Last Word on Benjamin Constant" (No-

vember 1, 1845), though highly complimentary and wishing
that he might agree with the circle his opponent represents
(Mme. Récamier), Sainte-Beuve nevertheless publishes a
further letter, which settles the case. Notes appended
after Mme. Récamier's death confirm his contention that
Constant employed wit and mockery to cover a lack of dignity and real feeling, and that there was a crying contradiction between the serious orator, sincere in support
of liberty, and the scoffer in society, a contradiction which
is explained by the letters of his youth. Whatever we may
be willing to excuse in a statesman, we have a right to
demand seriousness, while in Constant too large a part of
the man parodied the rest. The critic does not blame; he
observes.

Nothing could be more characteristic than this controversial piece. When sure he is right, Sainte-Beuve will
not retract or give himself out as vanquished, but will
stand his ground against all antagonists, even Mme.
Récamier; and he will fill his essay with allusions which
are perfectly obvious to one who knows the inside history,
but which look to the uninitiated like ordinary pleasant
compliments.

Daunou, Sainte-Beuve had known and visited for twenty
years, and with Fauriel, too, he had had personal, though
in this case not intimate, acquaintance. Both represent a
transition, the first holding more firmly to the critical and
historical views of the eighteenth century, and the second
being the most influential propagator of the tendencies of
the new age. In dealing with Daunou, the portraitist,
while passing over many details in a varied career, ex-
pands on the moments that paint the man, and, though a
friend, does not omit the "wrinkles and warts." The resulting image bears every evidence of reality. When we
come to Fauriel, it is the scholar, rather than the individual, that we contemplate, the scholar who, twenty years

ahead of his time, enamored of origins and seeking in all things the primitive, inoculated, more or less in private, the most distinguished minds of his day with new ideas in historical, critical and literary method. The whole development of Fauriel is presented in his relations with distinguished people, the school of Auteuil, Mme. de Staël, Constant, Villars, Cabanis, de Tracy, Baggensen, William Schlegel, Guizot, Thierry, and above all, in his relations with his closest friend, Manzoni, this friendship giving Sainte-Beuve occasion for a long digression on Manzoni's plays, pieces that make one blush for the French Romantic drama. The continuous and varied studies of Fauriel—Greek, Arabic, Italian, German, botany—take one's breath away. As to the writings, they are a trifle heavy, and the scaffolding seems inseparable from the monument; but these faults are apparent to all, and the critic insists rather on the inward and unostentatious merits. In regard to Fauriel's disputable theories, Sainte-Beuve sagely remarks: "Having no personal opinions of my own in such a matter, I confine myself to sketching in general terms the state of the question." The essay, thus saved from becoming a contribution to an antiquated and outgrown chapter of scholarship, retains its vitality in spite of time.

Many essays are purely occasional: it may be a review of some new publication, such as the charming piece on Louise Labé, the appreciation of Mérimée's *Civil Wars*, the portrait of Gresset, based on two volumes packed with fervent admiration for this minor poet and abuse of the Romantics, an admiration which Sainte-Beuve in an amused way finds "touching because it is disinterested": or it may be an introduction to a volume of letters of Mme. Roland or of Mlle. Aïssé,[4] or to the prose poems of Aloysius

---

4 Here we come upon a Mme. du Gravier of Orleans who supplied material by correspondence. We shall never know all Sainte-Beuve's relations of this sort, but each new discovery of a batch of letters increases our wonder.

Bertrand, or to a story of Töpffer, the introduction in each case being a loving portrait; or it may be something of quite temporary interest, a revival of *Bérénice* or of Lebrun's *Marie Stuart,* or a play by Scribe or Augier, or a story by Sue or Gogol, even the least of these having some touch of superior skill in the selection of salient episodes that bring the essence of the thing before us. Three times Sainte-Beuve reported an academic reception, and each time the purpose was to honor his patron Molé, the first occasion for compliment being naturally that on which Molé himself was received (1841) and the others being gatherings over which he presided, the receptions of de Vigny and of Vitet (both 1846).

Being in the Mazarine Library, Sainte-Beuve hunts up the lives of his predecessors, and thus comes upon "the first man with the soul of a librarian," Gabriel Naudé, who served Richelieu and Mazarin, an author whose style like his books is covered with cobwebs, a formless polyglot writer, yet a moralizing skeptic under the mask of a scholar, and worth the trouble which acquaintance with him entails. Labitte had attempted a resurrection, but this was hardly noticed. Naudé had long "entered into the darkness of those libraries he had so much loved and which were to be his tomb," yet he was so thoroughly revived by his successor at the Mazarine that he became for a time almost a familiar figure to cultivated Parisians. Sainte-Beuve takes a humorous pride in his bibliothecal ancestry, not stopping at Naudé, but going back to Callimachus, Apollonius and Varro.

Although admitting that criticism is of value only when applied to what is thoroughly known, Sainte-Beuve was induced by access to certain manuscripts lent by Sinner, a German friend of Leopardi, to write on the Italian poet an important essay embellished with translations. Some versions are given in rhythmical prose and others in couplets, the former being highly effective, while the latter are diffuse, though accurate enough, Sainte-Beuve himself modestly noting that his verse is rather a paraphrase than a close translation, a plaster cast in place of the original. The whole career of Leopardi is sympathetically followed, his skepticism being treated as "a natural and necessary progress of his thought, a somber and harmonious development of his talent and his character." He is the last of the ancients, arrived in the world too late. From another point of view, he is also a sort of "incredulous and atheistical Petrarch."

A study of Thiers (January 15, 1845) supplements the earlier *Globe* essays. Here the qualities of the historian are sought especially in his earliest writings, prize essays and journalistic and descriptive pages. In all may be found the alert, vigorous, fertile brain, together with a style vivacious, brilliant and fresh; the man thinks for himself and shuns declamation. Sainte-Beuve's own manner catches a sort of nervous animation from his subject, for he still not infrequently reflects the qualities of the author he is treating. Thiers makes us love the French Revolution, and he makes his critic vibrate with patriotic fervor. A postscript, based on the advance sheets of the *History of the Consulate*, is wholly enthusiastic. As to general principles, Sainte-Beuve combats, as usual, the idea of fatality in history, maintaining that any one of a thousand accidents could bring about an entirely different outcome. Suppose Napoleon drowned coming from Egypt, he suggests a few years later, or Chateaubriand dead of fever near Naumur; what a nineteenth century! The same opinion is emphasized in an essay on Thiers' friend, Mignet (March 15, 1846), who had fixed for the new generation the outline of the French Revolution. While admitting that history is an *art* and can be conceived only as the result of method and of a definite point of view, the

critic yet observes too much system in Mignet, a symmetry
of mechanism not found in reality, violating verisimilitude
and seeming too well arranged to be true. As an aside,
we may note the remark, not to be taken too seriously,
that all politicians are liars and that the unscrupulous are
commonly successful.

From the foregoing discussion, it will be obvious how
much Sainte-Beuve obtained from sources not accessible to
other biographers. He comes fresh from the dinner table
of Thiers or from a visit to Molé or Pasquier, or from the
salon of some lady who had been a girl under the Old
Régime; he recalls Mignet's and Fabre's lectures at the
Athénée in 1822, or Talma's *Han!* in place of the *Ah!* in
a former performance of Lebrun's *Marie Stuart*, or any
number of journalistic encounters, of which he might, if
so inclined, say *Pars magna fui;* he devours files of fifty-
year-old newspapers, hunts up the grandson of an
eighteenth century belle, writes in all directions for a scrap
of correspondence, a forgotten pamphlet, or a college record or reminiscence. Hence those vivid strokes by which
these portraits come to life and step out of their frames
to converse with us; hence, too, the actuality of the background, a past epoch vitally present. As there is more
reality in a collection of portraits than in a formal historical painting, so such informal essays seem to us more
effective than the connected history, and we recover a
richer territory from oblivion by these separate incursions
than by any regular invasion.

Sainte-Beuve, indeed, did not love details merely for
themselves, nor did he care for documents simply because
they had never been published. In every case, he sought
only the significant. With all his insistence upon accuracy
of detail, what he relished was, not information, but life.
Generally respecting the man of arid fact, he is yet sometimes amused at him.

Each branch of erudition, he says, is guarded by rather surly dogs; these are appeased, not by throwing them honey-cakes (beware of honey!) but by first offering some little dry stones. When they have digested a few of the stones, they say it is all right, and let you pass, even with your ideas, with your treasure. Once by, you need no longer bother with them, but proceed to join the clever people on beyond.

When he finds that a great historian has completely mis-judged the present, he imagines such blunders transferred into the past—one of those great discoveries, entirely new, and the more sure since no one can contradict. To Sainte-Beuve, on the contrary, life and experience replace the rigid methodology of the investigator. Formulas he has, but they are so flexible that they never distort the object to which they are applied, and in turn they are themselves never splintered by resisting surfaces upon which they cannot be forced to fit. Space and freedom are provided within a limited plot, and also sun and air and a soil fit for growth.

How often, too, in these portraits, along with the main personage, we get a glimpse of some entirely inconsider-able, yet interesting character! The retired lawyer who, though ignorant of Greek, devotes his last years to reading a Latin translation of Aristophanes and writing a com-mentary on it; the learned scholar "found seated in tears on the floor of his study in the midst of a thousand little pieces of paper, amongst which he was more undecided than the hero of Buridan"; Laënnec, distinguished physician, enthusiastically piping Breton airs on his flute to match the words of ballads recited by Fauriel; M. Cassat, former friend of André Chénier and publisher of a Parisian jour-nal, now shut up at Lausanne with his musty folios. know-ing his La Fontaine better than any editor in the world; each in his own way is alive. On other occasions, there may be offered a single incident that makes a person sud-

denly real; as in the case of Nodier, grown feeble, suddenly
at the entrance of the Institut recollecting the name of a
mountain that had momentarily escaped him and shouting
it vociferously to Sainte-Beuve already disappearing at the
further end of the double courtyard.

An additional element of vivacity is frequent metaphor
and comparison, not merely decorative, but illuminating.
The fact that Du Bartas is still read in Germany and Scandinavia may in itself be a mere dull fact, but not as thus
expressed: "His reputation is still found to-day freshly
enough maintained there, like those tropic elephants
wrecked, we know not how, and preserved amid the snows
of the north." One more characteristic example may be
quoted out of a thousand: "The Greeks had Homer on
their horizon, the Italians have Dante; an immense vista.
Our own distant horizon is a line flat enough. . . . The
age of Louis XIV easily remains, so far as language is concerned, the limit of our world: the hill has an admirable
contour, but it is rather close by."

In such images we perceive a surviving trace of Joseph
Delorme. We note also the statement that the subjects
selected for the portraits always had in them an element
of poetry or, at least, of charm. But, in the main, the
poetic youth was dead. To Guttinguer Sainte-Beuve
wrote in 1842: "Sad end for a poet; I was very little of
one; only for a season or two, and while youth sang
within." To himself he says: "I early lost, not my fire,
but my wings." The flower passes, the perfume, the grace
of sentiment. "Every elegiac poet must have felt bitterly
that it is not life, but youth, that is short." Even in 1846,
while commenting on the reasonable critic he has become,
he still loves and regrets his poetry.

Some years earlier (1843) he had portrayed the progress of this decline in those for whom criticism is a prelude and an ending:

Young, they have dreamed of literary glory in a form more brilliant, more ideal, more poetic; they attempt the lyric arena or the theater, they propose under their breath that which shall yield the triumph on the Capitol and the true laurel; or perhaps it is the novel that seduces us and summons us; we wish to dwell in the tenderest hearts and to be read by the most beautiful eyes. But miscalculations ensue, hindrances in the career, failures of talent, dull and obstinate refusals. We grow weary and, if we truly love literature, if solid knowledge has not ceased to increase and grow more delicate in the midst of the trials, and indeed by means of them, we are then prepared to enter what I call in a very general way criticism, that is to say, some branch of literary history or of the appreciation of literary works. Here it is that I generally await the youthful newcomers, so eager at the outset and so proud. Let them succeed in art and poetry, if they may; all our best wishes go with them; but on this point little advice may be given. Such palms are seized with main strength, and are not subject of discussion. Should the young men fail in the first object of their ambition, should they have bad luck in this first love, and if yet, having good brains, they sincerely cherish study, there is for them a resource and a consolation. Their return, even without any triumph, may have its charm; salvation is found in the shipwreck itself.

It was at the moment these words were written that Sainte-Beuve ceased publishing verses in the magazines. A group of *Poésies* had appeared in the *Revue de Paris* in October, 1841, and another group, *Imitations en Vers,* followed in December. The next October (1842), he added *Stances d'Amaury,* and in May, 1843, *Stances et Élégies tirées du portefeuille d'Amaury.*[5] Then in the *Revue des deux Mondes, Maria* (April 15, 1843) and the *Fontaine de Boileau* (September 1, 1843). This last, one of Sainte-Beuve's most accomplished productions in verse, describes the visit of a party from Count Molé's country place, *le Marais,* to the spring in question, a visit that offers occasion for literary reflections.

---

[5] These are all omitted from Michaut's bibliography.

Though the same law of beauty always rules
The form of talent varies with the time;
The poet molds to suit our present taste
A stuff eternal, ancient yet new born.

Here occurs also the celebrated recantation of the early repudiation of Boileau:

"O thou, whose law I dared one day and one alone deny." All these pieces are either incorporated in or added to the collections already published, and a goodly number, especially of the Amaury poems, belonged, as we have seen, to the *Livre d'Amour*.

Although Sainte-Beuve practically ceased to write verse, he retained in his nature enough of the poet to preserve him from a sort of deterioration to which the professional critic is especially liable. There come to both individuals and communities certain moments of high emotion and high thought which cannot be artificially produced and which cannot be indefinitely prolonged. These may be falsified by two kinds of parody, simulation and scoffing skepticism. Both were obnoxious to Sainte-Beuve. For simulation of high feeling he had an unerring perception, a really irritable sensibility, of which his defacing of "idols" was but one manifestation. Those critics, however, who prick the inflated bubble of simulation, are peculiarly subject to the other extreme, the mockery that destroys all faith in the reality of the high moments themselves. It is one of the features of Sainte-Beuve's true superiority that in him this faith remained unshaken. The occasions on which he yielded to the temptation to speak slightingly of anything actually earnest or lofty in human emotions or ideas, far as such might be from his own, are so few that they may properly be disregarded. He might smile, rather sadly, at outgrown enthusiasms, but he did not, with one or two exceptions, scoff at them. This perpetual honor paid to what is really exalted in man, exalted even when a trifle absurd, keeps the reader on a high intellectual plane; the vulgar—inevitable concomitant of our condition—appears as vulgar, the artificial is discriminated from the true, and the noble, whatever its flaws, is adequately admired for its superiority.

CHAPTER X

1840—1849

IN spite of his devotion to the *Revue des deux Mondes,* Sainte-Beuve had two serious quarrels with Buloz, the first in 1842, over an article on the Academy that offended his aristocratic friends, and the second in 1846, over the purchase of a share of stock. In both cases, he ceased contributing to the *Revue* for a time, and during the interval, published a few articles in the *Débats,* mostly book-reviews. The Revolution of 1848, coming without warning, found Sainte-Beuve writing on the seventeenth century and completing the third volume of his *Port-Royal.* He was an interested observer of events, until a radical journal found his name in a list of those paid from secret funds under the July Monarchy. Much disturbed, Sainte-Beuve, after trying in vain to get at the facts, determined to resign from the Mazarine Library. It was found later that an insignificant sum had been credited to Sainte-Beuve for the repair of a chimney. Meanwhile, he sought a position abroad, and from his friend, Charles Rogier, he obtained an appointment to the chair of French literature at Liège. This appointment stirred up in Belgium fierce opposition, led by Michiels, a wrong-headed egotist, who unjustly blamed the critic for his own literary failure in Paris. Having published *Port-Royal* in September, 1848, Sainte-Beuve opened his course October 30, and continued till July 13, 1849, giving each week one public lecture on Chateaubriand and two class lectures on the history of French literature. During the Easter holidays he visited Collombet and Mme. d'Arbouville at Lyons. In Liège, he worked enormously, and besides having an attack of writer's cramp, he suffered from lonesomeness and unsympathetic surroundings. After visiting Utrecht and Amersfoort (July) for manuscript material on Jansenism, he resigned his professorship and returned to Paris with the intention of publishing his course and then finishing *Port-Royal,* in preparation for which task he had spent a week in the library at Troyes (August) on his return from a second trip to Lyons. At Paris, Sainte-Beuve made his home with a friend, Dr. Paulin. While undecided as to his future, he received from Dr. Véron, editor of the *Constitutionnel,* a proposal that he should write for that journal a literary essay to be published each Monday at the rate of 125 francs each. After some hesitation, the offer was accepted, and the first *Lundi* appeared October 1, 1849, *Port-Royal* and the book on Chateaubriand being postponed to await some future period of leisure.

Every man before the public is obliged from time to time to assert himself and to maintain his rights and his dignity, but Sainte-Beuve's resentment at what he considered slights seems occasionally a trifle excessive. It was on grounds of hurt pride that he absolutely refused Pavie's plea, after the drowning of Léopoldine Hugo, to be reconciled through this deep wound (September, 1843). At some other moment, the appeal might have been effective, the man of moods sometimes resisting like iron, and again, when the bile gets dissipated, eager to make amends or, at least, ready to let bygones be bygones. Such inequalities of humor affected, not only Sainte-Beuve's friendships, but also his relations with the *Revue des deux Mondes.*

To this periodical he was truly devoted, and he several times exposed himself to bitter enmities by defending the editor. In 1840, when Walewski publicly attacked Buloz for rejecting, as head of the Théâtre Français, a comedy he had offered for performance there, Sainte-Beuve, after condemning the comedy itself as published (February 1, 1840), replied to the assault (February 15) in such sort that the victim nursed his rancor for twenty-five years, until, having attained high office, he could visit it on the critic with some effect. Furthermore, in 1844, Dumas grossly assailed the editor in a socialistic journal, and Sainte-Beuve again took up the defense, complimenting Buloz on his enemies, men who attacked him, not for his errors, but for his qualities, for his fight against the cor-

ruption of periodical literature and for his closing of the
doors against the barbarians. Others are aimed at in general terms, and it is interesting to remark some quotations
from "Literary Gladiators," a suppressed essay against
Victor Hugo. In the article in question, *La Revue en
1845,* the critic proceeds to lay down a program for the
future, having apparently been commissioned for this task.
A new period was indeed opening. Buloz, after a struggle
with his partners, the Bonnaire brothers, had secured control of the magazine and formed a stock company for its
financial support. It was at this time that the *Revue de
Paris* was discontinued and the whole effort concentrated
on the major periodical. One of Sainte-Beuve's efforts
was a vain appeal to George Sand to resume her contributions, although in his prospectus he was promising less
caprice and fancy, and more politics, philosophical and
literary criticism, voyages, studies of foreign lands, and
informative dissertations. He seems, indeed, to be a power
in the *Revue,* and yet he is unable to insert articles other
than his own, Buloz being absolute master. A campaign
of strategy in favor of Mme. Olivier was wrecked by the
dictator, and other friends fared quite as ill.

It was over two years earlier that Sainte-Beuve had had
his first serious row with the editor, a row so serious that
from July 1, 1842, to March 15, 1843, no article from his
pen appeared, and he even wrote to a friend that he no
longer had any organ of publicity. The occasion was certainly provoking enough to warrant all the anger displayed.
Without consulting Sainte-Beuve, Buloz had assigned a report on academic receptions to G. de Molènes, a clever lad
of twenty-one (May 1, 1842). With the patronizing arrogance of inexperience, the youth had reprimanded, as well
as benignantly approved, both de Tocqueville and Molé.
In his naïve clumsiness, he had even succeeded in being
offensive to Ballanche, de Barante, Chateaubriand and

Mme. Récamier. An undergraduate literary monthly might have been proud of such an article, but for the *Revue des deux Mondes* it was a disgrace and for Sainte-Beuve a humiliation. A single sample will suffice:

> A sigh of Saint Theresa or a word of Fénelon pleads more powerfully in favor of Christianity than all the dry and ungrateful arguments that fear, in conflict with skeptical instincts, inspires in Pascal. A single phrase of Mirabeau moves me more in favor of liberty than all M. de Tocqueville's metaphysics.

In his report of Molé's reception, Sainte-Beuve had made a point of the excitement of the audience at the Count's words *He said, He* being Napoleon. In the de Molènes article, we find this sentence:—

> There has been considerable mockery of the naïveté that the audience put into its expression of lively curiosity and confident admiration every time there came from the lips of M. Molé a word the Emperor had let fall.

Sainte-Beuve was furious. His most influential friends had been outraged and he himself had been ridiculed. He hurried to the office and let out upon Buloz such a blast as, he assures Olivier, the editor can never forget. No wonder that, after again joining the staff, he reserved for himself every academic appearance of Molé.

The second rupture, and this lasted over a year, came in the spring of 1846. This time the trouble was about a share that Sainte-Beuve had purchased on credit and which Buloz refused to give up until it had been paid for in full, Sainte-Beuve, on his part, considering the price demanded unreasonable. In his wrath, he not only left the *Revue*, but relinquished his stock, worth at the time 5,000 francs, though the market value soon rose to 25,000 francs. There was clearly a misunderstanding, for the version of the affair given by Buloz is entirely different from that given by Sainte-Beuve.

For a time, the critic wrote for the *Débats*, to which he had access through de Sacy, his colleague at the library. We have already noted his articles on classical subjects (1843-1847). To these he at this time added some half a dozen book reviews and two necrological notices of his Swiss friends Töpffer and Vinet, the latter, in spite of the frigid indifference of the editors, being praised as a sagacious, precise, clear-sighted critic, severe when necessary, but always obedient to the Christian spirit of charity. A charming and sympathetic portrait of Mme. de Staal-Delaunay (October, 1846) is a sort of prelude to the *Lundis*, as is also some gossipy comment on two unpublished letters of Prévost (July, 1847), an article wherein Sainte-Beuve becomes so eager for traits of character that he regrets lacking means of discriminating among a group of monks who seem at first sight so uniform. In connection with a review of the *Letters of Rancé* (September 29, 1846) it is interesting to compare an entry in a note-book: "September 13, 1846—Finished reading the Letters of Rancé and translated an idyll of Theocritus. Let us intermingle our pleasures." [1]

The *Débats*, resolute defender of the July Monarchy, had at one time been so obnoxious to Sainte-Beuve that he had hotly refused to have any connection with it, but he no longer felt any such repugnance. The government, while not very noble, seemed to him sensible, moderate, and on the whole, tolerable, rendering the people happy enough. His views on the various administrations differed little, indeed, from those of the *Revue*. In 1838, Molé had, for motives purely political, appointed Buloz, Royal Commissioner of the Théâtre Français, a post which the editor

---

[1] *Theocritus* appeared Nov. and Dec., 1846.

retained till 1848, though Guizot, in 1839, threatened to remove him if he did not cease to oppose his policies. Supporting Thiers in 1840 as the only available ministry and following this leader into the opposition in 1844, the editor got into trouble again with Guizot, who laid plans to ruin his magazine. To this time belongs Bonnaire's effort to sell out to the government, a project successfully resisted by Buloz. Every one of these perturbations may be traced in Sainte-Beuve's correspondence. While generally supporting his chief, he tended more and more toward settled authority, and in 1845 he wrote Labitte that the *Revue* was going wrong in politics, moving toward the Left, even the rabid Left. "I am not of that stripe any more," he adds, "in fact, I never was." Desiring to be just toward those he does not like, he reports that Guizot grows constantly bigger in the debate on the address. The leader to whom Sainte-Beuve gives almost complete adhesion is Count Molé.

Under the ministry of de Rémusat in 1847, the powers of Buloz at the Théâtre were increased. It was at this moment, and with a most enthusiastic portrait of this minister (as literary man, of course, and not as minister) that Sainte-Beuve returned to the *Revue* (October 1, 1847). Doubtless complaisance for Buloz was mingled with his real admiration for his own personal friend and former associate on the *Globe*. De Rémusat was, indeed, the intermediary in the attempted reconciliation of critic and editor. There must have been advances from the editorial office, for it is to be observed that, every time Sainte-Beuve broke with the *Revue*, the critics of that periodical seemed to take special pains to say flattering things about his books, with the object, it may be surmised, of winning him back. He, too, though his remuneration was not munificent, surely needed whatever extra money he could earn by writing. He told Reynaud, it is true, that he had to purchase rare books in order to use up his income, yet in 1844 he had written that, if he should send his resignation to Villemain, he would be again on the street, with only 1,000 francs a year from the Institut.

At any rate, he now came back with an article of laudation, in which a few critical objections are insinuated with a marvelous skill. In regard to a typical uncertainty in de Rémusat's philosophical doctrines, for example, he says: "He is one of those who, even if they have seized the truth, cannot, or perhaps will not simply hold on to it, but who still look behind them to see if there is not something else hidden there." He manages also to introduce a good word for Molé and Pasquier: "Before meeting them, I was not acquainted with justice of mind, moderate, prudent, truly politic, not going beyond the necessary, but ready to advance and to accept wisely." All of which can hardly be called disinterested, even if sincerely felt.

Since about 1844, Sainte-Beuve had, as a rule, dropped his old habit of beginning an essay with a lengthy introduction, and had substituted the abrupt opening which fixes attention at once upon the subject. Here, however, in harmony with de Rémusat's own manner, the manner of the *Globe*, he goes back to the page or two of preparatory reflections.

To what hazards, he says in the course of this passage, is not an historic figure subject when, escaping from actual witnesses, it passes into the hands of subtle commentators, of learned men without judgment, or, what is worse, of orators and charlatans in office, rhetoricians and sophists of all sorts, who trade without conscience in words? If we ourselves have been witnesses, able to compare our first sincere impressions with the usurping idol, we are seized with disgust, flung more than ever toward the natural and the real, toward that which is the subject of conversation and not of declamation.

What is best in every age, he proceeds, escapes and cannot be fixed in writing. "The approximate and the topsy-turvy make us suffer." A little further on, he states his method of approach: "To get well acquainted with any eminent character, a study of its origins and of its formation is of the highest importance."

One further quotation will show Sainte-Beuve's state of mind on the eve of the still unsuspected Revolution:

When young, when heart and mind are exalted, and when belief in the universality of reason prevails, one is tempted, even if clear-sighted and prudent, to think that human stupidity has finished its course and that the reign of truth is about to begin, while in reality such stupidity has only changed its dress with the times and, under one form or another, is forever our contemporary.

A few months before (May, 1845) had appeared in the *Journal des Savants* Sainte-Beuve's review of the *Poems of Francis I* which discusses love songs and wanders about among sixteenth-century imitations of the classics in a free and easy fashion quite unexpected in such surroundings. Cousin is reputed to have excluded so long as he lived his fellow academician from further contributions to this rigidly learned official periodical. The fact is, as Sainte-Beuve wrote to Lebrun, who repeatedly urged him to send in articles, that the critic was unwilling to submit his compositions to the censorship of a committee which included Cousin. He sees *clubs* in the distance, though these, as he admits, he probably exaggerates.

Still oblivious on the very verge of the upheaval, Sainte-Beuve published (January 1, 1848) an article on the *Chévalier de Méré*, typical *honnête homme* of the seventeenth century, the social ornament, with wit, taste, manners, good sense; an agreeable person, with no occupation, simply making himself and others happy, content to please, not for any advantage, but for the mere sake of pleasing; a character worth saving from the oblivion into which he had fallen.

All such delightful objects of contemplation were abruptly banished from men's minds by the Revolution of February, an outbreak that seemed quite as much of a surprise to its leaders as it was to the rest of the world. Sainte-Beuve's views of the movement are recorded in his note-books.

Feb. 24, 1848—What goings-on! what a dream! I looked for many things, but not so soon, nor of this sort. How insignificant now appears the wisdom of the wise! how vain the foresight of the prudent! I am tempted to believe in the nothingness of all judgment, and of mine in particular, I who pretend to judge others, and whose sight is so feeble. My pen, which flattered itself that it amounted to something, I am tempted to break in pieces forever, and write no more.

March, 1848—I have within me contradictory sentiments like different men in conflict:

I am curious, and the spectacle of human affairs entertains me;

I am an artist, and find things that are neatly done seductive. . . .

By instinct, I am at bottom Girondin and republican; my humor inclines to the populace, and with each public agitation, the old leaven stirs within me.

But I am forty-four years old; my health and my nerves are delicate; I have refined literary tastes and social likings; I have been settled for years, and my habits are in contradiction with my instincts.

I am rather old to begin over again, but I look on with interest and solicitude. This work is for the young.

Difference in age: in 1830-1832, I took these riots, these social commotions, very lightly; I was in love, a poet, passionate in politics to the point of rage; I strode forth, happy amid the storm, and sang.—To-day I look forward, I am concerned for the future, although that is no longer my affair. I go along with head bowed and with sorrow in my heart.

In crises like these, nothing is quicker to decline than civilization; in three weeks may be lost the results of several cen-

turies. Civilization, life, is a thing learned and invented. . . .
After a few years of peace, men forget this truth; they come to
think *culture* something innate, the same thing as *nature*. But
barbarism lurks always only a step away, and, as soon as you
give ground, it begins anew.

Then comes the murderous fighting of June 24, ''horrible day''; Lamartine and his colleagues have ruled by
anarchy, and at length lost their foothold in blood, in seas
of blood. Condemnation for wasted opportunities now replaces a momentary admiration for the heroic speech
of February 25, when, in the face of a raging mob, the
poet had refused to substitute the red flag for the tricolor,
and had swayed the rioters by his eloquence.

On that day, as we have seen, Sainte-Beuve had passed
the Hotel de Ville on his return from reading a chapter of
Port-Royal to the Oliviers. We are apt to think that the
whole of life is upset by a revolution, but we find that even
Thiers continued his Sunday dinners, two of which appear
in Sainte-Beuve's records; February 27, when it is noted
that the statesman is content with the situation, and April
2, when there was a discussion on the Roman republic,
Cousin espousing the cause of Cæsar, and Thiers and
Mignet that of Cicero, while Sainte-Beuve himself put in
a few words against the idea of fatality in history. Since
the public, however, was in no mood for literary articles,
the critic's occupation was gone, and he devoted himself
to completing and bringing out the third volume of *Port-Royal*.

The long interval between volumes had not been wholly
due to procrastination. A notice in the *Revue* (April 1,
1840) had stated that the work, which was to be in four
volumes, was finished, but must be revised by the author.
In 1842, after Sainte-Beuve has visited the rich Jansenist
library at Troyes, he expects soon to address Volume III
to Reuchlin; the next year, he is writing about a group of

Provinciales, but in 1844 the book is not yet ready, and in September, 1847, he is slowly finishing that third volume: not until 1848 is he able to announce that he is actually completing this task.

One curious reason for delay is the widespread public interest in the subject. Sainte-Beuve had once advised a young poet "to choose some spot not yet occupied, even if it be by the side of the road," "to have the right to say *This is mine.*" If mine and thine is "the first law of art," it was also, in the case of this work, a matter of sentiment. In 1842, the Academy having assigned Pascal as a prize subject, Cousin sought out the original manuscripts at the Bibliothèque Royale, discovered that the *Pensées* had been tampered with by the editors, and made his famous report on the subject. There followed such general excitement as only Cousin knew how to stimulate. "A great academic hunting party," Sainte-Beuve called the affair; everyone was going into it, eulogies, discoveries of manuscripts, projected editions, being the order of the day. "I let all pass," he adds, "having flung myself into my cloister precisely to avoid the high roads."

He nevertheless reviewed from advance sheets the edition of Faugère (July 1, 1844), in this article, as also in *Port-Royal,* defending the original *Pensées* on the ground that, not only would exact publication have been impossible at the time, but that too much literalness is also an infidelity. Pascal himself, he maintains, would have modified his notes before giving them out, and even though his friends were incapable of sympathy with his audacity, they yet knew better than we what would have been softened and omitted. Outside of this argument a characteristic passage may be mentioned. Placing himself within the thought and belief of Port-Royal, Sainte-Beuve draws an illuminating contrast, worth a volume of disquisition, the contrast between the Christian faith in Jesus Christ, the

Man-God, suffering for and with us, and the Greek conception of Diana in *Phædra,* who comes to console Hippolytus, yet without a tear and, unwilling to pollute her divinity, leaves him at the moment of death.

Another reason for delay was the assault on the Jesuits begun by Michelet and Quinet in 1843, continued by Sue in his *Wandering Jew* (1844), invading the Chamber of Deputies (1845), where a prolonged debate was held on freedom of teaching, and, of course, involving pulpit and press in animated controversy. Some of Sainte-Beuve's associates were among the assailants, and the *Revue* itself supported Michelet, but Collombet, the critic's friend, correspondent and helper, was a defender of the Jesuits. He himself wished to abstain from mixing in public religious quarrels. It was by mere fortuitous coincidence that his essay on de Maistre had the appearance of timeliness; the use of Pascal and Port-Royal as polemical material he would by no means sanction.

It was therefore not until September, 1848, a most inauspicious hour, that the third volume of *Port-Royal* appeared. The lack of public interest in the book may be inferred from the fact that the *Revue,* instead of giving it a separate article, includes it in a general notice of recent works (January 15, 1849). The author of this article, A. de Pontmartin, in a laudatory paragraph, asserts that no studies by Cousin, Faugère or Vinet have taken up Sainte-Beuve's field, such appropriation being in fact impossible, for he is "less like an owner who digs, plants and builds, than like a foraging bee, whose flight nothing can limit, and whose possessions extend wherever there is a flower to smell or a delicate essence to be gathered." Outside of Paris the work received more serious attention.

While Sainte-Beuve was thus preparing his volume for the press and observing the progress of political affairs, his entire life was upset by an unexpected incident. What he found out later was that 100 francs, spent for the repair of a chimney in his apartment at the Institut, had been entered in an account of secret funds as paid to him personally. The story made public at the time, however, was that he had received from the authorities a large sum of money, it being assumed, of course, that he had been paid for supporting the government with his pen. In the note-book under date of March 30, we read:

A frightful calumny has assailed me. Such is the reward of so many years of discretion, delicacy and disinterestedness. I am sending the minister my resignation, and a note to Jean Reynaud. I shall take up again my life of pain and labor, but also my entire liberty, the feeling of complete liberty.

In the private memorandum to Reynaud, an old associate in Saint-Simonianism, he denied ever having written, since the days of the *National,* a single political article or portion of a political article, or ever having praised the king or the royal family. Letters to the authorities, letters to the newspapers, letters and visits to everybody who might throw light on the subject, were of no avail. For consolation he reads Herodotus (April 9). The lesson of the eternal fragility of human fortune, "beautiful words on clemency, pity, peace, true after thousands of years," bring tears to his eyes; "it lifts up the heart and produces the effect of a delicious bath in a great Lydian river." After all, in spite of his agitation, he consented to remain at the library as long as his revolutionary friends, Carnot, Reynaud and Charton, retained control of the Ministry of Public Instruction, but being piqued that they had doubted him for an instant, he refused any public appointment offered as a mark of their confidence.

Meanwhile, he was hunting for another position. Switzerland suggested itself, but he found that country quite as upset as France. In June he wrote to a London friend asking if it were possible to find in England, either at London, Oxford or Edinburgh, means of honorable subsistence as professor of French literature, lecturing in French, for, though he read English, he did not speak it. The Seventeenth Century, Port-Royal, and the First Fifty Years of the Nineteenth Century are the subjects suggested. America, also, was considered as a refuge, and Ticknor (August 28) gives assurance of a warm welcome in Boston. "If it had not been for my mother, I would have gone," is Sainte-Beuve's marginal comment. In the midst of these inquiries, the office, by singular accident, sought the man. Charles Rogier, a former associate in the Saint-Simonian movement and a prominent leader in the Belgian revolution of 1830, was at this moment Minister of the Interior at Brussels. He it was who had in 1831 secured for Sainte-Beuve the appointment that the lover of Mme. Hugo had first accepted, and then declined. Now, through his brother, who represented Belgium at Paris, he asked the critic to recommend a candidate for a professorship of French literature at the University of Liège, and Sainte-Beuve offered himself. The appointment was made without delay; on September 6, the new professor having finally resigned his librarianship (September 3), arrived in Brussels, and the next day the decree of nomination appeared in the Belgian *Moniteur*.

At once a howl arose from a group of newspapers in Liège, Brussels and other towns, not simply the fault-finding with anything Rogier might do, to be naturally expected from the opposition, but more largely the virulent abuse of long-nursed personal hatred, combined with disappointed envy. Michiels, a megalomaniac with a persecution delusion, who, in his book *La France littéraire* (1840) had vilified all the leading writers of the day, because he ascribed his insuccess in Paris almost entirely to the machinations of those who had befriended him, and in the first rank Sainte-Beuve, now joined with two Belgian poets, who had coveted the professorship, to incite the public by every means against the newcomer. Why seek a foreigner to the exclusion of home talent? Let him show his degree of docteur-ès-lettres; he is secretly accepting 5,000 francs for articles in the government organ *L'Indépendance Belge;* far from being a writer of eminent talent, he cannot even write good French at all, and here all the violences of Balzac are repeated; above all, let him deny the authorship of the *Livre d'Amour,* that heap of "mystic obscenity"—a book, by the way, that obviously not one of these writers had seen.

Even a less sensitive man than Sainte-Beuve would have felt discomfort at exposure to such a vicious journalistic campaign. For the extent and bitterness of this hostility, slight compensation was offered by the newspapers that defended him, and by the small number of friendly greetings from colleagues. Though he expresses gratitude to Professor Théodore Lacordaire, brother of the famous preacher, and to M. Borguet, Rector of the University, for their kindness and helpfulness, he feels that the public and the students showed no enthusiasm, or even appreciation. They were polite and unresponsive, an attitude deadly to an artistic temperament. The recollections of an auditor (*L'Indépendance Belge,* August 14, 1904) shows that this indifference was the result of ignorance rather than ill-will. Sainte-Beuve was talking mostly over the heads of his hearers. In 1867 and again in 1904, Liège looked upon his course as one of the glories of the University.

After making his arrangements, Sainte-Beuve returned to Paris, but he was back in Liège early in October. The opening of the University (October 16) gave him an unfavorable impression. A fortnight later (October 30), having all these preliminary difficulties in mind and referring

315

to them indirectly, he opens his inaugural address with an appeal for good will, for a sympathetic response from the students. Why has he come among them? With no ingratitude to his own country, he can say without reserve that he has come to seek complete and true liberty. As he has already perhaps found from experience, such liberty has certain drawbacks, but when restrained within orderly limits, when respecting individual rights, it is worth every sacrifice. Of all the mottoes which have of late been so prodigally invented and blazoned abroad, there is but one that he would have the ambition to see inscribed over the portal of every man of letters, and of his own in particular: *Liberty and Dignity*.

Sainte-Beuve lectured three times a week, Mondays to the general public, including ladies, and Wednesdays and Fridays to the students alone. After Easter, he also had a class in composition for a half dozen preparing to teach French. *Chateaubriand and His Literary Group* was the fruit of the first series; from the second, he accumulated a mass of notes on which he could draw at need for the rest of his life. The salary amounted to about 5,000 francs, with 1,000 more allowed for expenses. The first course seems to have ended in May, but the others continued till July 13. Then after visiting Utrecht and Amersfoort (July 22-27) for unpublished Jansenist documents, Sainte-Beuve packed up his belongings and resigned, his letter of explanation being dated August 16. He did not after all abandon the professorship to his traducers, for his place was taken by another Frenchman, Auguste Baron.

Reviewing his experience at a later date (1867), Sainte-Beuve felt that at Liège he had gathered strength for his second critical career, gaining power, in an independent retreat, to criticize and judge—he always felt more independent at a distance from Paris—and further, trying out before his Monday audience a course in literature later continued in the Paris journals. At the time, he was unhappy and lonesome, finding no salon for conversation, and above all, no warmth of welcome. Not a student said, "I am glad you have come" or "I am sorry you are going to leave." Furthermore, the exile longed constantly for Paris, and by June he had fully determined to return. He suffered from overwork, as well as from isolation. In the solitude of his little house in the rue des Anges (No. 19), he toiled enormously, bringing on utter fatigue and a severe and persistent writer's cramp. The Easter holiday in April, which took him both to Paris and to Lyons, hardly interrupted his labors, for he was ever busy accumulating materials for his courses.

The lectures on Chateaubriand were completely written out and ready for publication. To Hachette Sainte-Beuve had written in February that he had in readiness the first volume of a *Literary History of the First Fifty Years of the Century*, which, with an additional volume of *Literary Portraits*, should give him enough revenue to pay his expenses for a year, while he was finishing the fourth volume of *Port-Royal*, designed at that time to complete the work. Following his investigations in Holland, a new stay at Troyes (August 11), on his way back from a second trip to Lyons, shows him actively engaged in carrying out this plan, Troyes being a rich depot of Jansenist manuscripts, upon which indeed he had drawn before. In June (1849), he had published in the *Revue des deux Mondes* two essays on Chênedollé, to which he subjoined a note about his public course at the University of Liège. "This course," he said, "will be brought out in book form by Hachette late this autumn under the title *History of the Literature of the Empire*, of which it will form the first volume." The preface and the dedication to Charles Rogier are indeed dated September, 1849, although *Chateaubriand and His Literary Group* did not actually appear till 1861; *Port-*

Royal itself was completed only in 1859. This change of plan did not come from any determination on the part of Sainte-Beuve; it was the result of a fresh opening provided by another.

The twenty-one lectures on Chateaubriand, while of great interest and value, do not, like the course on Port-Royal, mark an epoch in the critic's development. The mind that produced them is the mind already studied in the preceding chapters, and the political and literary opinions are identical with those of the recent *Portraits*. Sainte-Beuve follows Chateaubriand's career, not so thoroughly perhaps as we might wish, but still with a sagacious eye, and connects the works with the character and experience of the author. Every effort is made to discover and portray the *young* man at the time of his trip to America, not accepting later accounts, but eagerly seeking contemporary documents. In the *Essai sur les Révolutions* is found the primitive Chateaubriand, a substratum afterwards overlaid, concealed even from his own eyes by passing excitements, but persisting in spite of all. This book, indeed, supplies the key to all the others. Here the writer, though convinced of the social value of religion, is an unbeliever, and with this clew, the critic discerns, even beneath the later glorification of Faith, the skeptic lurking under the public advocate of Christianity.

This view has aroused controversy, and even called forth personal abuse. On such a matter one's judgment will, in truth, depend largely on what one selects for emphasis from the expressions of a complex and variable personality. While preparing his work, Sainte-Beuve had before him, as he tells us himself, the lectures on the same subject delivered by Vinet in 1844 at Lausanne. One passage in these Vinet lectures comes rather close to an accusation of affectation, but it contains a saving, though parenthetical, qualification:

318

His Christianity (I mean that of his books) is literary, his politics are literary, and the bond that unites the two is also literary. The whole, thoroughly sincere I believe, is the work of an artist. His life itself, his personality, bears the same character; he has composed it poetically, and of all his works, it is the best.

Thus Vinet insists upon Chateaubriand's sincerity, though admitting that a man ought not to be a poem. "The believer's imagination is more religious than his intellect," says the Swiss lecturer, adding, however, in regard to the "magic" of talent, that he does not think the man can exercise such magic without having submitted to it; the enchanter has been enchanted. The thought is completed in another passage in which it is said that Chateaubriand remained on the outside of Christianity and never crossed the threshold, that he dealt with phenomena rather than principles, and felt the external brilliance rather than the inward power.

Chateaubriand's pictorial power as a religious influence may, indeed, be viewed from various angles. The most competent judges, while appreciating his services in stimulating spiritual fervor, find his works a little unsafe and do not look upon him as altogether sound in doctrine or as a model of theological argument. In the view of Vinet, the Protestant pastor, the decorative emotionalism is what might be expected of a Catholic. Sainte-Beuve, applying the severe standards of Port-Royal, does not find it Christian at all. The most favorable opinion seems to be that it is more religious in intention than in execution.

In many points there is close accord between the views of Vinet and those of Sainte-Beuve. Outside of common admiration for the extraordinary individuality and appreciation of the imaginative marvels, there is also, as might be expected, agreement on the theatrical pose of the author and on his false and forced images. Vinet prefers the

319

Essai sur les Révolutions because it is natural, not in style indeed, but in substance; in the *Martyrs,* he finds the pagan mythology superior to the Christian marvels and he emphasizes the anachronisms; the *Itinéraire* and the *Dernier Abencérage* receive the highest praise; he entirely omits the politician, because he is speaking only of literature; in general, he views the character of Chateaubriand from a distance, so that it becomes idealized, and even in literary criticism, by stating the objections first and then his approval, he subordinates the faults to the merits and leaves the impression of high praise. Thus he finds the *Génie du Christianisme* incoherent but, being fused in the soul of the writer, it becomes a whole, a unity, a poem. If Vinet had analyzed and made us feel this unity, instead of merely stating it, his book would have been a masterly criticism; as it stands, when compared with Sainte-Beuve's more complete view, which embraces so much of the surroundings and sequences, it seems a trifle provincial.

From Vinet's manuscript Sainte-Beuve borrowed quotations, comparisons and ideas, and he often uses the same examples. Suggestions are sometimes expanded, sometimes condensed or passed over, sometimes traced out in an entirely new and often contrary development. The pages on *Atala* are a particularly close adaptation. On the other hand, Sainte-Beuve fills out his canvas with extracts from contemporary writings, correspondence, newspaper articles, obscure pamphlets, sometimes pertinaciously sought out, and, while his view is wider, his insight is at the same time more penetrating. The result, nevertheless, is not a satisfactory portrait of Chateaubriand; the fragments for the monument are assembled, but the monument itself is not constructed. "An Epicurean with a Catholic imagination" is, after all, a rather starved formula.

Chateaubriand's character exercised a powerful fascination over Sainte-Beuve, at the same time that it filled him with antipathy, impatience and revolt, the harmonies between the two being crossed at every point by discords. The critic appreciated what was elevated, generous and simple-minded; he sympathized with the tendency to solitude, melancholy and revery; he loved the miracles of imagination, the supreme art, the rhythm and color, the enchantment and intoxication; yet he is led to conclude that this emperor is a sort of Hadrian; he is "not one of the truly great artists of a great epoch, one of the very first, nor even one of the second rank for beauty, but is one of those who comes immediately after such, one of those who leave most abundant traces of themselves and most abundant remembrances on the slopes of a decadence, under the gaze of a posterity that no longer recognizes the truly beautiful." The terms of comparison, of course, are Homer, Virgil, Theocritus and their peers.

Early in the course are given the elements of Chateaubriand: (1) revery, *ennui*, the *mal de René*, seeking the infinite, painting vast spaces, the ocean, the desert, the human heart; (2) youth, delirium, romantic illusion, pagan desire; (3) honor, glory, chivalry, the prodigal and the brilliant, the noble, as opposed to the sordid and base. To these must be added imagination, an incomparable pen, and often a just judgment. At the end of the study, the qualities noted are untamed force joined to absurdities, sophisms and bad faith; elevation and a great primitive nature mingled with the vanity of a man of letters and with worldly pettiness; over all, a radiant, inspired imagination; Chateaubriand is "a great magician, a great enchanter."

A detailed criticism emphasizes the fact that this enchanter lacks unity, that he wrote passages rather than works, fragments, beautiful fragments, that could readily be transferred from one place to another. Negligent, without premeditation, he composed as he wrote, with precipitation and immature judgment. The sentiment is not equal to the expression, and he is often inexact: there is light, nay lightning, on the peaks; in the intervals nameless inadvertences and negligences.

Chateaubriand's youth, the epoch before 1814 when politics poisoned him, is his most attractive period. Sainte-Beuve sympathizes with his *ennui,* as weary of felicity as of misfortune, always wanting something different, seeking the intoxication of fresh sensations, incapable of happiness, yet insatiable for it, and rejecting it rather than be content. From America the young aristocrat rushes back, on learning of the arrest of the king. "There is in the human heart, and particularly in the heart of the poet, a certain need of instability and sudden change, so that in the case of even what is dearest and most desired, if much prolonged, one is happy of a break on the first occasion that offers, and above all if the renunciation can be made to appear a sacrifice." The poetic melancholy of René is seductive to Sainte-Beuve, for his own past feelings are brought to mind when he analyzes this malady of a whole generation, this satiety and disgust in advance of experience, arising from the fact that René is two persons of different age, one always interfering with the other. Mobile, in contrast to the fixity of Obermann, René gazes at, admires and cherishes his melancholy, and clothes the beautiful phantom in harmony and light.

The *Génie du Christianisme* is studied amid the circumstances of its appearance. Begun in the exaltation of a mystical crisis, its inspiration is sincere; yet, on the other hand, there was in 1800 a great rôle to be filled, that of poetic advocate of Christianity, and Chateaubriand knew how to stage his piece and appear with his diamond buckler and flaming sword. Thus it is that almost every word of Sainte-Beuve's praise is followed by a *yet* or a *but,* and robbed of its amenity. The objects of worldly interest presented by the champion are the superficial part that Christianity tolerates, but may well do without, the appeal being made especially to the young Catholics of the Salon, who look upon religion as something distinct from practice and life; it is the Romanticism of Christianity, which elicits, as in a museum, the cry: *How fine that is!*

The artificial arrangement, the declamatory and theatrical passages, the operatic mythology are intensified in *Les Martyrs,* a book which sometimes surpasses *Télémaque,* but never equals it. The *Itinéraire* is a search for images. "If he can find the finest phrase on the descendants of Saint Louis and of Robert the Strong, the finest phrase on Napoleon at Saint Helena, the finest on the tomb of Jesus Christ, the finest phrase on the coming republic, the finest and most splendid phrase on the ruin and the cataclysm of the old world; if he succeeds in that, he is content." Just as he traveled in foreign lands, so he wandered among books, reading enormously, yet never disinterestedly, always with an eye to getting something for his purpose. Glorious as his images are, they too often call upon us for admiration. "Look at me," they seem to say. Sometimes, too, they become mechanical, placed at the end of the passage, like the point of an old-fashioned epigram. And what, after all, have these images to do with Christianity?

In addition to such literary attractions and repulsions, there are the attractions and repulsions of personality. Chateaubriand was at times simple, frank, charming and, among friends, even modest, but his predominant trait was limitless egotism, which could be generous but not just. The man Sainte-Beuve could admire, but he detested the god. He speaks of Chateaubriand's powerful *retroactive* imagination that colored every object according to caprice and passion, and caused him not only to change his opinions, which is perfectly legitimate, but to deny he had ever held the view now abandoned, though previously expressed. If it were anyone else, we should say: "He lies." With Chateaubriand, we say: "He forgets." The politician, too, is treated without indulgence. After comparing a beautiful passage from Chateaubriand with one from Lamartine, the critic exclaims: "Noble poets, why have you not both remained faithful to the end, without ever staining the whiteness of your purity?"

The foregoing analysis will probably furnish evidence of two points: first, that Sainte-Beuve has not succeeded, if indeed he made the attempt, in finding the unifying force in Chateaubriand, though his phrase "retroactive imagination" might well furnish the key; and secondly, that he has carried out the promise of the two passages selected as epigraphs: (1) "It is useless longer to dissimulate the fact that the writers of our age have generally been ranked too high" (Chateaubriand); (2) "We do not desire to destroy a reputation; on the contrary, we wish to know precisely what it was that established the reputation we respect, and what are the true beauties that have redeemed all faults" (Voltaire).

Sainte-Beuve has been much blamed for disparaging Chateaubriand after having been admitted to the inner circle, but he was undoubtedly within his rights, and he did not betray any secrets learned at the Abbaye-au-Bois. The publication of Hortense Allart's account of her love affair with the sexagenarian beau has delighted even those who scold Sainte-Beuve while themselves indulging in far more scandalous indiscretions. The quotation from the *Memoirs* of a passage about a love intrigue at the end of the pilgrimage to Jerusalem, omitted by Chateaubriand in his final text, has furnished occasion for much execration, but the passage is unquestionably authentic; Sainte-Beuve had been allowed to copy it in 1834 and he had published it as a footnote without comment in 1836. If Chateaubriand had really cared to suppress the episode, he could readily have denied having written it.

The time had come, Sainte-Beuve thought, for real criticism to replace worship. "A sweet influence" had formerly paralyzed him, so that he was not free to speak in public of the idol. Now he was liberated from all bonds. Probably he went too far in his tendency to overturn the "statue," to emphasize spots on what was too immaculate to be human, but beyond this tendency, there was no ill-will, unless this be found in the footnotes, which were added at the time of publication. Here, doubtless in reaction against worshipers of the hero, he has sometimes been unduly severe in ascribing mean motives, and he also emptied into an appendix a mass of undigested jottings from his private note-books, which occasionally add to the impression of harshness. Nevertheless, he claims to have written merely as all Chateaubriand's friends and acquaintances, outside of his particular coterie, thought and spoke familiarly; another instance of the bounds that ought, perhaps, to separate written from spoken criticism.

Chateaubriand's pose and his distortions of truth in the direction of self-glorification, it was the critic's business to analyze and make intelligible as traits of character. We learn, indeed, of things that "a great talent will call up in the distance and create rather than relinquish," but it does not become entirely clear that the rôle, instead of being deliberately assumed, was rather the very character of the man himself, as inseparable from his earlier as from his later works. It is a peculiar feature of such individuals that they are at once artificial and sincere, not to say childlike. They are to a large extent sincere even in their pretensions, and really come to believe their own acting, their own prevarications. The average man may well exclaim: *The Charlatan!* but the critic should show that the theatrical part has become the reality, so that what contributes to the rôle is truth and what is incongruous is falsehood, the actor being so intent on his part that he makes it the measure of actuality and hardly any longer perceives his own subterfuges. The mind, under the influence of imagination and desire, peering through the mists of self-esteem, plays such tricks with facts, enlarging here, diminishing there, twisting chronology into an accomplice, that finally no proofs, even the strongest, can carry conviction of falsehood. We might perhaps conceive a Defoe-Chateaubriand coming to believe that all the episodes on the desert island were real, and thenceforth honestly maintaining that these experiences had actually happened to him. Later discoveries of printed sources for travels never undertaken do not upset this view.

Even in his most trenchant notes, Sainte-Beuve is by no means so cruel as Biré in the exposure of Victor Hugo, but it is perhaps a defect of his work that he has merely offered the elements of an analysis, without any sufficient conclusion. Was this the result aimed at? In one lecture, he says: "To be able to read a book, meanwhile judging it, without ceasing to enjoy it, is about the whole art of the critic." In addition, make comparisons, *Atala* with *Paul et Virginie* and *Manon Lescaut; René* with *Obermann* and *le Lepreux; les Martyrs* with the *Odyssey, Télémaque* and Milton; and a judgment will naturally result in each reader, formed from his own impressions. As for Chateaubriand's career, the most effective criticism is found in an extensive passage from the note-books presenting an ideal picture of what, had he chosen, this prince of writers might have been—"A Goethe-René"—as a guide and mentor to the new literary generation.

The insinuation that Sainte-Beuve was afraid to publish his work in 1849 is absurd. The reason he himself advances, lack of time, is in itself sufficient, particularly as this volume was to be but the first of a longer literary history. Beyond this fact, it may be noted that Vinet's lectures, *Études sur la Littérature Française au XIX Siècle,* appeared exactly at this moment (fall of 1849), and any publisher, if not the author himself, would naturally hesitate to launch a second treatment of the same subject. Moreover, the purpose of the book—to obtain money for temporary subsistence—was accomplished through the contract with the *Constitutionnel.* Although Sainte-Beuve again talked of publishing the work in 1851, what leisure he could obtain within the next few years was put upon *Port-Royal,* a task constantly growing heavier through the accumulation of fresh materials. When a little freedom was at last gained, Villemain took the field with his book on Chateaubriand (1858) and then de Marcellus (1859). The earliest convenient date of publication was therefore after the two final volumes of *Port-Royal* (1859) and at a sufficient interval from at least Villemain.

Meanwhile, the essential literary and political objections to Chateaubriand had been offered to the public during 1850 in three of the *Lundis,* which are, indeed, little more than a condensation of parts of the lectures, all the more forcible, be it said, for their condensation. The first (March 18) deals nominally with the *Memoirs,* but it is actually a study of Chateaubriand himself, his vanity, his talent as an enchanter, the several personages within him in conflict with the natural man, his misrepresentations and contradictions, his imagination substituting itself for sensibility, judgment and even memory. In the second (May 27), also attached to the *Memoirs,* the lover is considered, and here, far from representing the weakness for women as a fault, Sainte-Beuve regrets the omission of certain episodes whereby, though the pilgrim "might lose a little as Christian, crusader and show-piece," he would gain as poet and man. While setting forth Chateaubriand's perpetual inconstancy and his egotism and lack of delicacy in his love affairs (the pot calling the kettle black perhaps, but the kettle was nevertheless undoubtedly black), Sainte-Beuve contrasts the modern Satanism and sophistication of passion with its natural expression in Homer, and then with the decadence in Horace, wherein the idea of death appears, pleasure sharpened by a sense of the shortness of life. In *René,* on the other hand, we find the longing for eternity, to be seized in a moment, Christianity bringing not peace, but a sword that pierces the heart with bitter pain. *René* is always to Sainte-Beuve the one perfect work of Chateaubriand, and in his analysis of the malady we find the experience of one who had himself been stricken.

The third essay (September 30) deals with the statesman and politician. Entering political life with clangor, Chateaubriand, the poet abandoned by youth and left with an immense talent seeking occupation, took to public affairs as a last resort. There can, however, be no intermingling of poetry with political leadership, for the device *All or Nothing* is the antithesis of the true spirit of the statesman, which must make the best of each situation. If you are not in charge of public affairs, it is right enough to prefer the swallow or the bee to a bald-headed council. In itself poetry is adorable, but not as a means of decrying society and its interests. It has a right, this society, to demand seriousness of those who aspire to conduct it. Throughout the essay, Sainte-Beuve is merciless in unveiling the frivolity and pettiness of Chateaubriand's political motives. Whether justified or not, he certainly displayed no timidity. Why should he? At the same moment (July 1, 1850) in the *Revue des deux Mondes,* the egotism of Chateaubriand, who "thought only of himself," is the theme of an inflexibly severe article by Count Albert de Broglie.

Consideration of these essays has taken us a step beyond the decisive moment when Sainte-Beuve, quite unawares, crossed the threshold of a new career. Though completely

328

uncertain of the future, he had early resolved to resign his professorship. Famous as he was, he had yet no means of livelihood and no prospects. His quarrel with Buloz, while it did not shut him out from the *Revue des deux Mondes,* still made his situation there uncomfortable, and the pay was insufficient. The *Revue* itself had greatly changed. A glance over the pages at this date makes it evident that a new epoch had been entered, though neither Planche nor Sainte-Beuve seems to have realized the fact. The essay on Chênedollé (June 1 and 15, 1849) was published as No. LII of the old series of "Poets and Novelists of France," Planche's "Béranger" the next year being LIII. With "Mme. de Krudener" (September 15), which is quite in the old style, Sainte-Beuve ended, and he did not contribute again until 1863.

This last essay, a review of Eynard's biography, is a retraction—the critic is always willing to retract when truth seems to demand, but he grieves that he has lost an illusion. The charlatanism and self-advertisement of the lady in question, her tricks to push her novel *Valérie,* while ascribing its success to God, lead to the conclusion that her conversion is wholly the work of self-esteem and desire to shine. The last pages of the piece consist of a clever adaptation to the topic of the philosophy of Saint-Évremond. We may note that, when one of Sainte-Beuve's statements here was questioned, he replied that he had learned the detail from Mme. de Taucher, who had been present at the occurrence. The critic was never a safe man to assail on matters of fact.

For Chênedollé, Sainte-Beuve had access to the poet's private papers, and the essay, a by-product of the Liège lectures, is little more than a selection from correspondence and personal jottings, with connecting and explanatory remarks. The letters, which are grouped according to the writers of them, show especially the relations of the choice little society that included Mme. de Beaumont, Chateaubriand, Fontanes and Joubert, while from the material presented and from sympathetic comment emerges a most attractive personality, Chênedollé himself. The piece is an excursion into the byways. You cannot, remarks Sainte-Beuve elsewhere, know a country by rapidly traversing only the main roads; you must push your explorations into side-paths and even through thickets.

An autobiographical interpretation may be given to the observation that Chênedollé remained too long away from Paris and thus lost the influence he might have acquired at this center of intellectual life, a fault against which Sainte-Beuve himself was evidently on his guard. When the essay was published in the Chateaubriand volume (1861), the author slipped into a footnote, anonymously, a sonnet written in April at Liège, the first April he had experienced in the country, at least since childhood. In his memorandum to Jean Reynaud, he had written: "I have my weaknesses, as I have said: they are of the kind that gave King Solomon universal disgust and satiety." It has been suggested by some without evidence that Sainte-Beuve may have scandalized the people of Liège by improper associations, but in this sonnet he declares that he has been faithful to an absent love (Mme. d'Arbouville) and that he has renewed his innocence. His letters to the Oliviers confirm this assertion.

When Sainte-Beuve returned to Paris in August, 1849, he made his home with his friend, Dr. Armand Paulin,[2] in the rue Saint-Benoît, not far from the Institut and almost next door to the *Revue*. In the midst of his financial perplexities, his good angel was again Véron, a manager

---

[2] When Dr. Paulin died in September, 1857, Sainte-Beuve made an address at the grave. This is published, *Nouveaux Lundis*, vi, p. 455, with a hot answer to a Dr. Joulion, who had ridiculed the French style of the address in the *Evénement* (June 7, 1866).

who not only paid the artist, but who invented the framework for his appearance before the public. This remarkable promoter is assuredly deserving of kindly remembrance. After leaving the *Revue de Paris,* in which he had started Sainte-Beuve on literary portraits, he had become director of the Opera, where he had apparently learned to deal with the artistic temperament. In 1844, the *Constitutionnel* having fallen into hopeless decrepitude with only 5,600 subscribers, Véron bought the paper at auction and fifteen months later had a subscription list of 20,000 and advertisements amounting to 500,000 francs a year. The price of the paper had been cut in half and the pay of editors and contributors largely increased. To Eugène Sue 100,000 francs was offered for a *feuilleton* novel, the outcome being the *Wandering Jew.* Now, with his sure eye for public success, Véron proposed to Sainte-Beuve a series of weekly literary articles at 125 francs each. In his *Souvenirs d'un Bourgeois de Paris,* he says: "Twenty years later (*i.e.,* after the *Revue de Paris*) M. de Sainte-Beuve began again with me in the *Constitutionnel* a second literary campaign. On his return from Liège, after the Revolution of 1848, I solicited and urged him to accept my offer; I assured him that, especially just after our recent storms, the public would be interested in pure and true literature. He has often thanked me since."

Sainte-Beuve's own account is identical with the foregoing:

Scarcely back in Paris, I felt a great need of activity, after a year of severe study and solitude, but I did not know what to take up. M. Véron, director of the *Constitutionnel,* learning of my return, had the goodness to offer me the columns of his journal for each Monday. The proposal both flattered and frightened me. . . . I made all my objections (the difficulty, in the midst of political preoccupations, of interesting a large and varied public in pure literature) to M. Véron, who took the trouble to answer them, speaking as a man of taste with a feeling for literature and as a man of intelligence who knew his public. . . . At bottom, it was what I wanted.

The contract was made for a year, and the first *Lundi* appeared October 1, 1849.

CHAPTER XI

1849—1855

FROM the time that Sainte-Beuve began writing a weekly article for the *Constitutionnel,* he broke off all social relations and confined himself, as the immense labor demanded, to the production of his *Lundis.* His mother died November 17, 1850, and the following April he moved into the house, 11 rue Montparnasse, where he remained for the rest of his life. An attitude favorable to Louis Napoleon, especially exemplified in an attack on the Doctrinaires, *Les Regrets,* procured for him a place on the official *Moniteur* (Nov., 1854) when he left the *Constitutionnel* in consequence of Véron's retirement. Here he continued his *Lundis* without change or intermission, though in a rather less lively tone. He had previously (Sept. 6, 1852) refused an appointment by Fortoul as Villemain's successor in the chair of eloquence at the Sorbonne, but he accepted from the minister the grade of Officer in the Legion of Honor (Aug. 12, 1853). Named Professor of Latin Poetry at the Collège de France, on recommendation of the Faculty and of the Academy of Inscriptions, Sainte-Beuve discontinued his articles in the *Moniteur* (Jan. 8, 1855) and devoted himself to preparation for his new functions.

"In 1849," says Sainte-Beuve, "I undertook my campaign of the *Lundis* in the *Constitutionnel,* lasting three years, and for eight years thereafter I continued it a little less actively in the *Moniteur.* This campaign was broken by my attempted professorship at the Collège de France, a wretched affair, in which I was thwarted from the outset by physical violence; from this venture there came, nevertheless, my *Étude sur Virgile.* I made up for my failure by four years as professor at the École Normale, but this teaching, though very active, was behind closed doors, and

333

I have drawn from it nothing, or next to nothing, for the public (1861).''

The words ''a little less actively'' apply only to the period following the unhappy professorship. For five years and three months, Sainte-Beuve continued his *Lundis* with perfect regularity, first in the *Constitutionnel* (till November 29, 1852), and then in the *Moniteur* (till January 8, 1855). There were only three breaks in the sequence: an article was omitted, without the author's consent, April 15, 1850, but this lapse was made up by an extra article on Tuesday, September 24; there was another omission November 25, 1850, owing to the death of the critic's mother (November 17); and two articles in succession were given April 7 and 8, 1851, with none April 14, to allow time for moving. Such a record of uninterrupted literary production is astonishing, if not unprecedented.

''I, too, am of the *genus irritabile*'' is a confession found in a note (1861) to the essay on Chênedollé. Sainte-Beuve was, indeed, one of those artistic temperaments who need a manager for worldly success, but always revolt when the manager takes charge. Friction with his new editor could, therefore, hardly be long delayed. An article on Pliny, destined for the issue of April 15, 1850, failed to appear on that date, and the next day Sainte-Beuve wrote Véron a blazing remonstrance, withdrawing the article and throwing up his contract. What hurt him most was that, after all his efforts to produce his weekly essay on time, he was, without fault on his part, made to appear inexact in fulfilling his obligations to the public. Beyond this, since no warning of delay had been given, he feels that the cordial relations between author and editor, so essential to this kind of work, are over, ''the honeymoon evidently past.'' Véron will kindly publish an inclosed letter, and the writer will call to-morrow at four for the money remaining due, the cost of setting up the withdrawn article to be deducted, since it is only just that he should bear the expense of his own susceptibility. In this case, the susceptibility was supported by righteous indignation, but matters were adjusted, the editor had learned his lesson, and no further occasions for quarrel seem to have arisen.

From Liège Sainte-Beuve had written Collombet: "You follow your path. Alas! mine is not yet found. Will it ever be? How painful it is to be always obliged to begin over again!" Now, at length, the path has been found and, while intellectually it is a continuation, it is in all other respects a rupture with the past and a fresh beginning. Sainte-Beuve no longer had time either to visit or to correspond with his friends. The evening dinner hour, when a few familiars met at his table, was his only free moment, for during the day visitors had to be rigorously excluded. Throughout the correspondence of these years, the burden of his increasing labors is the repeated excuse when asking indulgence for apparent negligence. The letters to Collombet will best give the tone:

(July 4, 1850)—I have so much to do that I find time only for my task and all else must wait. (June 14, 1851)—Not a minute to myself; one piece of work finished, the next begins: thus I escape the torments of a soul that feeds upon itself. The work to which I am subjected is somewhat excessive; it smacks too much of the sin of Adam. (May 2, 1853)—My life is that of a man in a treadmill. You see the flour; may you find it good and praiseworthy.

On the other hand, work is his only pleasure; it is a necessity, for it occupies his mind. Even on Sundays he read proofs. "The harness rubs and chafes," he had written Olivier (1844), "and yet in the end you like it, while at the same time cursing it."

After his mother's death, he had no clear idea concerning his arrangements for the future, but must soon decide on a permanent habitation which he will never leave until carried out as his poor mother had been. Four months later he has moved into the house in the rue Montparnasse, a humble street not even dignified with sidewalks:

(June 24, 1852)—I have retired into the little house my mother occupied, where I expect to stay until carried out feet first. I live alone, or at least, without lodgers, and with a woman friend who kindly keeps house and relieves me of domestic cares; I do not go into society, and only emerge when it is necessary, to seek books, foraging, as I say. All my life is occupied with reading, writing and correcting proofs. You are the last one who needs to be told about such a régime of work; but the point in which my life differs from that of the Benedictine is that I introduce the steam-engine and everything is done with great rapidity. . . . I am giving a course in literature by snatches. All my subjects I select in concert with M. Véron, who, to be sure, enters very well into my ideas.

The woman friend whom Sainte-Beuve speaks of, Mme. de Vasquez, his first housekeeper, was also his mistress. She made herself highly disagreeable to persons who came to see him and, after her death, her father, a French peasant and not a Spaniard as Sainte-Beuve had been led to suppose, extorted from him a considerable sum of money, after which experience, the critic never committed that particular imprudence again.

The other writers on the *Constitutionnel* Sainte-Beuve knew but slightly, rarely seeing them and having no connection with the paper outside of his *Lundis*. At the *Moniteur* we find the same situation (1854). Here there were two directors, Turgan and Dalloz; the first he seldom met and the second, later his friend, he did not at this time know at all; he came in contact only with the printers.

Perhaps another man would have taken pains to keep up his social connections, but to Sainte-Beuve this complete break afforded a sort of independence which was grateful

to him as a critic. At the death of his mother, both Molé
and Pasquier sent letters of sympathy, an attention that
was appreciated, but that did not lure him back into aristocratic circles. He rarely even went to the Academy.
To Collombet he writes (July 4, 1850) : "It is painful for
me to be obliged at times to judge so roughly men I admire
and whom I have known; but working at a trade, I must
do the thing honestly and with all uprightness." What
has seemed to many a mere political breach, complicated
with a selfish desire for advancement under the new government, was, in reality, nothing but the natural outgrowth
of a new mode of life, which for several years offered no
prospects whatsoever of any public rewards. "By my work
and my economy," he writes Collombet (May 2, 1852),
"and these are matters on which I have fixed my attention
too late, I hope to acquire a moderate and modest independence for my years of inactivity and old age. To this
I have reduced all my prospects."

Such pecuniary motives would be sufficient to explain
the critic's repulse of the repeated efforts of Buloz to get
him to return to the *Revue*. These efforts ceased in 1851
and Planche was either permitted or incited to publish an
article on Sainte-Beuve (September 1), No. LV (and last)
of the *Poets, Novelists and Literary Historians of France*,
in which both praise and blame are awarded with an irritating condescension, evidently designed to wound. In the
last issue of 1853, however, there is a review of the past
twenty-five years, wherein there is a quotation from Sainte-
Beuve, "whose separation from us we deeply regret." In
1861 we find the critic as friendly with Buloz as though
there had been no breach.

It was not before December that any serious political
difference could have arisen, the *Revue* being throughout
this period conservative, approving the restriction of the
suffrage, and hoping for constitutional parliamentary gov-

ernment under the Prince-President, while Sainte-Beuve
cared nothing for forms, as long as the preservation of
civilization was assured through the stability of institutions, free on the one hand from anarchy, and on the other
from legitimist reaction. How completely his humanitarian
illusions had vanished is shown by one of his private notes,
written at Liège:

All my political ideas changed from the day I became convinced of the following moral observation: Mankind is a pretty
bad and insipid species; some men only are good, and these must
be constantly set apart, and stimulated with unremitting care, or
they will deteriorate.

In 1850, however, democracy appeared to be assured.
The essential, therefore, was adult education, a thought
developed in "Lectures du Soir" (January 21, 1850). For
the Dauphin, heir to the throne, Bossuet had written a
history; now the workmen of Paris had become the
Dauphin. Accepting the situation, Sainte-Beuve wants a
moderate and regular progress; he wants all that is best
in thought and all that is beautiful put within the reach
of this public, made to appear worthy of their love, the
only means of assuring the preservation of great traditions
being to place them, not in the keeping of some choice
Cénacle, but in the keeping of democracy itself.

Sainte-Beuve was by no means a political writer in any
ordinary sense, but he felt that criticism, protected by
power, helps in the common restoration. "Every time
that, after a long upset, the political order gets repaired,
and takes up its regular march anew, the literary order
tends to put itself in accord and to follow as best it can."
After the League, France had Henry IV and Malherbe;
after the Fronde, Louis XIV and Boileau; after the Revolution, Napoleon with Fontanes, Joubert and their group.
To himself and his fellow-critics had fallen a similar task.

As periods of revolution are always marked by declamation, abstract systems and vague generalities, the literary critic can be of public service by signalizing and condemning these faults and by insisting on simplicity, reality and precise statement, qualities which, indeed, would of themselves appeal to his disinterested taste. Throughout the *Lundis* of the first year, no other note is so insistent. At Lamartine's birth, all the fairies gave him their gifts, except the fairy of good sense, not vulgar good sense, to be sure, but tact, taste and delicate judgment. The Romanticism and eloquence of Lacordaire may be admired, but it is necessary to maintain the rights of neutrals, placed between extreme parties, unable to join either, but clinging to mitigated good sense and reason. Montalembert has come to stand against anarchy and gives evidence of abandoning system. Guizot is a systematic historian, who writes always with a political aim, holding a philosophy of history too logical to be true, and attempting to put his rigorous conclusions into practice. "For my part, when I have read some of these lofty lessons, so clear and absolute, in the *History of Civilization*, I quickly open a volume of Retz, to come back to the truth of human intrigues and mascarades." "In politics there are several different ways in which happenings may turn out. When the thing is done, only the result is seen. What occurred under our own eyes in February is a great example. The thing might have turned out in many different ways. Fifty years from now, it will perhaps be maintained (according to the method of the Doctrinaires) that the outcome was a necessity."

George Sand's pastoral romances are greeted with surprise and delight. May she never serve a party. "I always tremble when I see a philosophic idea as label to a romance." For the academic eulogy, it is time to lower the tone, not to seek applause by foreign ornaments and digressions, but by simplicity and truth. The sincerity of Barnave is noted and the absence of declamation. Eighteenth century memoirs are good reading because of their simplicity and freedom from false emphasis and pretension. Mme. du Deffand is praised for her clear, straight mind, without illusions, loving truth and reality and finding eloquence odious. *Gil Blas,* the epic of the ordinary man, is not a system, but merely mockery of the solemn and the false. From Chesterfield even a democracy may take lessons in politeness and discretion. Hamilton is never declamatory or overemphatic; Joubert is Athenian, a model of grace, moderation and ease.

The names used to illustrate this single tendency will give some idea of the way Sainte-Beuve flitted over the whole extent of French literature, with a venture, now and then, abroad; and he took pains at first never to present the same type of subject on any two successive Mondays. Sometimes his essay was suggested by some recently published book or by some personage or situation of present import. More frequently the motive seems to have been nothing but his own interest in a topic connected with his studies. Although the notes accumulated at Liège are not accessible, it seems probable that over half the essays were indebted to the material thus stored up, while not over a third deal with contemporary matters.

As usual, Sainte-Beuve did not adhere strictly to his original plan. For a long time, he tells us, he had wished the opportunity of being wholly a critic as he understood the function, with such maturity, and also perhaps such boldness, as had been acquired from age and experience. In the *Globe* and the *Revue de Paris,* he had written polemical criticism; then, in the *Revue des deux Mondes,* a criticism more neutral and impartial, but especially analytic and descriptive, with no conclusions; in the ruder times now come, he felt that he might be more daring, without failing in courtesy, and say at last plainly what seemed to be the truth about works and their authors.

Lamartine, Béranger and Guizot were the chief sufferers from this frankness, though the criticism in each case seems thoroughly just and pretty close to what posterity has approved. Merits are never lost sight of, and with George Sand and de Musset praise predominates. A notable example of justice is furnished by the essay on Balzac, written shortly after his death. Here, not a word betrays any enmity on account of the vicious attack on *Port-Royal*. Full credit is allowed to the genius of this most original and penetrating painter of manners; even some qualities of his style are praised, Asiatic and exaggerated as it often is; the characters live, but the author has less success in the action; a great observer, he yet invents as much as he observes; he is the prey of his work, rather than its master; and the critic, quite in the tenor of his post-revolutionary ideas, expresses the wish for a healthier and calmer literature.

As the Liège program included many minor writers of the Consulate and the Empire for whom time was lacking, Sainte-Beuve made several of the *Lundis* in a certain sense supplementary lectures to that course; others were excursions from *Port-Royal*, dealing with matters that could not be included there even as digressions; one little group deals with Napoleon, another with foreign literature; but the most numerous collection is based on French authors and French social life, particularly the eighteenth century. It is no arbitrary connection that is here indicated, for Sainte-Beuve himself, when returning to any field after various intervening essays, commonly reminds the reader of the relative matter in preceding pieces.

With the studies on Chateaubriand and his group may be included a lovely appreciation of Mme. Récamier, "the youngest of the Graces harnessing lions," whose fascination lives in Sainte-Beuve's essays as nowhere else. She is doubtless the starting point for a whole series of pieces on the salons of the eighteenth century, du Deffand, de Lespinasse, d'Epinay, Geoffrin and others. Literature is here simply the background upon which are drawn sketches of social life. The gossip concerning interesting personalities is like society chat about the living. We see Turgot playing battledore and shuttlecock with Mme. de Grafigny's niece, "who became Mme. Helvétius"; we hear of old M. Geoffrin reading the double-columned *Encyclopédie* straight across the page and finding it learned but rather abstruse; Voltaire, Rousseau and a host of others are shown in intimate glimpses, as they might have been known to frequenters of contemporary receptions and dinners. From memoirs and from letters, quotations, anecdotes and biographical details are selected with consummate skill and presented in a setting that displays all their significance and enhances their charm.

In the essay on Goethe and Bettina, there is a poetical picture of the tiny adorer, with her Italian imagination mingled with German revery and exaltation, the southern sentiment for art and nature enveloped in cloud and mist, "not without having passed through all the colors of the rainbow." It is not for such a portrait, however, that this piece is here singled out, but because its procedure is characteristic of so many of the *Lundis*. Looking through Bettina's eyes, or perchance using her as a point of departure and return, Sainte-Beuve expounds Goethe's universality, his study of every object, at once as naturalist and as poet, both in its reality and from the standpoint of the ideal, understanding everything excepting the Christian and the hero, the soul of Pascal and the soul of Leonidas. Nor is the essay confined to Goethe, as if one could not wander in chat, even when the chat is brief. Another object of Bettina's worship, Beethoven, also appears, figured as a sort of Milton, the reader being left to his own meditations on the kinship of genius deaf with genius blind.

One would like to linger over these early *Lundis;* the delightful account of Firdusi, based on Mohl's translation; the appreciation of the two Plinys; of Jeanne d'Arc, the sincere, sublime and natural peasant girl; of Fénelon, tolerant not in doctrine, but in character; of Barnave and Malesherbes, martyrs to the fury of '93; of Philippe de Commynes, master of political wisdom acquired, not from books, but from men and things, the best education for good brains. Every essay contains something memorable, and none, or next to none, have become antiquated or lost a jot of their vivacity of interest. But enumeration would be futile and discussion or description endless.

The two essays on Napoleon, however, must be mentioned, because Sainte-Beuve has been accused of writing them in the interest of the approaching Second Empire. Of this superficial accusation the dates alone would be a sufficient refutation, but the substance is still more decisive. Reviewing Thiers' latest volume (December 3, 1849), Sainte-Beuve finds Napoleon gigantic in no praiseworthy sense. "I know that nothing immortal would ever be done, if everything were not risked at a certain time for the great result; nor is it ill to have risked once or twice, but it is the disposition and the tendency to risk always that I find in Napoleon." At Erfurt, the Emperor, playing a rôle, ordered performances of Racine, but feared Molière, who unmasks the human comedy. Poetic enough is the vision of the future at Eylau: "The disaster of Russia was there before his eyes, in miniature, in a prophetic prospect." Yet the greatness is never veiled. In discussing Napoleon's *Memoirs* (December 17, 1849) the critic treats the Emperor as "author and as one of the masters of human speech." A literary education can spoil the natural expression of a strong nature, actions reflecting grandeur on the style; yet this military eloquence, needing for its effect the great deeds, is not to be imitated, and there is a place for Cicero after Cæsar. A third piece (January 14, 1850) is almost wholly an abstract of a volume on the Russian campaign, in which glory is shrouded under horror and agony.

Advising a young poet, Sainte-Beuve had once said that in every art success depended, not on doing something better than your predecessors, but on doing something different. To a certain extent he himself had already done something different in his novel, in his poems, and in his portraits, but it was in the *Lundis* that he at length attained his utmost success. "He has not had time to spoil his articles," said certain none too kind judges, and no doubt there is truth in the comment, though his wit surely had a far richer soul than mere brevity. "The time of systems is past," he remarks, "even in literature. The point is to have good sense, but without insipidity and tediousness, and to mingle with all sorts of ideas in order to judge them, or at least to talk about them freely and fittingly." To establish such familiar talk between himself and his readers, "to keep in constant touch with his public, to consult it, sometimes to listen to it," to be varied and entertaining, yet serious and full of substance, and, however time-worn the topic, always to gift it with novelty— such is the aim, such is the unquestioned achievement. Sainte-Beuve was always on the lookout for subjects susceptible of interest. Have Voltaire and Rousseau grown stale from overdiscussion? He will *surprise* them in some new attitude. He likes, as a rule, to present authors and epochs in a series of vivid episodes. Without destroying historical perspective, he makes all men contemporaries. His reflections are flavored with the wisdom of every age and every school, and they apply unmistakably to us. Soldiers, statesmen, authors, fine ladies, everyone with any mark of distinction, will bring some contribution to the reader's instruction or delight. Much has been said of the companionship of books; Horace and Montaigne are indeed tried friends whom no newcomer can replace; but among more modern writers, you can find no better company than Sainte-Beuve chatting to you of a Monday.

Occasionally an article was meditated in advance, sometimes even several weeks ahead of actual composition, but the usual procedure was to lay out the scheme on Sunday for the work of the succeeding week, and to write at once to Chéron for the necessary books. For the task he was performing, Sainte-Beuve had need of a secretary. We have seen that, soon after his return from Lausanne, a weakness of his eyes had made it necessary for him to employ a reader for the evenings, who also aided him in copying. Dourdain, Oger and the poet Lacaussade were his assistants before '48; at Liège he was served by a young Belgian; for most of the *Lundis* up to his Latin professorship, his secretary was Lacroix; to all of these he has paid his tribute and the first two were even celebrated in disguise in the *Pensées d'Août*. His secretaries, moreover, were not his only aids. Whenever a book, a pamphlet, a letter or a reminiscence was to be found, he wrote for information and help. Volunteers, such as Professor Egger, also offered their services. His most usual recourse, however, was to Chéron of the Bibliothèque Nationale, who, sometimes following the critic's indications, sometimes using his own vast stores of bibliographical knowledge, gathered packages of material, which were called for either by Sainte-Beuve himself or by Lacroix. The published correspondence shows, however, incomplete as it is, that, whoever the helper might be, Sainte-Beuve in general knew what he wanted and knew also where it was to be found. The most insignificant hamlet in the "goodly states and kingdoms" of print, he had either visited or surveyed from some neighboring eminence.

After his first year on the *Constitutionnel*, Sainte-Beuve permitted himself some liberties, as having already established a sort of intimacy with his readers and being assured of their favorable attention. At the beginning, it was not only in the case of Pliny that he feared lack of actuality, an excursion into antiquity which was not repeated, but even a venture into the seventeenth century was felt to require apology, the justification being some recent reprint of those older authors "who are still the most alive." As the series proceeds, however, contemporaries almost disappear, and the reader takes up an historical course in which the chapters, though not consecutive, are more or less connected by allusions and cross-references. Three-fifths of the essays of the second year deal with the eighteenth century. Yet the matter is not simply an old story retold, but always something new, perhaps additional information just come to light or, it may be, merely a fresh point of view or a novel emphasis or even just to revive an image. While Sainte-Beuve gives the necessary setting and a sufficient array of facts, he yet presupposes on the part of his readers a rather extensive knowledge of French literature and history, complimentary enough, even if at first a little bewildering. By the time the course has been followed for a year, however, a sufficient acquaintance with the principal personages has been gained to make one feel quite at home in this company. As annual subscription was the rule for newspapers of that day, Sainte-Beuve could count on readers who would not omit a single Monday. There is an art, perhaps intuitive rather than deliberate, in the unfolding of the apparently desultory succession of subjects.

While at first pieces are linked together merely by allusion and after an interval, there comes at the beginning of the second year a sequence of three essays on style, Mme. Caylus embodying that of the Age of Louis XIV, Rousseau that of the eighteenth century, and Camille Desmoulins that of the Revolutionary epoch. Soon we get two or three consecutive essays on the same topic, constituting, when taken together, a whole about as extensive as the earlier portraits, though done in a somewhat different manner and appealing to a wider audience. All are completely studied. Often, indeed, scores of volumes are consulted, so that, when the critic again takes a single treatise or novel to review, he feels that he is on a week's vacation.

Like others, he gets fatigued, and he once or twice acknowledges the fact and begs pardon. Sometimes he will write a piece merely for his own recreation. At other times, though not often, the article itself betrays a heaviness of disposition and lack of sparkle, but we are in turn recompensed, as in the early weeks of 1851, by an uninterrupted succession of studies characterized by exceptional brilliancy and charm. Such variations might be anticipated in any writer for the press; what is surprising here is the insignificant number of pages that the most exacting taste would be willing to forego. It is doubtful if there could be found, in all Sainte-Beuve's writings, any passage inserted merely to fill space.

In some respects Sainte-Beuve was a thorough journalist. Finding in the Bibliothèque Nationale the copy of Lubis' *History of the Restoration* in which Lamartine had marked passages for his secretary to copy, the reviewer cannot resist the impulse to publish his discovery and to expose the great poet's method of transferring such matter without acknowledgment and with but a few modifications of style to his own pages. A similar exposure is inflicted on an eighteenth century historian, whose themes are enfeebled versions of Tillemont and Saint-Simon. What will catch the public eye is preferred and what the public cannot digest is rejected, as in the refusal to discuss Renan's *Averroës*. Private papers or advance sheets are always welcome. An arresting way of saying things is constantly sought, particularly in the opening sentences of each article. The entertaining anecdote and the apt quotation are employed with skill. Though Sainte-Beuve will not refrain from citing his Latin authors, he now always translates in the interest of the unscholarly. It is indeed surprising how popular he can be, while maintaining a superior standard which may be fully relished only by the most highly cultured. As was proper enough, he tried, if not wholly to conform with the tone of the journal he wrote for, at least not to be openly discordant, an effort which brought him into antagonism with many of his former friends who detested the Empire. These he assailed with an urbanity often more irritating than frank blackguardism. In a like spirit he mingles literary compliment with condemnation. Planche reviewed Lamartine's *History of the Restoration* mercilessly in the *Revue des deux Mondes* (1854); Sainte-Beuve in his article is just as severe, but finds occasion to praise "those happy pages that escape amid the haste and the negligences of his genius."

The essay is apt to open abruptly, the subject stated at once, and if an introduction is employed, its purpose is to entice the reader into a subject that does not at first appear attractive. Enough biography is given to support the special view or impression that is to be emphasized, dates of birth, death and points of achievement being most carefully noted. Often indeed the essayist gives not only the date of an incident, but the age of protagonist at the moment, not trusting his reader to make the computation. The main facts of history we are supposed to know. We are to study everything in its best examples, to attach an exact idea to a name, to transform a mere name into a living man. Hence anecdotes, physical traits, characteristic incidents, vivacious phrases, and noteworthy selections from writings, for "it is thus that posterity abridges and will continue more and more to abridge.'' No one has the time to read all that Sainte-Beuve had read. Indeed he himself sometimes gets embarrassed by the mass of material. The impression, received from reading the chief works of Mme. de Genlis is, he tells us, all that he gives, for it would be rather bold to claim to have read them all: ''She surely would have invented the inkstand, if it had not been invented before.'' Masterpieces we are indeed supposed to be acquainted with, but we are glad to follow such a guide through the maze of secondary works in which French literature is so rich, journals, correspondence, memoirs, writings about society that penetrate and traverse literature in so many directions. Here we get introduced to salons, notable ladies, statesmen, soldiers, beaux, wits, a variegated and entertaining throng, each example, however, rendered perfectly distinct and individual. Writers of the second order are not disdained, for the light and graceful have a right to exist by the side of the great.

It is to Diderot that Sainte-Beuve returns, not as a model altogether, but as an inspiring example, to Diderot, who had the faculty, which is the critic's real triumph, of putting himself in the place of an author and reading according to the spirit that dictated the work. Warmed and inspired, he is the great modern journalist, the Homer of the type, intelligent, expansive, eloquent, open, friendly to all men and to all ideas. ''To each of us a guide and an example, writing for the public, addressing all, improvising, always hurried, going to reality, to the fact, even when he longs for revery; giving, giving, still giving, never storing up; *rather use yourself than rust* is his device. . . . He teaches us how we may reach posterity, in fragments it may be, from the midst of each day's shipwreck.''

After testing Sainte-Beuve on subjects which happen to be familiar, one acquires confidence in the justice of his impressions and in his skill in selecting exactly the points that ought to be distinguished and remembered. In a prejudiced and spiteful article in the *Revue de Paris* (June 1, 1854), Eugène Despois, finding fault with everything Sainte-Beuve had ever published, remarks that a reader who knows Voltaire only from the *Lundis* will be acquainted with many of his personal rows and private delinquencies, but will have no idea of the value of his works. This accusation cannot, indeed, be gainsaid, but who, one wonders, would come to Sainte-Beuve in utter ignorance of Voltaire? Disproportion in the assignment of space is likewise blamed, one essay for Buffon and three for Bernis. How true, wrangling pedant, how undeniably true! Yet many a reader is rather grateful to escape being again told that Voltaire was a great writer and is even willing himself to assume the responsibility of bulking Buffon incomparably larger than Bernis. The *Lundis* do not pretend to draw a chart of French literature; they are not even a course of formal lectures; they are merely a succession of entertaining and thoughtful personal talks. What is dead has the privilege of being stiff.

The theories of race, epoch and families of minds, here and there cropping out in these essays as devices for clarifying ideas rather than as scientific method, are not to be taken so seriously as some are inclined to interpret them. Arithmetical thinkers—estimable people, but not to be jested with—conceive life as a set of rigid formulas and are unwilling ever to modify a label once attached. With Sainte-Beuve the label varied with each new point of view and the formula was discarded the instant it did not obviously fit. Forcing facts into the mold of a preconceived theory always educes reprobation, for nothing is more distasteful to him than the abstract and the systematic in place of the real. It is true that he dreams of constructing a botany of minds, of relating individuals to the type, of preparing the elements for a natural history of human characters, but this thought is caressed, he tells us, in moments when he takes himself very seriously, a hint that ought to put us on our guard. Chateaubriand and Sieyès, Rabelais and Joubert, the practical man of business and the poet of chimerical talents, belong to antipathetic families of minds; Lacordaire is of the race made for certitude; Lamartine has a genius for the inexact; here is no geometric theory, but merely the genial application of a none too precise idea. All of us classify our acquaintances more or less in such fashion, and we feel no surprise if they sometimes overleap the bounds of definition. No more strict is Sainte-Beuve's search for qualities derived from ancestry or from native province, or for resemblances between brothers and sisters, or for character expressed in countenance, physique or dress. All such things taken together count in an estimate, but no single one is invariable, makes a law or could serve as a means for reconstructing a personality in the way a bone served Cuvier for his extinct animals. Here, too, Sainte-Beuve, though keen and skillful, goes in principle little beyond our daily distinction of Yankee and Southerner, or our interpretation of family traits or personal appearance.

It is the imprint of the epoch that seems to him most certainly distinguishable in the continuous stream of French literature. The sixteenth century, the period of Louis XIII, the Age of Louis XIV, the early eighteenth century, the time of the revery coming after Rousseau, the Revolution, the Empire, the Restoration, and even subdivisions of these, each is an aggregation of intellectual qualities and of moods perfectly distinct in itself, though not interdicting below the surface counter-currents and currents of survival and anticipation. We are all unescapably men of our time, either by attraction or repulsion, and yet, though each is intrinsically of his date and bears its mark, there is in the epoch, as epoch, no creative force. Genius remains inexplicable and essentially untrammeled, a divine gift. It is perhaps because Sainte-Beuve deals so habitually, not with the highest genius, but with minor writers and with general currents, that his emphasis on fashions of thought and speech is so pronounced. Such fashions commonly serve as palliations for faults of taste and sometimes furnish a characteristic lesson of humility. These people, he says, in reference to the perpetrators of some past absurdity, had the malady of their age; before disdaining them, let us ask if we have not the malady of ours; and having noted some previous reigning form of platitude, he adds: "Let us not flatter ourselves that we have not our own."

Paradoxical as the statement may seem, it is still a fact that one of Sainte-Beuve's most charming traits is his charity. Intimacy with Port-Royal had given him the habit of searching his own heart, so that, when he condemns another, he fixes his eye upon some similar shortcoming in himself. One of the poems in the *Livre d'Amour* tells us that, when attacked, he first felt resentment; then reflected, asking whether, though free from the fault ascribed to him, he may not have other faults; and so he is led to pardon. It had also long been his habit to take a favorite author and inquire: "What would he think of me?" Very often a general remark suggests a personal interpretation. "This Portrait of Fontenelle by La Bruyère," he says, "is a great lesson: it shows us how a skillful painter, a penetrating critic, may, when he tells the truth, be deceived because he does not tell the whole truth, because he does not sufficiently appreciate the fact that, in this bizarre and complex human organization, a thoroughly characteristic fault, freak or absurdity is never incompatible with superior qualities." Coming closer to his own case, he says in another place: "It befits those

who, living in calmer times, have not themselves escaped
literary contradictions and retractions, to show some indulgence for those of La Harpe.'' The following—who
can doubt it?—is pure autobiography:

> For a man of letters there is nothing so consoling as pro-
> duction, nothing that reconciles him better with others and with
> himself. Thought alone, solitary meditation, is doubtless also
> consoling; but such contemplative meditation demands in an
> ardent nature a sort of virtue, in order that it should not turn
> into bitterness and envy when it measures itself with others.
> Active labor, on the contrary, translated into works, distracts
> us from the perpetual comparison we are tempted to make be-
> tween ourselves and others less worthy, though perhaps often
> more favored, and it better fulfills the aim of life, which is to be
> or to believe oneself useful, and not to cut oneself off in an
> abnegation painful to sustain and not readily sincere.

It is certain that Sainte-Beuve has himself in mind when
he ascribes to Bussy-Rabutin ''that paternal solicitude of
the man of letters, unwilling that anything he had written
should perish, and desirous of such praise as might be
reaped even at a slight expense of reputation.'' Sometimes
we find even a direct personal confidence, as in the following on *amour-propre:* ''It would little befit us who
speak to be too severe, having felt it in our day and described it in our youth.'' There are other cases when the
personal experience is revealed only by search and comparison. Speaking of Mme. du Deffand's love for Horace
Walpole, Sainte-Beuve says: ''She loved Walpole as the
tenderest of mothers would have loved a son long lost and
suddenly found again. Thus many of these singular and
bizarre passions, in which there appears an abuse of sensibility, are only the revenge of nature punishing us for not
having done simple things at the right time.'' In one of
his private jottings (published, of course, with ''paternal
solicitude'') Sainte-Beuve tells us that, at the age of forty-

four, he had an indefinite longing for a young girl, a longing to gaze at her, to refresh his eyes and thoughts, to deck her out, to take walks with her under the trees, to see her happy—and he suddenly asks: "What is it I really want?" It is a daughter about fifteen years old. "My foresight fifteen years ago," he adds, "was at fault, or else I resisted Nature's insinuations, and to-day Nature recalls the fact. Our vicious and depraved tastes are often nothing but natural impulses gone astray and turned from their true import." Sainte-Beuve thus constrained his own self-condemnation to interpret a sentimental eccentricity of a blind old eighteenth-century lady.

Even in his attitude toward literary criticism itself, high as was his conception of its mission, is found a sort of indulgence akin to charity. In his view, the critic has a special sense. He admires Dr. Johnson for his good judgment, his striking way of saying things and his authority. Such authority he sought for himself, and yet he proclaims that there is no recipe for making a classic. Criticism can give advice, but inspiration escapes, being born as it pleases God. He would rejoin tradition, yet abolish models. We must not imitate, but be ourselves and aim high. The Temple of Taste must be enlarged, yet he has no pretension to be the architect. Authority does not involve infallibility. He tells us that some little pieces of Diderot have been called masterpieces, though by no means worthy of the title, all the while aware that the condemned qualification was applied in one of his own early essays. He can call Ducis the "innocent profaner of Shakespeare"; he can in turn appreciate all sorts of qualities and weary of them; use Pascal, for example, as an antidote to Bernardin de Saint-Pierre, love grandeur to-day and grace or wit to-morrow, seem unstable and even contradictory on many superficial points, but he is firm forever in what is fundamental, in an abhorrence of the *atheist*

354

spirit in literature, the spirit "which removes from all things the inward beauty, the *mens divinior.*"

Among books, too, he had his special personal friends and we are all advised to select such friends:

Whether it be Horace or any other who is our favorite author and who reflects our own thoughts in a rich maturity, to one at least of these good and antique minds we go to seek converse at any moment we choose, to seek a friendship that cannot deceive or ever fail us, to seek an habitual impression of serenity and amenity that reconciles us—and how often we feel the need! —with mankind and with ourselves.

While usually charitable toward human weaknesses, Sainte-Beuve will not condone vulgarity, dishonor or even open immorality. His touchstone is always something lofty and, while he does not often utter moral condemnation, he provokes it in the reader who, after all, is apt to take pleasure in thinking that the judgment passed is his own, rather than that of the critic. Wholesale praise or blame is never bestowed. To some, a man is all white or all black; to others, he is predominantly white or black; to Sainte-Beuve he is white here and black there. If the reader chooses to class the subject as one or the other, that is none of the critic's business; but beware of asserting that such a classification was intended. The critic will bluntly tell you: "I meant what I said, no more and no less; you have no right to make me a partisan of ideas that are yours."

The confusion of thought and the one-sidedness that lead to such misinterpretations irritated Sainte-Beuve. He has slight patience with those who strike a little aside from the point, or for those who employ vague words, or who abuse terms, or who become involved in vain, abstract philosophical expressions which give us the illusion of possessing ideas we do not have. Sainte-Beuve himself never uses a conventional language, but always attaches to his words a clearly felt and thought meaning. He actually hates vague and ambiguous terms. In the *Lundis,* indeed, he has even corrected some earlier faults, and he no longer indulges in round-about expressions. On this subject he says:

I formerly had a mannerism; I had brought myself to write with a certain turn of phrase, to caress and refine my thought; and I was rather proud of it. Necessity, great Muse that she is, forced me to an abrupt change: this very necessity that, in critical moments, causes the mute to speak and stammerers to articulate, obliged me, in an instant, to adopt a form of expression that was clean-cut, clear, and rapid, to speak to all the world in the language of all the world: for this requirement I am indeed grateful.

Indefatigable reader that he was, Sainte-Beuve could perceive that Huet, to take a striking instance, had read too much. Humanity likes to forget, and each generation wishes to reinvent, even if less well. It is Pascal, Descartes, Rousseau, men who have read little, who move the world. The composer of the weekly chat likes involuntary authors, those who write simply to preserve an experience; if he finds a book made without thought of its being a book, so much the better; even the mediocre writers of the Age of Louis XIV charm by their agreeable, familiar style, their negligences reproducing the spirit of conversation.

It seems as though Sainte-Beuve, largely shut out by his task from the highly prized pleasures of social intercourse, sought compensation for the reality he had abandoned in an imaginative reconstruction of the salons of the past. Though confessing himself somewhat of a stranger in the seventeenth century, he can go back as though he had lived in the eighteenth and frequent aristocratic gatherings with perfect freedom and without fear of annoyance.

Whereas contemporaries had to choose between Mme. du Deffand and Mlle. de Lespinasse, he is privileged to visit each in turn. He can forsake the frivolous as soon as they become too empty; nor does he have to listen to the philosophers beyond endurance; there is always some new society ready to offer entertainment. To the reader he communicates the "disinterested pleasure of living again in this choice company." It is indeed past life rather than literature that is mainly dealt with, or better, past life as seen through literature. When we are told that Buffon in his *Natural History* introduced into his description of the stag an account of a hunt so as to gain favor at court and thus enlarge the Jardin du Roi, how real a solemn old book becomes! All kinds of gossip Sainte-Beuve loves, yet he will not enlarge upon scandal, merely giving a hint to show that he is well informed, for he knows a vast number of discreditable stories that he does not tell. If Hecuba and Andromache are more purely poetic than Marie Antoinette, it is because there are no memoirs of the court of Priam, while we cannot help taking account of those concerning the court of Louis XVI. Of Ninon he remarks that "the succession of her lovers has been established about as exactly as that of the Assyrian or Egyptian kings," but what he impresses upon us is the civilizing magic of her social attraction. Indeed, the immense importance of the feminine influence on literature and good-breeding from the time of Mlle. Scudéry to that of Mme. Récamier is one of the predominant impressions left by this group of essays.

Human character revealed in the written word is thus the main interest. Louis XIV, with his good sense, and having the best education, that of events, writes the "style royal," and among authors he is truly the King; in Frederick the Great's works there is a superiority arising from force of soul; Napoleon and Richelieu show their greatness and are worthy of themselves even in wielding the pen; coming further down the scale, it is what Carrel did that made what he wrote memorable. In another region, good manners are expressed in urbanity, taste, unforced good-humor, finesse and purity of language. "Fénelon had not that irritability of good sense that makes one say *no* with vehemence." Lebrun-Pindare's bad character injured his poetry. Old virtues are fittingly expressed in old syntax and a springtime of discovery gives Amyot his freshness and grace.

Sainte-Beuve always attempts by quotation and by his own style to reflect the tone of his subject, light, serious, even heavy and pedantic, antique, classic, naïve, romantic and metaphorical, an infinite and highly artistic variety. His procedure is indicated in a significant essay on Walkenaer (May 31, 1852), in which this learned writer is criticized for *changing the tone* of his author, for instead of quoting, of borrowing "incomparable expressions," he translates, polishes and modernizes. While Walkenaer took notes and then wrote from these without verification, Sainte-Beuve always recurred to the original, his desk heaped with volumes, a hopeless pile to his secretary, but a mass wherefrom the master could select without hesitation the page he wanted and indicate the extract to be copied. His keenness for tone is frequently displayed in his discovery of the slightest traces of a diverse current in the productions of any epoch, such as the appearance of humanity and equality (presaging the era of philosophy) in writings of the dying Age of Louis XIV. A particular case of such sensibility is his noting with surprise in Mme. Lambert a passage of higher religious spirit than usual, a passage that proved to have been copied, as a friend afterwards informed him, from a life of Rancé. Sainte-Beuve possessed the critic's special sense.

That his keenness was now little exercised upon contemporaries need excite no wonder. The larger figures of the thirties and forties had all been discussed in previous essays, and the literary production of the early fifties was not imposing. There was a turn of the tide. Saint-Marc-Girardin, Sainte-Beuve noted, had been too successful in his efforts to cure his pupils of the malady of René; youths were no longer dreamers and poets, but positivists and utilitarians. Even in 1843 Nanteuil had sadly told Hugo that there were no more young men. There could be found, it is true, plenty of good poets (1852), but no vigorous original genius, Leconte de Lisle being rated as about the best. As academicians and others of prominence died, the critic might produce a sort of obituary portrait, interesting enough, though the subject was by no means preëminent. In writing, which is not wholly an art, said the critic, one must take account of the average public. These *Lundis,* we must not forget, were not intended primarily for posterity, but for the daily readers of the *Constitutionnel.*

On such daily readers Sainte-Beuve sought to exercise an indirect political influence. At first his tendencies are shown chiefly in his dislike of the fanatic, of the man of system who would construct an improved world in which we should all die of *ennui.* Nothing is more obnoxious than "abstract superstition," the abuse of analysis and the exaggerated application of mathematical methods in the social and moral sciences. Completely cured of humanitarianism, "the bauble of the age," he would come back to good sense and moderation. For the Revolution of 1830 his enthusiasm had faded long ago; both sides, he says, were foolish, and he repeats an old opinion that Carrel spoiled his career by sticking to his revolutionary friends. While frivolity and vice brought ruin to the *ancien régime,* the mob spirit is even worse, and a demagogue is only a reversed courtier without the polish. Monstrosities of style are parallel with political anarchy. Sainte-Beuve

has "no pretension to propose direct recipes for present
ills and inquietudes; there are no such remedies"; yet he
is always against excess and in favor of unity and order,
of a government that shall be moderate and humane, and
restorative through justice. Was the new administration
such a government? Sainte-Beuve said *yes*; the liberals as
a unit said *no*.

The critic's attitude toward individuals is well presented
in an explanation of his article on Montalembert (November 5, 1849):

I tried without flattery to depict him by the best and most
acceptable traits of his brilliant and militant eloquence; if you
only recall the moment and think that this article appeared in
the *Constitutionnel,* you will doubly appreciate my desire to be
agreeable to him. I was careful, moreover, to maintain the literary neutrality which I like to observe, especially in the face of
sharp-cut and absolute doctrines.

The day before the Coup d'État, Sainte-Beuve's article,
a piece of almost inspired innocence, dealt with Mme. de
Motteville. There is, however, no reason to believe that
he had the slightest suspicion of what was preparing,
though Véron, whom he always consulted about his topics,
might have known. The week after, Sieyès is the subject,
documents being furnished by Fortoul, Napoleon's minister
of education. Here the salve to the public is an insistence
on the proposition that, as a result of the Revolution of '89,
society without privileges has subsisted under all changes
of government. Two weeks later, with obvious and direct
application, an article on de Retz ends with the wish that
the agitators of the day would submit to necessity and take
up whist, or philosophy, or even write memoirs that would
inspire no desire to imitate their example. In another
place, Michaud is praised for his sage abstention from
politics in his old age. Throughout there is manifested a

special antipathy against the doctrinaire group. Guizot's deceptive eloquence in the Chamber was pernicious because failing to take account of a different atmosphere outside. The endless talk in parliaments excites frequent impatience. Let the liberals turn to literature. The humble Rollin is contrasted with those eloquent professors who take possession of their disciples and go into politics, and regrets are expressed that Cousin and Villemain—always pointed out when "eloquent professors" are in question—had not returned to teaching. The task is to awaken a love of letters in the positive and practical new generation; to awaken also patriotic fervor, for the people, entirely given over to private interests, need some political religion, "a remembrance or hope that shall be the soul of the nation," under Henry IV called the King, under Napoleon the Empire, and in the future by "some name not yet known."

While all such political views are merely incidental, they yet, even as asides, give to the essays a general atmosphere favorable to Louis Napoleon. The whole attitude is that of an absolutist. Finally, between a portrait of Gerbet and one of Bernardin de Saint-Pierre, appeared (August 23, 1852) the celebrated, perhaps we should say notorious, outburst, "Les Regrets." Here the opponents of the autocrat, among them many former friends, are accused of sulking because the new government is not *their* achievement. Regarding themselves as a privileged class representing right and justice, they suffer the pangs of lost power, being exactly on a plane in this respect with the ancient courtiers; and to make the stab more painful, Sainte-Beuve introduces a number of examples of fallen ministers. Allowing for principle, he does not advise espousing the imperial government, but deprecates obstinate resistance, praising Lamartine for devoting himself to literary production without any display of bitterness. All should be grateful to a stable government, of whatever

361

sort, which procures order, guarantees civilization, and allows the free development of men's faculties through labor. Another stab is the remark that the malady of *lost speech* is particularly painful to a government of orators. "Of all disposition of mind," concludes the new political mentor, "irony is the least intelligent; of all passions, petulance is the most petty."

Reproduced in the *Moniteur* and other official journals, this essay made a great stir, alienating almost all Sainte-Beuve's liberal friends. The attack could not justly be called treacherous, though many considered it so, but it was, to say the least, ungenerous. Not only at this time, but to the very last day, hundreds of able men suffered bitterly from the tyranny of the Empire. One may suspect that Sainte-Beuve secretly repented, for a note inserted when the piece was reprinted in volume VI of the *Lundis*, to the effect that the blow had been felt by the general staff of the salons, has a tone of bravado, rather than one of conviction, and many years after, he confesses in a letter to Schérer that he had yielded to an impulse and that he had not dreamed how serious the act would be.

The insinuation of pettiness was answered and completely confuted in a brilliant article in the *Débats* by Cuvillier-Fleury (September 26, 1852). This piece, "De la Critique expérimentale dans les œuvres de M. Sainte-Beuve," purports to be a general review of the *Portraits* and the *Lundis,* thus avoiding any difficulties with the censor. After much praise, the reviewer insists at considerable length on the changeableness of the critic, emphasizing each variation by quotation and example. Sainte-Beuve had broken with every one of his former associates and, by too much experimenting, had lost in elevation what he had gained in extent of surface. All this introductory part is an admirable preparation, and the fact that all the quotations are from *Portraits littéraires,* Vol. III, would show any careful reader that the general review was a mere pretext to cover the real point, a refutation of "Les Regrets." Who can believe, asks Cuvillier-Fleury, that our governors for thirty years, men whose task required elevation of soul and audacity, have been so grotesque and vulgar as to lament simply the external signs of authority? They would not indeed accept power under the imperial constitution. "They regret the honor and emotion of serious conflicts, the noble combats of political oratory in which the destiny of the country was involved, the illustrious arena of parliamentary discussion in which, during thirty years, the affairs of France were regulated with prudence, splendor, liberty and dignity." "Their regrets, whatever they may be, deserve respect rather than pity." What, indeed, does Sainte-Beuve know about the irritation of these choice souls? A final sugar coating is added in a reference to the "ingenious critic, the agreeable and profound scholar, the serious and charming writer"; but a feud was started which led to many subsequent blows by both combatants.

About two weeks after the appearance of "Les Regrets," Fortoul, minister of education, offered Sainte-Beuve the chair of eloquence (French literature) in the Sorbonne, made vacant by the retirement of Villemain. Political passion absent, no selection could have appeared more fitting, but under the circumstances, in spite of the fact that Fortoul, former disciple of Leroux and Lamennais, had for years been a personal friend of the critic, the element of pay for service rendered and for further service expected seemed altogether too obvious. Sainte-Beuve's refusal (September 6) was, however, based on other grounds: (1) he cannot "inherit from one he assassinates"—referring to his severe treatment of Villemain in an article on Bernardin de Saint-Pierre (September 6, 1852); (2) he is not fitted for public speech, lacking the force of the

orator, his nerves still suffering from his two attempts—
"I am wholly myself only pen in hand and in the silence
of my study"; (3) a professorship in the name of the
state demands habitual gravity and a past without frivolity, even poetic frivolity—a reason which recalls a remark
on Rivarol, "a man who had his Lisette was not quite fit
to defend high principles." The letter concludes: "Allow
me to serve the cause of letters as volunteer, attaching
them, as occasion presents, to the cause which I consider
that of society, order and practical happiness."

What Sainte-Beuve received from the government
through Fortoul was his engagement in November, 1854,
to continue his *Lundis* in the *Moniteur* when he relinquished his contract with the *Constitutionnel* on Véron's
retirement from the management. He was also named
Officer of the Legion of Honor (August 12, 1853), a distinction that involved validating the original decoration
conferred by Villemain in 1844 and at that time so
vehemently refused. All these favors contributed to
Sainte-Beuve's unpopularity with the liberals, to whom
he was indeed constantly giving offense. When he had
gone to Liège, he had been accused of deserting the Republic, while Belgium was hostile because he was a foreigner; his quick return irritated the Belgians and made
the Parisians sneer; his conservatism on the *Constitutionnel*
gave him the appearance of a time-server; and now his
connection with the official journal stamped him as a
renegade. Self-will and impulsiveness, indeed, kept him a
good part of the time in hot water, but, though imprudent
in his relations with the public and inconsiderate in his
treatment of old-time friends, he gives to the dispassionate
the impression of sincerity. His expressed hope that the
government would favor literature is the only indication
of ambition. Perhaps he dreamed that he might be to
Napoleon III what Boileau had been to Louis XIV, or

possibly what Fontanes had been to the First Empire, but there is no basis for such a suspicion beyond vague and unsupported guesswork. A wholly intelligible personal motive may be discerned in the fact that, while literary criticism was not wanted, Sainte-Beuve's occupation was gone: 1848 had wrecked his prospects; the new administration, on the contrary, was wholly favorable; it repressed agitation and by cutting politics out of journalism, left space for talk about books.

As though there were a purpose to close with brilliancy, the last three essays in the *Constitutionnel* (November 15, 22, 29, 1852) present a superb portrait of Benjamin Franklin, a piece of work upon which the critic lavished his best powers. On December 6 the series in the *Moniteur* opens with an attractive study of the Abbé Barthélemy and his *Voyage of Anacharsis.*

Up to this time, the *Moniteur* had not been noted for its attention to literature. The *feuilleton* itself was crushed by the weight of the political page, wherein the speeches to and by the Emperor, and the accounts of his doings, all with indications of applause, are a bit nauseating. In 1853 the size of the journal was changed from folio to full sheet, and on Mondays Sainte-Beuve usually occupied an entire page out of four, the article being in large type and making an imposing appearance. At first there are few other names of any literary distinction. Later Gautier did the dramatic *feuilleton,* Nisard and Mérimée occasionally contributed, and there is much more space given to books. When Sainte-Beuve began, Napoleon's *Memoirs* were being reprinted as a serial; then came some forgotten stories; in 1855 a translation of *Martin Chuzzlewit* runs for about a year and Ike Marvel's *Reveries of a Bachelor* is also reproduced. Sainte-Beuve, however, so long as his connection lasted, was the chief literary support of this paper.

Referring to his transfer in his opening article, the

critic announces that, since civilization is now assured by the will of one man, he will continue his course in literature without change in form or spirit. Appreciating the honor done him by members of the government, he will try to make his essays worthy of the *Moniteur,* and will sometimes coördinate them with the new régime. Under the present Empire criticism should equal that under the old. He will select subjects from the seventeenth and eighteenth centuries, without absolutely excluding contemporaries.

There is, indeed, in these *Lundis,* more uniformity and there are perhaps clearer traces of fatigue than in the previous ones. Sainte-Beuve is more leisurely; groups of two or three on the same subject predominate and, instead of seeking variety of manners, he dwells for considerable periods in the same epoch. He is sometimes oppressed by too strong a sense of propriety and merely alludes to a point of interest which he omits out of deference to his readers. The salons having been about exhausted, he now deals largely with public men and with more serious writers; yet the same procession of distinguished figures passes before us, preferably not authors, but men and women who represent the tone of good society, and the spoken language, or men of action who express their deeds in words. In 1854 Port-Royal seems again to have occupied Sainte-Beuve, and many essays are colored by researches connected with his book. Amidst such things, we find also odds and ends of studies, among which we are delighted to stumble on the fresh figure of Maucroix, which renews some of the earlier charm.

Notwithstanding some slight decline, the great qualities of Sainte-Beuve still persist. He never sees a confused mass, but always definite aspects, allied with one another and observed from well-chosen points of view. If Jacques could suck melancholy out of a song as a weasel sucks eggs, Sainte-Beuve had a parallel gift for sucking interesting matter out of forgotten books. He never merely repeats known facts and opinions, but always finds something new, if it be only an uncommon perspective. The quotations chosen are fresh and suggestive, while those everybody is supposed to know are merely referred to. The reader feels that he is getting something peculiar to Sainte-Beuve, not what any other critic might have said or could have said. A man is generally placed amid his contemporaries and a book fitted to the conditions of its time and discussed often, not for what it means to us, but for what it meant to its original readers. A favorite device is to trace a reputation through several generations, and then to establish the reality by means of facts, contemporary judgments, and the words and deeds of the person himself. Among minor writers, indeed, circumstances have much to do with reputation. Sainte-Beuve seeks in the past everything that has a distinct mark, and particularly the mark of an epoch. He records, not a list of achievements, but the principal occasions on which the whole originality of character is displayed. Passing distinguished men in review, he indicates certain features and underlines the traits, points out the contrasts and resemblances that present themselves and by maintaining the character of each object, fertilizes everything. And it is the better character that is preferred. By selecting the best and most elevated in the writings of celebrated men, he believes that he is truer, even from the standpoint of history. Excess of delicacy is less fatiguing than excess of brutality, and that which is vulgar, immoral, containing no principle of honor, is hateful. Opposites, however, are still suggested as a relief from over-indulgence in highly starched virtue.

One cannot help feeling how well Sainte-Beuve has read the books he discusses or mentions. And what limitless quantities he devoured! Think only of the portrait of Gibbon, involving as it did within a fortnight a reading

of the history, the autobiography, the correspondence, and
a search both through contemporary memoirs and letters
and through the comments of Guizot and other later
scholars—this preparation followed by the composition of
some forty thoughtful pages. If the result is sometimes
a little heavy, we find at other times the most vivid fascination, as witness the three essays on medieval chroniclers,
Villehardouin, Froissart and Joinville, the last read with
Homer open on the table, and all three rendered with a
naïve charm of style.

Sometimes an intimate confidence will still brighten a
page:

> Whoever in youth has conceived a romantic and tender ideal,
> and seen it wither before his eyes and break under his feet as
> he has advanced; whoever has more or less known errors, rash
> engagements and difficulties without issue, and has not sought
> to make of his faults a theory or a throne of pride; whoever
> (and the number is vast) has known the painful subjections of
> a literary life, even such as are honorable, and the weight of
> drudgery, in place of the light yoke of the Muses; such will have
> for the Abbé Prévost a special devotion, as toward an ancestor
> and an indulgent patron.

The political tone is little changed. Passing stabs at the
Doctrinaires are rather frequent: sophists and rhetoricians,
an intolerant clique eager to dominate, believing the world
going to the dogs when they do not rule. An oft repeated
doctrine is that the spirit of France always reflects the
spirit of the chiefs who guide the nation. Sainte-Beuve
was truly in the service of the new Empire; he even refers
to Louis Napoleon as "a writer one is proud to quote."
Yet some former social relations were continued, for
Pasquier furnished a document for April 4, 1853. "You
are not a man's enemy," says the critic, "because you see
his absurdities."

In regard to religion he goes farthest in the essay on the

anniversary of the *Génie du Christianisme* (April 17, 1854), inserting a passage wherein he says:

And we too (as after the Concordat) see the free concord and union of Church and State; and, from the particular point of view of the *Génie du Christianisme* which occupies us, is it not to be counted as a charming sign of a sweet influence regained and socially established, this image of the Virgin sent yesterday by the Emperor to our fleets, and received with gratitude as protectress and patron?

Now, while Sainte-Beuve as a writer for the *Moniteur* was somewhat restricted in his freedom, he was not obliged to say things he did not believe. Certainly he could not accept the Virgin as his own protectress; yet he upholds conciliation where old prejudices, as he calls them, could not be at once removed, and Bonaparte's Concordat seemed to him a masterly stroke of statesmanship. The Church, he maintains, is a rampart for the defense of society, to be supported even by the indifferent, advocacy of a state religion being thus merely a product of anti-revolutionary politics. But beyond such material aspects, there remained with Sainte-Beuve an abiding interest in religious feelings as factors in human nature. Religious writers, such as Bourdaloue and Fénelon, always attracted him for their subtle analysis of the soul. For his own part, he even in one place expresses the opinion that devotion to the Virgin and to the saints as intercessors between the crushed spirit and a terrible God might have saved Cowper from his mental torment. The embers of Port-Royal, indeed, could never be wholly extinguished by rationalism, however thorough. Above all, Sainte-Beuve had a constant and sincere admiration for Pascal, not only as a writer, but as a sublime personality. "After reading Pascal," he says, "one may remain an unbeliever, never again a mocker or blasphemer."

In these *Moniteur* essays the old literary disputes are

hardly touched. The critic may say: "About this group I uttered hard things in my youth when we were at war, but now, since rivalry has ceased, I can be just"; or he may assert that, "while prejudice and routine were broken by Romanticism, the great genius has not yet come." Criticism, he has learned, may be indulgent, but it is inexcusable to assign a quality opposite to that possessed. It actually hurts him when Lamartine calls Adolphe Dumas a Horace, or when Hugo calls M. Méry a Virgil. After all, these are by no means recent lessons. The piece on Chateaubriand cited above, while showing by means of the famous marginal comments to the *Essai sur les Révolutions* that René was not consistently a believer, concedes the sincerity of the emotion in which the *Génie* was begun and also the artistic sincerity of the whole work.

Here, in addition to one passage in quotation marks, several unacknowledged pages have been taken unchanged from the Liège lectures, a sign, one may say, of exhaustion. Indeed, while there still remained veins to be worked, five years of unintermitted prospecting had made choice more difficult, and there must have been felt, not only the fatigue of an endless task, but the monotony of always varying the ingredients. Vacations, too, were absent. Even a visit to Gerbet in Amiens (August, 1852) was in preparation for the eternal article. Another opening, therefore, could not but have been welcome.

Although Sainte-Beuve had refused an appointment to the Sorbonne, he was not unwilling to accept the professorship of Latin Poetry at the Collège de France, which, though bestowed like the other by the Emperor through his Minister of Education, required also a preliminary nomination by the Faculty of the Collège and by the Academy of Inscriptions, a procedure regarded as giving assurance of merit in the candidate, as well as security against political influence. Such nomination the critic received by an almost unanimous vote of both bodies. By an imperial decree signed Dec. 13, 1854, and published in the *Moniteur* the following day, "M. Sainte-Beuve, of the French Academy, is named Professor of Latin Poetry in the Imperial Collège of France, to replace M. Tissot, deceased."

Preparation of a course of lectures demanded discontinuance of the weekly article. The *Causéries*, scholarly always, but at this final moment without special distinction, ran along for four weeks longer, the final piece being a discussion of Fortoul's *Plan of Secondary Studies* (Jan. 8, 1855). Though bound to approval, Sainte-Beuve, nevertheless, here expressed his real convictions. He was no literary fanatic, for his early studies had given him a high regard for positive science and an unusual knowledge of the subject. Quite recently, in a perfectly non-contentious article, he had assigned the first rank in pure intelligence to the men named Archimedes or Newton or Lagrange. Now he asserts that Arago was right so long as he argued in favor of science; not when he attacked literature. The heart is with M. Girardin upholding classical studies, but reason and good sense must recognize the truth of the physicist's stand. It is indeed an absurdity to understand Homer and Virgil, yet know no truth of physical science. In discussing such educational plans, however, Sainte-Beuve is practically just as futile as others; the precise combination of scientific and classical training to be desired has not yet been found, and the debate is ever renewed afresh, as lively, as heated, as inconclusive to-day as it was in the time of Fortoul. In a sort of postscript to his discussion, Sainte-Beuve takes leave of his readers, thanking them for their good-will, begging leave to interrupt his regular communications, and announcing that he will be happy to resume when occasion offers.

The date in truth marks the close of a distinct epoch in

Sainte-Beuve's life, the epoch of the original *Lundis*. These he had begun to collect in 1851, publishing in that year four volumes, each containing the work of six months (twenty-six essays). Every year thereafter one or two additional volumes appeared, the eleventh in 1856 concluding the series and containing an index, later replaced with other matter. Volumes XII-XV (1857-1862) were appended as a result of circumstances, and the pieces were produced under different conditions. It is of some importance, indeed, that we should not consider the *Lundis* as a single continuous work, but the chief purpose of here mentioning these details of publication is to show that Sainte-Beuve himself at the age of fifty felt that something had been finished and that he was opening a new career.

CHAPTER XII

1855—1861

THE lectures of Sainte-Beuve as Professor of Latin Poetry at the Collège de France, begun in March, 1855, were interrupted by a prearranged political disturbance, and he found it impossible to continue beyond the second. In spite of repeated resignations, he was kept on the rolls as nominal professor until his death, though without salary and being represented by a substitute. The matter prepared for his course appeared in installments in the *Moniteur* and the *Revue Contemporaine,* and was then collected as a volume, the *Étude sur Virgile,* in 1857. For a time (1855-1856) Sainte-Beuve contributed critical articles every Saturday to the *Athenæum Français,* a weekly literary and scholarly journal; he then returned to the *Moniteur,* though writing irregularly and sometimes at long intervals. In 1857, he was appointed to a lectureship in the École Normale, where he taught for four years, giving two lessons a week, with the usual vacations. The leisure afforded by this consecutive teaching was devoted to the completion of *Port-Royal,* the final two volumes appearing in 1859. In 1861, gathering his Liège lectures on Chateaubriand, with additional notes, and throwing together at the end some articles connected with the subject and several pages of disconnected jottings, he produced two further volumes, *Chateaubriand and His Literary Group.* There was time also for social relaxation, and Sainte-Beuve emerges from his solitude with a new set of younger friends, most of them liberal in politics and anti-clerical, of whom Renan and Taine are the most important. He also became intimate with the Princess Mathilde and her brother, the Prince Napoléon (Plon-Plon). In September, 1861, he returned to the *Constitutionnel,* contracting to write a weekly article for a period of three years, for which he relinquished his place at the École Normale, as well as his leisurely essays in the *Moniteur* and some other literary prospects, in consideration of an indemnity of 25,000 francs.

On March 7, 1855, the *Moniteur* announced, as was customary for each new series of lectures, that "M. Sainte-Beuve will open his course on Latin poetry at the Collège de France on Friday, March 9, at half past twelve." On the ninth, the notice was repeated, with the additional information that the professor would deal with Virgil and the *Æneid* and that he would continue Wednesdays and Fridays at the same hour.

The opening lecture, later published as a pamphlet, gave in outline a history of the Collège de France and particularly of the chair of Latin poetry, which had been first held by Delille, though the subject had been treated without the title by Passerat, of whom a sort of portrait is thrown in. It was the second professor, Tissot, whom Sainte-Beuve succeeded, and among the substitutes of Tissot, the lecturer, loyal to a dear memory, pays a special tribute to one who would have been the natural successor and one whom he himself would have supported and applauded, "a friend, a young man distinguished by the diversity of his aptitudes, by the abundance and facility of his erudition, by his grace of pen and word, Charles Labitte, removed by death on the threshold of a brilliant career." It is as a "priest of Virgil" that the new professor conceives his function, an admirer applying historical and comparative methods, illustrating by Greek and modern parallels, and drawing from his subject a lesson of harmony, unity and good sense in an age of extravagance.

My literary principles, he continues (for I too have some, though I do not blazon them), my principles will appear, I hope, in the lively sentiment which I believe I possess for certain beauties and in my devotion to these. In our age wherein many systems and professions of faith have been made; wherein, on every occasion, the word belief has been introduced so prodigally in all sorts of philosophical, social and literary matters; I will not say that little faith actually exists; but rather that there is a more discreet religion which holds to the love of the beautiful, of the natural, of the fine and delicate in poetry. This the Greeks had; after them the Romans gathered more than one spark for their own flame; they in their turn held the torch. Some of these sparks, diminished but still vital, have passed even to us: may we never allow them to be extinguished.

Such sparks it is that he will bring together and revive; he may even become excited and passionate, for he has long put into this matter what ardor remained to him. Others may know the subject better than he, but no one loves it more.

There was nothing apparently either in subject or treatment that should stimulate the slightest opposition, but a band of resolute disturbers had concerted measures to make the course impossible and drive Sainte-Beuve from the chair. The speaker was interrupted with uproar, exclamations, invective, impertinent and abusive questions. One sou, it seems, was thrown at him, but hit a lady instead. The next Wednesday a second lecture met with a like reception. Other subjects, carried through by a determined orator, might survive a row, but how should the delicacy, stateliness and charm of Virgil be manifested in the midst of impudent turbulence? Refusing the assistance of the police, Sainte-Beuve relinquished the attempt and sent his resignation to Fortoul, though he held the nominal professorship until his death. For some years Martha, a painstaking scholar, supplied Sainte-Beuve's place, and when Martha secured another chair in 1865, his successor was the celebrated Gaston Boissier. In November, 1869, the place having become vacant by the critic's death, Boissier, being naturally first choice of both the Academy of Inscriptions and the Collège de France, was appointed to the professorship.

Sainte-Beuve not only sent his resignation to Fortoul, at which time he renounced all compensation, but he repeated it to Rouland (1857) and Duruy (1863), in both cases urging the appointment of Martha as an act of justice. At the time of his lectures, he even received threats in anonymous letters and, doubtless knowing the conspirator type from early experience, he carried a knife when he went out, a weapon which, Levallois assures us, he would not have hesitated to use if attacked. The specter of secret societies loomed large at this time, for a noted politician told Senior in 1853 that there were hundreds of thousands of members.

A book on Virgil was projected for October, but other work intervened, essays in the *Revue Contemporaine* and in the *Athenæum Français,* and the material was not in shape for publication till December. Then it began appearing fortnightly as a series of articles in the *Moniteur.* The first of this series, however, was a review of a new edition of Horace (December 3), an example—and none could be better—of Sainte-Beuve's original treatment of a worn subject, displaying that quality of genius which makes old ideas seem fresh and new. Here, not only does the critic bring out the qualities of the Roman poet, but he at the same time characterizes the French lyrists from Malherbe to Lamartine through their attitude toward their classic predecessor.

The series on Virgil opens December 17, 1855, and closes March 17, 1856. If we do not here get what the *Æneid* was absolutely, we get at least what it was to Sainte-Beuve; we get his appreciation of "that perfect and charming thing called the Virgilian genius." With his usual method, he paints the personality of the poet as nearly as he can by inference and divination, sets him in his epoch, tells what contemporaries and successors said of him, deduces from an elegy of Propertius his effect on Roman youth, and characterizes his poetry by its most illustrious admirers, an Augustus, a Chatham, a Fox or a Fénelon, "the last name standing for every man of taste and sentiment." "If the Apollo Belvidere should write, he would write like Virgil."

Sainte-Beuve always goes directly to the essential, a process that might be supposed commonplace, but, in truth, is so rare that, in itself, it is sufficient to give distinction. Few critics really direct themselves to the capital point or, except by accident, ever arrive there. Even the association of Virgil and Racine, so inevitable, gives the impression of novelty, almost of a discovery. The commentator's wide reading, too, provides a sort of originality. For example, explaining the word *facetum* applied to Virgil by Horace, he quotes La Fontaine: "*Gaiety* is to me not what excites laughter, but a certain charm, an agreeable air that can be given to all sorts of subjects."

An appeal to novelty, an appeal to live emotions at the moment of appearance is essential to every masterpiece:

For an epic poem any subject that offers a beautiful, noble and human material, a rich tradition, may be good to treat; even distance is not at all opposed to interest, and far from injuring, may serve the imagination of the poet by leaving him a freer course. Go back then as far as you like and widen the horizon; ascend to antiquities, to origins; take up again in portions even subjects already handled by others: but by some essential part, by some principal current of inspiration, let there be novelty, and application, *appropriation* of past things to the present, to the age of the world into which you have come, and to what is of a kind to interest in an elevated way the larger number of minds and souls: true and living success is at this price. To be alive at the time of birth is the first condition for living forever.

It is this principle, identical with the motive of most of the *Lundis*, that governs Sainte-Beuve's treatment of the Roman poet. He helps us to appreciate the actuality of the *Æneid*; he eloquently shows how Virgil's art embellished the Empire of Augustus and how the Empire inspired that art, an original Roman inspiration, the substance of Rome seen from the standpoint of Augustus himself.

At this point there was obviously occasion for some political allusion. All that Sainte-Beuve says is that, in spite of the advice of friends who warned him of the coming noisy interruption, he refused to omit this side of Virgil's inspiration. Had he been dealing with Cicero, he would have shown the orator's grief at the extinction of the Forum. Each loves the state of society most favorable to his special talent. "And it is therefore certain (even if the statement of the fact should, though I cannot see why, be displeasing to some) that the soul, the talent of Virgil found under Augustus the atmosphere most desired."

To comprehend the *Æneid* we need, instead of medieval allegory, a comparison with Homer, interpreted by the vast idea of a great national Roman poem. As example is better than any formula, Sainte-Beuve takes a first stroll through the epic before stopping at any particular book, telling the story with great skill, putting emphasis on features distinctly Roman and distinctly human, and rendering Virgil's "poetic morality" without addition or diminution. The most impressive aspect of this "poetic morality" displays human vicissitudes, triumph always incomplete and mingled with shadows, victor and vanquished confounded in one sad equality.

Virgil "borrowed from Greek and Roman tradition, and he did so with perfect taste, choice and discernment, a point easy and interesting to verify even without plunging into the infinite details of erudition"; but such matter, not being fitted to the *Moniteur,* was reserved for the *Revue Contemporaine,* in which the analysis of Book I appeared (October, November, 1856). The critic attempts to measure his subject, and "by *measuring* I mean assigning the exact part due to the man, to the individual talent, to the age, to the sources the author has drawn upon;

untangling and knowing what was in the air at the time
of the new creation and what preceded it; seeing clearly
all around it." Here the chief emphasis is on the borrowings from Homer; Eolus, for example, transformed into
a Roman centurion, religion becoming mythology, sophisti-
cated *after Cicero and Cæsar,* as one might say *after
Voltaire.* The simple doings of life, merely habitual in
Homer, are curiosities to Virgil; we believe the one, we
applaud the other. What we learn is not to admire either
Homer or Virgil less, but to admire both better, each in
his own order and period of civilization; for the Homeric
age and the age of Augustus or Louis XIV, the natural
man and the man to whom the abstract word is the most
familiar—both kinds are admirable, each in its place.
There are even hints that other often despised epochs are
precious, and the alert reader may note such expressions
as "the fine age of the Alexandrians," "the fine age of the
Ptolemies."

An analysis of Quintus Smyrnæus, originally five articles
in the *Moniteur* (May 12-June 23, 1856), is also included
in the Virgil volume, for Sainte-Beuve had been led by his
study of Virgil to read Quintus, and he had found him
better than his reputation. This impression is supported by
narrative and extracts. "A scrupulous historian of the old
legend," the critic follows the Trojan war as though the
episodes were reality, these far off things being believed
"on the faith of fame and of the Muses," as Cicero suggests. Here again, while showing a sufficient acquaintance
with the researches of modern scholars, and even with
pictures on Greek vases, Sainte-Beuve is above all the man
who has read and remembered his classics, and also, for
comparison and to show the universal resemblance of
human nature, his Goethe, his Tasso, his Chateaubriand.
As in the Virgil studies, all the earlier *Débats* articles are
drawn upon, particularly those on Theocritus, Meleager

379

and Apollonius. Much will always remain uncertain, but on controverted points, the judgment of Sainte-Beuve's taste may be felt, in the absence of positive evidence, preferable to much erudite hypothesis. The *Étude sur Virgile* appeared in 1857.

Meanwhile miscellaneous essays were appearing in the *Revue Contemporaine,* a rival of the *Revue des deux Mondes,* subsidized by the government, and in the *Athenæum Français,* a literary weekly on the model of its English homonym. To the first Sainte-Beuve contributed (1855-1858) half a dozen articles; for the second he wrote pretty continuously, at least once a fortnight, often every week, from July, 1855, to February, 1856, at which time he began his *Lundis* again in the *Moniteur,* though now without any effort at regularity. With few exceptions these essays are in the guise of book reviews, those that appeared in the *Athenæum* being four or five times the length of the usual critical article in that paper, always beginning in the place of honor on the front page, and almost invariably dealing more largely with the subject than with the book reviewed. The book itself, however, is always fairly considered, Sainte-Beuve being too honest a critic to neglect a plain duty, which is often disdained by the small fry of the profession.

The first piece in the *Athenæum* (July 28, 1855), a review of Maxime du Camp's *Chants Modernes,* is an example of good sense applied with severity, yet kindliness, by an expert to the absurdities and inexactitudes of an inexperienced and contemptuously self-sufficient literary partisan, a type by no means yet extinct. The critic wisely, but unavailingly, condemns the schools, and the schools within schools, of the French poetry of his day. Assuredly, he admits, the artist must be of his time. "To seek in the present to copy antiquity is to be the disciple of disciples. Let us study antiquity, as well as all ages previous to our own; let us enter their spirit to understand and admire justly; but let us seek in our works to express, if only in small part, the spirit of our own age, to say what has not been said before, or to say over, if necessary, the same things in a manner and with an accent which is our own." After asking "Why be realistic? Why be vulgar?" the critic cites with appreciation some of Du Camp's verses and finds fault with others, entering as in the olden days into technical details.

A little relaxation had evidently restored Sainte-Beuve's mental freshness, as may be felt in a charming portrait of Santeul, or in a vivacious account of Henry IV as a writer, or in the light touch with which Voiture is presented, or in the Homeric and Virgilian reminiscences clinging about Ronsard. In this last piece, he asks each great French author in turn, "Have you read Homer?" thus characterizing two centuries of French literature. The character of the man is the essential point in discussing the Marquis d'Argenson, one of whose comments enables us, through perceiving how persiflage dried up the heart of the mid-eighteenth century, to understand the success of Gresset's *Le Méchant,* which portrayed the type; by antithesis, it helps us also to understand the success of Rousseau. In most of these essays, too, vivacity of expression is renewed. We read, for example, of works "that have wearied the author before wearying the reader"; or again, of Amyot who, "without being aware, has given a Homeric air to Plutarch and made him talk a little like Nestor." The final piece is on Eugénie de Guérin, in whom Sainte-Beuve finds one of those devoted sisters he was so pleased to contemplate (cf. Pascal and Chateaubriand). Here there is no question of literary eminence; he simply perceives the "perfume of her soul" and he wishes to share his impressions with others.

At the time when Sainte-Beuve began writing for the

Athenæum, while also preparing the volume on Virgil, he
engaged as his secretary Jules Levallois, whom he had
previously aided in finding literary employment. Like
many others who came close to the critic, Levallois was
surprised at the extraordinary sureness of his memory and
the richness of his information. In a mass of printed
matter heaped on his table, Sainte-Beuve knew just where
to strike. As to actual composition, he liked to talk his
articles during the evening walk. At such times, he
warmed up, becoming angered at opposition, but the next
day, when dictating from a manuscript entirely in his own
hand and mostly illegible to others, he would readily accept
suggestions even as to style. Scrupulous as he was, the
practical journalist could not worry over minute niceties
of expression, as Flaubert did, and it is easy enough, without searching through many pages, to find repetitions in
the phraseology which a more fastidious stylist would have
avoided. Proofs were read with great care. In reprinting
in book form, the articles were never altered, but rectifica-
tions or new views were inserted in notes, attention being
sometimes called to a blunder as a sort of general warning
that such things were to be expected. The typographical
errors that escaped, though not usually important, are yet
sufficiently numerous to attract attention, Renan and Taine,
with better eyesight, being superior in such details.

Sainte-Beuve, according to Levallois, was fundamentally
sad, rarely smiling and never giving way to hearty laughter.
He worked all day, to the almost complete exclusion of
visitors, and for exercise took an evening walk. He did not
rise much before nine, when he took some chocolate. For
lunch he had a cup of tea and a bun, sharing the food
with his favorite cat. His dinner was plain and substantial, the drink being water reddened with a little wine.
Of pure wine a mere sip was taken at the end of the meal,
and on great occasions there might be some liqueur, but

never cognac or coffee. Sainte-Beuve, says Levallois, was a *gourmet*, not a *gourmand*, and it was one of his theories that a delicate taste in art implied also a delicate palate. The Doctrinaires, he maintained, would not perceive it if you fed them cardboard. Like them, Victor Hugo, it may be remembered, was absolutely heedless of what he swallowed.

At this time Sainte-Beuve would not bear contradiction, but his secretary could always win him over by praising one of his poems, the volume being at once sought out and the piece read with emotion. Lively quarrels over politics led Levallois, a liberal, to leave in 1859. The devoted Troubat, introduced by Champfleury and Dr. Veyne, followed in 1861, the interval being filled by Pons. Recognizing that three years was about the limit allowed a man of talent for sinking himself in the work of another, Sainte-Beuve aided in launching his secretaries on an independent literary career, and he has been generous in acknowledging his indebtedness to Lacaussade for information about English poetry, to Lacroix for happy remarks, to Pons for history, and to Levallois for critical judgments and for help on *Port-Royal*. "He was no more obliged to write such an article," says Troubat, "than Cousin or Villemain."

Another young man, Charles des Guerrois, who considered becoming Sainte-Beuve's secretary in the years immediately after 1848, has left interesting reminiscences. To him the *Livre d'Amour* was read from manuscript and he found it very attractive. He reports the saying: "When I have loved my friends a certain time, I love them no more; I detach myself without breaking with them, by the sole effect of time elapsed": the example being Marmier, with whom Sainte-Beuve had been like a brother but whom he now met without intimacy. The Abbé Gerbet, however, was greeted with effusive cordiality, as was also Pavie; but these were persons seldom seen. Nothing could be less justified, says des Guerrois, than the accusation of envy; he never surprised in Sainte-Beuve the slightest movement of jealousy. Of personal habits we learn that Sainte-Beuve had the ability to sleep and that he needed much sleep; he would even interrupt his work, throw himself on the bed and take a short nap. His walks were always in the street, never in the near-by Luxembourg Gardens. When he let himself go, he was gay.

The new articles in the *Moniteur,* in general quite as lively as those in the *Athenæum,* were written with a lack of constraint which indicates increasing independence. While mostly concerned with some recent publication, they seem often in choice of subject-matter purely personal, and even an essay prepared as an introduction to a volume of correspondence ("La Marquise de Créqui") is cut into parts and made to serve for three *Lundis.* Not infrequently the page or two of approach to the topic reappears and much liberty is taken in digression, such passages being often the most interesting parts of the essay. In a piece on some new correspondence of Voltaire, for example (October, 1856)—a piece that is both entertaining and full of ripe wisdom—after proclaiming that he would neither diminish the qualities of a great mind nor make a moral and philosophical idol of one who respected nothing or next to nothing, the critic continues:

Young people unconsciously, at the moment they actively enter life, seek in the celebrated men of the past and in popular names pretexts for their own passions and systems, vehicles for their own ideas and enthusiasms; whether they espouse and exalt such celebrities or disparage and insult them, it is only themselves that they have in mind; it is their own idea that they salute and praise, it is the opposite idea that they debase and affront. To see things as they are and to see men as they really have been is exercise for an intelligence that is disinterested, and an effect, I fear, of something like apathy.

384

Always faithful as a book reviewer, Sainte-Beuve will now occasionally, after a general criticism, detach a subordinate character (Abbé de Pons, Duc de Nevers) and produce an original portrait, or rather resuscitation. One of these minor characters not suggested, it is true, by any book, but who had relations with Port-Royal, is the Abbé de Marolles (December, 1857), a voluminous and incompetent translator, important solely as a collector of engravings. His comical lamentations over the bad reception of his books and his other innocent absurdities are pleasantly rendered, and we perceive that, if Sainte-Beuve often redresses the balance by presenting the bad qualities of commonly worshiped idols, he also takes pains to show the merits of a person generally ridiculed and despised. In quite another spirit, as was fitting, is his contempt for the vulgarity and meanness of Bossuet's secretary, the Abbé le Dieu—"Why," he asks, "should every scrap of manuscript be published?"—and his severe condemnation of La Beaumelle for falsifying an historical character by adding passages of his own to Frederick the Great's letters. Unfaithfulness that disfigured the type Sainte-Beuve could not tolerate. Of the Genevan scholar, Favre, he remarks: "An inexact or false statement did not irritate him." His own calm was always upset by such things.

There are series of essays on a single theme that run to fifty, seventy, a hundred pages: the life of the Duke de Rohan, the correspondence of Frederick the Great with his brother and sister, the literary friendships of the Marquise de Créqui, the character and military career of Marshal de Villars. In all, even when the topic is old, there is some fresh information or at least a new color; characters are vividly developed and documents, both published and unpublished, are skillfully used. Throughout, the prime interest is not literature, but life. It is the grandeur of Bossuet, priest and doctor rather than man of letters, standing for the established order as opposed to individual fancies; it is General Pelleport or General Friant, types of military honor and duty, free from self-seeking—"How many such are needed that we others may dream!" There is sympathy with Richelieu's "glorious patriotic tyranny" which produced a unified France, and with Frederick's faculty of seeing things as they really are; there is condemnation of the frivolity, persiflage and corruption of society just before the Revolution; there are quotations from Mme. de Tracy's girlish memories put alongside those of her "silver age" and leading to reflections on happiness as we grow old, all recipes vain in the absence of Christian belief; there are delightful chats on social life, "which is not extinct, as some say, but ever present where a mother with bright daughters entertains people of brains." How far we are from literary abstraction is manifested by the exclamation—and remember Sainte-Beuve's taste!—"Let Atticism itself perish, if it cannot be conserved but by the absence of life!"

The latter part of 1856 and the beginning of 1857 seems to have been a particularly vivacious period. Producing at his own convenience, sometimes weekly, sometimes fortnightly, sometimes at longer intervals, Sainte-Beuve appears to have renewed his vitality. The heaviest of his efforts is perhaps the portrait of de Rohan; the most sparkling, the chat on Tallemant and Bussy and that on the Abbé de Pons. A few phrases from the last will show how little the critic was now hampered by the awesome solemnity of the *Moniteur:* La Motte's version is "Homer as he would have been, had he had the honor of living in the later years of the reign of Louis the Great"; there are advanced minds "ripe from childhood for Addison's *Cato,* whom the *Iliad* wearies as much as *Tom Thumb*"; society ladies flattered themselves that they at length understood the question of the epic, as Fontenelle had already put them in the way of understanding physics—"they have since likewise understood many other questions."

Sainte-Beuve was obviously not overexerting himself on his *Lundis*. Instead of a volume to each half year, as had been the custom, two volumes more than suffice for all the articles from August, 1857, to August, 1861, when the series ceased. The surplus space in these volumes was filled with longer essays prepared as introductions to editions of Parny, Saint-Simon and Fléchier, models of their kind, giving, as they do, concerning the author and the conditions of composition exactly the information needed for an understanding and appreciation of the work that follows. For the year 1850 we count only four *Lundis*, with five for 1859, while at the end of March, 1860, they begin again with rather greater, though irregular frequency. To Reuchlin, Sainte-Beuve wrote (February 3, 1858) that, while faithful in thought to the past and to absent friends, he was lazy and inactive, fatiguing himself with letters, visits and trips, yet he adds: "The work in hand takes all strength and activity."

This work was of various sorts, but the chief reason for the slowing down of journalistic production was the appointment of Sainte-Beuve in 1857 to a lectureship at the École Normale, an active teaching position that, according to his own statement, occupied the greater part of his time. The place, with its modest salary of 6,000 francs, was offered as compensation for the professorship at the Collège de France, which had been definitely renounced, although the government refused to appoint a successor as requested.[1] After vainly urging Sainte-Beuve to resume

---

[1] Notwithstanding the fact that Sainte-Beuve had recently urged Rouland to remove his name from the list and that he considered himself professor merely by fiction, he yet in 1857 offered his vote to Renan for nomination as successor to Quatremère in the Chair of Hebrew.

his lectures on Latin poetry, Rouland, Minister of Public Instruction, at length named him to the École Normale. Here there could be no public disturbance. "Behind closed doors," as he puts it, Sainte Beuve delivered two lectures a week—Mondays and Saturdays—from April, 1858, to July, 1861. Beginning his first term with Malherbe and the seventeenth century, he went back the next fall to the origins and the Middle Ages, a part of his subject which he makes no pretense of knowing from first hand investigation. He was, however, familiar with the work of specialists and followed and quoted the best authorities then available, among his sources being essays by Magnin and Littré in the *Journal des Savants*. "Though dealing with this ancient period," he writes, "I cannot make my home there." The lectures were written with great care and, when needed, could be drawn upon for critical articles. Only three, however, were published in full—"De la tradition en littérature," "Malherbe," and "Origines de la langue, etc."—in the *Revue Contemporaine* and the *Revue Européenne*. These are first rate specimens of professorial discourse. Devoid of arrogance, yet showing a realization of the master's superiority in knowledge and experience, they are infused with friendly considerateness toward the views of immature but clever pupils. We have evidence that later, in writing *Nouveaux Lundis* which deal with the older literature, Sainte-Beuve had recourse to these lecture notes, just as, in the earlier *Lundis,* he often fell back upon the material amassed at Liège.

However conscientiously prepared, two lectures a week in a consecutive course on French literature (the critic told Goncourt that Bossuet furnished matter for twenty-two) left far more leisure than a constantly varied weekly article for the public press. Aided by his secretary, Levallois, Sainte-Beuve now pushed to completion the two final volumes of *Port-Royal,* the subject being as usual reflected

more or less in such *Moniteur* essays as were published
during this period; we find the allusions to Virgil and
Homer, so prominent up to the middle of 1856, now yielding place for a time to another atmosphere. When the correspondence of Agnès Arnault appears, the *Lundi* even
begins (March 1, 1858), "Who should speak of these letters
if not I?" and the review, which was reprinted as an appendix to *Port-Royal*, is entirely in the tone of the history.
For the concluding volumes, the old lectures were thoroughly revised, passages were transferred to new positions,
and much was entirely rewritten. Levallois speaks of
days, even nights of effort to verify the smallest detail. To Reuchlin, Sainte-Beuve writes (February 3,
1858) for a story of Leibnitz and Arnault that he recalls
from conversation. The same care was expended on the
correction of the proofs, some of these being even sent for
criticism of detail to a minute specialist. On April 1, 1859,
Sainte-Beuve writes that he is entirely absorbed by his
course at the school and by the printing of *Port-Royal*.
Shortly afterwards the completed work appeared.

Probably the most grateful of the reviews that greeted
it, a review for which Sainte-Beuve, as was his practice,
thanks the author (September 9, 1860), was that written
by Renan, which appeared in the *Débats* (August 28,
30). While, according to his custom, Renan makes the
work under consideration the point of departure for his
own theories about humanity, he insists on its interest and
charm, on its just observation and sure judgment, on its
accurate and living portraiture, and on the lofty philosophy
tacitly underlying its verdicts.

Another book which occupied Sainte-Beuve, but upon
which he expended much less effort, was *Chateaubriand and
His Literary Group,* which appeared in 1861. Here he
simply reprinted his Liège lectures, together with a large
number of more recent annotations, adding a series of dis-

connected remarks, and some articles on Chateaubriand's friends, which had appeared in magazines.

The latest of these articles, that on Guéneau de Mussey, published in the *Revue Européenne* (1850), shows Sainte-Beuve's constant alertness in picking up material. Finding the physician of the École Normale to be a son of Chateaubriand's friend, he secured from him, among other documents and family traditions, the letters René had written to the elder Mussey, and from these he made an essay which, modest as had been the subject, is not the least interesting addition to his book.

Another document, and one that drew forth much condemnation, was the account by Hortense Allart (anonymous, of course) of her relations with Chateaubriand in his old age. Admitting to various correspondents that there might be a legitimate difference of opinion upon the propriety of adding this record, Sainte-Beuve nevertheless maintains in both public and private writings, that his portrait of Chateaubriand is true, that it reflects what Pasquier, Molé and other friends, even Joubert, said in personal talk or letters, and that, while he took some pleasure indeed in unmasking the *man* and exposing the rôle, he yet represented Chateaubriand's attractive personal qualities, gave full weight to his social seduction, and, far from trying to break down his reputation, had presented him as the greatest writer of his age.[2]

The people who misunderstood his purpose were those with single-track minds, who could comprehend nothing but unmixed praise or blame, and who took out of a complex book only such passages as would fit their preconcep-

---

[2] The talk of Mme. Mohl, Mme. de Circourt and others reported by Senior supports Sainte-Beuve's portrait. Sainte-Beuve's fault consisted in blurting out what others kept for private conversation. His literary appreciation far surpassed that of the younger generation, for d'Haussonville, when asked where he put Chateaubriand, replied: "Nowhere; we cannot read him."

tions, whether favorable or unfavorable. This type is represented by Pontmartin, who reviewed the work in the *Correspondant* (January 25, 1861). He sets out with complete admiration for both the character and genius of Chateaubriand and, instead of discussing the facts, seeks in Sainte-Beuve's moral nature the various elements of perversity that lead to any unfavorable estimate of the hero. Amid these personalities, about the only bit of critical insight is the discovery of the fact—"invisible as the nose on a man's face or the cock on a steeple"—that the notes contain more disparagement than the original lectures. At all events, a majority of those most deeply offended by Sainte-Beuve's book were already for other reasons sufficiently hostile to its author.

Whatever valid objection Sainte-Beuve's opinions and mode of life might beget, this antagonism was in reality to a large extent partisan. Some of it, leaving out of consideration purely personal hatreds, was literary, cherished by adherents of the Romantic School, many of whom, however, like Champfleury and Gautier, now became close friends; part was social and religious, nursed by the forsaken salons, the anti-imperialistic aristocracy, and the church party, constantly receiving fresh occasion for irritation and finally becoming irreconcilable; part, and this includes also some of the foregoing, was political, varying in intensity among the legitimists, the doctrinaire liberals and the republicans.

Accepting the Empire, not with enthusiasm, but from the dictates of good sense, as the best practical solution of the troubles and difficulties in which France was entangled, Sainte-Beuve found no embarrassment in serving the government indirectly by attracting readers to its official organ. When he changed journals, he went from *Constitutionnel* to *Moniteur* or from *Moniteur* to *Constitutionnel,* and his rare magazine articles were contributed to the *Revue Con-*

temporaine so long as that was official, to the *Revue Européenne* when the subsidy was transferred to it, and again to the *Revue Contemporaine* after the absorption of its rival. His political sympathies betrayed themselves, as he justly says, "only intermittently and by fits and starts." They had, at any rate, but inappreciable influence on his literary judgments. On the other hand in a memoir to the Emperor, he urged, in vain, direct imperial encouragement of letters, so as to diminish the ill effects of "the desire for gain combined with the need of making a noise," and he served for several years as mouthpiece of a ministerial committee for awarding prizes offered to encourage dramatic compositions distinguished for moral and literary excellence as well as for public success, there being, it is true, few pieces that fulfilled the requirements. Sometimes he attempted conciliation, complimenting Guizot, Villemain and even Cousin, and seeking to abate the friction between the government and the Academy by writing introductions in the *Moniteur* to the orations pronounced at academic receptions (1856-1857). His support of the government, however, did not preclude considerable independence. Of Hugo, for example, he will say, even in the *Moniteur* and after *Les Châtiments:* "A great modern lyric poet is not more preoccupied to close each of his pieces with a clap of thunder or a stroke of the lash" (November 28, 1859); or again: "All the old voices are silent except one grand voice" (February 20, 1860); and he will discuss Hugo's idolater Flaubert and also Taine (1857) as tranquilly as though they had not been anathema to authority. Limayrac, political editor of the *Constitutionnel,* who, in an inspired article, lectured him for this heterodoxy, called forth a heated letter in which the critic threatens to withdraw open support, though remaining loyal to the Empire. Some years earlier (1853), when Mme. Sohms was banished as *persona non grata* to her imperial cousin, Sainte-Beuve had been one of two who ventured openly to bid her farewell at the railroad station: in 1860, he visited her at Aix-les-Bains and brought back a letter of reconciliation resulting in her return to Paris. While respectful to ministers of state, he is frank and unhesitating in the expression of grievances or objections.

True to his principle that each subject should be studied for what it is in itself and not as material for propaganda, Sainte-Beuve does not any longer introduce politics excepting incidentally and by insinuation. He abominates the Restoration; he has little respect for parliamentary government, a divided and disputed authority maintained by speeches (July Monarchy); to him real power is the finest thing that exists in the realm of action. In French history he especially admired Henry IV and Richelieu, Louis XIV and Napoleon, since all worked for strong government and for national glory. While realizing the savagery of warfare, he perceives a period in which a great nation is ripe for conquest. Waterloo fills him with patriotic anguish. Current events, even the Crimean War, are rarely mentioned, though he takes advantage of the public interest in things military to discourse on great leaders of the past such as Villars and Rohan (five articles and three articles, 1856). The most direct approach to the subject is an essay in the *Revue Contemporaine* (May, 1857) on Saint-Armand, in which the portraitist, by entering into the soldier's point of view and exalting certain heroic traits of character, stirs up admiration for a career in which one activity, here very lightly touched, was that of minister of war at the time of the Coup d'État.

That Sainte-Beuve's political views were shaped by personal interest, there is absolutely no evidence beyond the fact, which he states frankly enough, that, as every man prefers the form of government which favors the free exercise of his talents, he himself naturally appreciates the opportunities offered him by the Empire, not of course the petty professorships, but the demand of a stable society for his literary criticism. Undoubtedly he overestimated the Emperor personally, "a chief who has in his hand the power of Louis XIV and in his heart the democratic principles of the French Revolution." Only such a chief can foster social progress, since without him the general body would not move, assemblies retarding, rather than advancing good causes. A talent for government was to Sainte-Beuve as much a distinct gift as a talent for poetry or music or mathematics. Those who possessed this talent should be the rulers, and he recognized it, erroneously, in Louis Napoleon, whom he had never seen, but who, in his opinion, had "lifted high the flag of France" (April 9, 1860). Not that every thing was perfect; but "let us accept, and then strive to correct, to ameliorate; let us give up party and serve France, poor France." The idea was mistaken, perhaps, but it was not ungenerous.

Owing to the dynastic character of French politics, the different parties were kept socially separate and there were few drawing-rooms in which Republicans, Bonapartists, Orleanists and Legitimists rubbed elbows. Sainte-Beuve's support of the Empire, therefore, put a barrier between him and most of his former associates, yet it did not interfere with a number of warm friendships based upon those fundamental intellectual sympathies which are not inconsistent with divergent views. Old Lebrun, for example, academician and senator, is often visited and even more frequently consulted. The comparative leisure allowed by the appointment to the École Normale gave opportunity for social relations as well as for the completion of unfinished literary tasks, and it is chiefly with a fresh group of distinguished friends that Sainte-Beuve emerges from his seclusion. The *Lundis* of 1857 distinctly mark the passing of an old order and the advent of the new. On

May 11 appeared an appreciation of de Musset, just dead at the age of forty-seven, and on July 17 a commemoration of Béranger, on the occasion of the old bard's funeral. Meanwhile, the genius of Taine had been heralded (March 9, April 6), *Madame Bovary* had been praised and blamed (May 4) and Renan, who as yet has no article to himself, though often subject of passing eulogy, had been indicated as a model of the "learned scholar combined with the literary artist" (February 23).

De Musset and Béranger dead: how typical of a vanished past! Hugo, object of ancient enmity, was in exile, and upon his recent productions the critic's mouth was sealed, both by propriety and by a sacred promise;[3] de Vigny, long estranged, was living in his "ivory tower"; with Villemain and Lamartine relations were merely formal, though, in spite of much fault-finding, Sainte-Beuve never lost his admiration for the brilliancy of the one or his enthusiasm for the poetic genius of the other; Lamennais, recently dead, was but a memory and a regret, as was also the Chateaubriand-Récamier group, the offspring of which were soon to receive grievous offense from the publication of the Liège lectures; Ampère was living most of the time in Rome, occasionally returning to Paris during the summer, and George Sand hid herself in Berry, though she often begged for a visit and saw Sainte-Beuve at Magny's restaurant whenever she came to town; Buloz and the *Revue* were still distant; Thiers, who favored keeping

---

[3] Biré, in his *Souvenirs*, recounts an incident told him early in June, 1852, by Octave Lacroix, Sainte-Beuve's secretary. While the critic was dictating an article on Beaumarchais (June 14), a lady's card was handed him, the name being Viscountess Hugo. He grew pale and left the room. On his return, he said: "She goes to-morrow to Brussels with her daughter Adèle. She has asked me not to write anything against *him* while he is in exile. I promised and I will keep my promise." Even without such an incident, the reasons adduced by Sainte-Beuve in a letter of 1856, that he could neither laud nor blame without misunderstandings, would be a sufficient excuse for silence.

the Pope in Rome and who, at the same time, would not
serve under Louis Napoleon, was unvisited, though always
lauded as historian, and Cousin was a frequent object of
stinging sarcasm, mingled with high appreciation of his
great talents. Of the aristocracy, Mme. de Boigne was
still occasionally seen and with Pasquier Sainte-Beuve dined
a few days before the old statesman's death (1862). Many
undistinguished friends of former years Sainte-Beuve indeed clung to, but among the eminent hardly one remained
except Mérimée, not an intimate precisely, but at least a
close and sympathetic associate. In fact, the various
groups had so completely vanished out of Sainte-Beuve's
life that Gautier, a personal acquaintance, it is true, of
long standing, but only recently a familiar, and now a colleague on the *Moniteur,* gave the impression of being one
of "Uncle Beuve's" oldest friends. The flame that had
blazed around *Hernani* might smoulder, but its heat never
became quite extinct.

Of the new friends, the most important were Renan
and Taine. To neither of these could be applied the lament
uttered to Reuchlin (April 22, 1858) : "I do not know what
to say to these young people when the conversation is prolonged. I have not, as you have, the grain of gaiety you
mingle with your serious studies." Although both addressed Sainte-Beuve as "dear Master," prolonged conversation must have brought forth sufficient divergence of
opinion to make intercourse interesting. Sainte-Beuve admired the outright speech and the fighting spirit of this
pair, and there can be little doubt that the reaction upon
him of these professed but completely emancipated disciples
was quite as pronounced as any influence exercised by him
upon them. They could not, indeed, much modify the
mind and character of a man past fifty, but they could and
they did strengthen him in his political independence and
in his anticlericalism.

Renan Sainte-Beuve had known for several years. The younger man, when sending the critic his first book, *Averroës*, in 1852, had said in the accompanying letter: "Your writings contributed to my substituting, in place of the abstract aim I had pursued, the historical and critical research which is the true philosophy of our time." The volume could not be reviewed in the *Constitutionnel* unless some *slant* could be found to make the article timely, but Renan is frequently lauded in the *Lundis*—"scholar and artist combined"—and the letters exchanged display a rapidly increasing intimacy.

With Taine the acquaintance began in the same way, with a book, *Les Philosophes Français*, accompanied by a letter. A review of this and other works by the same author in the *Moniteur* (March 9, 16, 1857) led to a meeting, which quickly developed into a close friendship. "If I do moral physiology," wrote Taine (1867), "it is thanks to you." This "moral physiology," however, Sainte-Beuve could not accept in an excessive form. Content to have as a guide the sentiment of a formula, he will hesitate to articulate the last word, preferring the literary outlook to the scientific axiom. Appreciation of one who entered the lists fully armed could never silence criticism, and in this group, the Goncourts excepted, criticism, even severe criticism—a mark of the new epoch—did not engender enmity.[4]

---

[4] The essay on Taine opens as follows: "M. Taine is one of the young writers who has made a most marked début in recent times, or, to speak without ambiguity, his début has been the most resolute and the least groping seen in literature for many years. With him no experiments, nothing given over to the chances of youth: he has entered completely armed; he has taken his place with a firmness, a vigor of expression, a concentration and absoluteness of thought, which he has applied in turn to the most various subjects, and in all he has come out one and himself. He has willed and he has accomplished. He has talent and he has a system. I should like to render full justice to his talent and to discuss a few of his ideas. Predecessors who are already old, owe to the new men who count for

Another free-spoken critical writer introduced to the public by Sainte-Beuve—"I like to sound the first stroke of the bell"—was Schérer (October 29, 1860). Not yet a personal acquaintance nor a Parisian, but soon to settle at Versailles, he is welcomed and wisely counseled as a fellow-craftsman. Flaubert's *Madame Bovary* had been reviewed May 4, 1857. It is recognized that the main points of the story are admirably told and the personages well characterized, but why, it is asked, is there not a single good or pleasing person in the book? Truth is not all on the side of evil. The new literary signs noted in this review are science, the spirit of observation, maturity, force, a bit of hardness: "Everywhere I find anatomists and physiologists." Somewhat later (July 23, 1860) the Goncourt's are favorably mentioned, and we feel that the new circle is fast forming. Baudelaire, "one of the oldest of those I call my *young* friends," receives private advice in a letter of 1857—he is "Petrarchizing on the horrible," and while his skill and also his sufferings are appreciated, he is urged to consider his own words, "In the hardened brute the angel wakes," and cultivate the angel. Some of these remarks were repeated later in a public communication to the editor of the *Moniteur* (February 20, 1860). Here Sainte-Beuve is not dealing primarily with verse, but is advocating a hearing for the new school of novelists represented by the *Cathérine Overmeire* of Feydeau, this second choice being forced upon him because Flaubert had failed to follow up Mme. Bovary with another novel of contemporary life. Even while fighting for freedom of art,

---

something this first testimony of esteem, that they should pay attention to them and become well acquainted with them. To occupy oneself with those who begin to make their way, however, is a restorative, even when these young people have no youthful trait but their force, and come forth already entirely complete and ripe. In approaching them, it is necessary to be doubly on one's guard and to gird one's loins."

however, Sainte-Beuve censures the excesses of the realists. As professor, he is to maintain *taste* and *tradition*; as critic, to seek the *new,* vividness, ardor, youth, the future.

For this letter, Sainte-Beuve was attacked by Cuvillier-Fleury in the *Débats,* an attack that he repaid with interest at a somewhat later date. He did not mind receiving blows, he said, provided he could hit back, and his counter stroke, for all its finesse, was always a deadly thump. Here, after showing the early royalist affiliations of his victim (Cuvillier-Fleury had been tutor in the royal household), he sympathizes with the so-called liberal party for being obliged to endure this self-appointed official defender in the press, "taking on the airs of a veteran of liberty, distributing and weighing praise with a self-important tone and with a smile that he considers shrewd because it accompanies a preachment." Speaking a year later of the same opponent, Sainte-Beuve professes to harbor no personal rancor, being able to discuss his literary productions with impartiality, an impartiality that admits merits indeed, but certainly does not bear lightly on faults. The same spirit is shown in private letters concerning Villemain. To Bersot Sainte-Beuve writes: "I have no animosity in my heart"; and yet he cannot accept Villemain's assumed rôle, and he insists on using the dissecting knife, however disagreeable the operation. On the other hand, he corrects the estimate of a younger writer who has not allowed due credit for the distinguished critic's brilliant qualities; at the same time repudiating a too exalted estimate of himself. Such examples lead us to acquiesce in the statement of Levallois that Sainte-Beuve kept his taste above his passions.

Among the distinguished foreigners who sought out Sainte-Beuve was, of course, Matthew Arnold, who dined with him in a restaurant (doubtless Magny's) in August, 1859, afterwards passing to his house where he was regaled with the letters of de Musset and George Sand.[5] "His conversation," writes Arnold, "is about the best to be heard in France," and this after intercourse with Cousin and Villemain, both noted as brilliant talkers. Sainte-Beuve's oft expressed regret at his inability to talk entertainingly must have referred to the witty bandying of nothings in society or to futile attempts to interest such strangers as brought no reciprocal mental wealth.

It seems to have been in 1860 that Sainte-Beuve made the acquaintance of Princess Mathilde and Prince Napoleon, cousins of the Emperor, an acquaintance that soon became an intimate friendship, both imperial highnesses visiting the critic in his humble home. The origin of these relations is likely to have been an anonymous eulogy of their father, King Jerome, published in the *Moniteur* (July 6, 1860) on the occasion of his death, the authorship of the article being obviously no secret. Within a year, Sainte-Beuve was the most highly esteemed of the regular attendants at the Wednesdays in the rue Courcelles and he was also (beginning June, 1861) a frequent visitor to Saint-Gratien, the suburban seat of the Princess at Montmorency. It was he who introduced Taine in 1861 and Renan in 1862. Independently the Goncourts, after their book on the women of the eighteenth century, were initiated through an invitation to dine. Among the guests they found Gavarni, Chennevières and Nieuwerkirke. Others frequently met at her highness' dinners and receptions included Viollet-le-Duc, Charles Robin, Berthelot, Delacroix. Gautier was one of the most constant visitors, and later librarian. Flaubert, too, was nothing less than a fervent adorer. An attempt to exhaust the list would be futile.

It was a circle of artists and writers that the Princess gathered on these Wednesday evenings at her town house

---

[5] When Arnold visited Paris again in 1863, Sainte-Beuve presented him to the Princess, on an evening when the Prince was also present.

or entertained during the summer at her country seat. Women bored her, but clever men she liked and for them she reserved special hours. All the world might share her smile and feel her charm of manner, but it was with this group that she indulged in her free talk, though even here there were limits not to be passed. Too much libertinism was repressed and, though Flaubert might praise Victor Hugo, the Empire must not be assailed. One evening, for an offensive remark, About was dismissed without his dinner, and both Sainte-Beuve and Taine were finally banished for outraging family feelings.

During these years, however, not only was Sainte-Beuve an habitual guest of the Princess, but she also visited him familiarly at his home and occasionally dined there. When the critic prepared a verbal portrait to accompany an engraving in the *Galerie Bonaparte* (1862), she came to his room and sat opposite him at his table, talking while he took notes. This portrait, while of necessity presenting only her good qualities, is sufficiently accurate, and it even delicately suggests the defects. After sketching her physical traits, the writer speaks of her firm and decided intelligence, clear cut ideas, direct and impetuous character without subterfuge or subtlety. Her art studies, her charity, her sympathy with the unfortunate, her charm, her conversation which provoked and permitted contradiction, her loyalty to friendship—through such traits we come to appreciate the grand lady: "A nature rich, loyal and generous; one who, in the highest rank, joins the gift of beauty to the sacred fire of art; who has the courage of her convictions together with the charm of sentiment." She is "not only happy herself, but spreads happiness about her," leading "an existence ornate yet simple," and enjoying not only art and elegance, but also nature and friendship. "To see her in winter, each evening, in the endless and brilliant society that she receives, always at

hand and constantly prepared, speaking to each, varying
the greeting and the apt remark, she seems a born fashionable hostess; to find her in the country surrounded by a few
friends always the same, one would rather say that she is
made for an intimate circle and for a peaceful, cheery
and felicitous mode of life.'' The praise is almost un-
stinted, yet no one would be led to think of the Princess
as a rival of Mme. Récamier. There is always in the background some trace of the Bonaparte nature and some semi-
official tinge. We feel this shadow even in the most delicate of the writer's compliments: ''Her house is a sort
of ministry of the Graces.''

In return for this appreciation, the Princess sent Sainte-
Beuve a portrait of himself which she had taken the pains
to write:

In a certain district of Paris, there is a street less frequented
than the rest: at number 11 rue Montparnasse, I had an appointment, accepted with great joy; I carried away from my
visit yesterday the most charming memory. I found a delicious
little nest; I found fresh fragrance, solitude, not too much light;
in a long room a large table loaded with books—paper, pens;
not a spot of ink. In the midst of all this material lives a fine,
caustic insinuating mind, indulgent by goodness of heart as well
as by habit;—smiling at every little piece of malice and finding
such everywhere; accessible to every one, but guarding his own
preferences;—a philosopher in the mode of the ancient Greeks
—whom he much resembles in appearance;—a believer without
religion; a philosopher not without moments of indignation, an
observer through curiosity; on the whole, a mind that understands
all minds and explains all; and that has the rare good fortune
to have only enough passion to keep him just and impartial.
How could I fail to be proud at being able to occupy such a man
for several hours; of having inspired him with the desire to know
me well enough to give the public an appreciation of me sufficient to flatter the most fastidious.

If the Prince did not use such heightened terms, he yet
speaks of his lively and lasting friendship for Sainte-

Beuve, "a charming mind, critical above all, believing in socialism under a dictator." He indeed visited him familiarly and passed many hours in his little house, even disregarding the break with his sister and extending his visits to the very end. He associated Sainte-Beuve with him in editing the *Correspondence of Napoleon I* and, after the critic's death, which he regretted intensely, he refused to appoint another in his place on the editorial committee.

The little house in the rue Montparnasse was exceedingly modest, with a solemnly cold bourgeois reception room and, up a narrow stairway, Sainte-Beuve's sleeping apartment, which was also his work room, with table and book-cases, and, in the corners, heaps of newspapers and pamphlets in apparent confusion but all carefully marked and labeled. A flight further up was the main repository of books, many of which were rare and valuable. The absence of decorations and of elegance offended the Goncourts, to whom Sainte-Beuve, in house-coat and slippers, looked like a gouty janitor (1867).

The household, however, was not altogether that of the respectable middle-class. It consisted of a cook, a maid, a housekeeper, sometimes pressed into scribal service, a secretary, who had his lodgings outside, and a "little lady," from time to time changed, who also lived apart, but came frequently to dine. The secretary—Troubat from 1861 on —was originally employed at one hundred francs a month to work from 9 to 12 A. M. and from 7 to 9 P. M., but his labors soon grew to cover most of the day and his compensation was increased to two hundred francs. Such help was indispensable, for the bad hand and arm and the weak eyes incapacitated Sainte-Beuve to such an extent that often he could neither read nor write. The "little lady," whom gossip magnified into three, furnished a Bohemian element that ordinary visitors had to put up with, though she was excluded on state occasions, to which, indeed, neither secretary nor housekeeper was often admitted. Of the illicit consort there was no parade and no concealment.

Chastity was a virtue that Sainte-Beuve demanded neither of himself nor of others, a view by no means exceptional, if not always in public profession, at least often enough in practice, among the political and social leaders of the time, as well as among artists and literary men. When chastity was a matter of conscience, Sainte-Beuve appreciated it, but when it was a matter of mere convention or prudery, it irritated him. On the other hand, a flagrant discord offended him as something inartistic; he condemns the vices of Archbishop Harlay, and in the case of the Empress Catherine, he finds a great reign stained by the scandal of her infidelities. In general, however, irregularity in sexual relations was to him of so little consequence that, in his studies, he paid slight attention to such questions unless there were specially interesting developments. Passion, on the contrary, directed to a definite object, or to several in succession, excited his deepest interest and never failed to be signalized. In his talk he seems to have gossiped rather more extensively about the lower sort of relationship. To himself he ascribed the weakness of King Solomon, which though diminishing his flame, had not corrupted his heart, his meaning apparently being that he retained his honesty and his sympathy, together with a capacity for poetic emotion, which sensuality is apt to dull or destroy. His group in Hades was "that of the adulterers (*Moechi*) sad as Abbadona,[6] full of mystery and dreams even in the midst of pleasure, and forever pallid with a voluptuous sensibility." What excited his ire was any accusation against his character as an

---

6 Sainte-Beuve had read of Abbadona in Nodier, an angel who has penetrated with horror the mysteries of Satan. Nodier got the name from Klopstock.

honest man. When, to take only one case out of many, Laurentie insinuated that he must have received some benefit from a person of whom he had spoken slightingly, Sainte-Beuve blazed out in a note of unparalleled personal bitterness and direct insult. He is unsparing also in his condemnation of social cruelty, whether in reality or in a novel. The morality of *Aurélie* (a story by Pontmartin), he writes, "seems to me detestable, because it is inhuman." It is clear, on the whole, that Sainte-Beuve never allowed his sexual irregularities to interfere with his work, and he blames others who show such a weakness.

When he was in the rush of his weekly articles, he could not see his friends or even answer letters till the work was completed, usually Sundays and Mondays; and even in periods of respite, he was at times "captured by a succession of appointments and occupations," that were perhaps even more fatiguing, so that he often longed for repose. From time to time, the old dissatisfaction still crops out; his life is a failure, "might he find some retreat where he could write a little verse or devote himself to a chosen task, enjoying in the intervals the conversation of friends." This moment past, his only pleasure is plunging headlong into work, distracted, occupied, consoled by literary pursuits. His average condition, however, in these later years is one of moderate contentment. He has become reconciled to the absence of religious faith and seldom any longer complains that the only consolation, the hope of heaven, is not his. To George Sand he writes (1860) that he is neither happy nor unhappy. His temperament had come, indeed, to a condition of stable equilibrium.

A curious episode of this period is his correspondence with Adèle Couriard, one of those girls who write letters to men of eminence without any previous personal acquaintance. In this case, as in others, Sainte-Beuve fell an easy victim to the fascination of feminine handwriting. The first communication came from Geneva in 1856, Adèle being then twenty-five, and for four years (1857-1860) the old critic replied regularly, coquettishly mingling sentiment and romance with his self-analysis. He insists that he is not an extraordinary person, not a genius, but merely a skillful man of letters. Dealing with many topics, he has a sort of breadth, but is incapable of embracing a large space at once. He lacks energy of resolution and constancy in fulfilling duties, a weakness increased by his occupations: "This passing from one subject to another in things of the mind has its reverberation even in the heart." Yet, however wandering his caprice, he often, or rather always, comes back. More weary than sad, he desires repose, yet feels that he is not enough of a sage to find it a joy instead of a weight. At times his past dreams are revived, and he pictures the charms of a retired domestic life; so attractive to him, we note, when not compulsory. In fact, he poetizes even his analysis and there is perceptible an undercurrent of sentimental hope that something may come of the relationship. At length, however, he gets a bit tired of his little friend's moral and religious rigidity. The two met in 1862 with mutual disenchantment and the correspondence ceased. Six years later, a fresh letter, accompanying one of Mlle. Couriard's moral tales, calls forth from Sainte-Beuve a protest against being preached at. "Be yourself," he answers, "with the religious sentiments that harmonize with your nature, but which are not perhaps equally adapted to all. I would not lessen any one's belief, but why meddle thus with other people?" Two features are here typical—a long stretch of the sentimental and, at the end, a sudden resentment.

Meanwhile the articles in the *Moniteur* continue though without much regularity. Toward the end, they grow briefer, often not more than a dozen pages and rarely ex-

406

tending to the normal twenty. To information and well-chosen quotations from the book under review, Sainte-Beuve always adds something new and interesting from his reading, his reminiscences, or from unpublished sources. His personal recollections, in particular, become increasingly prominent, including such diverse persons as Mme. Récamier, Maurice de Guérin, Lamennais and de Tocqueville. The literary, as usual, is frequently subordinated to other interests. "Here," he says, talking of a new collection of letters by Mme. du Deffand, "here is a correspondence of a kind I love, one that initiates us into all the circumstances and the daily life of a delicate and polished society and that permits us to live therein for years by means of a few hours of reading."

The tone becomes now far less strenuous. He writes for a scattered group of sensible people who do not even know one another. He likes to find points of literary agreement with adversaries, for "that civilizes warfare." Professing himself unable to answer Schérer's strictures on Joseph de Maistre, he yet feels the man in de Maistre superior to the result of this exact analysis, for on reading some recently divulged correspondence, he feels himself anew under the charm.

Is it weakness, incertitude of judgment? I prefer to think not, for the basis of my opinion is the same; but I like all that pertains to the man when the man is distinguished and superior; I allow myself, and shall always allow myself, to be caught by curiosity to know the life and that masterpiece of a life—a great and powerful mind; before judging, I think only of understanding and enjoying, when I am in the presence of a lofty and brilliant personality.

In the life of literature, too, Sainte-Beuve is content without protest to record how things go. He can portray a typical bore, the Abbé Saint-Pierre (August, 1861), without irritation, simply recording his platitudes with an amused smile. The obscurities and eccentricities of past poets, such as Villon, are interpreted by the moderns as deep thoughts or as wonderful strokes of imagination. So be it. Addressing de Musset, he exclaims:

Thus it already happens to you (for we see this mysterious phenomenon take place right under our eyes), O most charming and most ardent of the poets of our age, you, whom I did not hesitate to hail as a genius when you were but eighteen years old, but who, in your brilliant writings, did not entirely fulfill your promise; who, in the midst of admirable bursts of passion, of ravishing outgushings of elegance and grace, scattered so many incongruities, blemishes and incoherences, and let fall so many desultory shreds! I perceive the time when all these things will be counted to your honor more than if you had better governed your talent and made full use of your generous gifts; and our descendants, reading you, will say: "So much the worse for us where we do not understand! There is surely some hidden meaning here." Thus they will say, and indeed they say so already, because they feel the need of making you all that you might have been; for you are the child of the age, its personification in their eyes, and where the uncertain model does not fully answer their ideal and is found wanting, there they themselves take a hand and complete you. And we too, who well know your strong and weak points, who have seen you appear, shine and die, we shall applaud, nay, we already applaud this beginning of an illusion, because, after all, your charming renown, if it a little outruns your works, will nevertheless no more than equal your genius—what that genius would have been if you had deigned to employ it fully and as an artist more completely master of his force.

On the other hand, the critic insists on high standards for the journeyman work of literature. Dealing with an ill-written book of literary history, he begs pardon for criticizing the style of the estimable historian, but the fault is common among those who study the seventeenth century. Such study requires long preparation begun in early youth, when a first general layer of knowledge of classic French should be unconsciously acquired. Upon this general knowledge, superficial if you choose, but at least delicate and light, are gradually to be added stronger and more marked colors; charming memoirs should be read, those of Mme. de Motteville, Mlle. de Montpensier, Cardinal de Retz, Mme. de Lafayette, Mme. de Caylus, the whole of Mme. de Sévigné; Saint-Simon should come last. So would be formed a second general layer, slowly suffusing the mind. Only upon this foundation, prepared with leisure, should the investigations of Monmerqué, Walckenaër and Cousin be set.

One must not pride oneself on being learned before being simply well educated (the great and detestable eccentricity of the moment and the peril of the future); proportion, tone and propriety should be observed; one will not begin by plunging head-first into the unpublished before having read what has been in print for two centuries, what no longer ago than yesterday was well known and formed the delight of every rich memory; a career should not be opened with discoveries in the seventeenth century; but if such be made, they should be set forth in a manner more simple, in closer harmony with the subject, more worthy of the seventeenth century itself; there should be no clash with it when coming to speak of it; talking about this polished society, as is done on every possible occasion, language should not be used which is calculated to make their hair stand on end.

After having thus vented the pain he has often felt in reading modern treatises on the great age, Sainte-Beuve indulgently adds high praise for the good sense, the application and the patient research of the author.

His own style, while based on the sort of reading here demanded, was by no means formal. He permitted himself licenses that would be faults in the uncultured and he uses many picturesque popular expressions, though always making it plain that he is aware of his deviation from strict correctness. A certain sort of ingenuity is "to shear an egg." He even invents phrases of his own on a popular pattern; if the accessories overwhelm the main subject, he will say, "The fish is drowned in the sauce." Sometimes he is exceedingly lively; for example, after citing a rough judgment emitted by Buffon, he says: "Buffon has put his finger—what am I saying?—he has put his four fingers and his thumb on the truth." Primness was an affectation utterly obnoxious to this lover of reality.

Yet the realist has not killed the poet, at least the poet in aspiration. "I once wrote," he says, "a great piece of foolishness: 'For a sonnet of Petrarch, I would go to Rome afoot.' . . . But why call this folly? I would say it again, and if one might make a pilgrim's vow on such a condition, it is my legs that would to-day be wanting rather than will and desire." Gray's melancholy has affinities with his own: "How well I understand the obstinate and sulking silence of profound poets who have reached a certain age and dried up; how well I understand the still affectionate rancor against that which one has loved so much and which will no more return, the pain of a soul orphaned of poetry and that will not be consoled."

A marked feature of these final *Lundis* and also of the correspondence of the period is the frequent mention of Goethe, who really takes the place of all former models. Writing to Mme. d'Agoult in 1866, he says: "Although in these past few years I have sought to know him better and to become penetrated with him, I am, in the study of this great nature, nothing but a novice and an aspirant." A few references will be illuminating: "The model and living type of intelligent and universal criticism" ("Werther," 1855); Sainte-Beuve is "one of the humblest and unworthiest of the great school of Goethe" (letter, August 31, 1857); "the great Goethe, master of criticism" (letter, February 20, 1860); "the greatest modern critic, and the greatest of all time'' (October 6, 1861). Speaking (1857) of Alfred de Musset, who precipitated himself into his poetry, Sainte-Beuve discovers here the opposite of Goethe, ''of that Goethe who detached himself in time from his creations, even from those originally the most intimate. . . . Goethe, from youth, even from the time of *Werther,* prepared himself to live more than eighty years.'' Though in this respect Sainte-Beuve could not follow the model, he still absorbed enough of the Olympian spirit, if not to differentiate the work of his final years from that of the earlier, at least somewhat to color it, the tone being in harmony with that natural to advancing age.

The last essay of this series in the *Moniteur* (August 26, 1861) is a review of the nineteenth volume of Thiers' history. Thus Sainte-Beuve ended here with the same historical series that had called forth his first important article in the *Globe* thirty-five years before. Thiers, indeed, is the only writer whom the critic follows continuously from his 'prentice days to his latest period. Attracted both by the subject and the author's mode of writing history, he praises his fairness, proportion, liveliness, accuracy and, at the end after many hesitations, his style, finding a passage to quote in which there is no fault.

Senior records Villemain's complaint that people in France read nothing but newspapers, a complaint that sounds strangely up-to-date. Sainte-Beuve, taking advantage of the situation, was a journalist, and an expert journalist. No view of his career can be adequate that does not take this fact into consideration as fundamental. He was rarely perfectly free in choice of subject or mode of treatment, but was obliged to accommodate himself to his public and to the character of his journal. The freedom he attained within these limits increases one's admiration for his skill. His eye was always alert for a piquant situation, and he knew how to press all the piquancy possible into his pages. Nine-tenths of the *Lundis* exemplify such an appeal to public interest, while they generally also possess permanent value. One unusually striking example will perhaps suffice. Lacordaire is received into the Academy, the first monk ever elected to that body. If the public had not been excited before, it would become excited on reading Sainte-Beuve's presentation of the situation (January 24, 1861), a Dominican delivering a funeral oration over de Tocqueville, with American democracy for his theme, and received by a heretic, the Calvinist Guizot, the most eloquent organ of regulated liberty—with the question of Rome and the Pope lurking in the background. At the same time, the critic is enabled to sketch some traits of the three eminent personages involved, while he also insinuates the political lesson that one should not forget the great common cause, "a strong society and a glorious France."

In this piece Sainte-Beuve repeats a remark of Lamennais about Montalembert and Lacordaire which he had quoted previously: "They are, nevertheless, eggs that I have hatched." Such use of a passage a second time is very unusual, for, up to this period, Sainte-Beuve is a marvel of variety. In the fifteen volumes of the *Lundis,* even though the same subject may reappear several times, there are assuredly not ten pages of repetition either of fact or of phrase.

According to Levallois, the *Lundis* were at first very popular, particularly those on the salons of the eighteenth century. When the critic began in the *Moniteur,* there was a diminution of public favor, partly from political feeling, and partly because the essays themselves had a touch of the solemn and official; but after the professorship episode, the public welcomed his articles, the row at his lectures having reacted in his favor and the essays themselves regaining their ease and lightness.

THE CONSTITUTIONNEL

Unquestionably Sainte-Beuve's collaboration was now regarded as highly valuable, so valuable that Persigny, Minister of the Interior, was most insistent in securing his services to give literary prestige to the *Constitutionnel*. Much urging was necessary, for Sainte-Beuve was loath to give up his professorship at the École Normale, since in three more years he would be eligible for a pension of 1,200 francs; moreover, Garnier, the publisher, had proposed a history of French literature in several volumes, which he would like to undertake; and furthermore, the pay offered, three hundred francs for an article, was what he had finally been getting from the *Moniteur* since the first of January. For relinquishing these advantages and signing a three-year contract for a weekly article, he demanded and received an indemnity of 25,000 francs. On September 16, 1861, he entered upon a new series of *Lundis* [7]

---

[7] Sainte-Beuve's changes of journal were curiously connected with a chapter of high finance under the Empire, and they indicate a sense of honesty that refuses all association with shady transactions. He left the *Constitutionnel* in 1854, when Véron sold the paper to Mirès, a speculator and promoter, who added it to a group of journals already owned by him and his associates and used to advertise and support his financial schemes. The *Constitutionnel* was at once offered to the ministry as a political organ and accepted. On Feb. 17, 1861, at the instance of Delangle, Minister of Justice, Mirès was arrested for dishonest dealings, and on July 11 he and an associate, Solar, were condemned to imprisonment for five years and to a fine of 3,000 francs each, though the next year the sentence was reversed on appeal. On account of rumors that high officials were interested in shielding Mirès, the affair caused such a scandal that the Minister of Justice published in the *Moniteur* (March 5, 1861) a letter to the Emperor assuring him that no facts connected with the case would be hushed up. This scandal so hurt the *Constitutionnel* that it lost subscribers every day. Véron, called by the board of directors again to take command, announced (Oct. 22, 1861) that the *Constitutionnel* would unite complete independence with sincere devotion to the government, but not finding such independence possible, he dropped out before the close of the year. As part of the plan for the rehabilitation of the *Constitutionnel*, Limayrac was taken over from the *Pays* to be the chief leader writer and Sainte-Beuve was induced to contribute his weekly literary article, the value attached to his collaboration being indicated by the fact

which, with irregularities and intermissions, including change of journals, continued to within a few days of his death.

---

that the critic's name is always printed in more prominent type than that used for any other contributor. For him only, when he took a vacation, is the fact announced, together with the date when his next article might be expected.

D'Anchald was at this time appointed manager of both *Pays* and *Constitutionnel*, giving the ministry, as was the custom, a resignation in blank. In November, 1862, on the change of governmental policy toward Italy, he was informed by the authorities that his resignation had been accepted, but he protested and appealed to the stockholders. In order to avoid open scandal, he was allowed to remain as manager, but August Chevalier, representing Persigny, was appointed political and literary director with authority to pass upon everything that should appear in the paper. This new editor told Senior (April 4, 1863) that the former manager had received a bribe of 60,000 francs for inserting an article opposed to the Emperor's Italian policy and presumed to have been written by Prince Napoleon, the article having been set up, but discovered and stopped just in time. On Feb. 10, 1863, d'Anchald published a letter on the front page discharging Chevalier, who at once asserted his rights in court, the judgment allowing him police assistance. On June 16 Mirès had a fight with Chevalier in the office, the police being called in to eject the intruder. "The row in the *Constitutionnel*," writes Sainte-Beuve to the Princess (June 18), "begins again between owners, managers and the political administrator." There was again a resort to the courts, and in 1866 the action taken by stockholders during the years 1863 and 1864 was nullified, a new meeting being called which appointed A. Ladrait de la Charrière manager. Mirès was again in control. On March 29, 1867, a new program was announced, and it was in connection with this change that Sainte-Beuve, who had gone beyond his original engagement for three years, ceased his connection with the *Constitutionnel* and returned later in the year to the *Moniteur*. The old editorial staff was at the same time largely replaced, though the critic's friend, Roqueplan, continued for several years to do the dramatic *feuilleton*. See Senior's *Conversations*, Viel-Castel's *Souvenirs*, Taxile Delord's *Histoire illustrée*, and *Moniteur* and *Constitutionnel* for these years, particularly report of a debate in the *Corps Législatif* on February 12, 1863 (*Moniteur*, February 15). Sainte-Beuve had no personal grudge against Mirès, for the financier once at least accompanied him to his home for a brief visit. It is perhaps to Mirès' credit that the stockholders of the *Constitutionnel* later complained that he was paying his editors too much, and he replied that he was not paying them nearly enough.

CHAPTER XIII

1861—1864

FROM September, 1861 to the end of 1864, Sainte-Beuve continued regularly, with brief intermissions, his series of weekly essays in the *Constitutionnel*. Though there is no sudden change, these *Nouveaux Lundis* differ in many respects from the earlier articles. Since his newspaper, while supporting the Empire, was unofficial and, as the organ of Persigny, anticlerical, the critic enjoyed greater freedom than in the *Moniteur*. He felt that he was engaged to a certain extent in a battle for liberty of thought and he consistently opposed intolerance both in religion and in literary taste. Among his articles, there are many studies of contemporaries, both of friends and opponents, and he takes the old man's privilege of reminiscence. Less attention is now given to plan, the subjects do not in general require extensive preparatory studies, ideas already used are unhesitatingly repeated, and a single phase of a topic is almost always preferred to a broader treatment. Toward the end the substance is not infrequently rather slight; Sainte-Beuve's supplies appear to be getting used up, and his articles, while still interesting in part, and sometimes throughout, show marks of fatigue. In addition to the weekly task, there was also an occasional introduction to some volume, usually published first as a magazine article, and in 1863 the critic began again to contribute occasionally to the *Revue des deux Mondes*, the pretext being invariably the recent death of some former literary friend. Bound down by such labor, Sainte-Beuve yet reserved scraps of time for social intercourse. He continued without intimacy relations with many old friends, chiefly at the Academy; toward his schoolmates and other undistinguished comrades, he constantly manifested an affectionate interest; but his real circle was the group of literary men and artists gathered around the Princess Mathilde and her brother, Prince Napoleon. Most of these men, together with a few others, assembled fortnightly at the Magny dinners, at which Sainte-Beuve was a sort of presiding spirit. Differing profoundly, yet moving in a common direction, they gave the critic a certain sentiment of support, lacking since his break with Romanticism. Between him and Renan the community of spirit was closest and the mutual admiration strongest. Politically Sainte-Beuve still supported the Empire, though with no enthusiasm. His chief aspiration was humanitarian social improvement under a philanthropic despot, and he did not hesitate in 1863 to vote for the Saint-Simonian Guéroult, an opponent of Persigny's official candidate. From October, 1864, at the solicitation of his friend, Prince Napoleon, he served on the governmental committee for the publication of the correspondence of Napoleon I.

"I begin again, in September, 1861, more actively than ever, a campaign of *Lundis* in the *Constitutionnel,* endeavoring to give them a character slightly different from the old ones. Forward! a final pull at the yoke, forward!" Such is Sainte-Beuve's own feeling as he entered upon his new task. There is, indeed, no line of absolute demarcation between the old *Lundis* and the new. It is the author's opinion that what he is now doing is much like his early work and that he has merely perfected his first manner. At least, the last fringe of the earlier series announces many of the qualities characteristic of their successors. He continues to review Thiers (volumes on Waterloo and Saint Helena), admiring his lucidity and his vivid, rapid style without a shadow of bombast. If the subject is Mme. de Sévigné, he again admires her brains, her style, her frankness, her character. He still calls for the definite word and the precise fact. The writings of Louis XIV have a royal, not a literary stamp, the king, wholly king. There exists a genius for governing, which is in the first rank of all human capacities. Napoleon as a critic of war is the Goethe of this branch, while others are the La Harpe, the Lessing, the Schlegel. Compared with the great thoughts of a Newton or a Laplace, how feeble are our strokes of wit! A portrait of Dagobert de Fontanille, a picturesque and original warrior of the Revolution, evokes the exclamation: "How miserable our pen wars in comparison! O to live and die like the men of duty and patriotism!"

There are, however, differences both in manner and intention. Reserving these for later treatment, it may here be noticed that Sainte-Beuve does not any longer take the color of the book he is reviewing, but regards it throughout more objectively, standing apart, describing, quoting, especially judging, sympathetically, indeed, but from his own inalterable point of view. He blames a certain critic because "he does not resist his author." Yet, at the same time, he grows more indulgent, as when, speaking of the transformations of Lamennais, he urges us (himself included) not to be astonished and scandalized, but to look into our own hearts and see if something parallel cannot be discovered there; and, before blaming a certain nobleman of the eighteenth century, he asks: "What might I have done amid such influences?" This indulgence, on the other hand, does not extend to inexactitude or concealment in the statement of facts. "Art is severe, scrupulous, inexorable, and criticism, her humble servant, does not recognize, when closely pressed, any timid solicitudes or complaisant retractions." It is the same with the expression of opinion. Though the tone has come to be that of a man who ceases to insist on persuading or exerting any specific influence, who finds his intellectual pleasure in neutrality and who states his views without anxiety to have them adopted, he is firm in his condemnation of the declamatory in expression, of looseness and confusion in thinking and, above all, of sect in criticism. He even blames a favorite author for misjudging William of Orange: "What was permissible in a sincere but narrow man like Arnauld or in a genius entirely oratorical like Bossuet, was not permissible in a sage like La Bruyère." The distinction here drawn is pure Sainte-Beuve.

What he himself selects as distinguishing his new essays

in the *Constitutionnel* is the endeavor to introduce a larger proportion of truth, to give his impressions with a freedom that would have been inappropriate in the *Moniteur*, "that is, in the vestibule of Cæsar's palace." Such previous constraint is evidenced by antipapal footnotes added in the published volumes. In this respect, and this was not the only one, he could allow himself to speak with greater frankness in the *Constitutionnel*, for the ministerial patron, Persigny, and all his editors were outspoken anticlericals. The writers in this journal Sainte-Beuve describes as "devoted defenders of a government we love and which, already good in itself and sufficiently glorious in its results, seems to us compatible with all desirable ameliorations" (January 12, 1863). Within such limits, he could speak his mind.

For his topics he is still obliged to consult what he believes to be the public taste: "I treat the subjects that present themselves, trying to do my task honestly and conscientiously, that's all." Sometimes he tests his readers, as in an article on the medieval drama, a test that evidently had an unfavorable outcome, for the experiment was not repeated. Current publications, though not infrequently a year or even several years old, furnished the point of departure. At times, the publication reviewed became a mere excuse for developing some portion of his subject, a particular instance being a group of books on Montaigne which give occasion for a disquisition on Montaigne as a traveler.

At first, the studies deal predominantly with the present or the recent past, but the topics drawn from former times soon grow more frequent and, within a few months, come to outnumber those dealing with his own epoch, a natural enough result, since, even granting some superior interest to what is contemporary, the productions of three centuries must outweigh those of fifty years.

From the outset, Sainte-Beuve made himself obnoxious to the clerical party. He opens this particular campaign with a review of Laprade's critical essays, characterizing the author as "a distinguished poet with a very limited range, but in no sense a critic." A friendship of twenty years was thus turned into enmity, and the ultimate results were most unfortunate.[1]

Two weeks later, the subject is another pillar of the Church, Veuillot, the violent and abusive, though able editor of the suppressed clerical organ, *L'Univers,* who is studied for his talents, but from the standpoint neither of an adherent nor of an adversary, an attitude displeasing to both parties. Hardly two months had passed, when it came the turn of Mme. Swetchine. This devout lady, who asked after her guests' souls as others might ask after their physical health, is analyzed as a case of temperament shaping a form of piety; admiration is tempered with criticism of her exaggerations and lack of taste, and, while she is appreciated as a religious writer, her followers are warned to be more moderate in their praise. The ensuing resent-

---

[1] In the *Correspondant* for November 25, 1861, Laprade published a violent poem, *Les Muses d' État*, in which he not only attacked Sainte-Beuve, which was safe enough, but also heaped abuse on the government, which was very dangerous even under the *Empire libéral.* The poet promises to authors who write vile, atheistical and servile books that they will, besides getting decorations and places, have crowns woven for them in six long columns of the *Moniteur* by the *Causeur du Lundi,* who even, in the school where future thinkers are trained, teaches this fine style to future professors. (As Sainte-Beuve was no longer either writing in the *Moniteur* or teaching in the École Normale, this passage must have been written before September). All the remainder of the piece—nine-tenths of it, at the least—is a violent general attack on the Empire, its organs and agents. At the end, the poet calls on the Muse to return to the walls of Troy, and "make Jupiter thunder—to kill fleas." Even the epigraph, *Circenses,* is an insult to the government. On December 14 Laprade was dismissed from his chair at Lyons. The December *Correspondant* says, through its secretary, that the verses were provoked by an article in the *Constitutionnel* by a colleague at the Academy (Sainte-Beuve), and it accuses Sainte-Beuve and two other professors of demanding Laprade's dis-

ment of these followers was expressed in what Sainte-Beuve terms insult and abuse.

The Doctrinaires and the salons are also favored with some further plain speaking. Immediately after Veuillot, Guizot is keenly analyzed and, though complimented as writer and orator, he still furnishes an example of the futility of oratory as a tool of government. The brilliant young Prévost-Paradol who, "disdaining experience, worships parliamentary institutions and makes an idol of England," comes a fortnight later. In his case, however, the political dispute could not interfere with a warm personal friendship. Sainte-Beuve later (April 11, 1864) speaks of the essays on Veuillot and Prévost-Paradol as attempts "to make the realm of letters neutral, not to render it forever inviolable like Delphi in antiquity—that would be asking too much of our customs and usages—but to make it at least more hospitable and friendly, so that each might be just to the others and not be pursued by polemical iniquities." His design, he confesses, had been very imperfectly executed. Within the year, Pont-

---

missal. Sainte-Beuve, however, declares in a footnote that he had nothing to do with the affair "absolutely and entirely." The article in the *Constitutionnel* (December 6), "De La Poésie Insecticide" (alluding to the flea-killing line), was signed by A. Gremier, one of the regular writers of political leaders. This editor speaks of Laprade as a mystic and dreamer suddenly become a false Juvenal, striking right and left in politics, art, literature and manners, yet with nothing to complain of, since he had a good place in the University. This he ought to have resigned before he ventured to attack the present government as corruption itself, perverting everything and suppressing honor, liberty and justice. In an official warning to the *Correspondant* (December 18), Persigny calls Laprade's piece an "abusive diatribe" against the established order and the sovereign that France had chosen. The decree of dismissal, proposed by Rouland, emphasizes the abuse of the sovereign, lack of fidelity to the government and violation of the oath of allegiance which every state functionary was obliged to take. There is not the slightest shred of evidence to connect Sainte-Beuve with Laprade's dismissal and his own statement must be taken as final. In 1872 Laprade himself wrote a letter defending Sainte-Beuve's memory against this "odious accusation."

martin, who represents the salons and a certain fashionable
religious type, is as courteously as possible made to appear
the mediocrity that he was. That Sainte-Beuve had a lance
to break with the writer who had turned a review of his
Chateaubriand into a string of personalities does not to any
marked degree interfere with his critical neutrality. It
is Pontmartin's methods, theories and style that are here
discussed, and it is remarked in passing and not without
example, how impolite and even obscene aristocratic society permits itself to become when it abuses its opponents.
A veiled observation at the end about fair and worthy
daughters of too celebrated mothers becoming wives of distinguished lawyers or becoming marchionesses and even
duchesses—"The thing has been seen"—must have
wounded several families besides the de Broglies, long ago
irritated by articles on Mme. de Staël, which her daughter,
the Duchess de Broglie did not wish written, and recently
offended anew by the critic's public opposition to the son's
election to the Academy. To have there one de Broglie
was, he maintained, a good thing; to have two at the same
time would be too much (February 2, 1863).

Plain speaking reaches its climax in a reprimand administered to Pontmartin (July 28, 1862) for a book in
which his wounded vanity avenging itself transgressed
every principle of decorum and even of simple decency, and
violated confidences in a mean betrayal of his own guests.
In thus giving general offense, the author could not omit
Sainte-Beuve, who is accused of stabbing friends in the
back, an accusation often repeated since, which here calls
forth the retort that, if the writer is not merely frivolous,
he is a calumniator.[2]

---

[2] In 1865, Sainte-Beuve remarks that Mlle. E. Drouet could even
reconcile "the critic of the *Samedis* with the critic of the *Lundis*";
and his note, printed in 1868, explains the first named as "M.
Armand de Pontmartin, with whom I believe I formerly had some
slight disagreement, long ago forgotten." *Nouveaux Lundis*, x, 117.

On the other hand, at a time when praise from Sainte-Beuve could make a reputation and when a mere mention was a highly appreciated honor, there is frequent favorable reference to the new generation—Renan, Taine, Flaubert, the Goncourts and a multitude of others. Any work well done might expect at least a word of approval. Few indeed of the younger men who approached Sainte-Beuve failed to be under some obligation to him, either for direct assistance in making their way, or at least for encouragement. Such favors, however, could not be extorted without desert. Several years earlier, Louise Colet had been rather peremptorily told to stop bothering him and to permit him to admire her in silence.

Meanwhile, his former friendships and his early experiences were not forgotten. These things had passed into history and the treatment of them is wholly historical. Some of his most interesting recollections are now given piecemeal to the public—his attendance on Guizot's lectures when the statesman was a professor, his impressions at Rome, his part in the publication of Lamennais' *Paroles d'un Croyant,* the Sunday afternoons in the parlor of Delécluze, the Fridays in the library of the elder Viollet-le-Duc, even the memory of unidentified social evenings, "so many blond heads, so many serious or inspired brows," a whole variegated picture of a vanished past. Not infrequently an essay will be rich in reminiscence, and the critic will even confess to the garrulousness of old age. Sometimes the persons concerned or their family or their admirers were offended, but Sainte-Beuve did not now much care. When a man he had known is presented as a piece of perfection, he will exclaim: "You'll have to wait till I'm dead to make me swallow that"; or again: "I do not like conventional portraits. The public likes them, however, and it is always a delicate matter to disturb what the public has viewed and what it wants; it seems as though, in putting back the warts and the spots, one had the express purpose of dirtying or outraging the image." In general, on the contrary, the result is rather a more lifelike portrait. "Having made my reserves," he says, "adduced certain corrections and, if you choose, indulged in a bit of mockery, I continue within my own limits to cherish admiration and respect for the character of the man and for the talent of the poet." The delightful essay on Béranger, indeed, from which these phrases are quoted, may be taken as a justification of the procedure, for without veiling any weaknesses, it leaves with us a final impression of the man's good sense, honesty, gayety, kindliness, wit and grace. In what we might call a bowdlerized portrait, Sainte-Beuve has simply put back the expurgated traits. In his own case, being even more frank about himself than about others, he has rendered the task of the expurgator impossible. There is no "statue" of Sainte-Beuve, but there is a distorted image that requires rectification.

A majority of these new *Lundis* betray an absence of strict plan, a feature resulting from a newly adopted method of construction, this being a practice that certainly does not go back to the days of Levallois (before 1859), but which seems to have been begun in the time of Pons and to have been fully developed when Troubat became secretary in October, 1861.

As previously, no time was wasted. On Tuesday, Wednesday and Thursday, Sainte-Beuve dictated the article for the next Monday, every doubtful fact being verified by immediate search and every doubtful word being hunted up in Bescherelle, a dictionary rich in quotations. Friday night the proofs were sent to the house and Sainte-Beuve went over them on Saturday, Troubat reading the copy aloud while the critic followed on the galley, correcting, substituting and adding new matter. On Sunday morning he examined a second proof, and in the afternoon he went to the newspaper office to make the final corrections. Finishing this task about six o'clock, he felt delivered, being mostly free till Tuesday, when the same process began again. Parallel with the dictation, from Monday till Friday, he read, took notes and ruminated his article for the following week, no insignificant task, for in addition to the books on the shelves at home, Troubat often brought as many as fifteen volumes from the Bibliothèque Impériale. Many essays were naturally in mind for weeks in advance and information was sometimes widely sought by letter. On Friday, to plan the ensuing essay, Sainte-Beuve shut himself in for the entire day, seeing nobody and stuffing cotton in his ears to exclude any noise that might break the charm. He called the process ''basting'' his article, for he emerged with an assemblage of papers, separately composed, but pinned together according to the order of thoughts to be followed.[3]

This scrappy method of construction, the results of which can be very clearly perceived in the new *Lundis,* is particularly well illustrated by four articles on Horace Vernet (May 18, 24, June 1, 8, 1863). In fact, the critic at one point confesses that he had been carried along farther than he had expected and appeals to his readers to permit him to continue. After the death of the patriotic painter (January 17), the family had placed in Sainte-Beuve's hands a collection of letters written from Africa, Syria and Russia, and this veritable prize for the journalist forms the kernel of the piece, but he begins, with some aid from artist friends, to comment on a few early paintings and on a group of engravings from the Print Collection. There

---

[3] Pons, secretary from 1859 to 1861, says that Sainte-Beuve wrote the whole article in one day on small sheets, and that he then went over it to polish and to remove every trace of rhetoric, sacrificing purism to ease and naturalness. There is no mention of this process of "basting," and its effects are not visible in the essays of that period.

follows a severe portrait of Gustave Planche, whose criticism of Vernet had been not only harsh but malignant. Of Planche it is said: "His youth was, of all those I have known, the most irreverent and the most devoid of the faculty of respect," and the same character continued throughout life. Thus we meander along until finally we come to the letters of travel, with pages of delightful quotation selected with the customary skill. How this stay-at-home critic appreciates the valiant voyager in strange lands! How the lively, honest, sympathetic character of Vernet emerges from the details as we proceed! A string of disconnected anecdotes is now tacked on, and the piece ends with an appeal to France to remain France, gaining all the elevation and depth she may, but not too much of the Empyrean, permitting herself two or three metaphysical abstractors for Sundays, but for working days relying on those who show native qualities and defects: "swaggering, heroism, gayety, sentiment, light humor, brilliant audacity, clear glance and practical good sense." We can almost see the eager penman scribbling his separate passages as the thoughts come, and then arranging them, pinning them together as the pattern suggests itself, "basting" the vesture of thought to be firmly stitched together, elaborated and embroidered as he sits at his table and dictates to Troubat.

Renan, we are told, could lay down his pen in the midst of a sentence, talk with a visitor and, at the end of the interview, resume his phrase at the point of interruption. It was not so with Sainte-Beuve. He worked himself into a sort of nervous tension or intellectual exaltation which would be spoiled by any intrusion. The excitement lasted beyond the moment of composition, and it is responsible for some of the irritated outbreaks which were so frequent. One reason given for absence from the Academy was that he would arrive excited over his article and be led to quarrel with his colleagues. Troubat found that these fits of anger would subside as quickly as they came, and he governed himself accordingly. Younger men, as a rule, got on better with Sainte-Beuve than men of his own age, excepting such of these as did not harbor resentment.

The literary level to which the critic lifted himself when he composed is made manifest in the difference between his essays and what is reported of his talk. If his conversation was sometimes a bit too free for delicate ears, there is not in his written work, even when he touches on scandal, the slightest trace of coarseness; and far beyond this negative merit, his literary atmosphere transforms everything and produces an effect quite different from the other. What we get from the Goncourts, it is true, is not his actual talk, but the effect of such talk on these hearers. It may, nevertheless, serve to illustrate the point. They record (November 8, 1862) that Sainte-Beuve spoke against Michelet with a sort of animosity and angry rancor. In the almost synchronous essay (March 10, 1862) we read:

I neither blame nor praise this historical method, the farthest, I confess, from my own taste and habitude; it is enough for me to say that M. Michelet has made it his own by force of will and talent, that he has carried it to a point where it has become unique, that in it he has finally become past master; and as advice is perfectly useless, I accept the man of knowledge, imagination and heart as he is; I accept him in the brilliant and risky products he gives us, regretting what offends me and paying homage to the wonderful passages from which I profit. . . . I capitulate, recognize his power, and simply ask not to be called upon to discuss it.

The turbid matter from the boiling cauldron below has been refined into something that gives the impression of tranquil artistic contemplation.[4]

---

[4] After a breach of twenty years, Sainte-Beuve's letters to Michelet from 1860 to 1869 are very friendly. The beginning of the breach coincides with Michelet's assaults on the Jesuits.

CHARACTERISTICS OF THE NEW LUNDIS

In spite of their great merits, in spite of occasional superiority, these new *Lundis* do not seem such an astonishing achievement as the earlier series. A single volume commonly furnishes the point of departure and many of the pieces are merely familiar chats on books of the day. Sainte-Beuve of course adds illustrative matter from his resources and sometimes even from special investigations, yet the impression of intense preparatory study no longer makes one marvel. In a majority of cases, he spreads a subject over two, three, and even four weeks. He frequently repeats not only ideas, but phrases already used, giving rise to a suspicion that he has taken out of their envelope some notes which have served the same purpose before. In the essay on Bossuet (May 19, 20, 1862), to give but one special case out of many, he tells again a story of Louis XIV and Mme. de Montespan and reproduces the very words of his former estimate: "The sovereign organ and interpreter of the established order." At times he seems to sum up opinions, as though putting his final stamp upon a subject, a good example being the rounding out with no essential change of his judgment on Benjamin Constant (January 27, 1862). The notes prepared for his classes at the École Normale—up to 1861 almost untouched —were now drawn upon. There will be future occasion to refer to this matter; here it will be sufficient to observe that, in the essay on Bossuet just mentioned, a passage discussing the influence of Latin on the great preacher smacks strongly of the professorial lecture, and in another place, the advice to read a little of La Bruyère at a time, but to read it frequently, calls up a vision of the classroom.

Not that there is the slightest diminution in interest. There is seldom an essay that can be called dull and hardly a page that has lost its savor, even when the subject seems least prepossessing. Who would not feel like skipping a

criticism of C. de Lafayette's long poem on country life?[5]
Yet here, a group of rather unimportant poets disposed of,
is found a charming discussion of Hesiod, Lucretius and
Virgil, while a French description of a barnyard is dignified by its companionship with the ancients. How dull
a subject seems a *Journal of the Health of Louis XIV!*
Yet Sainte-Beuve interprets the record, extracts parallel
matter from memoirs of the time, and brings the thing to
life. "The man," he finds, "was often ill; the king always
seemed in good health."

The openings—what musicians call the attack—would
furnish an admirable subject for study. Sharp-cut and
endlessly diversified, they invariably arrest attention.
"Most of his openings are happy," he said of Pontmartin,
proving that he himself gave special heed to this feature.
The endings, too, are highly skillful, for they are particularly designed to appear artless. They are almost always
entirely informal, avoiding climax, epigram or rounded
period. The author seems simply to stop talking, but, natural as the procedure seems, it is the result of art, the
last phrase inevitably suggesting reflections that the essay
is intended to impress. The reader fills out what the author has left unsaid.

Often the title suggests a large topic, but the critic, after
giving the setting in a few general remarks, proceeds to
develop only a phase of the subject which specially attracts him. From the Empress Catherine's *Memoirs,* for
instance, he strays into a consideration of her correspondence with Voltaire (April 7, 1862) ; two articles on Fou-
cault (November 17, 24, 1862) deal almost wholly with
the persecution of the Protestants; a general account of the
Greek Anthology (January 13, 1864) leads to selections
confined to a single poet, Leonidas of Tarentum, and then

---

[5] This poem was called to Sainte-Beuve's attention by Lebrun, a
personage who touches Sainte-Beuve's life at many points.

we pass to a discussion of the place of Greek in modern
culture; in the *History of Louvois* (January 18, 25, 1864),
Sainte-Beuve discovers documents that show Victor
Amadeus of Savoy to be "one of the most original characters of history," and, after devoting one essay to the
trickery employed by Louis XIV's minister in the acquisition of Strassbourg, he gives the second entirely to the
counter trickery of the wily Savoyard monarch. The procedure is, indeed, frequent enough to furnish a type, a
subdivision of which would be the essays in which a group
of books will be characterized and then some point or points
fully developed.

Always fond of anecdote, Sainte-Beuve, at about sixty,
is freer than ever in his reminiscences of persons and
happenings pertaining to his earlier days. "I act the part
of Nestor," he says, "and ramble along about olden times."
The difference between his recollections and those of others,
Lamartine for example, lies in their accuracy. When he
reviews the *History of the Restoration* by Viel-Castel (February 9, 16, 1862), not only does he give a group of miniature portraits, but he recalls the passions aroused by the
"White Terror," which the cold historian fails to render,
and in the second part he pictures Royer-Collard and
Pasquier as he had known them, the former in particular,
not described, but emerging vividly from a series of disconnected incidents, anecdotes and comments, as a loud-
spoken personage with an authoritative and dogmatic manner that lent effectiveness to lively and timely, but not over-
brilliant, epigrams. When the book under review treats of
Greece in 1863,[6] Sainte-Beuve recalls his youthful articles
in the *Globe,* written when that country was "a bleeding

---

[6] It will add to the interest of this review to know that the author
of the book was one of the most prominent leader writers for the
Constitutionnel and that, on April 5, the volume had been highly
lauded by his chief, Limayrac, on the front page of that journal.

heroine, a victim, a chained and palpitating Andromeda that fired the heart." The duel of Carrel and Girardin can be weighed calmly, his own experience on the field of honor unnamed, but lurking obviously in the background. When the subject is Viollet-le-Duc, the days of early Gothic enthusiasm come back, two young men arriving in a German town and without pause seeking out the narrowest street for a row of old houses, a doorway or a courtyard. What was so far in the past had become impersonal. Much in the poems, the Princess is told, is no longer himself (March 9, 1863); the *Chronique Parisienne,* so carefully concealed at the time, can now be publicly acknowledged (October 24, 1864); and of a volume of Boulay-Paty the remark can be recorded: "This book, I can say it to-day without embarrassment, is an imitation of *Joseph Delorme*" (1865). Sainte-Beuve's memory was marked by equilibrium and order, and each idea, says Troubat, seemed to have its pigeon-hole. He will recollect the talk of M. Manuel, an old clergyman at Lausanne, dead twenty-five years ago; or every detail of de Vigny's reception at the Academy; or the complete picture of Magnin surprised in the midst of his researches in the Royal Library. When he comes to speak of Jansenism, with a difference, he will recall Hugo's words about Port-Royal, uttered at his own Academic reception, "The Bible open before them in the church and the sun spread in the skies," and repeat a criticism made at the time in a private letter.

His association with the Romantic group is naturally one of the episodes of Sainte-Beuve's career to which he very often recurs. Whatever defects may be noted in Lamartine, de Vigny and de Musset, and whatever disparaging anecdotes may be told, these poets are always placed, as poets, on a height beyond the reach of detraction. Hugo, too, is invariably lauded, a sun that "reigns and dominates, and gilds or warms from afar." But imitators are warned that they have appeared too late. In literature there are decisive moments, the time to strike, when a book may be an event and make an epoch, but that moment past, even a good work falls flat. Lebrun-Pindare, for instance, a poet of transition with a real vein, published after his epoch and failed. Sainte-Beuve, proclaiming himself "a classicist of my own kind and in my own way," condemns those critics who measure everything by school rules and prefer a correct disciple to an original, though not necessarily very distinguished innovator. Romanticism was to him a movement in history, a general refreshing breath that passed upon souls, a "necessary and legitimate renovation in art, poetry, philosophy, history, criticism." But Sainte-Beuve is a champion of present and living literature. We should not read, reread and always admire the same thing, but seek truth and novelty. There are, indeed, specially happy ages, but never the literary Messiah. The true descendant of Racine was Voltaire, the descendants of Voltaire are the historians and critics of the nineteenth century, Thiers, Thierry, Guizot, Fauriel and, at the time of writing, Renan. "Enough of the Seventeenth Century," he exclaims over a volume on La Rochefoucauld, though anything really new on such a subject will always be welcome. When some letters of the Countess of Albany are published, he is happy to penetrate into a new social world, being fatigued with the old. Even antiquity can be maintained in its rank only by being related to modern civilization and to the march of the human spirit. To be fossilized in the old, not to be possessed by the present and the future, creates mere learned futilities. Let us live amid the wonders of modern times: "Prometheus has not ceased to press forward and to despoil the gods."

Sainte-Beuve could, he said, understand Eckermann's feelings of hero worship on first meeting Goethe from his own youthful feelings toward Chateaubriand and Lamar-

431

tine, only Eckermann, a born disciple, remained in subjection, while he himself, a born critic, emancipated himself. Yet, in spite of many jibes, he always manifested
toward the generation preceding his own, even toward
Cousin, traces of the deference of a younger man for his
elders. In one of his essays, he remarks: "I have lived
many literary lives, and I have passed pleasant hours of
conversation with cultured men of more than one school;
it seemed to me that I was one of their group, so long as
I talked with them." Yet he did not always feel capable
of entering new fields. "Each critic," he remarks in his
Chateaubriand volume "(be he also a poet), has only his
own reach: each of us has only a limited time, and this
past, he does not get renewed. The old critic retires and
shuts the blinds, or only opens them toward the sunset."
Sainte-Beuve did not become the old critic he pictures.
Whatever fixed standards and unchangeable ideas had developed from his studies and meditations, he was always
alert for literary novelty.

His attitude in this matter of new and old was, if the
analogy be not pushed too far, somewhat parallel with his
attitude toward his old and new friends. The old were
a part of his experience, a part of his developed personality, like a well-known book that does not need often to
be opened; to see them on rare occasions or in public was
sufficient; his real companionship was with the new.
Though not in their circle, he met Lamartine, Thiers,
Cousin, Ampère and many more at the Academy, Ampère
and Cousin, indeed, being his associates on the committee
for the *Dictionary*. Cousin, he says, was aware of his
admiration, and they talked, when they met, almost as
formerly, Sainte-Beuve now not hesitating to contradict
but, in his opinion, paying attention to the difference in
rank which he recognized. To Baudelaire he wrote (January 8, 1866) that Mme. Hugo was the only constant friend

remaining to him from the Romantic group, at the same time expressing his belief that, if he and Hugo should once come face to face, the old sentiments would revive, since they had never met without in a few moments understanding one another just as formerly; and to Verlaine (November 19, 1865), after thanks in the name of Joseph Delorme for favorable comment on *les Rayons Jaunes,* he proceeds to extol Lamartine whom the young poet had decried, adding that doubtless Hugo in his fraternal generosity would assent.

It was in 1864 that Lamartine, on the occasion of the new edition of Sainte-Beuve's complete poems, devoted two articles in his monthly *Familiar Course in Literature* (CI, CII) to his old-time friend. The form is a personal letter addressed to "My dear Sainte-Beuve," and in the midst of the quotations constituting three-quarters or more of the piece, there are many recollections of their relations in former days, among them being interviews with the mother in the little garden, rue Notre-Dame-des-Champs, and intimate walks and talks, "you in your outlook more mild, more modest, more sad than I," but exercising indescribable charm. Praise is awarded to the poetry, even to *les Rayons Jaunes,* but particularly to the *Lundis:* "I read assiduously the admirable articles that make the Monday *Constitutionnel* the foremost work of high literary criticism in France." Deeply touched, as well as flattered and exalted, Sainte-Beuve hastened to write his preliminary appreciation in a letter (July 31, 1864), not having time to call and express his thanks personally before the end of the week.

"I keep excellent friends," wrote Sainte-Beuve, "whom I never see," for absence and silence did not change his sentiments. The few hours he could now spare for society were given to the circle of the Princess and her brother. There had been enmity between brother and sister, but they became reconciled in the summer of 1862 through their common group of friends, a circle that Viel-Castel characterized as a crowd of "demagogic mediocrities," Sainte-Beuve himself being nothing but "an atheistic feuilletonist." It was this same group that formed the nucleus of the Magny dinners. Dr. Veyne, a fresh, jovial, generous physician, good Samaritan to many victims among the poor and particularly in the Bohemian world, desiring to divert the celebrated artist Gavarni, who was ill, proposed to Sainte-Beuve a fortnightly dinner to be held in the critic's habitual restaurant. As the proposal accorded with a desire Sainte-Beuve had long harbored, his adhesion was readily obtained, and the first reunion took place on Saturday, November 22, 1862, the guests being Gavarni, Sainte-Beuve, Dr. Veyne, Chennevières and the Goncourts. Others were gradually added, among the best known being Gautier, Renan, Taine, Schérer, Flaubert, Viollet-le-Duc, Nefftzer, editor of *le Temps*, Robin and Berthelot, scientists, with Nieuwerkerke, Chennevières and Saint-Victor to uphold the arts. Of these Nefftzer was the only one not in the circle of the Princess. Sainte-Beuve's old friend Olivier sometimes attended, and we have a glimpse or two even of George Sand.

Monday, Sainte-Beuve's free evening, was the usual time of meeting. There was naturally much general talk, for every one made confessions and the conversation wandered over a wide range. Occasionally some one would develop an idea, while the others would listen, until a discussion would be started, when all would talk at once, shout at each other and even get heated and angry. A quarrel over Homer almost caused a break between the Goncourts and Saint-Victor. Sainte-Beuve is looked upon as a sort of presiding spirit, the elder, the veteran, yet without special privileges. In September, 1863, he is the only one to defend Thiers against a massed attack. Generally he is represented as gossiping from the stores of his "immense and babbling memory" about perhaps Chateaubriand, the salon of Mme. Récamier, or Louis XVIII, Pasquier, de Musset, de Vigny, Planche, or some verses by Robespierre he had heard of from a Boulogne librarian, or again the tattle of the eighteenth century drawn from memoirs and tradition. A fair sample of the personal gossip is what he told of Hugo's physical force, a beard that ruined every razor, teeth that would crack a peach-stone, and eyes that from the tower of Notre-Dame could distinguish the color of Mme. Nodier's gown on the balcony of the Arsenal. For all these pictures we have to depend on the *Goncourt Journals,* and these brothers were imperfect "stenographers," giving too much froth and too little substance, listening with all their ears to an impulsive utterance never intended for anything but momentary effect, and then with righteous indignation setting it down for the purpose of later putting it in print. As a result, we receive an impression of disparaging anecdote, contemptuous aspersions and off-color talk which, according to the testimony of Taine and Renan, is utterly out of proportion. Of the serious discussions we get only glimpses. While grateful for what is given, we must regret this insufficiency, though, in truth, fairness would not call for such criticism, had not the diarists claimed the credit of being "stenographers."

Among the members of the Magny group, a half dozen may be selected to emphasize Sainte-Beuve's salient characteristics by contrast.

Gautier, now writing the dramatic and art *feuilleton* for the *Moniteur,* with an occasional book review and a still rarer poem, was the general favorite, "universally beloved," according to Sainte-Beuve's unusually fervent tribute. His charming ingenuousness never abandoned him. When named librarian of the Princess in 1868, his query was: "Has she a library?" It was he who transmitted to the new generation the appellations of 1830, "Father Hugo" and "Uncle Beuve," and while no one else addressed the critic with *tu*, all came to refer to him as "uncle." "Unlike ourselves," writes Sainte-Beuve, "whose nerves get the upper hand and are stronger than we, he never explodes." Confessing that he had been unjust to Gautier in the beginning, he now makes full amends. He sympathizes with the poet turned critic, treats with indulgence such a crochet as the opinion that Voltaire is not to be called a writer at all, and mingles the lightest kind of faultfinding with generous praise.[7] "The word inexpressible is no longer French since this new master of our vocabulary has been able to say everything." In contrast with "Uncle Beuve," Gautier was chiefly a painter in words. When the fairy tales of Perrault illustrated by Doré are reviewed by him (*Moniteur*, December 19, 1861), the article consists of a series of vivid descriptions of the pictures, descriptions which make us feel the poetry of the characters and situations, of Prince Charming, of Sleeping Beauty and the rest. Sainte-Beuve, with the same book before him (December 23), deals historically with his author, exhibiting a remarkable intuitive insight into the problems of folklore and, in the end—and here he shows that he has been talking with Renan—defending the fitness of fairy tales for children on the ground that the developing child should be allowed to pass in this natural way through the infancy of the race.

The Goncourts are both limited in outlook and supercilious in attitude. While Gautier is never sneered at by them, and Flaubert but rarely, Sainte-Beuve, Taine, Renan

---

[7] The whimsicality of Gautier appears plainly in a little incident. An umbrella found after he had called on Sainte-Beuve being naturally supposed his, he, when notified of the fact, replied: "I never use the bourgeois implement." For Sainte-Beuve, on the contrary, the despised object was a normal accompaniment.

and Mérimée are often treated with an air of contemptuous superiority. The brothers are rather surprised that Sainte-Beuve calls on them (October 18, 1861) for the purpose of making their "intellectual acquaintance," that he wants to know, and that, disquieted by their preoccupation with art, he gropes, questions, and tries to get them to talk. Such an effort astonishes them. They, on their part, measure everything by their own tastes, and are offended by Sainte-Beuve's plebeian, inartistic home and by his inelegant dress. To them Pasquier is a commonplace and overrated nonentity, while Sainte-Beuve, on the contrary, appreciates the skillful mediator, the inventor of means for solving difficulties, the type of wise moderation and indulgence in practical statesmanship, applying his experience to changing situations and managing men with varied good sense. "That," he adds, "is as good as a lively and stinging book." Distinct from critics who are all literature, Sainte-Beuve appreciated every type of intellectual mastery. "To form a state," he says, "requires a statesman, just as to write a poem requires a poet"; and again, "Talleyrand did not write his maxims, like La Rochefoucauld; he put them into practice." With the arrogance of specialists, these appreciative collectors held the critic's opinions of painters in contempt, though he never really ventured into art criticism, but only sought the traits of personalities or of schools as presented on canvas. The Goncourts would never have maintained with Sainte-Beuve that a great battle might be as much a classic as a tragedy and, considered as a masterpiece, should be just as thoroughly and widely known. Sainte-Beuve never, either in criticism or in disparaging gossip, seeks to assert his own superiority; the Goncourts almost always do, and there is nobody, even the Princess and Flaubert, who does not at some time or other get on their nerves. Dining with the Princess, they meet "a young scientist named Pasteur";

Sainte-Beuve, with the name, knows all the essential points of the young scientist's achievement. Arrogance and disdain are the offspring of narrow views and the progenitors of petty personal interpretations. When Sainte-Beuve remarks, and the remark can be found in a dozen of his essays, that there is "no posterity" for present-day writers, the Goncourts infer that the journalist must be envious of them as authors of books (February 19, 1869), and when he fails to review their *Madame Gervaisais,* as they had expected, an unfavorable review being to them better than silence, they never forgive the slight. Their entry of the critic's death in their diary is accompanied with a sneer. In their judgments, whether of men or of literary and artistic productions, they did not in the slightest degree aim at critical neutrality. It is not to be supposed that a critic like Sainte-Beuve, who tries to see a thing as it really is, will always succeed in his endeavor, but he is more likely to see true than one who looks at everything through a theory, through a prejudice or through exasperated and possibly diseased nerves.

Flaubert, realist as well as protagonist of painstaking minuteness, furnishes a further indirect antithesis. At the same time that Sainte-Beuve finds *Salammbo* grandiose and powerful, he finds it also artificial and theatrical, a sort of archæological poem, smelling of the lamp. By cultivating atrocity the author fatigues the nerves till they become insensible. Realism the critic likes, preferring a book that is, above all, life; yet he does not like the representation of what is repulsive, vulgar, flat and tiresome. Art needs sentiment, something indefinable that rectifies without falsifying. The theoretical problem, however, is insoluble; the only way to end the debate is by example, and the examples presented have the fault of disregarding elevated characters and of representing the world as vulgar and ignoble. "Represent things and persons as they are,"

the critic counsels, "but not more ugly and more evil. . . .
I do not even ask you to select; paint the truth; but do
not expressly choose the worst and prefer it to everything
else." In this "refinement of a blasé talent," his practiced
eye sees the end, rather than the beginning of a school.
Furthermore, the minute descriptions paint everything on
a single plane, making an inventory like that of an anti-
quarian or an auctioneer, and presenting an assemblage
of details that no eye would have time to perceive. Fromentin, on the contrary, describing a girl's room, gives just
what a lover would notice. It is indeed, as usual, the excess
of the method that offends Sainte-Beuve's taste. In fairness to his friend, he prints in an appendix a long defense
of *Salammbo,* which Flaubert had written, and there was
no interruption of friendship until the breach with the
Princess.

In an essay on Magnin, after remarking that in erudition, especially in that dealing with foreign literatures, the
pure Gallic race has been content to divine, to taste, to
touch and pass on, Sainte-Beuve exclaims: "O Taine, what
progress have you made since our time! Your stomach is
truly strong enough to digest stones, and your brains are
all the better for it." What Sainte-Beuve admired in
Taine was, indeed, a talent quite contrary to his own.
Writing to a priest who wished to launch a philosophical
work, he dwells on the unfavorable condition of the book
market, and then adds that to consult Taine would be useless, since he would consider only the merits of the abstract
ideas without regard to what might be opportune. It is
characteristic, too, that Taine did not attempt to modify his
manner according to the periodical in which he wrote, while
Sainte-Beuve adapted himself and observed the proprieties
the place demanded. Taine's inquiries, moreover, were all
conducted with some design; Sainte-Beuve's were largely
haphazard and free. Intellectual rigidity, in the one case,

stands opposed to flexibility, in the other. Yet it is chiefly to the example of Taine that we owe Sainte-Beuve's much too celebrated attempt to outline his method ("Essay on Chateaubriand," July 21, 1862).

This method, in comparison with the rigid system of the younger man, shrinks, we shall find, to slight enough dimensions.[8]

Although apparently fluctuating, moral science, says Sainte-Beuve, has its definite results. So far, as in botany before Jussieu and comparative anatomy before Cuvier, we have nothing but the description of individuals, and it is such observations of detail that the critic himself amasses. Some day, however, there will emerge a real science, classifying the larger families of minds and their subdivisions. Frequently, indeed, Sainte-Beuve assigns one of his subjects to the same family of minds as that to which some other belongs, but there is never a logical definition of such families. They are not, it is confessed, like families of animals, since there is too great a mobility of combinations, and man is so organized that the investigation, since this is really an art, can be carried on only by those who have a special vocation. Apparently a science that demands a gifted artist to wield its tools is but slightly scientific. Furthermore, every principle stated is followed by a *but,* which robs the results of all their rigidity and all their certainty. In natural history, any one with eyes can note the presence or absence of a feature that classifies the object studied. Sainte-Beuve, indeed, perceives that he has attaind no such method, and this perception makes him as a critic and, at bottom, as a scientific mind, superior to those who claim to have reached biological certitude in literary classification. What he presents, indeed, is rather

---

[8] Nevertheless, a physician, F. F. E. Voizard, has taken the pains to analyze a few of Sainte-Beuve's essays, each in the form of a medical report of a case.

a literary and historical mode of procedure than a scientific method, and a procedure, not preëxisting in theory, but growing out of his own practice. Instinctive at first, it was later consciously applied, and varied according to the subject.

This method then—if we must use the word—was somewhat like that of Taine, but with important differences. It begins with Race, *but* the root remains always obscure; that is, we gain by observing the parents, especially the mother, and also by observing sisters and brothers and children, in whom may sometimes be bared a quality more or less hidden in the great man by his very superiority. The search, however, must not be carried too far. Indeed, a fortnight after expounding the great theory (August 4), Sainte-Beuve has occasion to apply it to Racine; he seeks for brothers and sisters who may throw light on the dramatist's genius, and he finds these brothers and sisters, but he does not find the light. And later, in the case of Littré, he traces elements of character to father and mother, and then adds that "by a variation common in this complex and mobile physiological order," Littré's brother did not inherit these traits. On the other hand, qualities appear without antecedents; Gautier's taste for the decadent being "a mysterious element such as enters into every talent."

The second subject of study is the group of friends at the time the talent asserts itself; and here the case of Chateaubriand is supplemented by personal experience:

The critical group of the *Globe* around 1827 is well known, as well as the wholly poetical circle of the *Muse Française* in 1824 and the *Cénacle* in 1828. None of the young talents that lingered and lived in one of these groups has passed through it with impunity. . . . The truly great outgrow the group; they become themselves centers and others gather around them ("The truly great," as enumerated in other essays, were Hugo, Lamartine, de Musset and de Vigny). . . . There are talents that participate in several groups at the same time and do not cease to travel across successive media, perfecting, transforming or distorting themselves. (Here Sainte-Beuve without doubt placed himself.)

What has at length been gained by this "method"? Each work thus examined "acquires its full meaning—its historic meaning, its literary meaning—regains its true degree of originality, of novelty or imitation, and, in judging it, we run no risk of inventing false beauties and admiring awry, as is inevitable when we rely on pure rhetoric." Yet the judgments of taste are not to be excluded; there is a time for Quintillian, as well as a time for the historical student.

Other points are added: youth, the moment of excess becoming a fault; then decline, distortion, for few improve with age; then the author's ideas and mode of life, even if his writings are the opposite, for "nothing is more like a hole than a protuberance"; finally, disciples and opponents; all leading to a formula that defines a talent, the example being Chateaubriand, "an epicurean with a Catholic imagination." It may be said that this particular product of the scientific "method" has not been accepted as a geometric certainty. After all, the critic himself often insists that in physiological criticism there is always a residue of the unexplained—genius.

Sainte-Beuve's theory, in truth, is so flexible that, without discarding it, he can display all his critical powers, while Taine's is so absolute that he is excellent as a critic only when he frees himself from its trammels. The objection uttered in the first essay on Taine (1857) continues unanswerable, the objection that, knowing all the facts of race, environment and epoch, you could not predict the work of art or literature. In an even earlier criticism of another work, Sainte-Beuve had complained that certain forms, certain divisions, were more methodical, more scholastic, than the subject-matter allowed, and he had signalized it as a fault, a fault of which, in truth, he himself was never guilty, "to divide and subdivide his (the subject's) mind, his mode of thought and speech, to separate into various compartments what was never anything but a unit and should be accepted in its natural shape, in short, to treat too much as a book that which is a man."

His own attempt at method Sainte-Beuve really criticizes in his essay on Littré (1863). The nature of his own mind, he says, caused him to place Comte among those who "conceive the progress of society and that of the human understanding in a certain line which may be admitted in general without going so far as to adhere to it too closely in detail." In the realities of each day, too many exceptions belie the doctrine; and the formula of Comte, too absolutely applied, compromises the general results that otherwise one would be disposed to accept. Yet, even if the system leads to a slight forcing in the application of certain laws, true in a general sense, and to putting too much order and regularity into the varied elements of the past, still this fault is preferable to its opposite, too much confusion. Particularly in literature, however, a fresh experience without theory is best; "the truant surely gathers more flowers." Yet, even here, there are rules and summaries, artificial it is true, methods that resemble labor-saving machines, which abbreviate and sum up an interminable task.

When Sainte-Beuve comes to Taine's *History of English Literature* (May 30, 1864), he finds a book that does not leave things as they were before its appearance, yet he looks upon the doctrine of race, environment and epoch as nothing but common-sense, which such frivolous persons as himself will fail to apply as an exact system. Accepting the comparison of the human spirit with a river modified by everything in its course, Sainte-Beuve insists that the

443

drops of which this river is composed are not alike and that there is here something science has not explained, something perhaps inexplicable. In other words, the mass is always in Sainte-Beuve's interest subordinated to the infinitely variable individual. This is true humanism, inseparably linked with sensibility and humor. The spirit of abstraction and system makes itself felt even in Taine's energetic and hard style; "the man of science and intelligence should beware of fatiguing the man of taste."

"Literary criticism," says Sainte-Beuve (November 7, 1864), "cannot become a positive science"; it remains a delicate art, but profits by every scientific induction and every acquisition of history. This is the final conclusion. It is with certain rules that we lay siege to a writer, but these must be concealed. Now, at length, the critic even regrets for a moment the olden time when reading was a pleasure instead of a labor. "The historical point of view," we read in another essay, "is distinct from that of taste; neither should be sacrificed to the other, nor should the two be intermingled." And, in addition to taste, there is insight: "Those who give themselves the title philosophers, and who are really nothing but professors of the subject or reasoners in it, do not even guess what a height of true philosophy is attained naturally and with a single bound by certain of those natures that are called artists." Sainte-Beuve had in himself enough of the artist to dispense very generally with the method of the professor.

The historical critic of the group who excelled in literary art was Renan. It is indeed this feature that Sainte-Beuve chiefly stresses in his review of the *Life of Jesus* (September 7, 1863), this review being a supreme piece of insight, critical skill and journalistic tact in handling a difficult and even dangerous subject. In his letter of acknowledgment, Renan says (September 10): "You know, you understand everything, you see everything at first glance with a

justice and surety that astound. The exact amount of what
is known, of what is implied, the most delicate balance of
criticism is felt and divined as though you had given a
lifetime to these studies. . . . I feel that I only apply your
procedure to older histories.''

Some earlier articles on Renan (June, 1862) also exhibit
Sainte-Beuve's skill in analysis at its best. In Taine's
view, these pieces were not disinterested, the purpose being
to pave the way for the reopening of the course in Hebrew.
This purpose, indeed, there is no attempt to conceal, the
concluding passage, a picture of how Renan's opening lecture might have been received—all his distinguished opponents listening, though unconvinced—being a plea for
liberty of teaching. Disinterested, however, the essay really
is, for the aim, which appears here and there in a passage,
does not at all influence the portrait or the criticism. Apart
from any professorship, Renan would be the same; a critic
and artist; an intelligence, lofty and aristocratic and even
a trifle sacerdotal; a mystic, with faith, not in the supernatural, but in the divine. We are made aware that
Renan's view of a plan in the development of humanity
is not shared and that his attack on Béranger shows too
little of the ''Gallic spirit.'' On this last point the critic
says: ''In reading his article, I admitted at almost every
phrase that he was right, and yet I resisted when it came
to the whole: I am surely only semi-Gallic, but the semi-
Gallic part of me found an answer even to an intelligence
of such constant elevation and which joins so much sagacity
with so much delicacy.''

In discussing individual articles, the critic remarks that
his friend's essay on the Academy furnishes too ideal an
interpretation of the facts. As there is a *Lundi* on the
same topic, Pellison and d'Olivet's *History* (July 19, 1858),
a comparison of the two pieces may be instructive.

In the first place, Sainte-Beuve deals with the book,

distinguishing the style of Pellison from that of d'Olivet,
and later objecting to some remarks of the editor; Renan
simply names the editor, ignores d'Olivet completely, and
proceeds to praise the style of Pellison. Sainte-Beuve, too,
praises this style, but distinguishes between its formality
and the ease of a de Retz, aristocratically sure of being
right even in his negligences. The critic, moreover, gives
some biography of his author, showing how he acquired his
mode of writing and how he came to produce his work. For
the origin of the Academy, Renan is content to quote a passage; Sainte-Beuve tells the story and finds political as
well as literary reasons for Richelieu's foundation. He is
always concrete, exhibiting the Academy as sometimes
abreast of public taste, sometimes behind it, offering an
anecdote of Voiture and telling, among other details, how
the armchairs came to be introduced and how ladies first
gained admission to the public meetings, all this connected
with the subject, but drawn from other sources than the
work under review. There is not a trace of such gossipy
matter in Renan. He expatiates on the Academy as the one
enduring institution in France, a new power born to society,
the power of brains; he asserts that here, in contrast with
specialists of the other classes of the Institut, the man of
the world is represented in intellectual effort; and, in
closing, he glorifies the Academy as maintaining, against
the mercantile and the material, the qualities of delicacy,
taste and tact. In Sainte-Beuve's essay, on the other hand,
we are always close to reality. One of his main criticisms
—and this Matthew Arnold seized upon—is that the Academy has, though with reason enough, failed to carry out
one item in Richelieu's program, the judgment of conspicuous new literary productions, a thoroughly French
function, since in France people not only like to be moved
and pleased, but wish to be assured by some authority that
it is right to have experienced such feelings: generalization

always tied close to fact. His article—a talk rather than a piece—ends characteristically with greetings to the first installment of the new *Historical Dictionary*.

The same contrast between the philosophical enthusiast intent on principle, and the man of experience clinging to individual fact, may be found in essays on de Sacy, Guizot and Lamennais. In de Sacy, Renan finds the moralist in love with the past, settled upon the already accomplished, not the critic who concerns himself with origins, the primitive, that which is in process of evolution; he then preaches a sermon on materialism and, taking his author as an example, states his objections to the liberal school. Sainte-Beuve, from de Sacy's enthusiasm for Cicero and Bossuet, from his lyrical outburst over the catalogue of a fine library, from his admiration for *Télémaque* and his antipathy to La Rochefoucauld, makes the man's character real; and then he adds an anecdote of de Vigny reading to the Academy some pretentious verses of Adolphe Dumas, Sainte-Beuve himself exploding with impatience, while de Sacy, man of delicate taste, went home ill and did not recover for several days. It is the same with Guizot and Lamennais, Renan always tending toward his ruling ideas, Sainte-Beuve toward the individual case and the personal trait. It is men, Renan himself remarked, rather than the abstract march of events, which Sainte-Beuve's taste led him to take as the subject of his studies.[9]

In the foregoing pages, no attempt has been made to characterize any of the distinguished writers mentioned, excepting in so far as they might serve to illustrate certain qualities of Sainte-Beuve. Though so unlike, they were united in general tendency, and the critic, conscious of their support, grew daily more outspoken in his campaign

---

[9] Of Renan's Saint Francis, Sainte-Beuve wrote the Princess (September 6, 1866): "I would never dare to give the public such personal reveries as truth."

for liberty of thought. Firmly anticlerical, he was in no sense hostile to religion, though himself an unbeliever. Here and there in private correspondence, a slighting word may be found, but never in his published works, his sympathy with Christian sentiment being unfailing.

Perhaps the best example of his attitude is offered by his review of Guizot's *Meditations on the Christian Religion* (November 14, 1864), a review of which Guizot himself wrote: "It is impossible to speak in a better tone of ideas that one does not share." Sainte-Beuve does not argue but, after a respectful statement of the author's position, he presents an imaginary composite portrait of a skeptical philosopher studying the evolution of the world, not a portrait of himself, though representing well enough his own intellectual attitude toward religious and other sorts of Faith. "I make it a point of honor," he adds in a footnote, "to understand all phases, reserving the right to prefer that which, with my experience complete and my illusions dissipated, appears to me to contain the most truth."

Guizot was a Protestant; Lacordaire was a fervid preacher of the dominant creed, and in writing of him (March 23, 30, 1863) Sainte-Beuve, supported, he thinks, by no group excepting scattered persons of good sense, hesitates to express too feeble an admiration of this leader of a white militia and idol of electrified youth; but, he adds, it is the character, perhaps the weakness, of the critical spirit not to be able to hold its tongue. While expressing admiration for the talent, and respect for the character of Lacordaire, the critic energetically asserts as a certitude that the preacher's attitude toward science would be the death of wholesome studies and of the true modern spirit. In his condemnation of Goethe, Lacordaire "has happily mistaken his epoch." Sainte-Beuve upholds research as against traditional beliefs and urges the value of good sense, "not a fine theme for eloquence, appropriate only for a private room, not for a pulpit; addressed to a few in a low tone, not to an assembled crowd." France he finds above all moderate and opposed to fanaticism and hypocrisy, as shown in the revolt against the Congregation in the twenties. At the time of writing, however, the critic feels the danger of the clerical party "with its organization, its numerous means of propaganda, its well-served press, its commands so rapidly accepted and repeated by all its organs, its ready abuse, easily passing into calumny, and the great difficulty of reaching it with effective blows while at the same time properly respecting the religious element and attacking only the clerical."

A case in point was soon furnished by the rejection of Littré by the Academy in consequence of Dupanloup's public denunciation. In order to write with propriety articles involving criticism of his colleagues, Sainte-Beuve thought it necessary to resign from the Committee on the Dictionary, thus giving up an annual compensation of 1,200 francs. His scruples, however, were not shared by his associates, for his place was left vacant (1863), and he was reëlected the next year.

In the three articles (June 29, July 6, 7, 1863), the rejection itself is but twice mentioned, the effect being obtained by commendation of Littré as scholar, author and upright character. In his sobriety of statement, Sainte-Beuve strives to be in antithesis to those "who have talent, but also the ostentation and magniloquence of talent." A contemptible trick of the opposition elicits the comment, "Partisans do not recoil before these little infamies." Coming to the Dictionary, where the methodical linguistic knowledge of the philologist ought to be added to the taste of the Academy, he finds jealousy hiding below conscience in the charge of atheism: "Hush! there is nothing more respectable than conscience." This simple, modest man,

Littré, who refused place and honor, who worked regularly in his humble lodgings from 6 P. M. to 3 A. M., and who spent his vacations acting as charity physician to the needy, belongs to the group that seeks "to free humanity from illusions, vague disputes and vain solutions."

The next week's essay, the subject being some books on Molière, is characteristic of Sainte-Beuve's sly strategy.

Let us unwrinkle our brow with Molière, it begins. One tires of everything; one tires of hearing Turenne praised, of hearing Aristides called The Just, of hearing it said that the Great Age is the Great Age, Louis XIV the great king, that Bossuet is eloquence personified, Boileau good sense, Mme. de Sévigné grace, Mme. de Maintenon reason; one tires of Racine more readily than of coffee. In the long run, 'one is satiated even with honey,' says Pindar, 'even with the enchanting flowers of Aphrodite.' There is only a single thing in France in regard to which we seem nowhere near disuse or weariness, and that is, hearing good said of Molière.

We are apparently the width of the equator from controversy when, after a discussion of discoveries concerning Molière's early life, we come upon the following passage:

To love Molière is to be cured forever, let us not say of low and infamous hypocrisy, but of fanaticism, of intolerance, of hardness, of what makes one anathematize and curse; it is to bring a corrective even to admiration for Bossuet and for all those who, like him, triumph, even if only in words, over their enemy dead or dying; who usurp a sort of sacred form of speech and involuntarily suppose themselves to have the thunder in their own hands in place of the Most High. Eloquent and lofty race, you are far too grand for me.

The difference between Sainte-Beuve and his adversaries —most of his friends too, for that matter—was that he did not allow his partisanship to blind him to literary or personal merit. He was firm upon the point of difference, but,

450

in judging all other points, largely free from prejudice. That ill-will never colored an opinion would be a hazardous statement, but, if he finds true merit in an opponent, he seems always ready to recognize and proclaim it. Yet it was a battle in which he was engaged. To Renan he writes (1867) that he feels honored in being associated with him in an important reform, he coming too late and about to finish, while the younger man could long endure and fight. What that reform was we see by the conclusion of the final essay devoted to Taine's *History of English Literature* (June 13, 1864): "A moral progress remains to be made in this nineteenth century, which boasts of being an age of tolerance and which is only half so." This progress will lead us to honor all sincere seekers for truth, to put them all on an equal plane in distributing rewards, to make no discriminations, even if their results are by no means ours. Tolerance, indeed, is not indifference, but an active, virile and vigorous virtue, which has its roots in conviction. And it works both ways. In one of his footnotes, Sainte-Beuve tells an anecdote of a student who, for interrupting the free-thinking Adolphe Franck's discourse on toleration, was thrown out of the lecture hall by his classmates.

Intolerance in taste offended Sainte-Beuve quite as much as intolerance in religion. Over and over again, he censures those who make appreciation of one genius a club for attacking another. "Why these perpetual exclusions?" he asks. Toward those critics who assume a lofty tone and put themselves above their authors he is especially severe:

Are you Virgil, the pious and sensitive singer; there are those who will call you effeminate and altogether too tender. Are you Horace; there are those who will cast in your teeth even the purity and delicacy of your taste. If you are Shakespeare, some one will appear to call you a drunken savage. If you are Goethe, more than one Pharisee will proclaim you the most selfish of egotists. . . . Every talent, every gift you have received and exposed to view will some day discredit you and be used as a reproach or a nickname to humiliate you.

In general, "one is never more at home than when astride of a very narrow view." He himself, on the contrary, is ready for "the most diverse hospitalities," realizing that "there is more than one mansion for great and acute minds." If "each adorer has his saint and each saint his adorer," the result is bad only when carried to excess. "Love your subject, biographer or painter," he advises, "espouse it, embrace it, and, if there be doubt and contest, take its part, plead in its favor." If "too much openness of mind is better than too little," yet judgment must never be flabby. Of a certain critic he says: "I do not reproach him for impartiality or moderation, but for irresolution." For his own part, Sainte-Beuve can, for instance, strongly condemn certain features of La Harpe, and still quote him with approval, "though we flatter ourselves that we have buried him."

The critic could give praise neither to the man of learning without taste nor to the man of taste without learning. He could, indeed, admire de Sacy, who deliberately shut himself up in the seventeenth century and in the Golden Age of Latin literature; yet for himself he accepted and favored, though with reservations, the new methods of literary study. If taste groans over the critical, grammatical and philological apparatus of vast modern editions, science, taking the matter in hand, establishes her method and suffers neither selection nor exception; the work is worthy of all encouragement and praise. Preferring fact to system, Sainte-Beuve went, when he could, to the sources. His taste, he confesses, was for civilized, cultivated, classic ages and, when obliged to enter medieval literature, he had to force himself to study the rougher types; yet, making his reserves, he appreciates the subject-matter and admires

452

the spirit and the sap; not enough, to be sure, to content
Paulin Paris and other specialists. "Numerous and excellent critical works," says the critic, "leave to amateurs
and popularizers, like ourselves, nothing but the task of
painstaking reproduction and summarizing, though as we
proceed we intermingle some judgments and reflections."
The texts, which he analyzes with his usual skill, he has
read, and he finds much to commend, but when a passage
is equalled with Sophocles, he revolts—these medievalists
"have not read Sophocles, they are not on intimate terms
with Theocritus, and they are rather misty even in respect
to Boileau." In general, when Sainte-Beuve wandered
outside his own field, he went to the best authorities. He
never ventured among pictures without aid; for an aside
on the perturbations of the planets, he consults a member
of the Academy of Sciences; and in military affairs, he
falls back on the masters, considering a judgment final if
it may be traced to Napoleon. Even for Greek, Latin and
English, he always sought the support of special scholars.[10]

Buttressed by authority, he felt secure as to fact; but
inference is a far more delicate matter. Every moment
nature baffles a seemingly complete observation. Men are
more complex than is surmised, and one eminent quality
does not necessarily exclude other qualities not so fully
developed. "How the judgments of men," he exclaims,
"accord with their organization and spring directly from
their personality!" But Sainte-Beuve, aware of his own
variations, will not use himself as a standard. He knows
his own value, but he is truly modest. Renan's *admirable*
he rejects, as he had previously rejected the same praise
from George Sand and Adèle Couriard; and he will not
allow that he is first in any kind of literary work. When
Balzac arrogantly asserts that "to understand is to equal,"

---

[10] According to Pons, he had trouble in reading English poetry,
but we know the names of his aids.

453

Sainte-Beuve proclaims the axiom false. To understand a picture and appreciate the artist's talent does not make a painter, any more than to understand a campaign makes a general; the critic remains a critic, who should try to be as open and broad as possible. Not liking Alfieri, Sainte-Beuve yet appreciates him as a superior man; he will try to appreciate Michelet because of Renan's admiration; of Balzac, he will now say, "I have the fault, it may be, of not altogether admiring the celebrated novelist." He feels that he is not of the same family of minds, being more sensible to certain faults than to qualities, and in expressing this opinion, he admits that he doubtless judges himself. Owing to variations in human types, literary quarrels seem bound to arise, but let the weapon be the rapier, not the bludgeon.

Possibly in politics the bludgeon might be admitted, but Sainte-Beuve at least would not wield it. While largely sharing the views and the animosities of the *Constitutionnel*, he must have felt somewhat humiliated at its daily bickerings with the *Débats*, quite like the traditional altercations of village journalists. Still devoted to the government from good sense rather than from enthusiasm, he felt increasing disagreement with many of the imperial policies. "I had formed an ideal of the Empire," he wrote the Princess (December 19, 1862), "I had wished that the Emperor might each day do something unexpected, something new and grand." Disappointed in such hopes, he suffers "like an author whose play is spoiled by the actors." The total neglect of literature he considered a dangerous fault, since it drove the best writers into the opposition. Men of letters and politicians, he ventured to think, do not get on well together; personally they may be on friendly enough terms, but by race they are antipathetic (December 5, 1864). In the *Constitutionnel* he had wished to help along the liberal Empire, but had at length, July, 1863, gone back in dissatisfaction to individual literary criticism, no further praise of the Empire appearing for over two years. In the elections of 1863, while the *Constitutionnel* as Persigny's organ supported the minister's candidates and launched out against those of the opposition, especially Thiers, Sainte-Beuve in his district ignored the wishes of his superior and voted, not for the official candidate, nor yet for the doctrinaire Prévost-Paradol, but for Guéroult, an old Saint-Simonian, an anticlerical, devoted to Prince Napoleon, belonging to the opposition indeed, but without bitterness or suspicion. A *Lundi* on Guéroult (January 12, 1863) represents him as preferring, though not pre-occupied with forms of government, a liberal solution, yet willing to accept any benefits offered by autocracy and to coöperate frankly and sincerely for real social amelioration. The furtherance of what was best for the masses lay, in truth, always at the bottom of Sainte-Beuve's political principles; the Emperor aroused hopes because he seemed a meditative philanthropist. "In spite of all," says the critic (1865), "the principles of '89 are still mine"; and when a letter of de Tocqueville somewhat contemptuously traces the Revolution of '48 to the stomach of the nation, rather than to its mind and heart, his comment is: "There is nothing more respectable than the stomach, and no cry calls louder than that of misery."

At about this same time, Sainte-Beuve returned for an occasional article in the *Revue des deux Mondes,* and he writes to "My dear Buloz" as though there had been no estrangement. A portrait of Magnin (May 15, 1863) is largely in his old manner, but more crowded with recollections and anecdote. Equally reminiscent is his article on de Vigny (April 15, 1864) in which, in spite of high praise for the poet, he offended admirers by mockery of the pontifical character of their idol. The story of the English father-in-law, who knew that his daughter had

married a poet but could not recall de Vigny's name, is
naturally relished by the critic. Typical is a keen remark
that in de Vigny's mind ideas transmuted facts into something different from reality and that thereafter it was
impossible for any one to set him right. The prose works
are slightly appreciated. Buloz said: "You place him too
high as a poet and you do not allow him enough merit as
a novelist." It is, however, an early estimate reaffirmed.
The former rebellious spirit, too, reappeared in connection
with the Magnin article. In the absence of Buloz, the
manager had sought to delete a reference to Taine, for the
moment on bad terms with the *Revue,* but Sainte-Beuve,
though willing to accept advice, would not submit to
changes in his text. Asserting that, in journals not considered independent, he enjoyed perfect liberty, he adds:
"I have enough good sense to observe the proprieties of the
periodical for which I write."

Some of these notions of propriety are worth attention.
A passage from Benjamin Constant reviling journalism
might not be quoted in the newspaper, but could be added
when the essay was published in a volume. Uncomplimentary personalities, too, usually anonymous at the original appearance, have the names supplied in later footnotes. While often thought too free in personal anecdote
and in criticism of the living, Sainte-Beuve proclaims himself impelled to indulgence by his daily relations with
people. "If you need not fear to meet in the evening,"
he says, "the man you have judged in the morning, or
perhaps one of his intimates, you can with propriety speak
of him as you would of a writer of the past and, without
embarrassing your thought with all sorts of circumlocutions, call the false false and the puerile puerile." In
discussing the Academy, he thinks he uses "decorous liberty," and he more than once quotes d'Orsay's refusal of
a large sum for a volume of memoirs: "I will never betray

people with whom I have dined." Moral decorum is also insisted on. A passage in Mme. Roland is blamed as offensive to modesty, while this married lady's passion for Buzot is followed with intense interest. Sainte-Beuve suffers at the realistic substitute for the famous reply, "The Old Guard never surrenders"—a substitute glorified by Hugo in *Les Misérables*. Reversed rhetoric is as bad as the other. "There is not," we are told, "a dirty word in Homer."

The little gaps between theory and practice may be illustrated by an episode of 1864. In a review of various poets (April 21, 1862), Sainte-Beuve expresses admiration for Mickiewicz who, already old, nobly and proudly refused the proffered love of an adoring girl, as not befitting his years, and the critic contrasts a parallel refusal by Chateaubriand who, even in his abnegation, made a characteristic effort to trouble the heart of his worshiper, to leave there some trace of regret, some fatal drop to poison future happiness. When a young woman from Dijon—married, a mother, very provincial, but eager for intellectual guidance—wrote to Sainte-Beuve and then visited Paris expressly to talk with him, he received her cordially, asked her to dine at his house, and on her refusal—possibly dreaming of Hortense Allart and Chateaubriand—invited her to a restaurant. There, in a private room, immediately after the soup, he began to make love, but she plainly told him that the only love she desired from him was paternal affection. Much upset at this repulse and apparently chagrined at the absurdity of the unsuccessful sixty-year-old lover's rôle, Sainte-Beuve remained for a time silent, face in hands, but he soon recovered, accepted the situation, and continued to the end a kindly friend and an interested correspondent. Maxims not always followed, impulse, then return to reason—this is the character of the man though rarely of the writer. He could not but think of himself when he told the public that Pope, like most moralists, did not sufficiently practice his own maxims (June 13, 1864).

The rancor often ascribed to Sainte-Beuve is an error in interpretation. Without doubt, he was easily excited. The unbusinesslike handling of proofs at the Imprimerie Impériale wholly upset him and, if a printer made nonsense of his text, his wrath knew no bounds. The Goncourts speak of his nervous walk. He warned Troubat of his irritability and he frequently showed his quick temper, but the moments of impatience were soon over and even public quarrels, as those with Pontmartin, Cuvillier-Fleury and many others, were not always lasting. Barbey d'Aurevilly accused Sainte-Beuve of having him discharged from *le Pays* (November, 1862) on account of a bit of impudence, and he called the critic "a toad that wants to be a serpent." Not more than two months earlier Barbey had been "a friend," and Sainte-Beuve was much hurt at the accusation, which appears, indeed, to have no more foundation than that of his aiding to deprive Laprade of his professorship. He might talk against people; he did not try to hurt them in act.[11]

Though displaying much vivacity in speech, he subdued this when writing his essays. When irritated by the lack of critical faculty and the bad style of M. de Barthélemy, for instance, he says this in a footnote instead of in the text. Almost all his disagreeable personalities are thus relegated to the bottom of the page and kept out of the articles themselves. And this was not so much a necessity of journalism as a matter of literary taste. His taste, too, leads to neatness of expression. A writer has borrowed

---

[11] Barbey in his *Quarante Médaillons* (1864) blackguards nine-tenths of the members of the Academy and Sainte-Beuve is not so ill-treated as many others. *Joseph Delorme* is called a work of genius, while the critical essays are inspired by mere passion and prejudice, without judgment, taste or elevation. Such was the critic who replaced Sainte-Beuve on the *Constitutionnel.*

from him without acknowledgment; his note reads: "A passage in this introduction would lead to the supposition that one of the two, either M. Feuillet or I, had read the words of the other. If it had been I, I should have said so." The rarity of bitterness, even in footnotes, is really praiseworthy, considering the violence of the personal attacks to which he was subjected. "They insult," he writes the Princess (May 9, 1863), "believing perhaps that they are doing good."

In view of his general practice, the statement of the Goncourts that he wrote on Marie Antoinette in order to annoy the Empress is highly improbable. That Sainte-Beuve would have been pleased if what he wrote should annoy people he did not like and that he even modeled certain passages with such an aim, we can well believe, but only as a subordinate motive, the literary purpose predominating. Characteristic of the Goncourts' inability to get the exact point is their statement in another place that Sainte-Beuve projected a book on Mme. de Staël for the purpose of being disagreeable to de Broglie. The fact that we get from one of his own letters (March 15, 1868) is that the family's exorbitant pretention to perpetual ownership of all their grandmother's letters would drive him to the composition of a pendant to his *Chateaubriand* dealing with *Mme. de Staël and Her Literary Group,* the object being, not to annoy any one, but to present the truth. Enmities indeed did not dominate Sainte-Beuve and impair his art, and ill-humor did not make him unjust. At the back of his irritability, moreover, was a reserve of old-fashioned courtesy. When cut off from the free list of the *Moniteur,* he wrote the Minister of State, Walewski, an indignant letter, but it was polite; and to a proofreader at the Imprimerie Impériale an apology for a bit of impatience will be no less courteous.

In the opposite direction, that of kindheartedness, his

feelings were equally quick, as is shown by many letters of sympathy. And he did not forget the past. When his old teacher Gaillard died (1860), he recalled a friendship begun in 1818, and when Landry's son-in-law sought a position, an appeal to the educational authorities abounds in expressions of gratitude to the Landry family (1866). Barbe continues up to 1865 to receive his annual letter, Sellèque is told that a renewal of school friendships would be grateful if there could be a truce to work (1864), and Loudierre is publicly lauded as "a man of taste among the learned," one who might have made books as others do, "but preferred to make pupils" (1863). Furthermore, Sainte-Beuve was unusually kindly to struggling authors, to his secretaries in particular. He helped to launch Lacroix and Levallois; he aided Lacaussade and used his influence with Rouland in favor of an appointment for Pons. All of these he complimented in print and in doing so he was exceptional. When his name meant much, he wrote for Pons an introduction for an edition of Parny, and for Troubat one to an edition of Piron, a writer for whom he had to conquer a repugnance. When Mme. de Sohms, with her friends as collaborators, composed a gossipy weekly article for the *Constitutionnel* under the pseudonym Baron Stock, he corrected her proofs and lent Troubat to represent the fictitious Baron and to collect the easily earned pay, which equalled his own. M. de Pongerville, treated in the *Globe* as a mediocrity unworthy of the Academy, is now Sainte-Beuve's "dear and esteemed colleague"; de Sacy, in the text itself of the essays, is many times "My dear Sacy" and Janin is "our friend Janin"; even antipathetic persons apparently no longer awaken a really hostile feeling. If the scale sinks toward hatred, judgment and taste soon redress the balance.

The portraitist, indeed, enters into the intellectual life of his subject, and his curiosity is really sympathy; the critic stands apart and judges. Sainte-Beuve's eagerness to see the copy of La Bruyère annotated by the Countess of Albany might be called mere curiosity, yet the same impulse led him into the inner spirit of Eugénie de Guérin, Joseph de Maistre, Frederick the Great, and every sort of saint and sinner. Thus the portraitist and critic was, on the one hand, by his very professional procedure, led to an understanding of even distasteful personalities and, on the other, he was enabled to stand outside, not only of others, but of himself, and to contemplate his own character and actions, if not absolutely without prejudice, still with uncommon fairness. A study of other men's faults leads to bigotry; a study of one's own conduct begets tolerance. If Sainte-Beuve's ways, as he confesses, prevent him from entering into certain views, he does not decry any honest conviction, even though he may express disapproval. And in regard to that sort of patriotism which is nothing but national egotism, he is equally open minded. When a foreigner paints an unflattering picture of the French, he will ask himself: "Are we really like that?"

Sainte-Beuve had frequently spoken of the happiness of the man who could freely follow his taste in his studies without being obliged to produce his daily stint. To those whose fate it was to be overwhelmed by the burden and to feel the goad, he cries: "Thou shalt produce continuously and at the hour fixed, and however thy tastes may call thee hither and thither, thou shalt march only toward the assigned goal, and thou shalt labor from dawn till sunset." And yet he recognized that constraint and necessity were, on the whole, beneficial, and that there was a satisfaction in frequent production. From 1861 to the early part of 1865, his activities were concentrated on his essays for the *Constitutionnel*. So late as March of the latter year, he wrote Reuchlin: "Like a goat on a rope, I move in a narrow circle." He was able to call on the Goncourts only after two of a Monday afternoon, saying: "Come to see me early in the week; after that, I have my head in a bag." To Lescure he writes (April 30, 1864) that, after forty years, he ought to retire, but is condemned to continue indefinitely, with great danger to his nerves, his physique being horribly strained every week. "Each Tuesday morning I descend to the bottom of a well, not to emerge again till Friday evening at an uncertain hour." He is "not a gentleman, but a worker by the piece and by the hour."

As a consequence, he went to no receptions or formal dinners, except when invited by the Princess or her brother, and these dinners he reciprocated by small affairs at his house, where the guests were limited by space to five, all designated by the guest of honor.[12] Among such persons we find, at various times, George Sand, Berthelot, Flaubert, Dumas, Nisard, Émile de Girardin, de Sacy, Mérimée, Viollet-le-Duc, Nieuwerkerke, Delacroix, Sarcey, Schérer, Claretie, Coppée, Verlaine, d'Alton-Shée, the Goncourts, Renan, a list that might be largely extended. On Tuesdays he had his "little lady" and his secretary at table, and on Saturdays he often met another "little lady" for lunch at a restaurant. These Tuesday dinners were, Troubat says, gay. Sometimes Pantasides would come to read Greek, perhaps some shady passage from Aristophanes. The jovial Dr. Veyne, Sainte-Beuve's "minister of the interior," was a frequent guest, as well as the indispensable Chéron, of the Library, and to them the essay of the week was often read aloud for criticism, corrections being made on the spot. Everybody smoked but Sainte-Beuve, his housekeeper, Mme. Dufour, indulging even in cigars when she could get them. Every Sunday Camille Doucet, Director of Theaters for the Ministry of State, sent a box for some performance, and Sainte-Beuve attended with his

---

12 The Princess first dined at his house in June, 1863.

"family," taking great care that decorum should be observed in behavior and dress.

At the Academy, at the Magny dinners and at the house of the Princess, Sainte-Beuve kept in touch with most of the celebrities of the day. Sometimes, too, though rarely, he would of an afternoon accidentally meet on the crowded Boulevard his comrades in journalism, learn the gossip he might otherwise fail to hear, sharpen his wits with an exchange of repartees, and feel the pleasure of seeing "real good will on the worn and acute faces of intellectual workers." Returning to his unfashionable district, he would perhaps run into a gay crowd of the populace, and hear the cry: "Make room for the old fellow!" or "Respect old age!" disagreeable reminders indeed, but well intentioned. "O Paris, Paris!" exclaims Sainte-Beuve, "Paris of every epoch, Paris old and new, always anathematized, always regretted, and always the same! It is in thee that it is sweet to live, it is in thee that I wish to die!" (July 28, 1862). And again: "Paris, city of light, elegance, facility, in thee it is sweet to live, in thee I hope to die! Happy city, where one can get along even without happiness, where it is enough merely to feel that you are here!" "Ask the happy and lovable Auber," he adds, "who never leaves town."

Sainte-Beuve was, indeed, a thorough Parisian. He grew more and more averse to travel, though he could appreciate it in books, growing enthusiastic over descriptions of the Sahara and sympathizing with Montaigne's delight in new scenes and his love for the place he was going to, in contrast with Chateaubriand's hurry to get away from the place he was in. Moreover, though the critic visited great houses, he was completely plebeian, having even a weakness for organ-grinders, because "it is not ill that the poor should glean after the harvest." The _de_ in his family name he dropped. He thought that a man should make his own

463

way, not inherit distinction like de Broglie. His active
sympathy was always at the service of indigence, a poor
old scrubwoman, a struggling writer, a clerk, a policeman,
a laborer, with a family to support, seeking employment.
He makes a plea for certain of Rousseau's letters, full of
vulgar preoccupations, showing him "as little of the gentleman as possible," yet redeemed by sentiment (July 22,
1861). In externals, too, Sainte-Beuve was far removed
from elegance, though the old-fashioned bareness of his
house was getting modified through gifts of the artistic
Princess, pieces of fine furniture, rugs, a desk clock, a picture painted by her own hands. In the evenings, when
Troubat read aloud, Sainte-Beuve would sometimes doze,
his appearance at such times reminding his secretary of an
old woman, the resemblance to his mother being most striking. Any passage he wished to refer to he would order
marked, and he often took the book himself and with his
own hand wrote marginal comments.

In outward appearance Sainte-Beuve was completely
unaristocratic. The description of the Goncourts (1863)
is verified from many other sources; a little, round, rustic-
looking man, wearing countrified clothes, "dressed like
a provincial haberdasher," fond of bright-colored neck-
ties; high forehead, shiny bald head protected by a skull-
cap, bushy eyebrows, big eyes (Taine says they were
small; Zola finds them round and bulging); nose betoken-
ing curiosity and sensuality, large ugly mouth with an
attractive smile, cheeks prominent and rounded like great
knobs; resembling a provincial librarian fond of good
Burgundy. In his evening walks, always with cane or
umbrella, he noted all the little happenings on the way,
stopping now and then under a street lamp to jot down
some phrase that had come to him. To Taine he gave
the impression of timidity, his soft, insinuating speech
having in it something of the ecclesiastic who is also a

man of the world. Then there would come outbursts and explosions. The charm of his talk lay in little touches that built up a conception; there was in it nothing large and grand.

Never eloquent in the oratorical sense, Sainte-Beuve, as he grew older, became even more opposed to the slightest appearance of clap-trap, more sensitive to every trace of pose. Reference to the Muse seems theatrical and spoils the pleasure he takes in an otherwise sincere writer. Good sense, always fundamental with him, is now predominant. On the other hand, though writing no poetry himself, he still loved poetry and was especially friendly and encouraging to young versifiers. He not only greets Théodore de Banville as a successor of talent, and encourages François Coppée to pursue his original path, but in cases too numerous to mention, in acknowledging a first volume of some ambitious obscurity, he writes *Monsieur et cher poète*, though often advising: "Keep your poems for your own pleasure." He sympathizes with his friend Baudelaire, who like himself had "tasted the bitter fruit, full of ashes at the core" (March 27, 1865), yet he warns Verlaine (December 10, 1866) not to take "that brave and poor Baudelaire" as his point of departure to push still further along the same path. "Sounds are not exactly marble or stone to be engraved." Follow what is best in you, is the advice, and apply this to worthy subjects. In his present contemporaries, indeed, Sainte-Beuve found excellent poets, but none equal to Lamartine, Hugo, de Musset and de Vigny. Could this judgment be called a prejudice? As for himself, he knows his place. None of these great poets, he says, have written sonnets: "Entering this cage, the swans and eagles would have broken their wings. The sonnet was left for us who were birds of less lofty flight and of smaller span."

In addition to the Monday holiday, or rather half-holiday, Sainte-Beuve now gave himself each year at least a month of freedom. In 1862 there are no *Lundis* during the four weeks from June 16 to July 21; in 1863 there is a five weeks' interval from April 13 to May 18 and again one of three weeks from November 30 to December 21; in 1864 the gaps are from March 21 to April 11, three weeks, and from September 18 to October 24, five weeks. Of the April intermission in 1863, he wrote that he felt a bit let down and would suspend work for a month for rest and recuperation, and in December he passed a fortnight at Compiègne, the only time he was ever at court. It is reported that he read poems of Hugo to the Empress at her request and that, the critic having been writing for two years for the *Constitutionnel,* the Emperor complimented him by saying: "I always read your articles in the *Moniteur.*" While at Compiègne, Sainte-Beuve walked, talked, dined, saw dancing and spent his odd moments reading the grammatical work of Vaugelas. He wrote Troubat to have this author's *Quintus Curtius* ready for him to plunge into on his return home; he has had too much leisure and "his brain is famished."

This slight preparation, with the addition of some passages obviously drawn from a Normal School Lecture, furnished matter for two delightful chats on usage and on the life of words (December 21, 28, 1863). In March, 1864, when his eyes incapacitated him for work, he again took some old lectures of his École Normale course, the type being *explication des textes,* and made from them three *Lundis* on the *Cid* of Corneille (February 29-March 21), prefixing an essay reviewing a group of more or less recent books on the dramatist. Three weeks later, the next two essays are on Émile de Girardin, requiring little new reading, and to the end of the year, the critic spins out an extensive fabric from rather slender materials. He has become far less strenuous than in his early days, two, three and even four weeks being usually given to a single topic, and we often feel with him that he is getting to the bottom of his barrel. Large portions of essays, occasionally the whole, will be given to remarks on a number of books on a subject under consideration; there will often be several pages of detached or loosely connected thoughts in series; there will be even simple gleanings from a volume under review with next to nothing of the critic's own, though usually his full mind recalls plenty of incidents to illuminate the subject-matter. He will sometimes merely probe into a book, read a few chapters, examine certain portions. Except in the *Revue*, there are no longer any complete portraits, merely glimpses and sketches. The author, he once says, "has painted, drawn a picture, but as for us, we talk, we listen, we repeat what we have heard." When he has to do Taine's *English Literature* (three essays, June, 1864), he is occupied "like a galley-slave," yet most of his comment is digression and about half his space is devoted to a study of Pope, whom he greatly admired. It must not be thought, however, that these pieces lack interest. Not one but contains some page that the reader will mark for remembrance. Sometimes there will be a fine opening (*Marie Antoinette*, August 8, 1864), often a subtle analysis, a bit of ripe wisdom, a flash of insight, a digression into delightful fields.

On October 11, 1864, the *Moniteur* announced a new committee for editing the correspondence of Napoleon I. The chairman was Prince Napoleon, the members Walewski (Privy Council), Amédée Thierry (Senate), Comte de Laborde (Archives—the only member retained from the previous committee of fourteen), Sainte-Beuve (Academy) and Col. Favé (Aide-de-Camp). Regularly, every week, Sainte-Beuve attended meetings and took part in the discussions. His letters show that the task was no sinecure.

CHAPTER XIV

1865—1869

IN 1865 Sainte-Beuve was busily engaged in preparing some volumes for the *Encyclopédie Péreire,* an undertaking that fell through, so that he felt obliged to refund the money advanced for his labors. At the same time he continued with a few articles in the *Constitutionnel* and he wrote on Proudhon for the *Revue Contemporaine.* On April 28, 1865, he was appointed Senator with a stipend of 25,000 francs; he considered himself the representative of letters in the upper house. Some of the leisure thus secured he devoted to a new edition of *Port-Royal,* the whole work being gone over with infinite care. In 1867 he transferred from the *Constitutionnel* to the *Moniteur* on a favorable offer from Dalloz. He also took Cousin's place on the staff of the *Journal des Savants,* to which learned miscellany he contributed a few rather lengthy papers. He further wrote occasionally for the *Revue des deux Mondes,* one article causing a fuss with the de Broglies over some letters of Mme. de Staël. In December, 1865, Sainte-Beuve was smitten with the malady that finally caused his death, and he was never again able to go away from his house further than he could walk. In spite of severe suffering, he labored intensely, producing essays equal to anything he had previously done. On March 27, 1867, he had a dispute in the Senate over a disparaging reference to Renan, and on June 25 he made a speech on excluding certain books from a town library, the two incidents leading to a challenge, which he refused to consider. On Good Friday, 1868, occurred a dinner to Prince Napoleon, which excited noisy hostility in aristocratic and religious circles. To this year belong two senatorial speeches, one on the press, the other on the School of Medicine, in both of which his anticlerical utterances caused interruptions in the Senate, followed by denunciation on the one side and applause on the other, the students in medicine visiting his house in a body as a demonstration of approval. Refusing to join a new official journal, Sainte-Beuve remained with the *Moniteur* until, an article of his being censored by the management, he withdrew and joined the *Temps* in January, 1869. This act caused a breach with the Princess, who came to his house and made a scene. A sort of reconciliation was arranged just before the critic's death. In the *Temps* appeared groups of articles on Talleyrand, Mme. Desbordes-Valmore and General Jomini, the first group angering aristocratic society. The last time Sainte-Beuve left his quarter (April 29) was to vote for Gautier, who was candidate for a seat in the Academy; his last published article (Sept. 7) was a letter to the editor Nefftzer on the *Senatus-Consulte*. Sainte-Beuve died October 13, 1869, and was buried, without services of any sort, beside his mother in the Cemetery Montparnasse. Here, on May 10, 1903, a bust of him was unveiled, speeches being delivered by Gaston Deschamps and Jules Levallois. During the critic's lifetime, in 1859, a bust by Meusnier had been placed in the Public Library at Boulogne.

At the close of 1864, Sainte-Beuve's situation was highly unsatisfactory. He naturally felt that a successful literary man ought, as he entered his declining years, to have some established mode of life, a position of dignity and leisure which delivered him from drudgery; but to him nothing of the sort had come. In a letter to Calonne, who had asked for articles for the *Revue Contemporaine*, he complained (April 11) that the government discouraged literature and that, while still devoted to the Chief, he was obliged to look out for himself, and for this reason had written for the *Revue des deux Mondes* and would write for the *Contemporaine* when in September he could lighten his weekly task and get ahead of his work. At the expiration of his contract, he would modify his mode of life, now become unbearable. Yet when the time came, he continued his connection with the *Constitutionnel*, even writing the Princess (October 14), during a five weeks' intermission, that he was preparing his reëntrance, and telling Chéron (October 21) that he was returning to begin a new campaign. He hopes, however (November

17), to relax his chains a little toward the end of January. On February 8, he writes the Princess: "I have entered the last phase of my life," a laborious one about which he will not complain, but which requires abstention from social engagements; and he is to dine with "his new boss," Isaac Péreire. He had previously informed the Prince (January 28) that he was giving up journalism to write two volumes serving as an introduction to a projected encyclopædia.

Throughout the year 1865, indeed, unmistakable signs of a reversion to some of the sentiments of 1830 may be perceived, the humanitarian note, long subdued in Sainte-Beuve's writings, now again becoming distinctly audible. The first words in the *Revue Contemporaine* are an expression of the author's regret that he had been unable to show his esteem and regard by paying funeral honors to Enfantin (August 31, 1864) and Proudhon (January 19, 1865); the first, known in youth and appreciated for large-hearted generosity; the second, met at a later date, and respected for solid intelligence and moral uprightness. Advocates of conflicting systems—Saint-Simonianism and a special form of socialism—these two leaders joined hands only in a common aspiration toward social betterment, extinction of hereditary privilege, and alleviation of the lot of the poor. Though to the mature Sainte-Beuve Utopias made little appeal—every reform introducing new abuses and progress seeming slow and limping—yet his heart went out to every victim of oppression and to every sufferer from poverty. He therefore plunged with enthusiasm into the new undertaking, a series of volumes designed to afford a foundation for social regeneration, "a vast and noble project, a generous enterprise, which came very near execution, but was finally dissipated in smoke." Every Saturday he attended the meeting of editors in the rue de l'Université, returning home

470

laden with books and documents, planning and meditating his part in the immense task.

The vital spark of the undertaking and the man who brought Sainte-Beuve into it was the enthusiastic and chivalrous Charles Duveyrier, a former Saint-Simonian, writer for the *Globe* (1830-32), eloquent and mob-conquering leader of an apostolic mission to Belgium and England, dramatist, journalist, man of affairs and organizer, whose later ideas are set forth in one of the 1865 *Lundis* (September 4). To him civilization was "human perfectability in movement," a movement to be accelerated by the union of workers both of hand and brain. For the encyclopædia this *Diderot,* as Sainte-Beuve called him, sought to combine and conciliate dispersed and sometimes hostile writers, with the aim of conquering poverty, superstition and ignorance by education, and he dreamed of an institution that should be the home of research, discovery, generous ideas and social progress, a disinterested scheme which captured the imaginations of many eminent publicists—Renan was one—and which revived faded aspirations in the but slightly optimistic Sainte-Beuve.

Financial backing for the enterprise was furnished by the Péreire brothers, Émile and Isaac, both former Saint-Simonians and writers for the *Globe,* who had acquired great wealth through combining speculation, railroad building and banking, and who were now at the height of their prosperity. Isaac's son, Eugène, engineer, banker and founder of the omnibus company, was also one of the band. Many dreamers of 1830 had made their way in the world, and the old Saint-Simonian group now included financiers, senators, high administrative officials and leaders in every walk of life. One of these, Michel Chevalier, the economist, acted as chairman of the meetings, and it was in spite of his objections that Sainte-Beuve was made a member of the staff. As advance pay for the introductory volumes, the critic received 20,000 francs. By November, having nearly finished his *Proudhon*, he is eager to begin work, but delays ensued and, when Duveyrier died (November 10, 1866), the whole project fell to pieces. The sum Sainte-Beuve had received was returned in instalments, though no repayment was either asked or expected. Two slight passages appended to the Proudhon volume are all the literary results that Troubat could find for publication.

This volume on Proudhon, completely prepared by Sainte-Beuve, but brought out only after his death, is made up of four articles contributed to the *Revue Contemporaine* (October 15-December 1, 1865) under the title *Proudhon Studied in His Private Correspondence, First Part*, 1838-1848. The second part, which presented "almost insuperable difficulties," was never written, though preparation of it had been begun and even as late as January, 1868, the critic still awaits the time when health will permit him to complete it.

Few will share Taine's opinion that Sainte-Beuve had done nothing better. Over half the work consists of extracts from Proudhon's letters, the proper title being *Proudhon Expounded and Commented by Himself*. The construction, too, is weak, altogether too much of the essential matter being thrown into footnotes, and these not added later, but, with few exceptions, belonging to the original magazine articles. Yet a vast amount of effort had gone into the preparation. The critic's correspondence of 1865 shows an unremitting search for information and for documents. Sainte-Beuve sees or writes to Proudhon's friends, Bergmann, Darimon, Mme. Ackermann and others, and he follows every clew. Through his publisher, Garnier, he had himself met Proudhon in 1856; and in 1860 he had sent him, an exile in Brussels, a copy of *Port-Royal*. In spite of all efforts, however, the work lacks vividness of portraiture, and the reflections and digressions are seldom of the highest interest. Far above the average mediocrity of the *Revue Contemporaine,* these essays are below their author's usual standard.

What chiefly attracts attention here, as in the case of the encyclopædia, is a recurrence of youthful proclivities. In 1862, a comparison of a description by Proudhon with one by Maurice de Guérin (September 1) is purely literary; now attention is directed to social organization. Not that Sainte-Beuve can accept the maxim that income from property is robbery, or conceive the equality of talents, or deeply sympathize with the man of system and absolute doctrines, the combatant in whom logic banishes reason. The biographer may, indeed, go so far as to think that "property is a privilege, the title to which each generation ought to renew and justify by labor"; or he may admire Proudhon's contempt for place and his passion for the cause of the poor, and find a probable part of truth in his doctrines as interpreted and attenuated in his correspondence; but the main purpose of the articles was to break down barriers and prejudices, to diminish hatreds arising from ignorance, narrowness and hostility, to explain, if not to excuse, the disputant's irritations and extremes, and above all, to show the man, brave, honest, generous, and faithful to the end. In this effort lies the originality of the undertaking, especially on the morrow of Proudhon's death, when hatreds were so violent. The agitator, so ferocious in printed controversy, becomes more human when interpreted by his friendly letters. What is further characteristic is Sainte-Beuve's compassion that almost shares the struggles, revolt and sufferings of a man of the people, so poor that he was obliged to journey from Besançon to Paris on foot; typical also is the accompanying equitable judgment that condemns the spirit of class in the poor as well as in the rich. The critic's ideal of the social philosopher is one who, after viewing all things, examines each "with clearsighted and supreme impartiality, animated by the breath of universal sympathy."

When these articles came out in the magazine, the editor, Calonne, proud of his catch, placarded the author's name in big letters, a piece of vulgar advertising that aroused Sainte-Beuve's ire. He objected to industrialism in literature for himself quite as much as for Balzac, or any other.

Meanwhile, the *Constitutionnel* articles continued, weekly or fortnightly till April, and after that at uncertain intervals; for the second half year, only six; for the whole of 1866, but five; and the single *Lundi* for 1867, ending Sainte-Beuve's connection with the *Constitutionnel,* is dated January 28. For this series, too, no extensive preparation was required. Three essays are devoted to Zeller's lectures on history (January 16, 23, 30, 1866), a course delivered before the Princess and frequently attended by Sainte-Beuve, who had himself recommended the lecturer. To fill up space, the critic again has recourse to his normal school lectures on Bossuet, which seem to be here reproduced verbatim, a sentence at the beginning and end of a passage connecting the class lesson with the book under review. A piece on Grote's *Greece* is mostly a discussion of the Homeric question; two on Racine's last days are based on some letters recently received from Holland and are intended for *Port-Royal;* Louis XV, Saint-Simon, "the most prodigious of portrait painters and king of every historic gallery"; the correspondence of de Tocqueville and that between Marie Theresa and Marie Antoinette—such subjects could give little trouble to the well-stored mind. There are four essays on *Poetry in 1865* (June 12-July 3) wherein, among the younger set, no really distinguished poet is noted but Sully-Prudhomme, and the critic is somewhat bewildered by the exuberant and unfamiliar germination, mostly imitators of Gautier, Banville, Leconte de Lisle and Baudelaire. Toward the close of his connection with the *Constitutionnel*, he seizes an opportunity to give publicity to his friends, the Goncourts (May 14, 1866) and Saint-Victor (January 28, 1867).

When Sainte-Beuve thus relaxes, he is apt to grow more sparkling, but in attitude there is little change, as will appear from a few scattered quotations:

I have seen so many injustices and so many false judgments on persons who did not deserve them—believed because so often repeated—that I always leave in my mind a door half open to contradiction and doubt.

Disinterested pleasure of critical curiosity, final delight of those who have lived much in retirement, who have acted little and read a great deal! What could be more agreeable and more innocent, indeed, than to occupy oneself with studying almost affectionately the exact details of a vanished life, so as to catch a distinct image of a figure of the past and, in order to recompose and show her to others, giving all one's pains to a woman who is nothing to us, from whom nothing may be expected, but whose indefinable grace and smiling kindliness attract and charm us.

It is good to know Latin; to know mathematics is at least as high a mark of culture.

Sainte-Beuve still seeks to be just. In a note to the de Tocqueville essay, he says: "I see that I have not gone far enough in the praise that is his due." Nor does his sly malice fail. The Goncourts, who particularly strove to be rare, are two literary heretics: "And who indeed," he asks, "is not more or less heretical to-day?" Granting that there is a new discovery or two in a book

475

on La Bruyère, he does not find enough to demand that all the bells of Paris should be rung. Good sense is found at the bottom of every great reign. Visions in science are as insubstantial as in other subjects. Flammarion is allowed "to speak or rather sing" a quoted passage about the inhabitants of distant worlds, and after the quotation come the words: "But we, plain men, whom the supernatural always surprises, we ask his permission to hesitate and doubt a little in the presence of this new revelation which he propounds."

For his mode of life at this time Sainte-Beuve needed at least 20,000 francs a year, a modest enough sum, it would seem, for a man with a world-wide reputation, but a sum for which he was obliged actually to slave. Outside the weekly payment, his *Lundis* brought him in but little, for he sold the volumes outright, the first series to Garnier for 1,500 francs and later 2,000 francs each, and the second series to Lévy at the rate of 2,500 francs, not begrudging his publishers their handsome profits. From the strain of incessant journalistic production, the encyclopædia offered the first prospect of relief. What made this relief an actuality was his appointment to the Senate, April 28, 1865, the position carrying a salary of 25,000 francs. His acceptance of the post and his conduct as senator do not in the slightest deserve the vociferous condemnation vented by his enemies and often repeated from force of habit.

In 1857, we are told by Levallois, Sainte-Beuve thought it would dishonor him to accept such an appointment, because he would be expected to pay for it by renouncing his independence and performing such service in the press as might be demanded; but later, after sufficient service had been freely rendered, he felt that a reward for what was past could not rightfully restrict present or future liberty, and he became impatient when the appointment was delayed. He had served the Empire from promptings of reason, grateful for the chance to develop his faculties in peace. Recognition of some sort would, indeed, be agreeable, but he could not have thought of the Senate, had it not been suggested by others. General talk on his candidacy put him in an embarrassing situation not of his own making (April 3, 1865). It was especially irritating to have the matter discussed in the newspapers and to receive from abroad congratulations based upon a false report. When the decree of October 5, 1864, named seven senators, he congratulates one, Nieuwerkerke, who belonged to the circle of the Princess, but feels humiliated over another, probably Chabrier,[1] whom he thinks fit only for the madhouse, and he requests the Princess (October 12) and will ask the Prince to cease using their influence in "that affair." He is hurt at the putting off of literature and personally alienated from the Emperor, an attitude which seems a little sulky. The matter slumbers until Friday, April 28—then surprise, joy, gratitude! The next day the official notification is gracefully presented to him at the hands of the Princess herself, and the new senator sends the Emperor a letter of thanks, afterwards repeated in person at a public reception.

Congratulations rained upon him, and he was especially touched by letters from the students and from the mayor of Boulogne, a city to which his heart remained faithfully attached. In answering such communications, he never omits to delineate his functions as those of a sort of official representative of literature in the government. He even thinks that, if the appointment had been decided by the suffrage of all men of letters, his name would have

---

[1] Chabrier, who interrupted Sainte-Beuve's speech on public libraries (June 25, 1867) by a sarcastic query, had slight claims to the honor. The other six appointed were of such rank as to bar objection.

been found among the first ten. Indeed, his initial task over a year later (July 6, 1866) was to report a law on copyright.[2]

For the time being, however, he is not very active. "The Senate is hard at work," he writes (July 7, 1865), "work in which I have the appearance of taking part." What was really "a nightmare" was the preparation of an address as Director of the Academy on the prizes for virtue, an address which, after a preliminary reading at the table of the Princess, he delivered in July, getting as usual into a little controversy, this time because he compared a priest who merited one of the prizes with the Vicar of Wakefield; an insignificant enough straw, but indicating how the wind was blowing. People who could get horrified at the comparison of a Catholic with a Protestant were ready to lunge out on almost any pretext.

The Proudhon articles sufficiently attest Sainte-Beuve's independence, but two other incidents are significant enough to deserve mention. Before his appointment, he had flatly refused to write a review of the Emperor's book on Cæsar unless the editor of the *Constitutionnel* should give him absolute liberty to express his true opinion, an opinion which, judging from the reported talk in the office and from the opening passage dictated to Troubat, would have got everyone concerned into most serious trouble. The second incident was connected with the preparations for the Exposition of 1867. From Duruy, Minister of Instruction, Sainte-Beuve accepted the task of preparing a report on the literature of the preceding fifteen years, but when limitations were imposed, he refused to continue. "The good, the true and the beautiful," he wrote, "made up a fine but specious device";

---

2 The law Sainte-Beuve approved, not always its applications. In 1863, he had written: "Our new ideas on literary property, miserly, illiberal. jealous and niggardly ideas." Essay on Ducis.

as for himself, he sought the true, the true alone, and let the good and the beautiful take care of themselves. To manifest an absence of personal feeling, he suggested the names of others fit to take his place, but as a writer he ignored the exposition, except for a contribution on the Academy to the *Paris Guide*. Sainte-Beuve, grown old, had softened considerably, but in matters of what he considered literary conscience, the rebellious fire was always ready to flare up.

Rather frequently he was called upon to take the part of good sense against intolerance. In 1866, when Bergmann, Dean of the Faculty of Letters at Strassbourg, was cited before the Academic Council, for correcting the proofs of Proudhon's *Annotated Gospels*, Sainte-Beuve came vigorously to his defense in personal letters to every individual member of the Council and, if health had allowed, he would have burst out in the Senate. It was from this professor that the critic had received much material for his own essays on the eminent socialist and the affair moved him deeply. He also defended the *Figaro* (1866) when it was threatened with prosecution for an indiscretion, and he used his influence in favor of a printer who had been imprisoned and of a poor newsdealer who had incautiously sold copies of Rochefort's *La Lanterne* (1868). In such affairs he was not acting against the government, but appealing for mercy. Imprisonment for an offense of the press seemed to him "an infamy, a remnant of barbarism."

Besides defending those in trouble, Sainte-Beuve was tireless in securing help for the indigent and in seeking places and honors for the ambitious. For a man who lived amid books and whose every moment was intellectually precious, his activities actuated by the heart, his expenditure for others of his time, money and concentrated and sustained attention are truly extraordinary. His begging letters are numerous, and before writing such a letter, he personally investigated the case, and he follows the matter up sometimes for many months.

One of his chief occupations during the years 1866-67 was the preparation of a new edition of *Port-Royal*. It was Sainte-Beuve's practice never to drop a subject he had once treated. Pons tells us that every article became a nucleus to which was added everything that came to hand on the subject, letters, published essays, scraps of personal information, all carefully arranged and labeled, accumulations of material to which the secretaries applied the legal term *dossiers*. "When I have once treated a subject," writes the critic himself, "it becomes to a certain extent mine, and I then, whether I will or not, seem obliged to note and gather everything that relates to it." In reading the later essays, we can often trace in a single piece indications of reference to several such *dossiers*. We observe especially the critic's unfailing interest in any new light thrown on themes of earlier articles, on Benjamin Constant, for example, Chateaubriand, Fauriel, on the sixteenth century, or Boileau, Bayle, Voltaire; but the topic that above all preoccupied his mind was Port-Royal. New matter came to him from Holland; a scholar of Lyons, Chantelauze, sent to be used as an appendix a small treatise on de Retz, about which there is a vast amount of correspondence; there are fears that death or permanent incapacity may interrupt the task of revision; every text was verified anew, every authority, even the slightest statements, an enormous labor, "a big thorn," as Sainte-Beuve writes Levallois (December 5, 1867), and it is a relief to have it finished. In spite of all effort, however, blemishes remained. To a priest who in a rather severe but generally fair article had pointed out errors of detail, the author, though in the heat of his anticlerical campaign, wrote a letter of thanks (January

480

20, 1869), admitting the justice of every stricture and promising the proper corrections.

Old friends were fast disappearing: Duveyrier and Gavarni died in November, 1866, Baudelaire in September, 1867, and Dübner in October. For the unveiling of Dübner's tomb (October, 1868) Sainte-Beuve wrote a eulogy, which ill-health prevented him from reading. This scholar, whose friendship is called precious and upon whom he had often relied for final judgment on questions of classical erudition, seemed to him to have been ill-appreciated in France, and his remarks to this effect offended persons representing the Academy of Inscriptions, the University and the Imperial Press. Another would probably have kept silent on the subject or reserved his insinuations for a more fitting occasion, but it was Sainte-Beuve's habit to speak out what was on his mind, even at the risk of a row.

He had previously published in the *Constitutionnel* a necrological article on his old friend the Countess de Boigne (May 18, 1866). An estimate of Cousin appeared in the same paper (front page, January 14, 1867) at the time of the philosopher's death. This piece is not wholly laudatory, but "when applied to such eminent talents and such distinguished works, criticism always presupposes much praise and high esteem." Cousin was a force, an intellectual influence; he had "the need and the secret of predominance;" a fine and vital intelligence, he was "one of the most astonishing of meteors."

Cousin's vacant place on the staff of the *Journal des Savants* was now filled by Sainte-Beuve, who interrupted his revision of *Port-Royal* to write some articles on Du Bellay (April, June, August, 1867), returning to an old subject, not much changed in ideas, but far more deft and wholly ripened. Perhaps an essay like this, even better than an introduction to *Les Poètes Français* (1861), gives an idea of what Sainte-Beuve's projected *History of French Literature* might have been.

The next year he contributed two further articles, *Saint-Évremond* (February) and *Eugène Gandar* (October, November). The *Journal des Savants* was then more literary than it has since become, among the editors being Mérimée, Villemain, Mignet, Littré and others whose names were familiar to general readers. Sainte-Beuve's articles differ little from the *Lundis,* having the personal touch and the imaginative phrase. They may be considered *causeries* raised to a slightly more elevated, though by no means formal plane. The essay on Gandar, based on family and other personal letters is a little treatise on "how to become a perfect professor," a treatise in which Sainte-Beuve will not, like Quintillian and Rollin, omit domestic affections and love of the homeland. Having passed through the normal school and the school at Athens and having taught in various provincial faculties, Gandar had attained almost at the moment of his death the chair of letters in the Sorbonne. Though the subject was not great, the study of the professor as type is by no means uninteresting. In regard to all this work the writer constantly consulted his old friend Lebrun, who presided over this journal.

A study of another professor and a close friend of early years, J. J. Ampère, was also prepared for the *Journal des Savants,* but when read before the editorial board the reminiscences it contained of strictly private affairs were found unsuitable for so staid a journal, and the article was transferred to the *Revue des deux Mondes* (September 1, 1868).[3] "I am in certain respects a pupil of Ampère," says the critic, who was yet almost of the same

---

[3] The Gandar article was written to replace this one which, in spite of Lebrun's protests, Sainte-Beuve withdrew. Nothing could alter his determination to allow no changes in what he had written.

age, for he had regularly attended the professor's lectures. In a footnote he adds: "Ampère studied literary history by strata and zones; I study by individuals whom I afterward relate to groups." Regret is expressed that the course of lectures on French literature was never prepared for publication to remain as a monument. At the end, however, Sainte-Beuve doubts (his strong point) if it would after all have been best for Ampère to have thus confined a mind that found its chief happiness in excursions in every direction. Perhaps such a task, being against his nature, would have spoiled him; at any rate, he would have lived less. After all, a treatise on literary history is at best authoritative for no more than twenty-five years. Entirely admirable is the criticism of the *History of Rome*. "At the same time very frank and very humble," Sainte-Beuve confesses himself not a competent judge of the erudition, but vigorously expresses the objections of good sense. On Ampère's *Grammar,* so ill-treated by specialists, there is a passing remark that exhibits a trait of Sainte-Beuve's strenuous character: "I could not have slept peacefully under the strokes of criticism, either true or exaggerated, to which Ampère's grammatical attempt was exposed; I should have enjoyed no repose until I had had the matter out with my opponents."

Some months earlier, a bundle of letters, written by Mme. de Staël to Camille Jordan and possessed by the orator's grandson, came into Sainte-Beuve's hands through the agency of his friend Chantelauze of Lyons. The resulting article, unfitted for the *Moniteur* on account of Jordan's antagonism to Napoleon,[4] was published in the *Revue des deux Mondes* (March 1, 1868), running to the unusual length of fifty-two pages. For two months the critic worked on his theme, writing eagerly to Lyons for

---

[4] Lebrun was again consulted on the appropriateness of this piece for the *Journal des Savants.*

information on every detail. He always read a letter or a diary as a skilled actor reads a play, with a complete perception of the situation and of the relations of the persons involved, not only seeing every detail of externals, but penetrating to the heart of the matter. With unerring tact, he selects what is most significant, makes it the center of attention and adds almost imperceptible touches, till the characters stand out with astonishing reality. As has been previously remarked, the de Broglies, who assumed proprietary rights in their ancestress, made a great fuss over this publication, their procedure so exasperating Sainte-Beuve that, had he been younger, he would have felt in honor bound to produce a book on Mme. de Staël and her circle to emphasize his independence. Though he did not mind offending haughty aristocratic pretense, he deeply regretted displeasing a sister-in-law of Jordan's, humbly offered excuses, and was happy when she was appeased. In preparing the essay for reproduction in book form, he even omitted a note printed in the *Revue* which dealt with Camille Jordan's wife, the money she brought him, some of her unpleasing traits, and her second marriage. As for Mme. de Staël, he felt that all he had published was to her honor and, while he asked no thanks of her family (the rascal), he did not look for recriminations and reproaches.

The bulletin of Sainte-Beuve's health now becomes of import. Jules Claretie, visiting him late in 1865, is impressed with the youthfulness of his vivacity. "He speaks," says this admirer, "he warms up, he recounts, he recalls; so many persons, dates, reminiscences file past him at a gallop. . . . No other can talk thus, without hardness, with such fire, such verve, such flashes."[5] There must have been, however, some diminution of vitality, for

---

[5] Article in *L'Illustration*, Dec. 30, 1865, to accompany a full-page portrait (frontispiece to the present volume) initiating a series, *Gallerie des Sommités Contemporaines*. The article is given wholly

an entry in a note-book reads: "At my age, Horace, Montaigne and Bayle were dead, and they are my masters: I might as well die." Yet up to the close of 1865, Sainte-Beuve had suffered only minor maladies, a bad hand, a bad knee, bad eyes, a cold that confined him to the house, with hardly a premonition of his real illness. At last, on December 28, he writes Dr. Piogey that, though he had hardly expected to need a physician, he may after all require a surgeon for a slight operation. In January, 1866, he is sad and suffering great pain; the operation, painful but not serious, to relieve the stoppage of a passage, incapacitates him and he cannot bear the jolting of a carriage. In March, he is completely well again. In August, his health is not bad, but he suffers minor discomforts, not to say infirmities, including a bad right arm; needs care; is good enough for the housed life of a man of letters. As the year drags on, he even attends some Magny dinners. But on December 13, he suffered the stoppage of urine which incapacitated him for the rest of his life. The real cause, stone in the bladder, he suspected, as did also Dr. Veyne, but he continued to undergo the futile operations advised by the surgeons he consulted. He writes Levallois that he is seriously ill, but without great pain, and does not dream of literary production. As senator, he can be ill without financial worry, and for this relief he is full of gratitude to the Princess, who indeed frequently cheered him by her visits.

On January 1, 1867, he writes that the newspapers made him more dangerously ill than he actually was, and that they now make him more thoroughly cured. His infirmity does not depart, he is seriously ill and fears the condition is permanent. It is distressing and subjugating,

---

to praise, but this is discriminating. The next *Sommité*, Jules Janin, whom Sainte-Beuve so greatly admired, is called by his interviewer "a writer of the second class."

but on March 6 he goes to the Princess for a Wednesday evening social gathering. In May he is a little better and can work. The next month he is about the same, able to go from armchair to table. In August his health is good enough, but again he cannot bear the jolting of the carriage. In September he does not budge and is scarcely alive. In November his ill health does not prevent work, but is an obstacle to all pleasure and suppresses animation. On the fourteenth the Goncourts, attending a dinner given the Princess by Sainte-Beuve at his house, report, with no trace of sympathy, that he was in great pain, which he tried vainly to hide. In December he has not been out twice since the affair in the Senate (June 25), and has no strength or capacity of attention. Then comes great pain (December 11), and the Goncourts find him very ill in bed (December 29), but resigned and read to by his secretary, though he himself writes that he can hardly talk, being in a state of habitual torpor.

About the beginning of January, 1868, he begins to feel really better, soon he can walk again, though only for a short distance, and he goes out for a stroll each evening at about six; but he is seldom in the Senate, on account of ill health. The speech of May 19 brings back his pains, though a week later he is better and expects to occupy the summer with work. It is the evenings he would like to shorten or suppress, the hours in which he used to enjoy the pleasures of society, now so heavy that he "enters long silences." The summer brings back his suffering, and in July he can neither walk nor sit without pain. He tries the carriage again, but is obliged to get out at once. In August he does not budge from his room, but by the end of the month he makes his solitary round of the Boulevards. His only good days are those free from pain. In October he writes that he is an invalid and rarely leave the house—he could not even deliver in person his address on Dübner—and in December he says that he has not much pain, though the inconvenience continues. Very often he tells his correspondent that he feels a slowing up of mental processes, fatigue, stagnation; he is not prompt to rebound as formerly, he beats only one wing, he has no go in him.

Standing by itself, this sanitary report would be of slight interest, but set alongside the work accomplished in the midst of these sufferings, it fills us with astonishment at the intellectual vitality that could dominate depressing ill health and intense physical suffering. Besides revising *Port-Royal*, Sainte-Beuve during these years (1867-1868), wrote essays of high quality that run beyond two volumes, and he delivered important speeches in the Senate which, for accuracy of statement and appropriateness of form, were prepared with no less care than that bestowed on his purely literary work.

At the time Sainte-Beuve entered the Senate, the leader who represented his ideas, Prince Napoleon, had retired. Wedded to an Italian princess, the Prince had consistently favored Italian unity and opposed the temporal power of the Pope. Several times his indiscreet oratory had caused the Emperor to send him on foreign tours. For a speech in Corsica at the dedication of a monument to Napoleon I (April, 1865), he had received a public rebuke, and in anger he had relinquished all public employment and withdrawn to Prangins in Switzerland, where he intended to spend three years, having no desire to reënter politics. He was often in Paris, however, and he also wrote anti-clerical letters maintaining his theory that the priest, while free and respected in his church, should be without influence in the state. In 1868 he sent Sainte-Beuve for insertion in the *Siècle* an article on the Roman expedition of October, 1867, and Garibaldi's defeat at Mentana, which, with Sainte-Beuve's letter to the editor, was interdicted at the moment of going to press.

As Mérimée did not take his senatorial duties very seriously, Sainte-Beuve considered himself the special governmental representative of literature and the press, and his first activities were in this line. The fact that his chief opponents belonged to the clerical group led him on to attacks upon this "odious" party, as he called it in his letters. To quote his autobiography: "The rôle he has filled and which has made of him the defender of free thought has been less the result of deliberate choice than of an irresistible impulse."

Much of the debate in the Senate had been purely academic, since the only authority allowed that body was to pass upon the constitutionality of bills sent up by the lower house; but on March 14, 1866, the Emperor enlarged these powers by granting the right to send back any measure not approved and thus delay its enactment for a year. Possessed of such limited functions, the senators naturally talked on everything under the sun, with negligible effect on public policy.

In 1864 (March 18) Bonnechose, Archbishop of Rouen, had attacked Renan, and when Delangle, Minister of Justice, declared that no law had been broken by the Hebrew scholar's appointment, a senator had cried out that the law ought to be changed. At that time, of course, Sainte-Beuve was not present, but on March 29, 1867, in the course of a discussion on primary schools, Ségur d'Aguesseau, digressing in every direction, happened to reproach Rouland, former Minister of Education, for "a scandalous nomination." Sainte-Beuve, interrupting with a heated protest, was properly enough called to order by President Troplong, who remarked that no names had been mentioned; but others rose to denounce "immorality and irreligion," accompanied by shouts of approval and calls for order, and Sainte-Beuve, too, continued, amidst a general hostile hubbub, his defense of liberty of thought. "You are not here for that," bawled Lacaze, and for some time longer the din continued, some making their reprobation heard and others, Sainte-Beuve among them, being inaudible.

The incident seems to have had a bad effect on the critic's health, and his next public appearance in the Senate was June 25, when he spoke against a petition to exclude certain books from a library at Saint-Étienne, among these being works by Voltaire, Rousseau, Proudhon, Michelet, Renan, George Sand and Balzac. He even defended Pelletan, whom he calls an adversary. The whole argument is based upon principles of fairness, justice, conciliation and expediency, the Empire protecting the loyal Left as well as the Right. Nothing could be more courteous, until turning to Lacaze, whom he cannot name a colleague, he calls up the insult of the March session and starts a parliamentary row of almost equal proportions. To those who condemn his attitude as unfaithful to the government, Sainte-Beuve's answer is that the Emperor, when appointing him, must have expected in the discussions a discordant note, discordant, but at the same time sincere. A few days later (June 30) Lacaze sent a challenge through Heekeren, the man who had killed Pushkin. In an exchange of letters, Sainte-Beuve rejects the view that Lacaze had been offended, insisting, on the contrary, that by arrogating to himself the right to dictate the expression of the speaker's thought, he had really been the aggressor, and the absurdity of the challenge is emphasized by a point-blank refusal to allow the controversy to be transferred "to any sphere where reason is no longer free." This correspondence, which appeared at the time in the press, was published by the critic in a pamphlet, together with his speech and the *Moniteur's* account of the two episodes. Public mockery, which the duelists had expected to fall on Saint-Beuve, was in the end reflected upon themselves as bullies of a rather brutal sort. The feeble state of the critic's health was well known and memory of his youthful duel with Dubois had recently been refreshed by Claretie quite accidentally in the *Figaro* (February 15, 1867).

About a month before Sainte-Beuve's second speech in the Senate, an incident took place which aroused a vast deal of foolish clamor. About twice a year the critic was accustomed to invite Prince Napoleon to dine at his house, just as he also invited the Princess, his practice being to have the guest of honor name the other guests. This time the Prince indicated About, Flaubert, Renan, Robin and Taine, and, as he had numerous engagements, he thoughtlessly set April 10 as the date, this happening to be Good Friday. In 1854 Senior noted that on Good Friday there are no dinners and that no one calls or receives, the theory being that it is a day of mortification; but that, nevertheless, it was the custom for fashionable people to drive in the Bois and for the rabble to turn the Champs Élysées into a sort of carnival fair. That Sainte-Beuve and his friends had thrown this etiquette to the winds and dined on the consecrated day was instantly seized upon by the clerical newspapers, always on the alert for scandal and conflict, and the affair was treated as a "demonstration" against Christianity. Sainte-Beuve, according to his practice, said nothing, but he was vigorously defended by some of his friends, notably by Schérer in the *Temps*. It was assuredly nobody's business, yet fashionable society and a majority of the Senate, both already sufficiently hostile, were stirred to further heated antagonism.

On May 7, 1868, Sainte-Beuve spoke for about an hour on a new law regulating the press. His discourse came at the close of a four days' discussion. Rouher, the Chief Minister, had just answered some objections in an impromptu speech, so lively that three orators who were to have preceded Sainte-Beuve relinquished their intention and the Senate was impatient to vote. Whatever interest might have been taken in the speech that Saint-Beuve read was dissipated by his opening statement that, intending to vote for the law, he simply wished to point out some imperfections in the measure. Under the circumstances it was but natural, without the malice imputed by the speaker and his friends, that his voice should be drowned by general conversation. Three times the few who wished to hear, backed by the presiding officer, called in vain for order, and Sainte-Beuve plodded along inaudible to the end. It was only when published that the oration produced any effect. It abounds, indeed, in political wisdom. Representing the generous idea of the Emperor as spoiled by the illiberal application of subordinates, the orator insists upon the folly of restrictions and petty vexations imposed upon journalists of the highest type, and demands absolute tolerance and full liberty of speech, showing from historical parallels that, while the march toward liberalism may be slowed up or accelerated according to circumstances, the direction cannot without peril be changed. That one of the great faults of the Empire was its vacillation in this regard, and particularly its uncertainty concerning the temporal power, seems now to be generally conceded.

Easily the best of Sainte-Beuve's three speeches is that on liberty of teaching (May 19, 1868) a defense of the Medical School by a former student and an appeal for tolerance, not only for Protestants and Jews, but also for free-thinkers and all members of the great diocese devoted to science. "In physiology, as in every other science," maintains the orator, "facts resulting from observation and experiment must be accepted, whatever they may be; the deductions then to be drawn from such facts are the affair of the individual.'' Defending ''the government to which we are all devoted,'' Sainte-Beuve, in the face of interruptions, assails the clerical party as a menace to the State. Here he is truly eloquent:

Ominous party, encroaching, devouring, insatiable party, ungrateful from its very nature, since it believes all free gifts merely its due! The more you yield, the more it takes; all you have given is no satisfaction, but only a point of departure for further demands. You heap upon it benefactions, and it will not even utter thanks. You send the army to Rome, within an inch of final downfall, you save the temporal power; next day you request that the wisest, most reasonable ecclesiastic in France be made a cardinal . . . you are refused with pleasure. And at the same time, in a letter addressed to the most compromising, the most turbulent of the French prelates [Dupanloup], means are found to insult one of your ministers [Duruy], to demand his discharge, a thing never seen in the memory of any king of ancient France during the centuries of Gallican religion.

This party covets to-day the instruction of youth, all instruction; even where it has no footing, it presumes to dictate rules, to narrow the bounds. . . . Any one who goes beyond certain conclusions that befit it is denounced to fathers of families and covered with mud, as soon as he displeases and refuses to obey the party.

Sire, Sire, I cry (and would that my voice, which is the echo of thousands, might be strong enough to be heard), Sire, redouble your wise firmness; hold good, Sire; keep respectful, keep at a distance these dangerous allies, imperious and self-interested, who have always been to those who have listened to them counselors of disaster.

This eloquence, as is demonstrated by Sainte-Beuve's private letters, in addition to his published articles, is the product of conviction, and it was a petty as well as a purblind spirit that saw in it merely an ambition for popularity among the liberal students. A group of about two hundred from the School of Medicine, in fact, visited Sainte-Beuve's house (May 27) and were conducted to his backyard so as to avoid conflict with the police. In a brief address he urged study as the only guarantee for the future, above all study of the natural sciences, physics, chemistry and physiology. "Study, gentlemen," he concluded, "work, work to cure some day our ills of body and of mind . . . avoid above all giving your enemies any hold upon you." The excitement and exertion of this public service brought on new attacks of suffering, which disabled the critic for the remainder of the year. All three speeches were published by Lévy in the form of pamphlets. Montalembert called Saint-Beuve a renegade, and the critic tranquilly inserted in the new editions of his *Portraits Contemporains* a psychological analysis of the type of mind that engendered such insults.

While preparing his speech on the press, Sainte-Beuve had written the Princess (March 12) that he was upset because obliged by his position to speak on the new law, of which he could say nothing good, and that he longed to go back to his books and pass his days among the dead. "O, to return to pure literary study without all this noise" (April 3). The preparation of the speeches, indeed, interrupted the composition of essays, for no *Lundis* appeared between March 16 and June 8, 1868.

The previous year there had been an interval of eight months between the last essay in the *Constitutionnel* (January 28) and the first of a new series in the *Moniteur* (September 16). In March, 1865, replying to Feydeau, who wanted articles for his journal, Sainte-Beuve had said that, though his contract with the *Constitutionnel* was ended, he could not abandon the paper. In December there are seals on the office and it is guarded by the police. If Granier de Cassagnac is appointed editor, "Good night." In March, 1866, the critic is entirely ab-

sent from the *Constitutionnel* and at the end of the year
he is absolutely retired from the daily press. He had
good reason for dissatisfaction. As a result of law-suits,
the speculator Mirès had regained control of the *Constitutionnel,* making it at the same time not only the organ
of the reactionary minister of Foreign Affairs, de Moustier, but also, as Sainte-Beuve complained to the Princess,
an advertising machine, a purely money-making undertaking. The critic retired, and a new program, with his
name left out, was published March 29, 1867.

At this moment Dalloz, proprietor of the *Moniteur,* having offered what Sainte-Beuve calls an advantageous contract, the critic joined that journal, a transfer that made,
Claretie says in the gossipy *Figaro* (February 15, 1867),
about as much noise as the departure of Mlle. Pearl, for
Sainte-Beuve is always listened to and knows how to
make the public listen. He has become Olympian in the
best sense. "It is something," adds the lively chronicler,
"to dare say, if not the whole truth, at least a large part
of the truth."

There appeared in the official journal nine articles, a
series which was then interrupted by illness. It really
gives the reader a friendly thrill when, in the Monday
table of contents at the head of the first column, his eye
falls on *Variétés* by Sainte-Beuve, and on the line under
this, *Feuilleton* by Théophile Gautier. Of the nine essays
in the *Moniteur,* only the last, that on Virgil (December
2), treats a literary subject. The others are: in September,
two portraits of minor personages of the Revolution and
the Empire; in October, a portrait of Marshal Saxe in
three essays; in November a portrait of the Comte de
Clermont, also in three essays, this last of the Condés
being treated as a personification of the decadence of the
old régime. The whole group, fresh, gossipy and rich
in appropriate moralizing, is as interesting as anything

Sainte-Beuve had done. The article on Virgil manifests a persistent love for the master-poet, and in some pages, which should be added to the volume of 1857, it presents a striking case of one of those imitations that completely transform the Homeric manner into the Virgilian.

Resuming with two articles in March, 1868, one a discussion of spelling reform and the other an eighteenth century portrait, the critic continued in June with an article on a general of the First Empire, followed by a series of three running through July on the *Memoirs* of Malouet, a portait with much interesting digression; in September he added a penetrating study of Lamennais based upon newly published material (two essays), a model of indulgence and tolerance, in which experience paints reality, without the illusions of imagination and feeling. This group ended with a fresh essay on the poet Charles Loyson (November 21), an acquaintance of early years.

The foolish treatment of the press by the government had alienated all the best journalists. Now, the Chief Minister, Rouher, brought matters to a culmination by establishing an official journal and taking governmental patronage away from the *Moniteur*. When the maneuvers had become apparent to Sainte-Beuve in June, he had resolved not to stay to have his articles censored. In August he perceived that Dalloz had lost the game, though the matter was not absolutely decided till near the end of September. To Rouher, who brought pressure to bear to get him to join the new *Journal Officiel*, Sainte-Beuve wrote that, though legally free, he felt morally bound to Dalloz. Private correspondence shows that desire for freedom was the preponderating motive. The keenness of his disappointment when this hope was frustrated explains the last of Sainte-Beuve's sudden leaps, of those apparent reversals of attitude which so disconcerted observers from the outside while seeming to the critic himself only a perfectly natural continuation of a line of conduct.

The initial article sent to the new *Moniteur* (for December 28), a review of lectures on poetry by P. Albert, is first of all a defense of Duruy, Minister of Education, whose scheme for the secondary teaching of girls had been violently attacked by Dupanloup, backed by all the bishops of France and approved even by the Pope. As to the lectures themselves, Sainte-Beuve praises the replacing of conventional rhetoric by new views, with suitable omissions for girls, such a course marking a date in public instruction, "the popularization, elegant and lofty, of the sanest and most advanced literary criticism." This might pass, but Pointel, the new associate of Dalloz, demanded the omission of a passage ridiculing the rage of the Clericals, especially the Bishop of Montpellier, "an eagle's cry—as though it were a question of saving the Capitol." Nothing enraged Sainte-Beuve quite so much as insistence on a change in an article he had written. The tyrant of the *Revue des Deux Mondes*, Buloz, "in his single person more inflexible than Minos, Eacus and Rhadamanthus," might mutilate the copy of others, but not Sainte-Beuve's. Even Littré had been unable to secure the modification of a passage dealing with the poverty of his parents. Here was a still more burning question, the question of fanaticism, and Dalloz was so informed. In the emancipated journal the critic had expected "no yoke"; while hoping to keep the editor's friendship, he withdraws not only his article, but his collaboration: "Decidedly I retire."

The article was sent to the *Temps* where, set from the proofs of the *Moniteur*, it appeared January 4, 1869.

Writing in 1863, Sainte-Beuve had addressed the editors of the *Temps* as "partisans of frank and full liberty, who hide from yourselves none of its perils, none of the chances to which it may lead, but who in a virile way prefer even the storm to stagnation, conflict to possession, and who, in virtue of a philosophy long meditated in its hardihood, believe wholly in the triumph of the best in humanity.''

Here at last the critic could be assured of full liberty, even if his views disagreed with those of the staff. Nefftzer, the manager, and Schérer, the chief critical writer, were personal friends and members of the Magny circle, and though the contributors included such extremists as the exiles Louis Blanc and Edgar Quinet, Sainte-Beuve felt that he was not assuming an attitude of hostility to the Empire. Finding that an article in which he defended a minister in his own way and with his own reasons could be inserted in nothing but an opposition paper, he maintains his independence as a man of letters, joins that paper, and looks to render service that could not be performed if he were bound. He ''quits officialism, nothing more, nothing less.''

Sainte-Beuve's view was not shared by the Princess, who was, Viel-Castel says, a fanatic on the subject of the Bonaparte family. In this case her fanaticism seems to have been further stimulated by the talk of Rouher, who was angered at Sainte-Beuve's defection from his new journal. She had paid her usual Sunday visit (January 3) and chatted pleasantly for an hour. The next day the article appeared in the *Temps*. In the afternoon she suddenly burst unheralded upon the rue Montparnasse and, if we may judge from the words ''Vassal of the Empire,'' uttered to Troubat while the master of the house was absent for a moment, there must have ensued a tempestuous scene. A violent tirade *in absentia peccatoris* two days later at her own house, reported by the Goncourts, shows to what lengths her invective could carry her.

The social gatherings at the house of the Princess, where he found ''the graces and smiles of life,'' had been Sainte-

Beuve's greatest happiness. When illness kept him at home, the goal of his dreams was there. "I often think of the rue de Courcelles," he writes, "of Zeller's course, of the non-official evenings, of the mornings in the studio ——of all I am deprived of"; and he hopes some change will permit him to taste again what was formerly his joy. It is a pleasure merely to listen to reports from Gautier and Flaubert. At length this last social tie was broken.

A fortnight later Sainte-Beuve writes:

I seek, and I question myself in vain, I cannot discover any personal wrong I have committed against your Highness.

You had accustomed me, Princess, to a wholly different sort of friendship—so different that I have not been able to consider Monday's interview as other than an extraordinary accident, something not from you, but from another.

For my part, I have put the mark after the Sunday visit. It is on that day at half past five that for me the book closes: will it ever again be opened?

I know what I owe for many favors, for so many recollections, for so many proffers of friendship, the proofs of which are all about me and will not cease to surround me. The amazement that seized me Monday and from which I have scarcely yet recovered will pass. All that preceded lives and will continue to live. In this regard, at least, I shall hold fast a faith that so often fails me in other things; even when I can no longer hope, I shall still trust, and a voice within will murmur in the depths of me: *"No, it is not possible."*

When, however, three months later, the Princess made some advances toward a reconciliation, Sainte-Beuve replied to her emissary, Charles-Edward, that he had already gone too far. As in the case of the Cénacle, as in the case of Mme. Récamier, and how many others, his emancipation seemed finally to be dearer to him than his friendship. Just before his death, there was an exchange of messages; but, in truth, another intimacy had been removed from the actual and placed in the chamber of recollections. Flaubert's adoration caused him to break with Sainte-Beuve, but all the others in the circle, even the Goncourts, continued to visit him. The Prince, too, saw no great harm in Sainte-Beuve's action. As formerly, he came familiarly to the house; he held political consultations; he would have led the funeral procession if distance from Paris at the moment had not prevented; and he inserted in his book on the Bonapartes a feeling tribute to the intellect and character of his friend.

Insulted by Granier de Cassagnac in the *Pays,* Sainte-Beuve followed his "supreme law" and did not answer, advising his friends to keep a like silence. His articles themselves, franker than ever, would furnish sufficient justification.

These articles he continued fortnightly (Tuesdays) in the *Temps*. There are three series extending to July 13, each the work of a master who no longer needs to exert himself. Perhaps there is extant no more wonderful performance by a dying man in almost constant agony.

The first series deals with Talleyrand, and while the portrait gives full credit to the charming exterior of the man, to his "superior mind, clear good sense and exquisite taste," and even on occasions to sincerity, it especially emphasizes his habitual venality and consummate corruption. As the critic had said before, a public man may have vices, but these must not govern his conduct. This insistence on the "reptiles at the bottom of the cavern" behind the decorated outside offended a fashionable society that had learned to admire Talleyrand, and when Sainte-Beuve accused Bonaparte's minister of instigating the slaughter of the Duc d'Enghien, and pictured him abstracting from the archives and destroying the evidence of this political crime, the *Temps* was even threatened with a lawsuit. "At the first word of this declaration of war," Sainte-Beuve, having the textual proofs, was ready to write a supplementary

499

article. Though willing to let each individual follow his own line and though himself with no desire for proselytism, he was yet, as he confesses, intractable when attacked.

As to Talleyrand's carefully prepared death, then a subject of bitter controversy, Sainte-Beuve simply pictures the fashionable crowd in the antechamber rushing off with the inspiring news of the reconciliation with the Church and, without discussing the vexed question of sincerity, he employs the much more effective device of telling how his own Jansenists used sternly to demand, in such cases of conversion, the restitution, as far as possible, of ill-gotten wealth. To Jules Claretie he wrote (April 7, 1869) that he had prepared the pieces without prejudice, he neither loves nor hastes, but simply studies and analyzes, with reflections as he goes along. A certain ripe negligence is indicated by the fact that he intended to write one or two articles, but was carried on by the subject to five. His skill has now become second nature. The picture of Talleyrand wearing an iron brace on his lame leg and imperiously striking the metal with his cane to attract attention is only one example of those unforgettable touches, so easy for the unskillful to pass over, but which the master painter seizes as a gauge of reality.

The subject of the second series (four articles), a foil to the aristocratic Talleyrand, was Madame Desbordes-Valmore, whose husband and son had provided the family letters. "The life of a woman," remarks the critic, "her biography, properly speaking, is not to be written"; and indeed he knew more than he told, though an early love affair might be guessed by an attentive reader. What comes to the fore is the heart-breaking poverty and misery undergone by this *"Mater dolorosa* of poetry," her inexhaustible plebeian sympathy with the suffering and oppressed, her bosom never so full of her own pain as not to be open to the pain of others. It was a kindred spirit that animated the tenderness of the portraitist. To him Mme. Valmore had written in 1855: "You are the one I always call upon and always will call upon to relieve misery, when I can give nothing. I have led you to relieve so many." In this essay, however, Sainte-Beuve never personally appears; he makes no use of letters written to himself, but depends wholly on the correspondence with others. On the literary side there is full appreciation of the sensibility of the poetess, without the slightest claim to a rank higher than her desert, the praise of her work, indeed, being expressed in quotations from Lamartine, Raspail, de Vigny, Béranger, Brizeux and, as a climax, Victor Hugo. None of these estimates, however, is lovelier than the critic's own remark, a remark which bares the very fountainhead of her charm, that, in the midst of the most vulgar details of existence, "something set itself singing within her."

If Sainte-Beuve had written a history of nineteenth century literature, he would doubtless have proportioned his space according to the importance of the authors, but a newspaper essayist is under no such obligation. Occasion, materials at disposal, public interest, even his own mood, are governing motives. The Valmore family thanked, instead of vilifying, the critic for his work. "They offer a model," he wrote, "and he had not met a second such case in his literary career."

The work for the *Temps* concludes with five essays on General Jomini, a thorough and well-constructed study which involved serious preparation and the use of documents provided by the general's son. It might at first sight seem strange that Sainte-Beuve should thus devote himself to a purely military career, for Jomini's sole reputation was in the theory and practice of strategy and tactics, matters about which the critic professes utter incompetence; but the author's purpose was, not only to paint a portrait and to present an epoch viewed in a new perspective, not only to pay a personal tribute to a friend from whom he had learned much, but primarily to dissipate a prejudice, so that youthful military students might profit by Jomini's teachings without patriotic disquietude and so that France might accept the man without repulsion. This general had abandoned Napoleon and taken service under the Emperor of Russia. For this desertion the reader is gradually prepared, attention being first drawn to Jomini's Swiss extraction, his real patriotism of the heart belonging to the mother country, while the wars of France were merely a game he loved to play; then all allowance is made for the egotism of instinctive talent seeking an opening for its exercise, yet always repressed; and finally condemnation is aroused for the unjust and irritating hostility of Berthier.

Here, as in the Talleyrand articles, we observe Sainte-Beuve's emancipation. In the official press he could not have pictured as he now did the arbitrary character and the military and political mistakes of Napoleon I; nor could he, after showing how the Emperor had allowed Jomini to be crushed by government officials, have remarked that an absolute ruler is to a certain extent responsible for the injustices and insults inflicted in his name upon sensitive souls, adding the words: "That was true in the time of Napoleon; that remains true to-day."

These last words embody a personal grievance. Just three months before the appearance of this article (June 29), Sainte-Beuve had himself, on the occasion of Gautier's rejection by the Academy (April 29), been insulted by Rouher, Minister of State, whom he had met in the street when returning from the unfortunate sitting. Angered at a governmental interference to which he ascribed his friend's defeat, he had expressed himself with great vivacity, and Rouher had haughtily replied: "The Emperor will no longer receive the academicians; he will continue their pay, that's all."

Among other personal matters appearing in the Jomini essays are recollections of old Lausanne friends, the general having been a native of Vaud. Characteristic ideas also abound, expressed now with perfect calm. "When a person clearly possesses a superior talent," says the critic, "it is rare that other talents should not for that very reason be denied him: this is human nature and it belongs to every age." The art of war has been treated only in recent times because criticism does not precede, but follows masterpieces. Under the warrior's glory, the excesses and horrors are plainly seen. As to the discussion of campaigns, Sainte-Beuve does not presume to give his own opinion, but merely voices the judgment of experts. Even for those who care neither for Jomini nor for the art of war, there are attractive passages of tolerant and ripe wisdom, and while this last work is not a climax to Sainte-Beuve's literary career, it is fully worthy of him at his best.

Returning some letters of Proudhon to Bergmann and keeping others (April 27, 1868), Sainte-Beuve still hoped, as soon as the affair in the Senate was over, to set to work again on this subject. He was also busy with a new edition of the *Portraits contemporains,* adding many annotations. He is overloaded with work (November 2, 1868), all his time is occupied (January, 1869); his health, which is not reëstablished, retards everything (February); but he works as much as possible (March). An essay on Ronsard was planned for the *Journal des Savants,* but put off on account of illness. While engaged on Talleyrand, he read the Goncourts' *Madame Gervaisais,* and began an article on the modern novel, but when a report was brought him that the Goncourts had said to the Princess: "He is going to roast us," he put aside his article in anger, with the words: "I never roast anybody"; indignation of the authentic critic over the incomprehension that debases the standard of his art. Another task was the revision with additions of an article from the *Portraits contemporains* on Mme. Tastu for a *Gallerie de Femmes Célèbres* collected from the *Lundis* by Garnier. This essay, the last he completed, is interesting as showing his continued love of poetry, even of such as is not of the first rank.[6] While verse had long abandoned him and while what he had "somewhat vaingloriously called his song" is extinguished, "the sentiment is always present, if only in the form of regret, and to recall it touches an always living fiber" (May 14, 1869). The last thing attempted was a piece on d'Alton Shée's *Mémoirs,* of which a dozen pages were dictated. Endeavoring one day, though weary and in pain, to add a line to the manuscript, he murmured "I cannot," and laid down his pen.

For the final three years, he was shut out from all external social life. He could walk slowly for short distances, but could not ride in any vehicle. To the Senate he went only twice in 1868, on the occasions of his speeches, and he seldom attended the Academy. His last visit (April 29, 1869) was to do his part toward the election of Gautier. The Goncourts tell of a dinner at Sainte-Beuve's house (December 21, 1868), at which the Princess was present, and where the whole evening was spent in the effort to get the academician Pongerville to tell his two favorite stories, so as to secure his vote for Théo as a reward for an appreciation of these. At the election Sainte-Beuve attempted a deal in which Gautier's friends were to receive votes in return for giving their support to the candidate of Thiers, but the plan was wrecked by the obstinate self-confidence of the imperial party, a defeat that

[6] In its revised form, it seems not to have been reprinted.

Sainte-Beuve took much to heart. This occasion was not only his last visit to the Academy, but it was also the last time he went beyond the limits of his immediate neighborhood.

Friends, however, continued to visit him to the very end. In 1867, his next door neighbor having died, he leased the vacant house, in order to assure quiet, and joined it to his own, thus acquiring a larger reception room. It was here that Marie Sasse and Maurel gave a concert with Reyer at the piano (May, 1869), an instrument hired for the occasion, for Sainte-Beuve had none of his own, being in no sense musical. He had seldom gone to the opera and, though not without taste for melody, seems to have been more intent upon the words than upon the music. He was at least sufficiently interested in the lyric stage to put into one of his essays a few words condemning the barbarism of the Parisian reception of *Tannhäuser*. Another social gathering worth chronicling is a dinner to Mlle. Favart, who publicly recited Sainte-Beuve's *Larmes de Racine* at the Théâtre Français on the great poet's birthday (December 21, 1868). The director of the theater, Édouard Thierry, was also a guest, as well as the habitual Veyne and Chéron. Unable to go out, Sainte-Beuve thus had scraps of entertainment brought to him, and every favor was paid with a letter of gratitude.

Not an article in the press, indeed, severe though the criticism might be, provided it was honest, but called forth a note of acknowledgment and thanks, for on such matters of courtesy Sainte-Beuve was punctilious. On the other hand, when his account of Proudhon's youth is called a romance, he tells the writer bluntly that to disparage predecessors is a raw and pedantic procedure; seeking truth in common, the last comer rectifies, but does not suppress or deny those who have gone before. Leagues for various purposes Sainte-Beuve refuses to join, on the ground that he is able to think only individually. He also refuses to compose a preface for a volume of poems, as incompatible with the character of a self-respecting critic. To Biré, on the occasion of one of his denunciatory books on Victor Hugo, he writes: "I do not believe that Hugo was systematically malevolent," adding that it is good, on the other hand, to correct errors.

When *Hernani* was revived, Sainte-Beuve congratulated Mme. Hugo, regretting that, nailed to his chair, he could not be present to show that he did not wish to lose his rank among the veterans of 1830 (June 29, 1867).[7] It is a delight to talk Switzerland with visitors. While some "want logic in ethics and find too much pious folly in the Sermon on the Mount," he "personally leans toward this side of the admirable sermon" (April 6, 1869). He is one who "in aging returns in thought to his first literary pleasures and adorations." Yet he keeps moving with the current. We find a letter to his "dear friend" Ernest Daudet, containing praise and criticism of *Marthe Varades* (June 23, 1868), and one to Zola, who had repeatedly asked an opinion on *Thérèse Raquin*. To this book Sainte-Beuve's objections may be summed up in the sentence, "Art, reduced to truth pure and simple, seems to me to depart from truth" (June 10, 1868). Zola had lauded the critic in the *Figaro* (February 9, 1867). Characteristically it was the anatomical method, the dissection of intelligences that he had chiefly admired. The first *Lundi*, according to his view, had been begun in the medical school. Sainte-Beuve himself thought otherwise. A love of exactitude and such excellence of method as might have gone into his writings was the debt to his medical training which he acknowledged.

The critic's intuition seems almost infallible. As early

---

[7] Troubat by oversight dates this letter 1869. Mme. Hugo died in 1868.

as 1867, he appreciated the scholarly preëminence of Gaston Paris and Paul Meyer, and he scented, without actual knowledge, the inexactitude of de la Villemarqué. Yet he will not trust himself beyond his limits. For German, he would "suck the marrow after a learned friend had broken the bones" (February, 1869). Not sure of the nuance of some colloquial expressions in an English book on Talleyrand, he consults his old aid William Hughes (February 19, 1869). Of the things of the North, he rather regretfully confesses ignorance: "I feel I have been too much a homekeeping critic" (March 23, 1869).

Almost all his Magny friends visited him from time to time. "The dear Goncourts have come to say good-by" (June 20, 1868), and he wishes their novel full success. Mérimée and Giraud have also been to dine with him. So also we get glimpses of Garsonnet, old acquaintance of Royer-Collard; of Milbert, adorer of Rachel; of Mme. Blanchecotte, Gautier, Viollet-le-Duc, Prévost-Paradol, Renan, Prince Napoleon; of Paul Grimblot, full of Greek, Latin and Sanscrit; of Émile Barrault, an old Saint-Simonian; and of Rochebilière, librarian of Sainte-Geneviève, master of the seventeenth century, always ready to discuss Bossuet, Bourdaloue and other great preachers, while the host takes notes. Pantasides must not be forgotten, a Greek, ignorant of his own age, but at home in ancient Athens, living from five franc private lessons and the correction of texts for Didot, and getting innocuous pleasure from dominoes at the Café d'Alençon. Louise Colet, now a neighbor, also dropped in occasionally and usually bothered Sainte-Beuve by her unrestrained explosiveness. More demure were the three domestic cats, Jolie, Vieille and Maigriotte, who survived their master only to disappear, as all household pets did, in the pitiless days of the siege.

Particularly to be noted are three old fellow-students

SAINTE-BEUVE

of Charlemagne, all of whom, to Troubat's amazement, used *tu* to the great man. Of these the closest friend was Loudierre, with whom intimate letters, some unprintable, had been exchanged in youth. Now a retired professor, for whom the critic had obtained the cross of the Legion of Honor—Chéron had been one of his pupils—he was still ready to quarrel over Latin and Greek texts, perhaps the placing of a comma in a passage in Virgil, matters ever alive and important to Sainte-Beuve. A second of these companions was Potier, son of a famous actor and himself a dramatic writer and comedian, now blind, but nevertheless vivacious. The most interesting of the three was Nestor Roqueplan, dramatic critic of the *Constitutionnel,* ranking with Sainte-Beuve and Limayrac as a brilliant talker, noted in youth as a dandy and epicure, and always an eccentric character. Alphonse Karr tells us (*Livre de Bord*) that, when a friend tried to borrow money from Nestor, he would exclaim: "I lend money, become a creditor! No, no! I have had creditors myself, and found them so disgusting that I have sworn for my part never to be a creditor, never!"

Another visitor, who came regularly every Tuesday afternoon, was Sainte-Beuve's cousin d'Alton Shée, whose grandparents, uncles and aunts had entertained his childhood at Boulogne. Hereditary member of the House of Peers, d'Alton Shée had scandalized the Royalists in 1847 by declaring in a speech: "I am neither Catholic nor Christian." A founder of the Jockey Club, he had led a riotous youth—to a servant who once on a Wednesday asked at what time to waken him, he had answered "Friday." In 1848 he had fought on the barricades; he had supported Ledru-Rollin, and still a republican and a socialist, he had stood unsuccessfully for deputy in the elections of 1869. Like Potier he was now blind, but full of vivacity and an inexhaustible talker.

508

Unlike his cousin, Sainte-Beuve was a friend of the
Empire, and remained so to the end. The substance of
his Senate speeches he had often expressed both in conversation and correspondence, and sometimes in his published essays. The government, he thought, had alienated
all the intellect of France, Catholic as well as free-thinking,
and the writers for the official press were persons with
whom no self-respecting man would wish to be associated,
an opinion which he doubltess did not insist upon in the
presence of Gautier or Roqueplan. Rouher's famous exclamation, "Italy will never enter Rome, never!" seemed
to him most ominous. He found the Empire very sick
(August 11, 1868) and, as he loved it and was a part of it,
he suffered. Perhaps, though he would not have advised
such a measure some years ago, it might help matters to
frankly proclaim a constitutional ministry. In September, 1869, the Emperor in a *Senatus-Consulte* yielded
grudgingly to the liberal demands of the Chamber. The
Prince came direct from the Senate to Sainte-Beuve's
house, declaring the thing "execrable," and Sainte-Beuve
sent to the *Temps* a letter, his last published composition
(September 7), expressing the views he had expected, had
health permitted, to present in a senatorial speech. This
communication, the only one from his pen wherein he
emerges from his special function of defender of free-
speech and enters general politics, is a warning of the
imminent danger of revolution. The Empire had utterly
neglected men of letters, had alienated the Academy, the
University, the Institut, even the artists, and to all remon-
strances had replied with the unvarying refrain: "What
is that to us?" Here lies a chance to regain public favor,
and Sainte-Beuve calls on the Ministry to do the thing
completely without irritating reserves, to accept the whole
development, to follow up the liberal idea in its true spirit.
Instead of yielding step by step, as in a retreat, the Gov-

ernment should put itself at the head of the liberal column
and lead the movement.

Although Sainte-Beuve voted for Jules Ferry against
the clerical Cochin, he was in fact by no means hostile to
the rule of Napoleon III, however irritated he might become
at the influence of the Empress and her advisers. It was
the truest good-will that led him to point out a fatal fault.
Intellectual nullity in authority was a political peril and,
politics aside, if restrictions were to drive science to Berlin, he foresaw sad days for France. He was perhaps
happy in not surviving the imperial régime.

Altered in appearance and voice by constant pain, he
still made every effort to be agreeable to his visitors, for,
as far as was possible, Sainte-Beuve was a good humored
invalid. In 1866 he had written the Princess (January
24): "There are two ways of getting along in illness;
the medical, according to rules and prognostics, and in this
respect I am coming on all right. But according to the
other way, that of the patient, I am far from what is desirable." He rarely complains, though he fears he may
never again get to Saint-Gratien (June 14, 1866). "But
I will not be ungrateful, whatever happens," he writes
(July 25, 1867), "and on the whole, fortune has not ill-
treated me. It has, in fact, treated me better than an infinite number of my fellows who are as good as myself or
better; I have had days that, by their distinction and their
adorned delightfulness, count by themselves more than
many ordinary years." In a stagnant life he has the tranquil pleasure of recollections. Being much read to, he
finds many amusing things in this daily torrent of ink
(January 8, 1868). Seneca says that pain is no evil. "I
do my best to believe it." Work makes the hours pass,
but the end of the day is dull. In 1869, the heat of July
brings on severe pain; by September, the intensity of the
malady has terribly increased and he passes from crisis

to crisis. The Prince sees him just before leaving for Prangins. At this time, if he sits, he must use two stools in place of a chair. In October Mérimée, Lebrun and Doucet drop in after an Academy meeting, and Sainte-Beuve, in bed and never again to rise, humorously invites the "respectable" Lebrun to dine at some indefinite future time. Even the physicians still give Troubat hope, but on October 13 all is over. The final struggle, lasting many hours and giving proof of astonishing vitality, was watched by a faithful group, Dr. Veyne, Paul Chéron, Pantasides, Troubat and a devoted old servant, Marie Chicot.

Announcing in the *Revue des deux Mondes* (October 15) the extinction of this "luminous intelligence," Ch. de Mazade justly said: "M. Sainte-Beuve had in him nothing of the soldier, and he has ended like a soldier, firm in heart and mind, surrendering arms only in the presence of implacable death, that last and only enemy over whom mind cannot triumph."

According to Sainte-Beuve's wish, following the example of his compatriot Daunou, there were no ceremonies either at the home or at the grave. Six thousand persons crowded into the rue Montparnasse; a procession, distinguished and humble walking side by side, followed the body to the cemetery, and they were there simply dismissed with thanks by Lacaussade, one of the executors.

Never before had the newspapers given so much space to the passing of a literary man. There were a few discordant notes, but these were drowned in the general chorus. The *Constitutionnel, Figaro, Liberté* and *Siècle* gave columns of gossip, biography and stories. Paul Dalloz in the *Moniteur* remembers "the charming hours his conversation gave us," excuses his defection on the ground of ill-health, and calls Sainte-Beuve a "master writer." The *Gaulois* tells of the aged errand-man weeping when he heard of the critic's illness and exclaiming: "If you should die, there would be nothing left for me to do but to kill myself, for you are my only means of subsistence." Prévost-Paradol in the *Débats,* putting aside "political differences," pictures the "antique sage," courageous in the presence of death and distracted from pain by talk of things of the mind, a critic "impartial in spite of appearances," uniting the "irritability of the poet" with sane judgment, and thus attaining equilibrium. And finally, Planquette in the *Journal de Paris* says: "French literature has just met an irreparable loss. . . . Since Goethe, our age has not produced so great a critic and it has produced few such great minds."

The most important estimates, however, estimates that are, from the contemporary point of view, final, are found in an essay by Taine, in the *Débats* (October 17) and in one by Schérer in the *Temps.*

"He lived to think," says Taine, "at least such was his object in the last thirty years of his life." The "little malices, passing irritations, apparent complaisances" were "but waves on a constant current, and behind all was that marvelous knowledge. *Volupté,* the poems and the *Portraits* are only studies and promises; the real work consists of *Port-Royal* and the *Lundis.* In the usual histories, one sees only facts, actions and results; in *Port-Royal,* the preparation, the internal conflicts and agitations, the causes of the external movements. The *Lundis* every one has read: they never cease to please and, when re-read, are always new." Naturally Taine finds Sainte-Beuve's chief title with posterity to be "the introduction of the procedures of natural history into literary study." In conclusion, he says, and he asserts that he weighs his words exactly: "In France in this century, he has been one of the five or six most useful servants of the human mind."

In the *Temps* of the same date, Schérer, in a more specific study, treats, in a way that can hardly be improved upon, Sainte-Beuve's development and the phases of his work. Although the author knows that many think the contrary, he insists that no critic was ever less influenced by considerations foreign to literature itself, a literary conscience constraining him to be just. The *Lundis* are called, without hesitation, "one of the most extraordinary books that literary history holds in memory."

The work, continues Schérer, is as astonishing by its extent as by the variety of its subjects; as prodigious by the labor that gave it birth as by the talent shown in it. Everything is here: ancients and contemporaries, the most serious by the side of the most frivolous, foreigners as well as French, prose and poetry, eloquence and history; Bourdaloue and d'Aguesseau elbow Musset and Parny; moreover, vast original research, use of documents, curious digging into unexplored domains; and furthermore, a marvelous exactitude. It needed personal acquaintance with Sainte-Beuve to reveal the almost morbid importance he attached to the spelling of a proper name, to a reference, to a date. He must see everything with his own eyes, verify everything. He had truly the religion of letters.

In spite of a few errors and many reticences, this admirable essay summarizes the impression left by the work of Sainte-Beuve in a manner almost wholly satisfactory. With this death a literary epoch is perceived to have closed. "He who had passed away was the last of the *littérateurs* in the old sense of the word, of those writers who occupied themselves wholly with things of the mind. The new epoch would demand either amusement or practical results." As a literary critic, Sainte-Beuve had by his achievement consigned all his predecessors to oblivion (an exaggeration, of course), and until a new criticism appears, "we cannot imagine a literary judgment under a form different from that of which he has given the model."

Let us not insist upon any *model*. When a thing has been supremely well done, it is best not to try to do it over in imitation. Homer, Dante, Shakespeare, on their plane —Horace, Montaigne, Pope, on theirs—Sainte-Beuve, on his—are not to be copied. Their qualities, however, so far as attainable, are a fit object of emulation. If we are to have trustworthy critics, their taste must, like Sainte-Beuve's, be trained through wide and intimate acquaintance with the best literature of all ages; they must have exact and full knowledge of the subject they are treating; and they must be gifted with the good sense to seize the point at issue and to disengage it from all its vague surroundings; above all, they must possess that real humanity which enters into and lives other lives than their own, free from hard and narrow antagonism, and entirely disinterested in aim.

INDEX

INDEX

516

INDEX

THE END

LEADING FIGURES IN LETTERS AND ARTS

ARIEL—The Life of Shelley
By ANDRÉ MAUROIS.
Translated by Ella D'Arcy $2.50
 The extraordinary and true romance of Shelley's life in a biography with all the brilliance of a great novel. With portrait.

A PORTRAIT OF GEORGE MOORE—In a Study of His Work
By JOHN FREEMAN $5.00
 The unique character and personality of George Moore as revealed in a keen and careful study of his writings, which also permits an estimate of his literary accomplishments.

HAIL AND FAREWELL—A Trilogy
By GEORGE MOORE   Each volume, $2.50
 An autobiographical series. Volume I, "Ave"; Volume II, "Salve"; Volume III, "Vale." Astonishingly frank description of the author's own experiences and the men and women with whom he associated.

ERNEST RENAN
By LEWIS FREEMAN MOTT $4.00
 The first complete and judicial estimate in English of the man who was a storm center in French intellectual circles.

THE TRUTH ABOUT MY FATHER
By LEON L. TOLSTOI $2.00
 Important and very intimate light on the personal life behind Tolstoi's writings and beliefs.

ECHO DE PARIS
By LAURENCE HOUSMAN $1.00
 A faithful record of a lunch party in Paris in the 90's at which Oscar Wilde displayed all his great conversational gifts.

D. APPLETON AND COMPANY
New York   **London**

461